Walking Through The Psalms This Year

John Schultz

Walking Through The Psalms This Year
Author: John Schultz

Published by JJ Publications
Toccoa Falls College
PO Box 800771
Toccoa Falls, GA, 30598
United States of America

Third Edition, 2006

Manufactured in the United States of America

ISBN 978-1-4116-8899-5

Preface

Growing up in the Netherlands in a Christian Reformed Church, the Psalms, as hymns to be sung, became part of my cultural and religious heritage. It was the singing of these Psalms with their almost Gregorian tunes that drew me back to the church after I met the Lord Jesus in a personal way during a Youth Retreat.

Years later, while in the jungle of Irian Jaya (Papua), Indonesia, I turned to the Psalms for my personal devotions and wrote extensive notes on each of them over a period of time.

Recently, I returned again to this Treasury of David, as Spurgeon calls them, and began to write a daily devotional on each Psalm. In doing so, I received the first and greatest blessing myself. It is my prayer that some of this blessing will flow over in your life as you go through this daily devotional.

The text used is the New International Version, unless otherwise indicated.

For more complete commentaries on the Psalms and other Bible books, go to www.bible-commentaries.com

John Schultz

"A daily walk through the Psalms with John Schultz is an experience not to be missed. It is spiritually invigorating and soul refreshing. One year on and you'll never be the same again."

Dr. Sam Gordon, international Bible teacher, Trans World Radio

"Walking Through The Psalms This Year is an excellent and insightful daily devotional which takes one through the Psalms each day. I have no doubt it will be a significant experience to anyone who follows John Schultz through the Psalms. His background in the Netherlands Reformed Church, where the Psalms were sung every week, and his experience in the jungles of Irian Jaya, combine to make him a Christian with a deep love and insight into the Psalms."

Dr. D. James Kennedy, Ph.D. Senior Minister Coral Ridge Presbyterian Church.

"A daily devotional based upon the Psalms can certainly turn our hearts and minds to the Lord. While John Schultz was serving the Lord in the beautiful yet dangerous jungles of West Papua (formerly Irian Jaya), God gave him the unique context for the thoughts he shares in Walking Through The Psalms This Year. John's keen insights and powerful applications help us appreciate God's glory, understand God's beauty, and worship God's majesty. I wholeheartedly recommend this thoughtful devotional guide to The Christian and Missionary Alliance family and to the larger Christian community."

Dr. Peter N. Nanfelt (President of The Christian and Missionary Alliance 1998-2005)

"In my many years of travel and speaking, missionaries have played a special role in my life. Thus, how good to see a devotional of the Psalms from a seasoned missionary. The rich truths gleaned from the Scriptures during John Schultz's years of serving our Lord in the field will encourage and strengthen you in your own place of calling."

Ravi Zacharias, author and speaker

Psalm 1
"Blessed is the man…"

Like the Sermon on the Mount, the Book of Psalms opens with a blessing. As we can choose to be saved so we can choose to be blessed. This Psalm mentions two kinds of persons, one who has accepted what Jesus has done for him and who wants to act upon it, and one who walks away from God's grace and is swept away by the current of life's temptations.

I say "swept away" but actually there is decline and stagnation in this rat race. Walking on the wrong path leads to standstill and, eventually, to sitting down. Wrong choices will lead to a dead end.

The alternative is to walk with God and to take the Bible seriously. To many people the law of God is not a delight and even fewer people meditate upon the Bible day and night. The only way to delight in God's Word is to delight in God and love Him with all our heart.

We will appreciate the Book if we know the Author.

If we make knowing the Bible our serious business, some amazing things will happen. We will be free from peer pressure. We will "not walk in the counsel of the wicked or stand in the way of sinners or sit in the seat of mockers."

We will lead fruitful lives and always be successful in the important things of life. "Whatever he does prospers."

We will occupy one of the highest offices in the universe and become members of God's supreme court. "The wicked will not stand in the judgment, nor sinners in the assembly of the righteous."

Picture the two paths depicted in this Psalm, one going down to futility, the other leading to the highest bench in creation. The difference is in the love for One Book and for its Author.

Psalm 2

"Kiss the Son, lest he be angry."

Psalm One emphasizes our relationship with God and His Word. The Second Psalm places us in the world in which wars are fought and politics govern nations. We have long since moved away from David's world, from the age in which each nation had his own deity and Israel alone confessed to be governed by God Almighty, the Lord of heaven and earth. In our time, kings and queens no longer reign by the grace of God, even though their titles may say so.

David may have written this Psalm on the occasion of his conquest of the city of Jerusalem, one of the last pockets of resistance by the original inhabitants of Canaan. It is just as difficult for us in our time to imagine ourselves in a theocracy, in which humans are directly governed by God, without significant human intervention, as it is to form an objective opinion about David's ethnic cleansing of the land of Israel, which is what the capture of Jerusalem amounted to. When we hear the words "conquest" and "ethnic cleansing," we think of world wars and crimes against humanity. Our modern day tolerance in a pluralistic society prevents us from finding any justification for David's deeds that form the basis of this Psalm.

It may also prevent us from getting the divine message this Psalm proclaims. Since the kings of the earth are no longer there or have anything to say, we do not discern that the powers that be "take their stand against the LORD and against his Anointed one." A president may profess to be a born-again Christian, but that does not make a nation "One under God."

David knew that God had appointed him as His representative on earth. He knew that there were powers behind the secular political bodies that were directed against God and His revelation in Christ. Although he did not know Jesus as the Christ, he spoke of an "Anointed one," which is the literal meaning of the word "Christ."

David knew that the solution to the problems of this world lay in embracing this Christ. We have no hope that every single human being on earth would ever come to this point, but that does not invalidate the premise.

We will either be the subject of God's scorn and scoffing, or Christ will embrace us if we allow Him to.

"Blessed are all who take refuge in him."

Psalm 3

"But you are a shield around me, O LORD; you bestow glory on me and lift up my head."

Surgical interventions may save lives but they leave scars. David wrote this Psalm as he was fleeing for his life from a *coup d'état* by his son, Absalom. David knew that this flight was part of the punishment he had brought upon himself by his sin of adultery with Bathsheba and the murder of her husband, Uriah. When David confessed his sin, God forgave him and spared his life. But David spent the rest of his life dealing with this forgiveness. God may have forgiven him, but David must have found it very hard to forgive himself. The scars of his sins were there to remain.

This Psalm was probably written on the occasion of David's first night outside the palace. As a fugitive, he turned to God and he discovered that, not only, did God protect and honor him, but that God Himself was that protection. Let us pause and allow the wonder of this discovery to penetrate: God guarantees, with His own Person, David's safety; He is the shield that covers David. What does this mean to someone who had to flee for his life because of his own fault? David must have been overwhelmed by the realization of what God's forgiveness would bring about. The greatest joy one can experience is the discovery that Christ died specifically for those things about which we feel so guilty.

In the three images David uses in verse 3, "a shield," "my glory" and "the lifter up of my head," he says: "God is my protection, my honor and my courage to face life." The lifting up of the head takes away the feeling of shame David must have had.

With these words David, unwittingly, proclaims the Gospel. If God is our shield, the arrows and bullets that are fired upon us will hit Him instead of us. There is no better image to describe what Christ did for us. "He was pierced for our transgressions, he was crushed for our iniquities; the punishment that brought us peace was upon him, and by his wounds we are healed" (Isaiah 53:6).

David was the object of God's severe mercy. Though he may not have understood this, he was correct in stating: "From the LORD comes deliverance. May your blessing be on your people." Those words are written for us. The only hope for healing of our guilt is an act of divine intervention.

Psalm 4

"Let the light of your face shine upon us, O LORD."

We are not told when David wrote this Psalm. Some think that it may have been during the same period he wrote the previous Psalm, when he was fleeing from Absalom.

David was obviously between a rock and a hard place. The words "distress" and "shame" point in the direction of physical and emotional stress. We read that he asks God, "Give me relief from my distress." The Hebrew words he penned down literally mean "Help me to breathe in a narrow place." He addresses God as "my righteous God," or, as the KJV renders it: "God of my righteousness." That is a beautiful title. David recognizes God as the source of his righteousness. He understands his righteousness comes from outside himself and that he cannot boast about anything within himself. It is the imputed righteousness, resulting from the death of Jesus Christ on the cross of Golgotha that is the basis of our prayers and of God's answer. David did not know the facts of salvation as we know them, but the Holy Spirit gave him the intuitive understanding as to how the relationship with God works. In his petitioning God's righteousness, he actually appealed to what God has done for him. This brought him to the understanding that, if God performed this overwhelming miracle of his justification, His meeting David's lesser needs would be child's play. This is an Old Testament paraphrase of what Paul would later say: "If God is for us, who can be against us? ... Who will bring any charge against those whom God has chosen? It is God who justifies. Who is he that condemns?"

David was on the right track by, first of all, trying to solve the problem of his own iniquity by appealing to God's righteousness, and then by praying for deliverance from the outside pressure. God's righteousness will deny the devil access to His children's lives. This is our defense against those who accuse us.

Psalm 5:1-6

"In the morning, O LORD, you hear my voice; in the morning I lay my requests before you and wait in expectation."

It is good to begin the day with God. We are not told anything about the circumstances during which David wrote this Psalm, except for the fact that he awoke in the morning and faced a new and difficult day. He admits that he does not know how to cope with his problems. David looks at the problems that are facing him and puts them before God, asking Him to listen. In doing so, he puts into practice the admonition of Proverbs: "Trust in the LORD with all your heart and lean not on your own understanding; in all your ways acknowledge him, and he will make your paths straight" (Prov. 3:5,6). David trusts in the Lord, he does not lean on his own understanding, and he acknowledges Him in his ways. It is important that he does this in the morning. He does not ask the Lord to pick up the pieces at the end of the day, but he consults the Lord before he acts.

This Psalm is David's morning prayer. The first thing he does, as he awakes in the morning, is to seek God's face. The Old Testament believers did not merely address God with words; they would come to the altar and present their sacrifice. The RSV translates this verse: "In the morning I prepare a sacrifice for thee, and watch." Every prayer is based upon a sacrifice. Prayer is never merely a matter of arranging words in their right order before God. Without the sacrifice of our Lord Jesus Christ no prayer would be possible. Our words are based upon the shed blood of Christ, which makes our speaking to God a prayer. Whether David personally brought a morning sacrifice or whether he identifies with the public sacrifice, which was brought every morning, does not make a real difference. In either case he begins the day on the basis of God's reconciliation.

Begin your day with prayer!

Psalm 5:7-12

"But I, by your great mercy, will come into your house; in reverence will I bow down toward your holy temple. Lead me, O LORD, in your righteousness because of my enemies--make straight your way before me."

Prayer is the unique way in which we can communicate and commune with God.

The great British preacher, Charles Spurgeon, saw in this Psalm the essence of all prayer in which our words are directed to a God who listens and who pays attention to what we say. And Luther thought this Psalm indicates that David's feelings were actually too intense to be put into words, so that he didn't know what to say to God or how to say it.

Prayer comes in all kinds of forms and modes. Some people have mastered the art of saying prayers of beauty and eloquence. King Solomon gives us an example of such an eloquent prayer at the dedication of the temple in Jerusalem (see II Chronicles 6:13-42). God answered that prayer because we read: "When Solomon finished praying, fire came down from heaven and consumed the burnt offering and the sacrifices, and the glory of the LORD filled the temple" (II Chronicles 7:1).

This doesn't mean, however that God only listens to eloquent prayers. When, for instance, Moses saw how God punished his sister Miriam with leprosy he cried out to the LORD, "O God, please heal her!" (Numbers 12:13). And God did. When Nehemiah stood before King Artaxerxes with a heavy burden for the city of Jerusalem that lay in ruin and the king asked him: "What is it you want?" we read: "Then I prayed to the God of heaven" (Nehemiah 2:4). Nehemiah was scared out of his wits by the king's question. There was no time to close his eyes and fold his hands; he shot up a silent prayer to God: "Help!" and God heard.

What all these prayers have in common is that they were directed to God. When we use prayer for any other purpose, we fail. Some Pharisees prayed on street corners so people would see them and believe them to be pious people (Matthew 6:5). Some use prayer to criticize or flatter other people; they act as if they are talking to God but they are actually addressing people within earshot. Prayer that is not a means of fellowship with God is no prayer at all.

We find, therefore, the following ground rules of prayer in this Psalm:
- Prayer must be directed to God in the full recognition of who He is.
- Prayer involves our whole being: body, soul, and spirit.
- Prayer must be based on the sacrifice of our Lord Jesus Christ.
- Prayer is most effective in the morning when we are refreshed from sleep.
- Prayer should be accompanied by faith that expects an answer.

Psalm 6

"My soul is in anguish. How long, O LORD, how long?"

This Psalm is written in a minor key. It contains the complaint of a sick, or even a dying person. This is the first Psalm in a series called "Penitential Psalms." The early church treated them as Psalms related to the crucifixion of Christ. We have to read this Psalm against that background, otherwise it degenerates into the complaint of a sick man and nothing more.

There are some thoughts in this Psalm that are fundamental for our comprehension of God's purpose for suffering. There may be a connection between suffering and a specific sin, but this is not always the case. Suffering in this Psalm is personified as an enemy. In David's case, God permitted this enemy to work in David's body to achieve God's goal. We do not read, however, what the cause of suffering is or what goal is to be reached.

In general, we can trace all suffering and death back to sin and to the power of the devil. Before sin entered the world, death had no place in God's creation. This does not mean that we should go on a guilt trip every time we, or any of our loved ones fall ill. We live in a sinful world and we breathe in its pollution.

David was not able, as we are, to draw a line from his own pain to the suffering of Christ on the cross. But what he wrote points prophetically to the experience of Jesus, who "took up our infirmities and carried our sorrows ... [who] was pierced for our transgressions [and] crushed for our iniquities; the punishment that brought us peace was upon him, and by his wounds we are healed" (Isaiah 53:4,5).

David's prayer has been answered by God for each of His children. If we belong to Jesus Christ, sickness is no longer a punishment for our sins. "The punishment that brought us peace was upon him" (Isaiah 53:5). This can never be undone. If God allows sickness in our lives, we must take this as an opportunity to examine ourselves. If there are sins which we have not yet laid upon Jesus, God may use sickness to draw our attention to the fact. C. S. Lewis, in his book *The Problem of Pain*, states: "God whispers to us to us in our pleasures, He speaks to us in our conscience; but He shouts to us in our pain."

Psalm 7:1-5

"O LORD my God, if I have done this and there is guilt on my hands--if I have done evil to him who is at peace with me or without cause have robbed my foe--then let my enemy pursue and overtake me; let him trample my life to the ground and make me sleep in the dust."

In the judicial system of the United States there has been deep concern about people who were convicted on the basis of circumstantial evidence and punished for crimes they never committed. Some innocent people have spent years in prison and some may have been executed, though not guilty. Fear of punishing the innocent has allowed some of the guilty ones to go scot-free.

We don't know what charges were brought against David, but the accusations had evidently been serious enough for him to bring his case before the Lord.

Our problem is that no one is completely without guilt in this world. Consciously or unconsciously we carry a sense of guilt with us that can weigh heavily on our hearts. Some of our guilt feeling may have nothing to do with deeds we committed. Some people go through life with a basset hound look on their face without having any specific reason for it.

But it can be a terrible burden to be accused of things we have not done. To live under a cloud of accusation can deprive us of any incentive for living a normal happy life. David did the only thing one can do under such circumstances; he brought the matter before the Lord. He declared willingness to take responsibility for his mistakes but refused to plead guilty to things he hadn't done. The apostle Paul did this when the Jews falsely accused him. Standing before Governor Festus, he said: "I am now standing before Caesar's court, where I ought to be tried. I have not done any wrong to the Jews, as you yourself know very well. If, however, I am guilty of doing anything deserving death, I do not refuse to die. But if the charges brought against me by these Jews are not true, no one has the right to hand me over to them. I appeal to Caesar!" (Acts 25:10,11). We have a better appeal than Paul's.

We will all ultimately condemn ourselves when confronted by the glory of God. After all, sin is more than doing the wrong thing. In Paul's words: "All have sinned and fall short of the glory of God" (Romans 3:23). But God will not unjustly condemn us of crimes we didn't commit. And ultimately, He will share His glory with us. We read about the New Jerusalem, the Bride of Christ: "It shone with the glory of God" (Revelation 21:11). If we are falsely accused we can bear it, waiting patiently till that glory envelops us.

Psalm 7:6-17

"O righteous God, who searches minds and hearts, bring to an end the violence of the wicked and make the righteous secure."

David, probably, wrote this Psalm while a fugitive from King Saul who tried to kill him. The poem beautifully expresses the emotions of being shaken by overwhelming circumstances. Its irregular rhythm reminds us of a stream that runs over a bed of rocks. It sounds syncopated with the beat on the wrong note in every measure. The composer Beethoven used this method very effectively in his compositions to give expression to his anger. David shows a very human reaction of fear and he deals with it in a healthy manner; he sings it out to God.

Saul's persecution of David was completely unjustified. David had never done anything to substantiate Saul's jealousy. But David knew that Saul wanted to kill him and that he had the means to do so.

We may have less reason for our fears than David, but that does not make them less real for us. If we feel like fleeing from our circumstance as David did, we may want to follow his example and flee toward God. If we flee to God we put a distance between the enemy and ourselves. Remember that our actual struggle, in the words of the apostle Paul, "is not against flesh and blood, but against the rulers, against the authorities, against the powers of this dark world and against the spiritual forces of evil in the heavenly realms" (Ephesians 6:12,13).

Ironically, David was in danger because God's anointing was upon him. Some of our conflicts are the logical results of God's grace in our life. The devil often reacts only when the Holy Spirit's work becomes evident in a person's life.

David may not have been guilty of the charges against him, but he was also not as righteous as he thought himself to be. But God covered him with a righteousness that was not his own. He does the same with us in imputing the righteousness of Jesus Christ to us. Taking our refuge in Him will make us understand how unshakable our position is in Him and we will join David in saying: "I will give thanks to the LORD because of his righteousness and will sing praise to the name of the LORD Most High."

Psalm 8:1-2

"From the lips of children and infants you have ordained praise."

Jesus quoted these words in the temple on the day of His triumphal entry in Jerusalem. On the day the Lord of glory returned to His temple, the children sang and shouted: "Hosanna to the Son of David." The priests and the teachers of the law were indignant and told Jesus to keep them quiet. He answered them: "Yes, have you never read, 'From the lips of children and infants you have ordained praise'?" (see Matthew 21:15, 16).

The Hebrew word used for "praise," actually means "strength." The praise referred to here as coming from the lips of the children is the loud cry of a baby that comes out of its mother's womb and sucks in the first breath of life. God hears a note of praise in this. To Him it sounds like "Hallelujah."

The text becomes even stranger when we see that God ordained this loud cry, this first sign of life, "because of [His] enemies, to silence the foe and the avenger." God uses this raw cry of a newborn baby to silence Satan! Even more, God bases His strength upon it! We are talking about the Almighty God here. He is the one who created the universe, the Lord of heaven and earth.

Anyone who has ever seen the birth of a child cannot fail to be overwhelmed by the tremendous beauty of this mystery. One human being comes out of another and it is alive! Nothing better illustrates the miracle of life itself than that first cry of a baby. Nothing glorifies God more than this. It is music in God's ear. Satan hates children, he hates births, and he hates life. Since we all come into this world through the miracle of birth and we glorified God with the first breath we took, we ought to know on whose side we are.

For a baby praising God at the moment of birth is not a matter of choice; it is a reflex. It is the infant's sign of being alive. Our breath stays with us until we breathe our last. We will inhale and exhale millions of times during our years on earth, but we will never match the "Hallelujah" of our first breath-- unless we make a serious effort. We breathe often without being conscious of it. If we are, it means that there is something wrong. We also seldom realize why God allows us to breathe. The key to our understanding of the mystery is in the last verse of the Book of Psalms: "Let everything that has breath praise the LORD. Hallelujah" (Psalm 150:6).

Psalm 8:3-9

"What is man that you are mindful of him, the son of man that you care for him?"

This short Psalm is one of the great gems in the Book of Psalms. David looks up at the night sky and sees things that had been hidden from him in the light of the day.

He recognizes that God is the God of the infinite great and of the infinite small. He is the God of the constellations and the God of the atoms.

As human beings we cannot conceive of the limitlessness of either entities. Our perception is limited to averages. Our ear can hear only tones that are within a certain scale and our eye cannot see that which is too big or too small for us. David speaks of space and of infants. Those two categories do not mark the boundaries of God's strength, but they are sufficient in David's demonstration of God's greatness.

When David looks into the night sky and he observes a small child, he stands in awe before the One who created both.

Modern man feels lost in a hostile world. He tries to conquer the space in which he lives. Redeemed man sees the harmony between himself and all of creation. The difference in view lies in a relationship with God.

David asks God the question: "What is man that you are mindful of him, the son of man that you care for him?" The answer he gives to his own question is: "You made him a little lower than the heavenly beings." The Hebrew words can also be translated: "You made him almost like God." God has made man His masterpiece of creation and He has even greater plans for those who love Him than David suspected.

God's plan for man is richly exposed in the person of Jesus Christ, God who became man in order to be a sacrifice for our sins. The author of the Epistle to the Hebrews elaborates on this by saying that Jesus was, in fact, lower than the angels when He died on the cross, but He is "now crowned with glory and honor." That glory is our destination if we identify ourselves with Jesus Christ.

We should learn to see in the dark, as David did. We will realize the miracle of our creation and our destination and we will exclaim: "O LORD, our Lord, how majestic is your name in all the earth!"

Psalm 8:3-9

"You made him ruler over the works of your hands; you put everything under his feet: all flocks and herds, and the beasts of the field, the birds of the air, and the fish of the sea, all that swim the paths of the seas."

To some of us, taking a closer look at the meaning of the words "You crowned him with glory and honor" may be disappointing. Receiving the promise that we will be kings and rule with Jesus Christ in His Kingdom, we envision ruling over other human beings, not taking care of flocks and herds, the beasts of the field, birds and fish.

God's mandate to Adam and Eve had been to be fruitful and rule over the earth. We read: "God blessed them and said to them, 'Be fruitful and increase in number; fill the earth and subdue it. Rule over the fish of the sea and the birds of the air and over every living creature that moves on the ground.' Then God said, 'I give you every seed-bearing plant on the face of the whole earth and every tree that has fruit with seed in it. They will be yours for food. And to all the beasts of the earth and all the birds of the air and all the creatures that move on the ground-- everything that has the breath of life in it-- I give every green plant for food.' And it was so" (Genesis 1:28-30).

Adam wasn't even declared to be the head of his wife! It wasn't until our first parents had sinned that God said to Eve: "Your desire will be for your husband, and he will rule over you" (Genesis 3:16). Evidently, God's original plan for mankind was for every individual to be directly accountable to Him alone. All forms of human government are the result of the fall. Abolition of every kind of government in our present condition would lead to anarchy. But that doesn't mean that governments will remain eternally. When Jesus Christ returns as King of kings and Lord of lords and we reign with Him, God will be all in all.

At present we may have some authority over fellow humans but we have little or no authority over the animal world. The wild boar and the grisly bear in the forest will not answer our call. If they do, we better flee for our life! The time will come, however, when "the wolf will live with the lamb, the leopard will lie down with the goat, the calf and the lion and the yearling together; and a little child will lead them" (Isaiah 11:6). That is the glory God has in mind for us.

Psalm 9

"I will praise you, O LORD, with all my heart ... My enemies turn back; they stumble and perish before you".

It seems difficult to reconcile the words in the title of this Psalm, *To the tune of The Death of the Son* with the contents of praise. We don't know if the son who died was the baby that was born as a result of David's adulterous affair with Bathsheba. If it was, David was to be blamed for this death and his enemies had every reason to attack him. The wording *"I will praise you, O LORD, with all my heart"* suggests a determination to praise rather than a mere emotional impulse. David made up his mind to praise God.

David uses praise as a weapon. He feels under attack, probably not merely by fellow human beings, but by the powers of darkness. And he takes recourse to praise to counter the attack.

Praise is not always a matter of spontaneous and relaxed fellowship with God. There are moments when one has to force oneself to utter words of praise to God because circumstances push us into the opposite direction. Paul and Silas are the classic examples of this in their imprisonment in Philippi. "About midnight Paul and Silas were praying and singing hymns to God, and the other prisoners were listening to them" (Acts 16:25). When Corrie and Betsie ten Boom were in a Nazi concentration camp during World War II, they decided to praise God for their circumstance, including the fleas that had invaded their barracks. Praise can be a form of resistance, when we realize that Satan has overstepped his boundaries and we decide to oppose him.

David recognizes that his defense is effective. David understands that God covers him with a righteousness that is not his own and that this is his protection against demonic opposition.

Praise is an act of the will. We can set ourselves to praise and mobilize our will, our mind and our emotions to this end. Just as loving can be an act of the will, ("Love the LORD your God with all your heart and with all your soul and with all your strength" is a command!), so can praise be. If we wait till we are in the mood for praise, we will have very little of it. We should have enough control over ourselves not to become the prey of our own moods. If we are governed by our emotions alone, we have lost the initiative in our life, and that can become the beginning of depression. We deceive ourselves if we think that we cannot govern our emotions. We will come to the conclusion that praise is reasonable if we see through the deception of the enemy. The reality belongs to Christ, and praise confirms our relationship to this reality.

Psalm 10

"Why, O LORD, do you stand far off?"

This Psalm is usually considered to be a continuation of the previous one. Yet, the content seems to be the opposite of Psalm Nine. David had scored points against the enemy by using praise as a weapon, but although the foe backed off, he was not defeated. This brings David to ask a question which is as old as the existence of evil in the world: "Why does God not do anything against it?"

The impression we may sometimes have–as if God is far away–is, of course, an optical illusion. Two factors play a role in this: the feeling of estrangement, which is the result of sin, and the limitation of our vision. We are the ones who are hiding and who have removed ourselves from the presence of God, not the other way around. In Christ Jesus God is with us: Immanuel. Also, our vision is limited to only a few years, which is less than a fraction of eternity. If God waits four hundred years before He brings judgment upon His people, we think that He does not do anything. In our opinion, help that is not given immediately is no help at all. Man is ephemeral, a dayfly. Both good and evil men suffer from this illusion.

The freedom God gives to human beings is, in itself, a kind of judgment. The wicked will run against the wall and thus will declare judgment on himself.

The wicked builds his security upon a very small foundation. He bases his conclusion upon the experience of the few years in which he was not shaken. This shortsightedness is also the ground for his supposition that there is no God and there will be no judgment. We always express our inner convictions accurately and consistently in the way we act. When the wicked man robs his neighbor he is expressing his philosophy of life. In the same way, one's love for his neighbor demonstrates his love for God.

The interesting, and for us, incomprehensible feature in this is that our prayers and the dawning of our spiritual understanding are not redundant and fruitless, because it is in response to our prayer that God arises. How this all fits together, I do not know. It appears that the helpless victim and the fatherless have a deeper insight into God's character than anybody else. It seems ironic, but they find themselves in a privileged position. We must keep on reminding ourselves of the fact that things are not what they seem to be. Only God sees reality objectively. When God seems far away, it is up to us to draw nigh and declare our trust in Him. When darkness closes in, keep on trusting, keep on praying, keep on praising. The end will justify us.

Psalm 11
"When the foundations are being destroyed, what can the righteous do?"

David had his share of persecutions. In his early years, King Saul considered him a rival to the throne who must be exterminated. Toward the end of his life, David's own son, Absalom, tried to kill him. In some instances, not only David's own life was involved, but the lives of others also, like when Saul massacred the members of the priest family who had, unwittingly, assisted David in escaping. It may have been at that occasion that David wrote this Psalm.

When a government that is supposed to uphold the law, rather commits injustice, it means that the foundation upon which a nation is built is crumbling. Many historic examples of such governments can be cited and some exist in our day.

The question in such situations, "What can the righteous do?" is a pertinent one. David was given the advice: "Flee like a bird to your mountain." David's answer is, "How then can you say to me, I take refuge in the LORD."

There are times when fleeing injustice promoted by governments is advisable. Some European Jews managed to escape Hitler's "Final Solution," thus saving their lives. David actually did flee from Saul and Absalom, but the important part was not from whom he fled but to whom. God always wants us to flee toward Him in all of our circumstances. We live in a world in which the foundation is, in most cases, not built upon the justice of God. Sometimes Christians can make a difference but more often they are the helpless victims.

Our fleeing to God brings us into a position in which we can intercede, but above all, it keeps us from becoming depressed by the daily news bulletin. The best thing we can do in a world that is falling apart is to strengthen ourselves in our fellowship with God. The realization that it is not God who causes the world to crumble, will keep us from losing our sanity. "For the LORD is righteous, he loves justice; upright men will see his face." As we see His face, we may even make a difference for the people around us when they see His light shine through us.

Most of us do not have to flee and our lives may not be in danger. This does not mean that the pressures of life do not crowd in upon us. Even if our lives have not been shaken to the very foundation, we must keep the line of communication open. God's righteousness often reveals itself in the small things of daily life. If we learn to relate our daily pressures to God, if we know Him in all our ways, we will not be shaken when the world is shaken to its foundation.

Psalm 12

"Help, LORD, for the godly are no more; the faithful have vanished from among men."

In the previous Psalm David painted a broad picture of a society that was no longer based upon the law of God and its justice. In this Psalm the crumbling of the foundations is worked out in the lives of individuals.

It is our relationship with God that governs our relationship with our fellowmen. The first and greatest commandment of the Bible is to love God with all our heart and the second, which is the immediate result of the first, to love our neighbor as ourselves (Matthew 22:37-39). All social ills can be traced back to an absence of a relationship with God.

Lack of fellowship with God also alienates us from our fellowmen. David wrote this Psalm while feeling lonely and forsaken. Being a social creature, he needed the company of his fellowmen. Fellowship with God is, of course, the most important and fundamental thing in life. But, even if we have an intimate fellowship with God, we need interaction with other people in order to live a healthy and well-balanced life. God intends it to be so that God's love reaches us through the lives of other people and that others learn to experience His love through us. David suffered from the fact that he was alone.

Living as a Christian among ungodly people can be as detrimental to our happiness as living alone. The Psalm opens with the statement that "the godly are no more," and its conclusion is that the wrong people form the upper crust of society, and moral values have turned topsy-turvy. Oppression and deceit have received "high ratings."

The marks of the society that surrounded David were lying and flattering for the purpose of deceiving. David contrasts this with the Word of God, which is, he says, "like silver refined in a furnace of clay, purified seven times." Any comparison between human speech and God's Word is doomed to failure. No word that has creative power has ever come from the mouth of man. But the failure is even greater when words lose their meaning or when they acquire a meaning that is opposite of what seems to be expressed. The meaning of our words will prove our sincerity or the lack of it. We demonstrate whether we are genuine or fake by what we say.

May God grant that no one can say when looking at us: "Help, LORD, for the godly are no more; the faithful have vanished from among men." Rather, "Let the word of Christ dwell in you richly as you teach and admonish one another with all wisdom" (Col 3:16).

Psalm 13

"How long, O LORD? Will you forget me forever? But I trust in your unfailing love; my heart rejoices in your salvation."

In this Psalm it seems that David reached the bottom in, what could medically be called, a clinical depression. And in his despair he asked "How long, O LORD?" "How long?" is a question that, actually, can only be asked by persons who live on earth within the boundaries of time. In heaven, in eternity, there are no long or short times.

David had lost the sense of God's presence, which he normally possessed, and, incorrectly, he blamed God for this. It is, of course, impossible for the omniscient God to forget, or for the omnipresent One to hide Himself.

Our emotions are never constant; we all have our ups and downs, even in our relationship with God. But they are *our* ups and downs and not God's. David ascribes to God what is normal for sinful man, but which is impossible for a holy God. David projects the frustrations of his own soul upon the character of God. In a sense, this is a healthy exercise; it expresses the essence of the work of redemption Jesus accomplished for us. He took upon Himself the blame that we should have borne. This is what we mean when we say that we lay our sins on Jesus. If we reproach God, unjustly, that He forgets us and that He hides Himself from us, God accepts this and forgives us our sins. David may not have understood this clearly, but the Holy Spirit uses these words to give a clear picture of the reality of our redemption. David's cry is a shadow of Jesus' cry on the cross: " 'Eloi, Eloi, lama sabachthani?'-- which means, 'My God, my God, why have you forsaken me?' " The question is too deep for us to be able to give the answer! So, David's "How long, O LORD?" actually accentuates what God does, and this turns out to be the salvation of humanity.

With the request that God give light to his eyes, David returns to reality. This sense of reality is the first answer to his prayer. The danger of passing through an extended period of depression is that we begin to see the break of our fellowship with God, with all its disastrous results, as a normal condition. The light should never go out of our spiritual eyes. We should keep our eyes on God's reality, lest we lose our grip on life.

David began to see that God had not abandoned him. God's presence is a reality, whether we experience it as such or not. Waking up to it will help us to praise Him as David did.

Psalm 14

"Oh, that salvation for Israel would come out of Zion!"

The evangelist D. L. Moody was once handed a slip of paper just before he entered the pulpit. The note had only the word "fool" written on it. Moody read the note aloud and then commented: "I have heard of anonymous letters, in which people send a message without signing their names, but this is the first time in my life that I receive an anonymous letter without the message and only the signature." He then opened his Bible and started to preach from the text: "The fool says in his heart, 'There is no God.'"

Verse One "The fool says in his heart, 'There is no God'" is not the declaration of an atheist, a person who in all honesty cannot bring himself to believe in the existence of a God. It is the statement of someone who repeats to himself "No God! No God!" Those are the words of someone who represses what he knows to be true because he does not want to have his behavior governed by a moral code that would be in accordance with an acknowledgment of God. A person may confess with his mouth that he believes in God and deny Him with his life. The world and the church are full of this kind of people.

God actually pities that kind of people. David states: "The LORD looks down from heaven on the sons of men to see if there are any who understand, any who seek God." But looking down from heaven, God only sees a lost humanity, without any exception. Among the whole population of this world there is not one individual who swims upstream; the current of evil carries everyone away. "All have sinned and fall short of the glory of God" (Romans 3:23). There is not merely the problem of social injustice, of oppression of one class by another, of one individual by another. It is not merely a matter of moral failure of some individual; we all fall short of the glory of God. God wants us to be as glorious as He is, but we are not.

God's compassion for lost humanity was worked out in His plan of salvation for this world, in the sacrifice of Jesus Christ in our stead. Salvation does come out of Zion! Refusing the payment for our sins by the blood of Christ qualifies us as fools. If we accept what He did for us when He died on the cross and rose from the dead, He will lead us to glory and we will be where God wants us to be.

Psalm 15

"LORD, who may dwell in your sanctuary?"

Psalm Fourteen began by showing us a world in which no one was good; it concluded with the longing for salvation to come from Zion. In this Psalm we find ourselves in Zion, where salvation appears.

God's throne is in heaven, but there was also a place in Zion where God was present above the cover of the Ark of the Covenant in the tabernacle and later in the temple. When David asks the question, "LORD, who may dwell in your sanctuary? Who may live on your holy hill?" he refers to this place on earth. With that question David actually reverses the roles. God came to us, so that we would come to Him! We ought never get used to this miracle. The question is, "Who can have fellowship with God?"

There is a danger that we read this Psalm in a wrong way. Jesus makes the point in the parable of the Pharisee and the tax collector in which the one listed for God what he did in his efforts to climb God's holy hill. The other one simply asked for forgiveness for his sins. Jesus says: "I tell you that this man, rather than the other, went home justified before God. For everyone who exalts himself will be humbled, and he who humbles himself will be exalted" (Luke 18:10-14). If we see fellowship with God as an effort man makes to climb up to where God is, we misunderstand what is being written here. The Psalm begins with God who lives in a tabernacle; that is, God came down to us, we are not climbing up to Him.

David gives us a list of dos and don'ts, but this does not mean that we can work our way up toward God. God came down to us to lift us up to Himself. If we have fellowship with God, the Holy Spirit will begin bearing fruit in our lives. Our fellowship with God will determine our walk in life, and our walk in life will strengthen our fellowship with God. This is not a circle but rather a spiral, because there is an ascending line in it. We may simply take in faith what God offers us and thank Him for it.

Psalm 16:1-4

"I said to the LORD, 'You are my Lord; apart from you I have no good thing'. "

The title of this Psalm states that it is "a miklam of David." Some Bible scholars believe that it means something written in letters of gold. It is true that Psalm Sixteen is one of the golden Psalms in the book, not in the least because, in the New Testament it is quoted twice in connection with the resurrection of our Lord Jesus Christ (Acts 2:25-28; 13:25).

David concentrates upon the positive aspect of God's protection, which is the intimacy of fellowship with God as a person. This fellowship begins with taking refuge in God.

As we have seen before, fleeing to God is a reaction of the soul upon the realization of the dangers that surround us in this hostile world. When we flee to God and take refuge in Him, we give up our right to protect ourselves. Fleeing to God, therefore, means surrender to Him. God does not impose His will upon us; but if we give ourselves to God so that He can do with us what He wants, He will give Himself to us in return. This act of surrender makes David exclaim: "You are my Lord; apart from you I have no good thing." We consider these words to be among some of the most delightful statements in the Bible. They speak, first of all of possession. A person, who gives all to God, discovers that he possesses all. This is satisfaction to the highest degree. Elsewhere in the Psalms a poet says: "Whom have I in heaven but you? And earth has nothing I desire besides you" (Psalm 73:25).

The words also speak of a decision David made. He has decided not to take pleasure in anything, or enjoy anything, unless God is at the center of it. This decision is at the basis of the Psalm; it is the rock upon which he stands. This limits the number of things he can enjoy, but at the same time it opens up some wide perspectives; for he finds himself immediately among a large group of people with whom he can have a fellowship of faith.

Sin brought about a separation between man and God, as well as between men and men. When fellowship with God is restored, brotherly love is also reactivated. This love will increase, as love for God deepens. When the Holy Spirit came upon the Christians at Pentecost, the hearts of men were fused together in deep brotherly love. We see again that the love for God is closely linked to love for our fellowmen. If we have no good thing apart from the Lord, all our delight will also be in "the saints who are in the land," that is, in our brothers and sisters in Christ.

Psalm 16:5-11

"LORD, you have assigned me my portion and my cup; you have made my lot secure. The boundary lines have fallen for me in pleasant places; surely I have a delightful inheritance."

Every Israelite who heard David's words knew that he was referring to the division of Canaan. A large part of the Book of Joshua deals with the allotment of the land to the different tribes of Israel (Joshua, Chapters 13-21). While Israel was in Egypt they had been slaves without identity. When God led them out they began a journey of freedom and dignity. On the night of Passover, while the angel of death meted out punishment to the Egyptians and the Israelites were protected by the blood of the lamb, a nation was born. When they entered the place of God's promise they took possession of what God had promised them. God had rehabilitated and made slaves into landowners.

When David wrote this Psalm, all this was ancient history. He had not conquered the land. The inheritance he talked about had been in his family for almost five centuries. But David had woken up to the realization of the meaning to him personally of what God had done for his people. The prophet Samuel had visited his parental home and anointed him to be the future king of Israel. We read: "From that day on the Spirit of the LORD came upon David in power" (I Samuel 16:13). He had had a personal encounter with God, which made him realize who he was, where he was, and what he possessed.

But in speaking about his heritage, David referred to much more than the place his family inherited. When the Holy Spirit touched his life he received a portion and a cup, a gift and an experience of fellowship with God of which his house and his farm were only vague images. In forgiving our sins through the Blood of the Lamb and in freeing us from the slavery of sin, God has restored to us a freedom and dignity, of which what Israel experienced is only a shadow. The inheritance that is given to us is unbelievably great-- it is God Himself.

Peter writes: "Praise be to the God and Father of our Lord Jesus Christ! In his great mercy he has given us new birth into a living hope through the resurrection of Jesus Christ from the dead, and into an inheritance that can never perish, spoil or fade-kept in heaven for you, who through faith are shielded by God's power until the coming of the salvation that is ready to be revealed in the last time" (I Peter 1:3-5). Can anything be more delightful?

Psalm 16:5-11

"You will not abandon me to the grave, nor will you let your Holy one see decay. You have made known to me the path of life; you will fill me with joy in your presence, with eternal pleasures at your right hand."

It is generally understood that these words are a prophecy about the resurrection of our Lord Jesus Christ, but David may have intended to say something quite different. He knew that he would die one day. He may have been gravely ill and God healed him. When he realized that God extended his life on earth it caused him such joy and intensified his fellowship with God.

The experience told him, however, that God had more in mind than a temporal postponement of the inevitable. He understood that God and death were incompatible. His experience of God's presence made him comprehend that, although death is all we can see at the end of life on earth, death cannot be the end; there must be life after death.

The phrase: "You have made known to me the path of life," says more than only that Jesus would rise from the dead and that a resurrection exists. The point is that the resurrection from the dead has consequences, not only for our body, but also our life. If death is not the end of life, if there is a resurrection, the fact will also influence life before death. Death robs life of its meaning; resurrection imparts content and quality to life. That is "the path of life" which leads to resurrection and glory. "The path of the righteous is like the first gleam of dawn, shining ever brighter till the full light of day" (Proverbs 4:18).

The knowledge of Jesus' victory over death will inject hope in our present life and also hope in death. We can say with David: "Therefore my heart is glad, and my glory rejoices; My flesh also will rest in hope" (NKJV).

There is of course a difference between the more or less limited kind of fellowship we experience with God while we are here on earth, living in a mortal body, and the boundless fellowship we will have with Him in our resurrection body; but it is not a difference of principle. The God we will see then is the same one who reveals Himself to us now. He changes not, but we will change. There is, therefore, no reason that we would not get a good foretaste while still on earth of the joy and eternal pleasures of which we will drink with full draughts in eternity. The least we can do is rejoice in the hope; that is realistic.

Psalm 17:1-13

"As for the deeds of men--by the word of your lips I have kept myself from the ways of the violent. My steps have held to your paths; my feet have not slipped. I call on you, O God, for you will answer me; give ear to me and hear my prayer."

In the first two verses David pleads a righteous cause at which he looks from a distance. He does not state exactly what the problem is. Evidently he was being accused of things that he had not done, and because he was convinced of his innocence he felt completely free to address himself to God in prayer.

There is always a close connection between our conduct and our prayers. Prayer can be hindered by what we do. Peter warns husbands that their prayers can be hindered if their relationship with their wives is not what it should be. We read: "Husbands, in the same way be considerate as you live with your wives, and treat them with respect as the weaker partner and as heirs with you of the gracious gift of life, so that nothing will hinder your prayers" (I Peter 3:7).

The apostle John also speaks about conditions in which "our hearts do not condemn us." He writes: "This then is how we know that we belong to the truth, and how we set our hearts at rest in his presence whenever our hearts condemn us. For God is greater than our hearts, and he knows everything. Dear friends, if our hearts do not condemn us, we have confidence before God and receive from him anything we ask, because we obey his commands and do what pleases him" (I John 3:19-22). These New Testament quotes are probably the best illustration of what David is saying here.

It is sometimes difficult to rid ourselves of all guilt feelings. Some people have a more tender conscience than others, but that is not the point. We have all sinned and fallen short of the glory of God (Romans 3:23). But that is not the point either. God wants us to be perfect and we will be perfect one day if we allow the Holy Spirit to do His work in us. But God knows our present condition and He accepts us as we are-- covered by the righteousness of Jesus Christ. Our prayers will not rise up to God's throne if we keep anything we have done from being covered by Jesus' blood. Every sin we confess will be wiped off the slate and our prayers will be heard and answered.

Psalm 17:14-17

"As for me, I will see Your face in righteousness; I shall be satisfied when I awake in Your likeness."

In making his "righteous plea," David does not appeal to a righteousness outside himself, as he did in earlier Psalms. This does not mean, however, that he boasts concerning his own righteousness. Our right relationship with God will give us, eventually, an integrity that will become self-evident and that does not have to be analyzed daily.

We are not told under what circumstances David wrote this Psalm. He does not reveal the identity of his enemies. It is quite likely that he was fleeing from Saul at that time and that Saul's men had surrounded his hiding place. David had received God's promise that, one day, he would be the king of Israel. His circumstances, however, seemed to contradict that possibility. When we consider the dire straits in which David found himself, we must assert this prayer is a beautiful model for all who call upon the Lord when life has become impossible.

It is an overwhelming experience to be cleared of all guilt by God Himself; it is awful when a man thinks himself to be innocent and he does not realize what his position before God actually is. There is in the background of David's argument the assurance that there is for him "no condemnation in Jesus Christ" (Romans 8:1).

There is always a great emotional relief when we understand that our circumstances are temporal and that nothing we experience, however painful, can stand in the way between us and the goal God wants to achieve with us. Often it is difficult to discern God's hand in our circumstances, and to believe that "in all things God works for the good of those who love Him" (Romans 8:28) may call for more faith than we can muster. But when we know that beyond the horizon of our life on earth God's glory awaits us, we will be lifted up above the pressures of the present.

David knew that one day he would wake up in eternity, look into the face of God, and be transformed by His glory. We may share in David's hope, whatever our circumstances today.

Psalm 18:1-6

"I love you, O LORD, my strength."

The eighteenth Psalm is David's personal testimony. David, probably, wrote this Psalm at the end of his life as an overview of his whole life. Yet, the character of the Psalm is not the words of an old man; it sparkles with vitality and energy. The statement "I love you, O LORD, my strength" is the conclusion of a lifetime.

Loving God is a unique phenomenon, reserved exclusively for the Judeo-Christian faith. Love for God is not found in any other world religion. All human love is derived from the character of God. "We love because He first loved us" (I John 4:19).

David had a tumultuous life behind him, from shepherd boy to fugitive, to guerilla leader, to king. He understood that the purpose of all his experiences was that the love for God in his life would grow and ripen.

The purpose of all our experiences, especially as Christians, is that we would "love the LORD our God with all our heart and with all our soul and with all our strength" (Deut 6:5).

David had many narrow escapes in his life. At one point he said to his friend Jonathan: "There is only a step between me and death" (I Samuel 20:3). This Psalm is a hymn of praise for God's intervention in those moments, any of which could have been his last. People who have had a close brush with death have a greater appreciation of life. We seldom realize that there always is only one step between life and death! No one can be sure of being alive the next day. Between heart attacks and car accidents, every human life hangs by a thread. The person who thinks differently has put his head in the sand like an ostrich. If our safety is not in God and in our fellowship with Him, we are always vulnerable and our lives are in constant danger. David's life had always been in danger, whether Saul wanted to kill him or not, but the anointing oil Samuel had poured upon his head to indicate that God had set him apart to be a king had made him invincible. Looking back on his life, David came to the conclusion that God had kept him safe in all the rough sailings. And he confesses that his life had been marked by a deep love for the Lord who saw him through it all.

David's love for God had energized him to the point where he called God "my strength." Loving God with all our heart and with all our soul and with all our strength will make us realize that He gives us what it takes to love Him. If we do not love Him we will have no excuse.

Psalm 18:1-6
"I love you, O LORD."

Loving God should be the greatest priority in our life. Love is, at the same time, a choice and a commandment. The Great Commandment, as Jesus calls it is: "Love the LORD your God with all your heart and with all your soul and with all your strength" (Deut 6:5). Jesus adds to this: "and with all your mind" (Mark 12:30). It seems contradictory that loving God can be both a choice and a command. Love that is not spontaneous is no love at all. God created man for the purpose of sharing His love with us and being loved in return. We can understand some of God's deepest longing that man He had created would come to Him and surrender to Him in love. In Paradise, God gave Adam the choice between the tree of life and the tree of knowledge, between loving Him and not loving Him. Adam chose not to love God. The sin he committed separated us all from God. After sin entered the world, love comes to us as a command, because this is the only hope of salvation. It remains true, though, that loving God is always a choice. It is an act of the will that makes us state: "I want to love the Lord my God with all my heart and soul and strength." It is never a matter of mere emotions; it is always an act of the will. For us, loving God is an act of obedience but also of surrender. We cannot love God and keep on living for ourselves and for our own ambitions. Loving God means giving up the right to self, to the way we spend our time with God and the time we spend on ourselves.

Loving God ought to have priority over all other goals in life. It should have priority over all other loves. We must love God first, before we love our spouse, our children, our friends. If we love God with all our heart and with all our soul and with all our strength, God will reach His goal with us. What more can we expect from life?

Psalm 18:7-19

"He reached down from on high and took hold of me; he drew me out of deep waters."

Verses 7-15 give an awesome description of the phenomena that accompanied God's intervention in answer to David's prayer. It is difficult to determine whether David describes supernatural interventions or natural disasters. We must be careful not to jump to conclusions. We tend to think that God will not stop the world, simply because we ask Him to. But the Bible does record supernatural events that occurred in answer to human prayer. During the exodus of Israel from Egypt and the subsequent conquest of Canaan natural phenomena of tremendous proportions took place that resulted in the drying up of the Red Sea, and the Jordan River, as well as the meteorite rain and the standing still of the sun. Yet, we take it for granted that God would never do anything along that line in our behalf.

It would be a tremendous experience if a thunderstorm burst loose immediately after we pray. David sensed the wrath of God for his enemies as expressed in an earthquake, in a volcanic eruption, in a sun eclipse, and in a thunderstorm with severe lightning. Imagine that someone calls to God for help, and all nature around him bursts loose, while he himself remains standing, "quietly among the raging waves."

In the midst of the awesome storm of all the elements of nature, David is aware of the presence of the Lord. He describes God as mounted on the cherubim.

God does not reveal Himself in the same manner to everyone. Elijah recognized Him in the small still voice, not in the thunderstorm or the earthquake (I Kings 19:11-13). The character of God's revelation to us may also depend upon the measure of our faith.

Had David only looked at his circumstances, he would have been completely stunned and bewildered. People hated him and tried to cut off every human way of escape. There was no hope for David on the horizontal level. But God reached down from on high and saved him vertically. When David finds himself in a spacious place, he experiences salvation both horizontally and vertically. Space is three-dimensional.

The depth dimension is not God's supernatural intervention, but His love for David. "He rescued me because he delighted in me." Yet, David's experience, with all its awesome manifestations of God's might, is nothing in comparison with our salvation. "This is how God showed his love among us: He sent his one and only Son into the world that we might live through him" (I John 4:19). Christ's birth in Bethlehem was more earth shocking than all of the mighty phenomena of nature in this Psalm.

Psalm 18:20-24

"The LORD has dealt with me according to my righteousness."

Looking at David's life, we cannot say with any benevolence that David's life had always been above reproach. Seen in the light of history, his sin with Bathsheba puts even his victory over Goliath in the shadow. In Shakespeare's words: "The evil that men do lives after them; the good is oft interred with their bones." We may not assume that David conveniently forgot the dark spots in his life as the end approached for him. When David says, "the LORD has dealt with me according to my righteousness," he speaks about a righteousness that comes to him from outside, what the apostle Paul in his Epistle to the Romans calls "imputed righteousness."

David's testimony in this Psalm consists of two miracles God has wrought for him. He has been delivered from his enemies and he has been delivered from himself. The latter delivery is by far the greater. We are, after all, our own worst enemies. It is not only, or primarily, the devil who tries to destroy the church of Jesus Christ; Christians do this also.

God wants us to be delivered from the mastery of sin in our lives. The poison in us is more deadly than any outward opposition. The fact that God justifies us is our greatest source of joy. It is also the basis of all other deliverances and victories.

God has made provisions for this deliverance in the death of our Lord Jesus Christ. All we have to do is ask Him to apply this to our lives. The fact that God deals with us according to the righteousness and cleanness that He has bestowed upon us Himself is a miracle that we will probably never fully comprehend. Once we possess the righteousness of Jesus Christ, the Holy Spirit will lead us on the path of righteousness and keep us from unrighteousness.

Obedience to the leading of the Spirit of God is of the greatest importance in our fellowship with God.

Psalm 18:25-29

"To the faithful you show yourself faithful, to the blameless you show yourself blameless, to the pure you show yourself pure, but to the crooked you show yourself shrewd."

It sounds as if David says that God is good to us if we are good to Him, and if we are not good, He will become angry. Our nature rebels against this kind of primitive representation of God's character. God is eternal and unchanging; He is not subject to mood changes and He is not influenced by circumstances as we are. This means that God's attitude toward us is not determined by our attitude toward Him. It is, however, true that our concept of God and our understanding of who He is changes with a change of our attitude toward Him.

If we accept the fact that Jesus died for our sins, there will be a change of heart to the point that our heart will no longer condemn us. A good example is the prophet Isaiah. When Isaiah encountered God and confessed his sinful condition, God cleansed him by touching his lips with a coal from the altar. This inner change enabled him to hear God's call for volunteers and he answered: "Here I am, send me!" (Isaiah 6:1-8).

David discovered in the same way the cleansing of his inner being and he recognizes the purity of God.

Our representation of God is often completely off the mark. We suspect God of having ulterior motives, and of doing the same kind of devious things we would do ourselves. The cleansing of our life will purify our vision of God and will lead us to discover His faithfulness, His goodness, and His purity. Few people really believe that God is one hundred percent good and that He is perfect love.

We must allow ourselves to be purified by the blood of Jesus Christ and by the influence of the Holy Spirit in order to see God as He is. Jesus says: "Blessed are the pure in heart, for they will see God (Matthew 5:8). And the writer of the Epistle to the Hebrews states: "Make every effort to live in peace with all men and to be holy; without holiness no one will see the Lord" (Hebrews 12:14).

Our discovery will certainly increase our intimacy with God. Inasmuch as it deepens, so will the experiences of life deepen our character. Thus the spiral whirls on high.

Psalm 18:30-50

"You give me your shield of victory, and your right hand sustains me; you stoop down to make me great."

In the last section of this beautiful Psalm David gives us a digest of his experiences with God throughout his life. Each of the images is a worthy topic for study. Nobody was more amazed about what happened to him than David himself. He never considered it to be a matter of course that he had come to such a high position in this world. He recognized always that the power that had brought him there was God's, not his. This is the secret of true humility.

When David mentions God's shield of victory, and His sustaining right hand he speaks of a fragile life that needs support. A human being, also a man of God, is a bundle of contradictions. God's victory is our shield. The fact that we are saved gives us the right to be protected from the Evil One.

In saying "you stoop down to make me great" David utters more than he could understand himself. David could not have known how deeply God would stoop down, not only to make him great, but also to rehabilitate every human being who confesses his sin before Him. David could not have had any inkling about the humiliation of our Lord Jesus Christ at the cross of Golgotha. From our side, we ought to get more insight in the impact upon our lives of Jesus' condescension, as expressed in His own words: "My Father will honor the one who serves me" (John 12:26). David realized that God had made him great, but he did not understand how; we, on the other hand, know how God did it, but we do not pause often enough to grasp the implications.

The understanding that Jesus came down to earth, emptying Himself of His heavenly glory and stooping down to wash our feet, is the key to a life of victory over sin. It is a great honor if a person receives a decoration for bravery in service. But the greatest decoration a human being can receive is the crown God will place on the head of every person who receives the salvation Jesus made available when He stooped down to touch our lives.

Psalm 19:1-6

"The heavens declare the glory of God; the skies proclaim the work of his hands."

When David exalted the glory of God in Psalm Eight, he was looking up into the evening sky. This Psalm is written in broad daylight. We stand in the sunlight to witness the marriage of the sun and the earth; the sun is the bridegroom and the earth is the bride.

David did not have a primitive concept of the world. His universe does not have a square and flat earth with the sun walking around it. When he sings an ode to the heavens and to space, he may not have known how huge the dimensions of space are, but our ideas of infinity are not much greater than his were. Looking into space, he sings: "The heavens declare the glory of God; the skies proclaim the work of his hands." David must have known that there were more starry skies than the human eye could see and he knew where it all originated.

A person who cannot see the hand of God in the universe is too dense to be called human. The prophet Isaiah said: " 'To whom will you compare me? Or who is my equal?' says the Holy one. 'Lift your eyes and look to the heavens: Who created all these? He who brings out the starry host one by one, and calls them each by name. Because of his great power and mighty strength, not one of them is missing' " (Isaiah 40:25,26).

David describes in beautiful poetry the rise, orbit, and setting of the sun. He depicts this as a bridegroom who takes his bride. The Living Bible paraphrases this magnificently: "The sun lives in the heavens where God placed it and moves out across the skies as radiant as a bridegroom going to his wedding, or as joyous as an athlete looking forward to a race!" There is exuberance, joy, power, and energy in the image of the bridegroom and the champion running the race.

Almost unnoticeably, David has drawn us away from the impersonal greatness of nature to the level of human experience of tenderness, love, competition, victory, and joy. The orbit of the sun has been presented to us in images of various human relations.

We can see the glory of God in the creation of which we are a part. God surrounds us with beauty so that we would be drawn to the beauty of His person. May the sunrise or the sunset we look at evoke in us a longing to personally know the One who invented all this! The Bible calls Him, "the Sun of Righteousness."

Psalm 19:7-14

"The law of the LORD is perfect ... more precious than gold, than much pure gold ... sweeter than honey ... in keeping them there is great reward."

To the casual reader, the transition from nature to the law seems to be a complete change of subject, quite unrelated. David demonstrates that people who believe this suffer from an optical illusion, and he shows that knowledge of the law of the Lord is a logical next step on the same path the sun is traveling. Paul uses the same kind of language as David, when he says: "For God, who said, 'Let light shine out of darkness,' made his light shine in our hearts to give us the light of the knowledge of the glory of God in the face of Christ" (II Corinthians 4:6). The light is not the same, but God who makes it shine is the same God. It is much easier to recognize God in creation, once we have met Him personally in Christ. Without this personal encounter, the recognition of God as Creator lacks depth and meaning. A personal relationship with the Creator expresses itself in our understanding of the law of God, and our obedience to it.

Most people consider the law something to be broken, a limitation of freedom. David uses the word in the widest sense possible. Laws are necessary for our existence. Without the law of gravity, for instance, we would not be able to live on our planet. Without a moral law, life becomes chaotic.

The law David describes, what he calls "perfect," "more precious than gold," "sweeter than honey," is the expression of the character of God. As the laws of nature enable us to live physically, so the moral code of God's Word enables us to live spiritually.

We all know, however, that nature is far from perfect. God's moral law may be perfect and sweet, but we are not what God wants us to be. David prays, therefore, "Keep your servant also from willful sins; may they not rule over me." The word "willful" in Hebrew has the meaning of arrogance. The root of the problem, as David realizes correctly, is the human will. Presumption, arrogance, or willful sins all speak of more than human weakness or giving in to temptation; there is resistance and rebellion in man's heart that has to be dealt with. David confesses that there are sins in his life that he is not willing to give up, but he asks the Lord to change his will.

Psalm 20

"May the LORD answer you when you are in distress; may the name of the God of Jacob protect you."

We don't know for what occasion this Psalm of David was written. Some people believe that it was written for David, rather than by David. It is, obviously, a beautiful prayer for someone who is loved. The Psalm opens with the prayer: "May the LORD answer you when you are in distress; may the name of the God of Jacob protect you." Another Bible Version reads: "May the LORD answer you in the day of trouble. May the name of the God of Jacob defend you."

Days of trouble appear in everybody's life. This Psalm, therefore, has a wide application. We can pray this Psalm as a prayer for many of our loved ones. If we are parents of children, we want our children to learn to pray. We can teach our children all kinds of things, but there are things they will have to learn by themselves. We cannot teach them intimacy with God. If we really love our children, their spiritual life and their relationship with God will be our greatest concern in our intercession for them. We cannot leave them a better gift than the example of our own constant, intimate fellowship with the Lord.

The Psalmist continues: "May he remember all your sacrifices and accept your burnt offerings." The sacrifices that were brought in David's day are no longer required. We know that the Old Testament sacrifices are all fulfilled in the death of Jesus Christ on the cross, where He became a sacrifice for our sin. But the sacrifices, mentioned in this Psalm are not directly related to sin. The Hebrew words used refer to the grain offerings and the burnt offerings that were brought to the temple as acts of worship. In the Old Testament days, they were regarded as acts of gratitude, as a recognition of God's grace, which required a response.

The apostle Paul puts it in a framework that fits our time, when he writes: "Therefore, I urge you, brothers, in view of God's mercy, to offer your bodies as living sacrifices, holy and pleasing to God-this is your spiritual act of worship" (Romans 12:1). It ought to be our prayer for those we love, our children, parents, relatives, and friends, that they would arrive at this point of recognition of God's grace, where they offer their bodies to God as a sacrifice of thanksgiving. The best guarantee that our prayer will be answered is to set the example and bring that sacrifice ourselves. My prayer for you is that God may remember all your sacrifices and accept your burnt offerings.

Psalm 21

"O LORD, the king rejoices in your strength. How great is his joy in the victories you give! You have granted him the desire of his heart and have not withheld the request of his lips."

Although this Psalm is written in the third person, David, probably, speaks about himself as he addresses God. This gives this Psalm a character of importance and royal dignity. David knows himself to be subjected to the authority of God, but he speaks as someone who has honor and dignity, and possessing royal power.

Fellowship with God endows us with honor and dignity. In the Book of Revelation the apostle John gives this doxology, "To him who loves us and has freed us from our sins by his blood, and has made us to be a kingdom and priests to serve his God and Father-- to him be glory and power for ever and ever! Amen" (Revelation 1:5,6). People who know God are important people.

But in the final analysis, this Psalm is, of course, a prophecy about our Lord Jesus Christ Himself. This explains the fact that David speaks, simultaneously, about himself and about someone else.

A sinful man enjoys power, as if it is something that originates from within himself. The person, who loves God, rejoices in God's power, and he acknowledges and recognizes that that which he possesses has its origin in a source outside himself, in the power of God.

The dignity David possessed was given to him in answer to prayer. God gave to David that which he needed most. There is in every human heart a longing for God, but not everybody is aware of this, or acknowledges it.

God comes to us with rich blessings. The essence of revelation is not that we approach God, but that He comes to us. This point is nowhere brought home so forcefully as in the parable of the Prodigal Son, where the father runs toward his son when the son is still far off. In Jesus' own words: "But while he was still a long way off, his father saw him and was filled with compassion for him; he ran to his son, threw his arms around him and kissed him" (Luke 15:20). In the context of the parable the boy repented of his sin.

Although this Psalm does not mention repentance, we must read this into it. If we turn from our disastrous ways and turn to God, He will pour His richest blessings out upon us. But pardon of sin is only the beginning of a stream of endless benefits that God has in store for us. We begin by realizing that our guilt is gone, and this is followed by a sensation of well-being, and the knowledge of being loved and honored. We only know what it means to be human in the exercise of fellowship with God, where we learn that God loves us personally.

Psalm 22:1-21

"My God, my God, why have you forsaken me? Why are you so far from saving me, so far from the words of my groaning?"

We cannot read this Psalm without remembering the suffering of our Lord Jesus Christ on the cross. In both the Gospel of Matthew and Mark, we read that Jesus cried: " 'Eloi, Eloi, lama sabachthani?'-- which means, 'My God, my God, why have you forsaken me?' " (Matthew 27:46; Mark 15:34). Jesus may have quoted the whole Psalm to Himself when He hung on the cross.

We know nothing about the circumstances under which David wrote this Psalm. It is obvious, however, that the text of this poem far surpasses anything that David could ever have experienced personally. This Psalm is one of the clearest illustrations of what Peter says about the Old Testament prophets and their writing: "Concerning this salvation, the prophets, who spoke of the grace that was to come to you, searched intently and with the greatest care, trying to find out the time and circumstances to which the Spirit of Christ in them was pointing when he predicted the sufferings of Christ and the glories that would follow" (I Peter 1:10,11).

For David, the cry "My God, my God, why have you forsaken me?" was the expression of a feeling, not an objective fact. This depressive exclamation indicates that David had, at least temporarily, lost contact with God. But God had promised: "I will never leave you nor forsake you" (Joshua 1:5). David's heartrending cry indicates that he was not conscious of any sin.

But that which for David was the expression, maybe to a point of exaggeration, of a difficult situation, was the ultimate reality for our Lord Jesus Christ. The whole crucifixion takes place between Verses 1 and 21 of this Psalm.

There are two paradoxes in this Psalm and in the way Jesus quoted it. If God really had forsaken Jesus at the cross, why did Jesus call Him "My God?" The second paradox is that Jesus uses the written Word of God's revelation to give expression to the fact that God had forsaken Him! When Jesus took upon Himself our sins, the unity between His spirit and His soul was broken, and thus the awareness of God's presence disappeared.

During His suffering, Jesus felt Himself unable to formulate a prayer of His own. The Spirit Himself interceded for Him with groans that words could not express (Romans 8:26). He always does this for people who are unable to pray themselves. We owe our salvation to the fact that Jesus specifically quoted these words.

Psalm 22:22-31

"You who fear the LORD, praise him! All you descendants of Jacob, honor him! Revere him, all you descendants of Israel! For he has not despised or disdained the suffering of the afflicted one; he has not hidden his face from him but has listened to his cry for help."

The second part of this Psalm makes us realize that David's desperate cry was, actually, a prayer. Verses 22-31 express the joy that is generated by God's answer. David knew, that although, he could not experience God's presence, God was not dead. He had said earlier: "Yet you are enthroned as the Holy one." The little word "yet" makes all the difference between what we feel and what we know to be reality.

It is good to remember that none of our desperate circumstances are permanent. There will be an end to everything we experience on earth, whether good or bad. Jesus' suffering at the cross was, at the same time the deepest point of horror in the history of the universe, and it was also the crucial victory over sin and death. It was God's solution to the problem of sin. The decisive factor is the love of Him who gave Himself willingly to take upon Himself the sin of others.

David says some beautiful things about Israel's relationship to God. Israel's history can be looked at from two different angles. On the one hand there is the thread of disobedience, rebellion, and hardening of heart; on the other hand, there are the facts of the exodus, the miracles of the journey through the desert, and the conquest of Canaan. God is enthroned as the Holy One; He is the praise of Israel, but He also "came to that which was His own, but his own did not receive Him" (John 1:11). The crucifixion was the ultimate demonstration of this rejection. Yet, in spite of the dark pages in Israel's history, we can say that it is the history of salvation. God revealed His glory to them, and the sacrifices and praise of Israel went up to Him as a pleasing odor. Israel's praise may not always have sounded clear and pure, but God identifies His eternal omnipotence with their feeble efforts. He bases His throne upon their poor performances.

Frail human beings called to God and He answered them. The faith of one man avails more than can be undone by the unbelief of many. For instance, the tiny kingdom of the Netherlands owes its independence to the faith of William of Orange I and of a handful of Reformed Christians.

Because Jesus left His divine glory behind and came to this demon-filled earth sharing our hunger, shame, and misery, and became victorious in those circumstances, we now become partakers of His divine nature. If this is not a reason to praise the Lord, what is?

Psalm 23:1-4

"The LORD is my shepherd."

The twenty-third Psalm is, undoubtedly, one of the most famous poems in world literature.

David sublimates this personal experience in this Psalm. He sees that the role he played as a shepherd is a projection of the work of God.

The smell of nature, the greenness of the grass and the stillness of the water give great charm to this Psalm and it leads us into the quietness that restores the soul.

But the calm of this Psalm has a deceptive character. This is not the harmony of Paradise. David lived in a world that was torn by human sin. Need and want lie in wait. There are crooked paths of unrighteousness, and there is the stillness and darkness of death. God does not take away these evil things for David, but the presence of the Shepherd compensates for them and leads to victory. Evil, however, is not only a reality that surrounds David, it is also in his own soul. The best description of a sheep's nature is given by the prophet Isaiah: "We all, like sheep, have gone astray, each of us has turned to his own way" (Isaiah 53:6). The Bible compares men to sheep, because they are lost. When David calls the Lord his Shepherd, he confesses that he is the sheep that is lost. The fact that God is our shepherd means our salvation and our restoration.

The restoration highlights the physical aspect of the experience, although this cannot be separated from the mental, emotional, and spiritual in man. The remarkable implication of David's words is the acknowledgment of the spiritual relationship: "the Lord is my shepherd" has an immediate effect upon the physical needs of man. God is interested in our physical well-being because He loves us. And it is amazing what green grass and quiet water can do to a person's emotions. Our soul needs trees! But a person does not become morally good because he does a lot of walking. God restores our soul by leading us in the path of righteousness. If the Lord is our shepherd, there will be a moral change that takes place in our lives. He makes us partakers of His Name; which means that we will start to resemble Him in the way we live and act. "For His Name's sake" also implies that it is God who sanctifies us. He does this, first of all, not for our sakes, but for His own sake. God saves us, not because we are worth much in our present condition, but because of His Name. We are valuable for God, even in our fallen state, because we are the bearers of His image and He loves us.

Psalm 23:5-6

"You prepare a table before me in the presence of my enemies …Surely goodness and love will follow me all the days of my life."

The second picture David uses in Psalm Twenty-Three is of a guest sitting at his host's table. God invites David as His guest and asks him to sit at His table in order to honor him. We will probably never fully comprehend the fact that the Almighty desires to honor us. One of the most amazing pronouncements of our Lord Jesus Christ is: "My Father will honor the one who serves me" (John 12:26[b]).

This invitation is also a guarantee of protection. The table is prepared "in the presence of my enemies." While being surrounded by fierce foes, David sits down quietly at God's table to eat and drink and have fellowship. The presence of the Lord was the most perfect protection against all who were after David's life. However strange this may seem, in this demon-possessed world, we can sit at God's table and celebrate with Him. What David eats at the Lord's table is the food that feeds our human spirit. In this respect, most people starve to death. Only Jesus Christ can give us the real food.

God's invitation to David implies that there is a certain equality between God and man. The Spirit of God and the spirit of man share, so to speak, the same substance. There are those in the Bible, who are called "God's friend."

God anoints David. Anointing in the Old Testament had a special meaning as a preparation for a specific task. In the New Testament, it was sometimes practiced to honor a guest. In the Bible, oil is usually symbolic of the Holy Spirit. When God invites us as His guest of honor, He pours the Holy Spirit out upon us. The abundance of wine also points in the direction of a show of honor. It may seem strange to us that a cup should overflow in order to prove this point, but we can understand that God does not want us to taste only teaspoons full of His joy. Both the oil and the wine are symbols of the fullness of the Holy Spirit. This fullness is the essence of the feast.

One of the results of intimate fellowship with God is that we leave a trail of blessing behind us. "Goodness and love will follow" in our footsteps. The implication is that those blessings are not meant for us but for others; otherwise, they would not follow us in our path, but they would walk beside us. We receive God's goodness and love while sitting at His table; the surplus of our joy and fulfillment overflows to the ones who come after us.

Psalm 24:1-6

"Who may ascend the hill of the LORD? Who may stand in his holy place?"

This Psalm was probably composed when the ark was brought over from its temporary residence to Jerusalem. As it was placed in the tent David had pitched for it, a choir sang: "The earth is the LORD's, and everything in it, the world, and all who live in it; for he founded it upon the seas and established it upon the waters." Israel far surpassed any other nation on earth in their understanding of God as the creator of heaven and earth. The ark was only a symbol of the glory of God, a glory that far surpassed our human comprehension.

The world, as God created it, contains an abundance of blessing for man and beast. Even after the fall and the curse, we still live on a good earth. God is Lord of the earth and Lord of all blessings.

The words: "The earth is the LORD's," only has meaning for us if we apply it to ourselves. If we confess that we are God's property, the picture begins to have meaning for us. A person who understands and accepts that he belongs to God spirit, soul, and body, understands something of God's claim upon the lives of those who live in this world.

This does not mean that we automatically have fellowship with Him. The experience of fellowship is represented in the image of the mountain we must climb. It sounds as if fellowship with God would demand the most strenuous effort on our part. The question is not whether we are able to reach the top, but whether we are worthy to even try the climb. He does not ask: "Who *can* ascend the hill of the LORD?" but "who *may*...?"

We picture ourselves as standing at the foot of the mountain and God living at the summit. Compared to this, the climbing of Mount Everest is easy!

Our climbing to the top depends on the way we live in the valley. "He who has clean hands and a pure heart who does not lift up his soul to an idol or swear by what is false" speaks about the goal for which we live. These are the factors, which determine whether God will have fellowship with us, or not. Purity of heart, however, is a result of our knowing God, not a prerequisite. If we know Jesus, we are already on top of the mountain. As the apostle Paul puts it: "Because of his great love for us, God, who is rich in mercy, made us alive with Christ even when we were dead in transgressions-it is by grace you have been saved. And God raised us up with Christ and seated us with him in the heavenly realms in Christ Jesus" (Ephesians 2:4-7).

Psalm 24:7-10

"Lift up your heads, O you gates; be lifted up, you ancient doors, that the King of glory may come in."

As the ark neared the gates of the city of Jerusalem, two choirs sang an antiphonal chorus, a question-and-answer hymn to accompany the pageant. The gates of Jerusalem were, poetically, addressed as if they were persons who were told to lift up their heads, or open up for the arrival of the Ark of the Covenant which symbolized the presence of God.

We see a parallel of this heavenly scene take place on earth when Jesus entered the city of Jerusalem. Matthew reports: "When Jesus entered Jerusalem, the whole city was stirred and asked, 'Who is this?' The crowds answered, 'This is Jesus, the prophet from Nazareth in Galilee' " (Matthew 21:10,11). Here the gates of Zion cry out. Is this a rebuke to men because they keep quiet? The gates have to be opened by human hands to let the King of glory enter human lives.

Prophetically, this Psalm predicts what happened on the day of Christ's ascension to heaven. The disciples saw Jesus being taken up to heaven before their eyes, but a cloud hid from their view what happened when the Lord arrived at the gates of heaven. Choirs of angels must have sung as the Lord of glory entered into the eternal glory.

As the ark, symbol of God's glory, entered Jerusalem, so Jesus wants to enter our heart.

This Psalm expresses anew how solemn and glorious the experience of our conversion actually is, and what eternal life will be forever after. The Apostle Paul calls this: "Christ in you, the hope of glory" (Colossians 1:27b).

We don't really know what glory is, do we? No one can give a definition of glory, except in negative terms. We know that sin makes us miss the glory of God. As the apostle Paul states: "All have sinned and fall short of the glory of God" (Romans 3:23). According to Isaiah, glory is synonymous with holiness. The seraphs in Isaiah's vision chant: "Holy, holy, holy is the LORD Almighty; the whole earth is full of his glory" (Isaiah 6:3).

"Who is this King of glory?" expresses some of the mystery of human life. Man is born in this world with an emptiness in his life, which can only be filled by an encounter with the King. To discover the answer to the question: "Who is this King...?" means achieving the goal of our lives.

Psalm 25:1-3

"To you, O LORD, I lift up my soul; in you I trust, O my God. Do not let me be put to shame, nor let my enemies triumph over me. No one whose hope is in you will ever be put to shame."

This Psalm is the first in a series of seven acrostic Psalms; each verse begins with a letter of the Hebrew alphabet. The Hebrew alphabet has twenty-two letters. In a way, this Psalm is irregular in that some letters are missing and others are used more than once. This may have been done on purpose to corroborate the irregular, up-and-down emotions expressed in the poem. David moved through a whole gamut of feelings, from guilt to uncertainty, to faith and intimacy with God, and back again to guilt feelings.

No one is completely even-tempered. Someone once, jokingly, told me that he was a very even-tempered person, always angry! We all have our ups and downs as part of our being human, which makes it easier to identify with David in his change of moods.

"To you, O LORD, I lift up my soul" is as the lifting up of a wave offering. The priests had to lift some pieces of the sacrifice and wave it before the Lord in order to indicate that it belonged to the Lord, and then put it down for human consumption. This is what David does here with his intellect, his emotions, and his will. He shows his willingness to surrender it all into death, while at the same time life on earth goes on for him. He uses his mind, but from now on it belongs to God; he has his own emotions, and makes his own decisions, but something has changed drastically. He promises to obey; he has lifted his anchor and allows himself to be taken up in the current of God's will, without control, without a rudder he himself can steer.

If we do this, we will sometimes ask if God knows what He is doing with our lives. Lifting up our soul to the Lord is an act of faith. We cannot see what the consequences will be, but we trust God. If God is who we believe He is, He is totally reliable, and this discovery is at the core of all our experiences with Him.

God promises that the outcome will be all right. We will not be put to shame. Shame is for people who keep controlling their own lives and mess it up

Psalm 25:4-7

"Remember, O LORD, your great mercy and love, for they are from of old. Remember not the sins of my youth and my rebellious ways; according to your love remember me, for you are good, O LORD."

Verses 4-7 contain a moving prayer for guidance and insight. "Show me your ways, O LORD, teach me your paths," suggests not only that we ought to obey God's command, but also that we would understand something of the "why" of God's guidance.

David asks here that God would become intimate with him and give him insight into His secrets. In dealing with Abraham, God said: "Shall I hide from Abraham what I am about to do?" (Genesis 18:17). David asks to become God's friend, for friends share in each other's secrets. Jesus also gave this definition of friendship, when He said: "I no longer call you servants, because a servant does not know his master's business. Instead, I have called you friends, for everything that I learned from my Father I have made known to you" (John 15:15).

Understanding God's motives in guiding us is useless without our obedience. When we know the truth, we have to practice it. God will not take the trouble to reveal things to us if we do not surrender to His will first.

When David says: "Remember, O LORD," he projects his own limitations upon God. It is redundant to remind God of His mercy and love. God knows Himself, and it is His Spirit who reminds us of God's love and mercy. As a puny creature, living in time and space, David reminds God that He is eternal! The Almighty must have smiled when David came up with these lines. Yet, there is something touching in it when a man says to God: "You are just like I am." David may have been wrong in taking forgetfulness as the point of comparison between God and himself, but as far as the principle of comparing goes he was right: we are like God and He is like us. At the same time, any comparison between God and us will bring out the enormous difference-- God is eternal and we are temporal.

God's mercy and love are placed against the background of His eternity, and so the right perspective becomes evident. Seeing our human need stimulates God's compassion. Isn't this amazing that that, which is a result of the fall, can evoke in God reactions of goodness and compassion? God looked down upon our world and was moved with compassion to the point that He came down to earth in Jesus Christ to take our sins upon Himself and to carry sin and sickness away. We cannot give a richer content to the word "mercy" than this. God has demonstrated His love to us.

Psalm 25:8-22

"The LORD confides in those who fear him."

These words capture the essence of this Psalm. The NKJV renders the Hebrew text literally: "The secret of the LORD is with those who fear Him." The words convey a relationship of intimacy and love. God knows, of course, all our secrets, but it is the sharing with Him of what lives deep inside us that will give depth and meaning to our fellowship with Him. From His side, God will communicate to us His secrets in the measure in which we can receive them. Our capacity in this will grow with the measure of our love for Him. It is only possible to have intimate fellowship with the Father as we are in Christ. For someone who is still "at home in the body, and away from the Lord" (II Corinthians 5:6), it is always difficult to understand that such fellowship with God is possible and that we can communicate with Him as a friend. The relationship in which God confides in us speaks of an intimacy that surpasses all other relationships on earth.

When we read: "he makes his covenant known to them," it does not mean that there are secret clauses in God's covenant, but that one enters into the experience of the covenant. Jeremiah prophesied about this: " 'The time is coming,' declares the LORD, 'when I will make a new covenant with the house of Israel and with the house of Judah. It will not be like the covenant I made with their forefathers ... This is the covenant I will make with the house of Israel after that time,' declares the LORD. 'I will put my law in their minds and write it on their hearts. I will be their God, and they will be my people. No longer will a man teach his neighbor, or a man his brother, saying, ' 'Know the LORD,' ' because they will all know me, from the least of them to the greatest,' declares the LORD. 'For I will forgive their wickedness and will remember their sins no more' " (Jeremiah 31:31-34). God's law becomes an inner reality in the person who is born again of the Holy Spirit. For a Christian knowing the Lord is not something that comes automatically. We gain the experience as we obey God on a daily basis and see God answering our prayers. Fellowship with God will make us into normal, well-balanced human beings who can go through life with a well-defined goal before them. Intimacy with God is a very practical thing. It is not something mystical and out-of-this-world, and it keeps us away from the Evil One.

Psalm 26

"Test me, O LORD, and try me, examine my heart and my mind; for your love is ever before me, and I walk continually in your truth."

The theme of this Psalm is innocence. Wanting to prove innocence, however, often masks a feeling of uncertainty and guilt. But David does not flaunt his own righteousness when he says: "I wash my hands in innocence, and go about your altar."

We can picture the Old Testament setting in the tabernacle and later in the temple. The washbasin and the altar, which stood at the entrance of the sanctuary, do not point to a sinless nature. Blood and water are symbols of cleansing, and they imply that there is sin, which has to be atoned for in order to restore fellowship with God. David's innocence rested on the fact that another creature paid his debt by dying in his place. On the basis of the sacrifice that was brought on the altar, David asks God to vindicate him.

We live in a world in which people seldom honor each other. Sin not only isolates us, but it also robs us of the honor that God wants to give us as human beings who are created in His image. Sin has made this world an abnormal habitat for mankind. This world is not what God created it to be and we are not what we were meant to be.

David knew the tension between being covered by the sacrifice on the altar and purified by the water of the washbasin, and living in the polluted atmosphere of sin. He has not surrendered himself to sinful desires; his trust in God kept him from this. Now he asks God for a visible demonstration of that which he knows to be true in the invisible world. He asks for his crown.

Then he takes another step forward. He asks the Lord to examine his heart and mind. The point is, of course, not that God would have to examine us in order to come to the conclusion that we were already pure. The Holy Spirit penetrates into the depths of our being and chases away all traces of darkness, so that we have no corner in which to hide.

The apostle John defines this innocence: "This then is how we know that we belong to the truth, and how we set our hearts at rest in his presence whenever our hearts condemn us. For God is greater than our hearts, and he knows everything. Dear friends, if our hearts do not condemn us, we have confidence before God and receive from him anything we ask, because we obey his commands and do what pleases him" (1 John 3:19-22).

Psalm 27:1-3

"The LORD is my light and my salvation--whom shall I fear? The LORD is the stronghold of my life--of whom shall I be afraid?"

David finds himself in a world of evil people, enemies who are after his life. The contrast between the darkness that surrounds him, and the light that God made shine in his soul, gives to this Psalm a delightful glow.

The Apostle John made the objective statement: "God is light; in him there is no darkness at all" (I John 1:5). David makes this into a subjective experience when he says: "The LORD is my light and my salvation." God not only saves us, but our salvation cannot be separated from the person of God, and it can only be experienced in fellowship with Him. An illustration that remotely approaches this truth is in the marriage of the British writer C. S. Lewis to an American lady. Lewis was a bachelor who had no intention of ever getting married, but he married Joy Davidman in order to save her from being expelled from England. God saves us by entering into a vital relationship with us.

Light and salvation are used as synonyms. We are saved by God's light. God makes His light shine upon us. Without God, we live in darkness. There is a strong suggestion of a parallel with the first day of creation. The Apostle Paul draws this parallel by saying: "For God, who said, 'Let light shine out of darkness,' made his light shine in our hearts to give us the light of the knowledge of the glory of God in the face of Christ" (II Corinthians 4:6). We usually react to this light with an initial shock, because the light discovers our darkness. Light becomes only salvation if there is a confession of sin. In the prologue to his Gospel, the Apostle John connects life with light when he says: "In him [Christ] was life, and that life was the light of men" (John 1:4).

We see a greater perspective as David's words are placed against the background of darkness, more specifically, the powers of darkness. And David was, obviously, quite aware of the presence of demonic powers. Light and salvation, therefore, take on proportions of a power encounter. Over against the awful threat of the devil stands the power of the light and the salvation in Jesus Christ.

God's light that shines upon our lives is not only our salvation, but also our protection, our defense and our weapon.

Psalm 27:4-6

"One thing I ask of the LORD, this is what I seek: that I may dwell in the house of the LORD all the days of my life, to gaze upon the beauty of the LORD and to seek him in his temple."

We live in a complex world. Some people simplify their existence by ignoring life's complications. It is a victory and it shows depth of wisdom if we can reduce life's complexities to some basic factors, as David does here. He says: "One thing I ask of the LORD, this is what I seek..." The greatest discovery we can make in life is the understanding of what is basic. Jesus said to Martha: "Martha, Martha, you are worried and upset about many things, but only one thing is needed." (Luke 10:41,42). The merchant who was looking for fine pearls understood this; that is the reason he went away and sold everything he had and bought the pearl of great value (Matthew 13:45,46). Moses grasped this when he prayed God to show him His glory (Exodus 33:18-23).

Seeking this one thing means to be willing to give up everything else. Blessed is the man who stakes everything on one throw to gain this one thing.

David discovered that fellowship with God is not only important as a means to achieve a goal, but that it is also desirable for its own sake. Even if the result would not be our deliverance and victory, it would be worth everything to know God. It is true, of course, that our relationship with God and our salvation can never be separated, but a bond of intimacy with God would be of the utmost importance, even if it meant our own defeat. In Jesus' life this was true in a sense; His fellowship with the Father led to His suffering and death on the cross. But, at the end, this became the greatest victory and deliverance of all.

The one thing David seeks is "to gaze upon the beauty of the Lord." The word "beauty" is surprising in this context. God is beautiful; He is the source of all beauty. In his vision of God upon His throne, the Apostle John writes: "And the one who sat there had the appearance of jasper and carnelian. A rainbow, resembling an emerald, encircled the throne" (Revelation 4:3). Nothing more beautiful and colorful can be imagined. God's beauty is the expression of His holiness, His character. God has given us the capacity to appreciate glory and beauty, and also to understand why things are beautiful. We understand beauty if we see the relationship with what we observe in God's love and majesty.

Psalm 27:4-6

"For in the day of trouble he will keep me safe in his dwelling; he will hide me in the shelter of his tabernacle and set me high upon a rock."

David had made fellowship with God the highest priority of his life. As we saw yesterday, he stated that it was for him the only thing of importance. He wanted "to gaze upon the beauty of the LORD." This, he asked in anticipation of "the day of trouble." The sequence of these thoughts is striking. David knew that trouble would come. In a way it had come already. People were out to get him and "devour [his] flesh." In order to face the crisis to come, he wanted to first saturate himself with "the beauty of the LORD."

We all know that life is not fair; life can be very ugly. In spite of all the beautiful things we experience we know that there is injustice, cruelty, and crime in human relations. Sin has permeated life to the core. Some days are worse than others, but none are completely free of it. Loved ones can be snatched away in car accidents; spouses can be lost to cancer. How do we arm ourselves against that? Unless we have caught a glimpse of the beauty of the LORD we will not be able to face the day of trouble when it overwhelms us. Trusting God in times of trouble will give us the experience of being completely safe. God hides us from the consequences of disaster in His own shelter, in the Holy of Holies. Even more than David, "we have confidence to enter the Most Holy Place by the blood of Jesus" (Hebrews 10:19).

Our family has had its share of trouble. One of our sons lost his twelve-year-old son; our youngest daughter lost her thirty-eight-year old husband, both to brain tumors. When our grandson Travis went to heaven, his parents were able to sing the doxology and when our daughter lost her husband and we were gathered around his deathbed, she sang: "My Jesus, I love Thee!" Our children must have seen the beauty of the LORD before tragedy struck, and God protected them against despair.

God doesn't spare us "the slings and arrows of outrageous fortune," but He wraps His arms around us and wipes away our tears. We owe it to ourselves to make seeking His face the top priority of our life. Without a vision of His beauty we will not survive when the day of trouble comes.

Psalm 27:7-12
"My heart says of you, 'Seek his face!' Your face, LORD, I will seek."

After the exuberance and shouts of joy in the previous verses David seems to take a step back. It seems as if the victory and assurance have slipped away. It indicates a case of changing moods, which proves that it is common to man to be inconsistent in his feelings. There is no sign of despair or even of doubt, but we can say that David's vision has dimmed. He wanted to have the subjective experience that God answered him. Even a ship that is tied to an anchor is not immune to the waves. The victory our Lord Jesus Christ has won for us does not necessarily protect us against "ups-and downs." We may be sure, however, that God answers, and His grace is not to be doubted. If we were perfect there would be no need for grace, and God's answer is an answer of grace, which means forgiveness of sin, healing, and restoration.

"My heart says of you, 'Seek his face!' Your face, LORD, I will seek." The Living Bible paraphrases this: "My heart has heard you say, 'Come and talk with me, O my people.' And my heart responds, 'Lord, I am coming.' " God takes the initiative and creates in the human heart the desire to see His face. Seeking God's face can be dangerous to our health. When Moses asked God: "Now show me your glory," God answered: "you cannot see my face, for no one may see me and live." (Exodus 33:18-20). Yet, God told David to seek His face. And we know that, ultimately, God wants us to see His face. We read in Revelation: "The throne of God and of the Lamb will be in the city, and his servants will serve him. They will see his face, and his name will be on their foreheads" (Revelation 22:3,4).

There is an element of dying in our search to see God's face. The physical reality as John describes it cannot be achieved on earth, but the eyes of our faith can focus more clearly on the face of God as we make seeking His face the greatest priority of our life. It is as John the Baptist testified: "He must become greater; I must become less" (John 3:30). Seeking God's face is costly, but it is worth the price.

Psalm 27:7-12

"Hear my voice when I call, O LORD; be merciful to me and answer me."

When we read the first six verses of this Psalm we get the impression that David had reached the highest point anyone can reach in his spiritual life. He had overcome fear; he experienced intimate fellowship with God, and he had been victorious over his enemies.

But, as we saw yesterday, David's mountaintop experience was not lasting. When the facts of daily life began to press in upon him it seemed as if he lost his grip on the experience of God's presence. In our own spiritual life we can certainly relate to David's experience. Our emotional makeup makes us subject to mood changes and we ought never to make our feelings the thermometer of our spiritual reality. That is why the Bible speaks of our "hope as an anchor for the soul, firm and secure. It enters the inner sanctuary behind the curtain, where Jesus, who went before us, has entered on our behalf" (Hebrews 6:16).

One day Jesus took three of His disciples to the top of a high mountain, where they saw Him being transfigured. They saw the light of God's glory shine upon Him, and they heard the voice of God the Father calling out from heaven. Peter wanted to stay there, but Jesus took them down to the valley, where they saw a father and his son who was demon possessed (Mark 2:2-27). God allows us a few precious experiences on top of the mountain, but our daily life is lived in the valley. When David descended into his valley of conflicting emotions, he knew that his mountaintop experience had not been in vain. It gave him what he needed to face the reality of darkness; it helped him to apply victory where it must be applied, in the details of daily life. It gave him hope and perseverance to wait.

We must treasure our moments of intimacy and ecstasy with God, but we cannot dwell on them for everyday life. They help us to see through the drudgery and the routine to the day when God will take us beyond the highest mountain on earth.

Psalm 27:13-14

"I am still confident of this: I will see the goodness of the LORD in the land of the living. Wait for the LORD; be strong and take heart and wait for the LORD."

"Goodness" is not the word to describe the sinful world in which we live. Our relationships are out of alignment: parents neglect their children, and oppressors, foes, false witnesses, and violent men abound. Injustice is practiced under the guise of justice. The law is used to commit murder and cover up crime.

It is against this background that we have to see David's exclamation in verse 13: "I am still confident of this: I will see the goodness of the LORD in the land of the living." The phrase "in the land of the living" does not refer to heaven, as some people think. David speaks about life on this planet. This diminishes in no way our hope of glory to come. We should, however, not leave this world in the hands of the devil without a strong voice of protest. Our God is the God of our today!

Waiting for the Lord is a way of life; it is an attitude of faith and confidence. When we wait for the Lord, we express the conviction that the appearance of things visible is deceptive. God will change this visible world. The Apostle John wrote: "He who was seated on the throne said, 'I am making everything new!' " (Revelation 21:5). This promise casts its shadow ahead upon our lives.

Waiting for the Lord and being strong are synonymous. We tend to weaken and lose courage and we easily become depressed under the pressure the enemy puts upon us. God is not far away. He is like a parent who has gone out for a moment and who will be right back.

A missionary in Indonesia had taken his wife and young boy on a trek of several days in the jungle. During that time they had had no contact with the outside world, for they had no two-way radio they could take on the trail. The mission leadership was unaware of the fact that they were making this trip, and they became concerned when for several days there was no answer to the radio roll call. So a mission airplane was dispatched to see what had happened. When the missionary and his wife approached their mission station, their young boy ran ahead and was just in time to see the plane land on the airstrip. The pilot asked the boy where his parents were. "They are in the jungle," he said. "Are you here alone?" "Yes," answered the boy. This started a rumor that this family had taken off to the jungle and left their little boy alone at home. The young boy should have said that the parents were coming along on the trail and he had just run ahead. He should have said: "They are on the way; they will be right here!" God is not far, even if it appears that way.

Psalm 27:13-14

"Wait for the LORD; be strong and take heart and wait for the LORD."

Waiting can be one of the most frustrating experiences in human life, especially waiting for someone who is late. It is certainly one of the most difficult ones. David was aware of this, because he said that it takes strength and courage to be able to wait.

Waiting for the Lord is even more difficult than any other kind of waiting we are required to do. When we wait for the Lord we think that He ought to be there, but He isn't; or at least we are not aware of His presence. David was confident that he would experience God's goodness during his life on earth, but he was still waiting for it.

Waiting for the Lord also implies an acknowledgment that God's schedule is different from ours. It means cancellation of our own plans and activities in order to adjust to God's schedule. That usually means a major reprogramming, a fundamental reorganization of our way of living. That takes courage and trust. If we wait for the Lord we confess that His schedule is better than ours and that His plans are worth the trouble of waiting for.

We know, however, that God is omnipresent, meaning that He is everywhere. How can we wait for someone who is already there? Maybe God is there, but we aren't! That means that not we are waiting for God, but God is waiting for us to get where He wants us to be.

Waiting for God involves an act of surrender, not only of our time, but of our plans, our initiatives--- of everything we are.

Waiting for God is an expression of trust. By waiting for God we express that we believe that God is reliable, even if outward circumstances appear to testify to the contrary.

Waiting for God determines the difference between success and failure. King Saul forfeited his crown because he didn't wait, but took things in his own hand (see I Samuel 11:7-14).

Waiting for God can be a form of praise. When the dark clouds of terror moved in, Habakkuk reacted by saying: "Yet I will wait patiently for the day of calamity to come on the nation invading us. Though the fig tree does not bud and there are no grapes on the vines, though the olive crop fails and the fields produce no food, though there are no sheep in the pen and no cattle in the stalls, yet I will rejoice in the LORD, I will be joyful in God my Savior" (Habakkuk 3:16-18). If we believe that God created time, we should be able to trust Him with it.

Psalm 28

"To you I call, O LORD my Rock; do not turn a deaf ear to me. For if you remain silent, I will be like those who have gone down to the pit."

When David wrote this Psalm, he was, obviously, under great pressure. The Psalm sounds like a cry for help, and there is a world of emotions in this prayer. This is the prayer of a man whose life is in danger. Yet, there is in this Psalm a treasure of hidden beauty that is not visible on the surface. The first striking thought is in the words "remain silent." Moses taught the people of Israel "that man does not live on bread alone but on every word that comes from the mouth of the LORD" (Deuteronomy 8:3). David is right when he says that it would be man's spiritual and physical undoing if God would no longer speak.

God began to speak to man immediately after he had fallen into sin. He called man to Himself. "But the LORD God called to the man, 'Where are you?' " (Genesis 3:9). In those cases in which God no longer speaks to man, we see that man has hardened himself.

Objectively considered, the fact that David calls upon God is a guarantee that God will keep on speaking to him. David's impression that God had ceased to speak to him is an illusion based on the fact that David used his feelings as the sole thermometer for his relationship with God.

There is, of course, a difference between David's relationship with God and ours. The writer to the Hebrews says: "In the past God spoke to our forefathers through the prophets at many times and in various ways, but in these last days he has spoken to us by his Son" (Hebrews 1:1,2). If, at some moment no prophetic message came through, people thought that God remained silent, but God's revelation in Jesus Christ to us is constant and continuous. When the pressures of life drown out the voice of God in our lives, we must make every effort to return to the place of reality where we can hear Him. That place is for us in the written Word of God. There must be in every one of our days a time when we can be alone with God and listen to what He says to us through His Word. If we are too busy to take out time for those moments, it is not God's fault. When we are too hurried to hear, it does not mean that God is silent. If He were, we would be dead.

Psalm 29

"The voice of the LORD is over the waters; the God of glory thunders."

In this Psalm, God is glorified because He disrupts the balance of nature. One would think that a Psalm that describes a thunderstorm would be completely played out on earth. But the Psalm begins in heaven: "In the splendor of his holiness." David wanted to draw a line between earth and heaven in order to put things on earth in their right perspective.

A thunderstorm is a majestic event on earth. Shafts of lightning and peals of thunder are part of God's glory in heaven, according to John's account in Revelation. Describing the vision of God's throne, he says: "From the throne came flashes of lightning, rumblings and peals of thunder" (Revelation 4:5). The question is, would there have been thunderstorms on earth if man had not fallen in sin? The accumulation of electricity in the sky, and the brutal discharge of it, would probably not have taken place in a perfect well-balanced universe. This kind of revelation of God's glory, therefore, may be related to an imbalance in nature caused by human sin. This is a strange thought, especially if we realize that flashes of lightning and peals of thunder are an integral part of God's glory in heaven.

What God is saying to us in this Psalm is that sin has not made it impossible for Him to reveal Himself to us via a creation that has rebelled against His sovereignty. We find in God's speaking elements of wrath and of judgment. Ever since the fall, nature which ought to be subjected to our rule has turned itself against us. The mystery consists in the fact that God communicates to us via those hostile elements. That which on earth seems to be destruction and demolition appears in heaven as the essence of glory. That is why man has a tendency to hold God responsible for the evil in the world, when actually, all God's glory does is to unmask the essence of evil. The storm David describes is very destructive; yet, it is a revelation of God's glory. The two elements seem difficult to reconcile. God's glory can be very harmful to us. Evidently, demolition is necessary before anything constructive can take place. The first result of the coming of the Word of God to us in the form of a thunderstorm is that our house of cards collapses. Salvation consists of our falling flat on our faces and accepting God's judgment. The reconstruction of our life by the Holy Spirit will be more glorious than we can imagine.

Psalm 30

"Weeping may remain for a night, but rejoicing comes in the morning."

David wrote this beautiful Psalm for the dedication of the temple, as the heading indicates. David himself never lived to see this day, but he had lived for it all his life. And, at the end of his life, when he gave the actual task for the construction to his son Solomon, everything was ready.

Looking back over his life, David remembers the desperate situations in which he had reason to fear for his life. For several years, Saul was close at David's heels to kill him. Although David was a national hero and a brave man, he had been under severe emotional stress. God had anointed him as pretender to the throne of Israel, when he was still a young boy, but the way to the throne had not been smooth and easy. Even after he had become king, his life had been in danger from time to time. It had been a long dark night filled with a bad dream.

But the all-consuming passion of his life had been to restore to the people of Israel the worship of God, in the form of a house of prayer where the presence of God was manifested. David had lived for that and saved up his riches to be able to finance that project. But David would not be allowed to see the realization of his dream. What the writer of the epistle to the Hebrews says about the heroes of faith can be applied to David here also: "All these people were still living by faith when they died. They did not receive the things promised; they only saw them and welcomed them from a distance. These were all commended for their faith, yet none of them received what had been promised. God had planned something better for us so that only together with us would they be made perfect" (Hebrews 11:13,39,40).

Our life may be different from David's, but his passion may be ours. Like him, we can seek first God's kingdom and his righteousness (Matthew 6:33), and we will realize that God wipes away the tears we shed in the dark. We are living toward the morning, when the sunshine of God's love and grace will wake us to a glory we cannot even imagine today.

Psalm 31

"Into your hands I commit my spirit; redeem me, O LORD, the God of truth."

The words: "Into your hands I commit my spirit" have become famous because Jesus quoted them when He hung on the cross. Luke reports: "Jesus called out with a loud voice, 'Father, into your hands I commit my spirit.' When he had said this, he breathed his last"(Luke 23:46). Jesus' last words before His death were a quote from God's written Word. In the context of this Psalm, David does no more than express his confidence that God will protect him. David did not mean that his spirit would leave his body and take his abode with God, ending his earthly life. The opposite was true; he wanted to stay alive. In Jesus' mouth these words acquire a greater meaning.

The word "commit" is actually borrowed from a financial transaction. It refers to a mandate, a deposit as a trust for protection.

We know very little about ourselves and the way we function. The apostle Paul distinguishes three parts that make up our humanity: spirit, soul, and body. To the Thessalonians, he writes: "May your whole spirit, soul and body be kept blameless at the coming of our Lord Jesus Christ" (I Thessalonians 5:23,24). Most of what we know about ourselves concerns our body. Our soul harbors recesses in which secrets are hidden that our conscious mind does not even know. The soul is the seat of our emotions, our will, and our thought process. That leaves the spirit. Without living fellowship with God, our human spirit is dead. Through repentance, conversion, and regeneration, the Holy Spirit brings our spirit back to life, so we can have communion with God.

It is the spirit, the organ that allows us to know spiritual reality that we must entrust to God for His safekeeping. If we do not surrender it to God, the truth of God will not inhabit us and make us the free human beings God wants us to be. Real freedom and truth are intimately related. Jesus says: "The truth will set you free" (John 8:32). Our spirit, under the guidance of the Holy Spirit, must govern our daily life. If our spirit is not in charge, we will be the slaves of the desires and lusts of our body. We can only glorify God in our body if we commit our spirit in God's hand.

Psalm 32:1-5

"Then I acknowledged my sin to you and did not cover up my iniquity. I said, 'I will confess my transgressions to the LORD'--and you forgave the guilt of my sin."

We could call this Psalm "The Psychology of Forgiveness." David confesses his sin. Some Bible scholars believe that this is a reference to his sin with Bathsheba and the murder of her husband Uriah. But we can be sure that David committed other sins in his life also. For a while David carried a sense of guilt with him, but after he decided to tell God everything he had done, his guilt was gone. That is the reason this Psalm begins with the word "Blessed." God will not forgive the sins we do not confess to him. We condemn ourselves to carry our guilt with us unless we confess. Confession is the key to blessing.

The Bible establishes a direct link between forgiveness and salvation. In his song of praise the priest Zechariah says: "to give his people the knowledge of salvation through the forgiveness of their sins" (Luke 1:77). And Jeremiah writes: " 'No longer will a man teach his neighbor, or a man his brother, saying, ' 'Know the LORD,' ' because they will all know me, from the least of them to the greatest,' declares the LORD. 'For I will forgive their wickedness and will remember their sins no more' " (Jeremiah 31:34). So forgiveness is the key to man's redemption and salvation.

Confession of sin occupies an important place in this process, but we are wrong if we think that confession brings about forgiveness. For David forgiveness took the form of an animal sacrifice, the blood of which was poured out at the foot of the altar. Forgiveness of sin is only possible on the basis of the sacrifice of Jesus Christ at the cross of Golgotha. Confession opens up the source of forgiveness for us. We may, therefore, say that this Psalm is, in the first place, a prophecy of the blessedness that is revealed to us in Jesus Christ. God accepts us, not because we better our life, or because we adhere to the rules, but solely because He accepts the payment Jesus Christ made for our sin. Our lives will be bettered and we will obey the rules, but that is not what produces blessing. It is the blessing that produces the change.

Psalm 32:6-11

"I will instruct you and teach you in the way you should go; I will counsel you and watch over you."

Some Bible scholars put the words "I will instruct you and teach you" in the mouth of God. It seems to fit better into the context of this Psalm if we let David be the speaker. The Psalm is called *"A Maskil,"* which we interpret to mean a poem for the purpose of instruction. David learned a lesson in the confession of his sin that he wants to pass on to others. It is difficult to convey to others the joys of blessing and the experience of freedom that is contained in the forgiveness of sin. If we turn away from God and try to go our own way, we are turned into the most hopeless addicts on this planet. Sin enslaves more than drugs or alcohol. As Jesus says: "I tell you the truth, everyone who sins is a slave to sin ... So if the Son sets you free, you will be free indeed" (John 8:34,36). It is this freedom in Christ that David wants to pass on to others.

David issues the warning: "Do not be like the horse or the mule, which have no understanding but must be controlled by bit and bridle." The comparison with an animal is not very flattering. A horse or a mule is trained by man to render service. Such training would be dehumanizing for us. David's intention is to emphasize voluntary surrender. A man who serves out of love augments his human dignity. A man who rebels against God lowers himself to the level of an animal. The question is not if we can stand against God or not. Such a supposition is ridiculous. Our sins make us less human, and unconfessed sin lowers us to the level of an animal. Confession enhances our human dignity, and fellowship with God makes us partakers of the divine nature and of His glory.

If we could see for one moment what God wants to do with our life, we would not hesitate at all to come to Him and allow Him to do His redeeming work in us. The Holy Spirit even wants to help us in confessing our sins. Without the Spirit of God, we would not even be able to say: "I am sorry!"

Psalm 33:1-5

"Sing joyfully to the LORD, you righteous; it is fitting for the upright to praise him. Praise the LORD with the harp; make music to him on the ten-stringed lyre. Sing to him a new song; play skillfully, and shout for joy."

The joy and praise in these verses is very inspiring. The poem differs from other pieces of art in that it has to be "to the Lord." Most pieces of art are the product of a human genius. In this respect the hymn of praise differs from other art forms. Not very many artists have put their talents on God's altar. There are two prerequisites to produce a hymn of praise: one has to be righteous, that is the artist has to be clothed with God's righteousness, and one has to sing "to the Lord." The meaning of this admonition is, probably, best explained by the Apostle Paul, when he writes to the Corinthian church: "Let him who boasts boast in the Lord" (I Corinthians 1:31). The Living Bible expresses best the emotions of the Hebrew with its paraphrase: "Let all the joys of the godly well up in praise to the Lord." Praise belongs to the godly; joy and righteousness go hand in hand. Just as faith and good works cannot be separated, so do righteousness and praise go together.

The righteous are admonished to sing joyfully, and to shout for joy, and to accompany this hymn with the accompaniment of various musical instruments, such as the harp and the ten-stringed lyre. The idea is that the music should sound beautiful and that it be played skillfully. This pre-supposes preparation and rehearsal. It is naïve to suppose that, in spiritual things, only spontaneity is desired. It takes a lot of rehearsal and great skill to produce something that is worth listening to; yet, the final product has to sound as if it is produced spontaneously.

Praising God is an art that has to be learned; it requires practice. We must make up our minds and set ourselves to it to master the skill of praise. This does not mean that everyone has to learn to excel in playing an instrument or we all must learn to sing. But it does mean that we have to cultivate an attitude of praise. The words "make a joyful noise" are often used to excuse sloppiness and carelessness in praise. We must learn to excel.

This excellence is not for the benefit of the public at large. We do not praise God in order to receive praise from man. We should not strive for applause, but for the Lord's assessment: "Well done!"

If we could for one moment see God as He really is, praise would flow naturally from our lives. Since the whole earth is full of His glory, let's open our eyes and hone our skills.

Psalm 33:6-9

"By the word of the LORD were the heavens made, for he spoke, and it came to be; he commanded, and it stood firm."

We can see that God's word is the truth, by the fact that He uses it to create. We will never be able to describe exhaustively the profound meaning of God's speaking. Our own ability to express our feelings and thoughts in words is only a vague shadow of God's revelation of His secrets. God's Word is the truth. He says exactly who He is; His Word proves to us that He is the truth.

According to the Psalmist, God's faithfulness is demonstrated in His works. What is meant is not only that God called everything into being but also sustained His creation. The writer to the Hebrews states that Christ is "sustaining all things by his powerful word" (Hebrews 1:3). The Word of God, therefore, is not only the source of the existence of all that is created, but also the power by which all things function.

Some people wrongly believe that God created all things, but that nature is like a clock that runs by itself without any outside help. It is God's presence that sustains His creation. That is the content of God's faithfulness. The sun rises and sets at certain fixed times. Everything moves according to a predetermined velocity. There is always enough oxygen for man and beast, and the earth produces its fruit. This is evidence of the faithfulness of God.

This is in sharp contrast with the "déjà vu" attitude of the writer of Ecclesiastes, who wrote: " 'Meaningless! Meaningless! 'Utterly meaningless! Everything is meaningless.' What does man gain from all his labor at which he toils under the sun? Generations come and generations go, but the earth remains forever. The sun rises and the sun sets, and hurries back to where it rises. All things are wearisome, more than one can say. The eye never has enough of seeing, nor the ear its fill of hearing. What has been will be again, what has been done will be done again; there is nothing new under the sun" (Ecclesiastes 1:2-5,8,9). There is nothing meaningless and wearisome in the Word of God that sustains His creation.

Even people who give no thought to God in their lives build upon this faithfulness of God. If, for example, a person promises to meet someone on Monday at 7 p.m. under the clock of the bank building, he may not realize that without the faithfulness of God there would be no Monday, nor the hour of seven, or even the clock.

Without the Word of God the atoms in our body would not hold together. There would be no atoms!

Psalm 33:10-22

"From heaven the LORD looks down and sees all mankind; from his dwelling place he watches all who live on earth-- he who forms the hearts of all, who considers everything they do."

George Orwell, in his book *1984*, coined the phrase: "Big Brother is watching you!" It catches the terror of a totalitarian state in which the conduct of every individual was regulated and controlled by the secret police. God's looking down from heaven has nothing in common with Big Brother's watching. The purpose of dictatorship is to suppress freedom and individuality; God's intent is to lead us into freedom and joy.

If human beings have a hard time with this, it is because of the condition of their heart. Our planet is populated by people who are in a state of rebellion against their Creator. Man lives under the illusion that he would be a match for God in a confrontation.

The Psalmist states: "The LORD foils the plans of the nations; he thwarts the purposes of the peoples." Twice in world history God foiled the plans of the nations and thwarted the purposes of the peoples: in Noah's flood, and in the confusion at the tower of Babel. People who rise up against God are doomed to fail. This is the issue that determines the course of history. World history rushes toward Armageddon, where the Antichrist will be crushed by the overwhelming power of the Lamb of God. Man's counsel is temporal; God's counsel is eternal. The Word of God will never become outdated. It stands firm from generation to generation. The Gospel is eternal.

God not only knows all the secret plans we make, but He invented the whole web of thought and planning, which we try to use against our Creator. We do not understand the process of our own thinking. God comprehends completely all human thinking. The actual problem is that man, with his limited knowledge, thinks that he will be a match for the omniscient God. The fact, however, that our knowledge and understanding are limited, does not diminish the quality of that part of the truth that we can grasp. We may not know it all, but what we can know is real.

What we can say about human knowledge can also be said about human power. We set our power over against God's omniscience. Human power and authority is derived from God's omnipotence. To think that we, as human beings, could in any way be a threat to the power of God is ludicrous. No conventional or nuclear arms will have any effect upon the Almighty God. God's omnipotence cannot be expressed in horsepower, or as being overcome by anything that is superior to His might.

Why don't we become realists so we can enter into God's freedom and joy!

Psalm 34:1-6

"I sought the LORD, and he answered me; he delivered me from all my fears. This poor man called, and the LORD heard him; he saved him out of all his troubles."

The troubles David speaks about in this Psalm were of his own making. King Saul tried to kill him and he therefore fled to Philistine country to seek asylum at the court of King Abimelech. But David was less than popular among the Philistines. In his panic, he fled to Gath, the birthplace of the Goliath, the giant he had killed. In fleeing for his life from Saul, he arrived at the headquarters of his archenemies. David went from the frying pan into the fire. In order to save his life, he faked insanity.

David's conduct poses all kinds of ethical questions that are difficult to answer. He told outright lies to both his friends and his enemies. David's relationship with God, at this point, was not what it should have been. He had no tender conscience towards God. When God saved him from a dangerous situation, it was not because he was innocent. God saved him because he was a sinner, not a saint. Nothing of what David had done could be classified as intentional sin. All of it was the result of the pressure of circumstances. He had not placed himself under God's protection, and that was the reason he found himself caught in the snares of the enemy. We cannot draw the lesson from this that it is not important to have a clear conscience, but we may conclude--and this is the important message of this Psalm--that if we fail morally, we have no reason to remain lying on the ground. We should never, *never*, give in to the devil's declaration that all is lost when we fall. Surrendering to Satan's deception ought to be inconceivable to us. This Psalm has to be read against this background of forgiveness and rehabilitation. It gives a deeper meaning to the word "grace." David certainly did not deserve to be saved. But then, who does?

When we consider the circumstances that caused David to write this Psalm, we wonder about its exuberance. It is overwhelming to realize that God is able to create such a sublime situation out of the condition of a weak, fearful, and dubious reaction of a refugee, a situation which was the result of his own failures.

It is at the point of our deepest failure that we begin to understand the marvel of God's grace. It is, in every respect, undeserved favor. Very much undeserved!

Psalm 34:7-16

"The angel of the LORD encamps around those who fear him, and he delivers them."

Very few people have seen an angel. Consequently, we know very little about angels and much of what people say about them must be considered nonsense. The idea that the souls of the dead become angels in heaven has no basis in the Bible.

Angels belong to a separate category of creatures. As far as we know they are spiritual beings who may appear to humans in a human form, but they do not possess a body as we do. The writer of the Epistle to the Hebrews states: "Are not all angels ministering spirits sent to serve those who will inherit salvation?" (Hebrews 1:14).

The fact that angels are mostly invisible to the human eye does not make their existence a myth. The Bible assures us, not only that they exist, but that they perform an important duty in guiding us through life on earth and protecting us when we place ourselves under God's protection.

As we saw in our previous meditation, David had allowed himself to get into deep trouble by leaving the path of truth. He had lied to the priests of Nob and faked insanity at the Philistine court. When he cried out to God to bail him out, he was not only saved from a certain death, but he made a discovery that humbled him for the rest of his life.

Some missionaries have reported that native people who intended to kill them saw them surrounded by angels that protected them, which prevented the attackers from carrying out their plans. We do not read that Abimelech who evicted David from his court, thinking he was a lunatic saw an angel. But David ascribed his salvation to angelic protection.

The angel David refers to, however, is called "the angel of the LORD," whom the Bible identifies with Yahweh, or Jehovah, God Himself. He is the manifestation of our Lord Jesus Christ in the Old Testament. When David cried for help, God did not send an angel to bail him out; He came Himself! He took personal charge of David's salvation, as He does with ours. Even in times of trouble of our own making, He pledges His help; it is ours for the asking. That is reason enough to extol the LORD at all times and have His praise always on our lips.

Psalm 34:7-16

"Taste and see that the LORD is good; blessed is the man who takes refuge in him."

With the words "Taste and see that the LORD is good," David appeals to our senses. He says that God's goodness can be appreciated by our five senses. Some theologians teach that God is good, but that we can only accept this fact in blind faith, because those facts cannot be substantiated. But David tells us that God's goodness is not a mere subjective experience. We cannot say that what we eat is a matter of taste alone. Food is an objective substance, whether we like the taste of it or not. Subjectivity is not excluded, but it cannot exist without the objective substance. So it is with the tasting and in the seeing of the goodness of the Lord.

"Taste" supposes eating and enjoying, but also being fed and staying alive, being nourished and built up by what we eat. If we taste the goodness of the Lord, this goodness will become part of us. C. S. Lewis preambles one of the chapters in his book *Miracles* with the ditty: "It is a funny thing, as funny as can be, but what Mrs. B. eats, turns into Mrs. B." God is good. Jesus confirms this by saying to the rich young man "No one is good except God alone" (Luke 18:19). Goodness is God's exclusive attribute which no man possesses unless he enters into fellowship with Him.

People often tend to project our human malice and hostility upon God. David had a personal experience of God's goodness and he invites us to experience this goodness in our own lives. It is the presence of evil in this world that will often make us lose the trail of God's goodness, and make us hold God responsible for the existence of evil. A French atheist even came to the conclusion: "If there is a God, He is the devil!" James answer to this is: "Don't be deceived, my dear brothers. Every good and perfect gift is from above, coming down from the Father of the heavenly lights, who does not change like shifting shadows" (James 1:16,17).

The Bible invites us to partake of God's goodness. Jesus says "I tell you the truth, unless you eat the flesh of the Son of Man and drink his blood, you have no life in you. Whoever eats my flesh and drinks my blood has eternal life, and I will raise him up at the last day. For my flesh is real food and my blood is real drink. Whoever eats my flesh and drinks my blood remains in me, and I in him" (John 6:53-57). If we feed on Jesus Christ, God's goodness will become flesh and blood in us. It is worthwhile to taste it.

Psalm 34:17-22

"The LORD is close to the brokenhearted and saves those who are crushed in spirit."

We looked at David's circumstances that formed the basis for the writing of this Psalm. It is common for man to seek his own way out of his difficulties. This leads to broken hearts and crushed spirits. When David finally realized what he had done, first with the priests of Nob, and then at Achish' court, he saw the broken pieces, not only around him but also in his own heart. We owe this Psalm to the miracle God wrought for him in this condition. David tells us that God always does this kind of thing. God saves us from situations in which we have landed by our own fault, from catastrophes of our own creation. The embarrassing part is that there are so many of them.

God is not in the heartbreaking business. There are numerous factors that can break the human heart and most of them have to do with love that has gone wrong, either in that it was spurned or taken away. Rebuff by a person we love can be a crushing experience. Even worse is when the one we love is taken away by death. Love is meant to enrich the heart, not to break it. Yet, the human relationships that enhance and deepen our humanity can hurt and devastate us.

The deepest hurts, however, are of our own making. Human love can only exist on the basis of God's love. The apostle John states: "We love because he first loved us (I John 4:19). The things we do that impair our relationship with God are the ones that hurt us most. Sin is the ultimate heartbreaker. When David sought his own way out of his predicaments and allowed his actions to be governed by fear, instead of being guided by God's Spirit, he ended up with the pieces.

The miracle is that God is in the business of healing the broken hearted. He does not glue the pieces together, but He provides us with a new heart and a newborn spirit. God promises: "I will give them an undivided heart and put a new spirit in them; I will remove from them their heart of stone and give them a heart of flesh" (Ezekiel 11:19). Whether our heart is broken and our spirit crushed by spurning of love or loss of a loved one, or by our own fumbling and stumbling, God can heal, renew, and restore. He will do it for the asking.

Psalm 35:1-4[a]

"Say to my soul, 'I am your salvation.' May those who seek my life be disgraced and put to shame; may those who plot my ruin be turned back in dismay."

We don't know what the danger was to David's life that caused the writing of this Psalm. It may have been the attack of King Saul upon him when he played the harp and Saul, in his madness, hurled his spear at David, wanting to pin him against the wall (I Samuel 18:10,11).

Some people think that David sounds too belligerent in this Psalm, a belligerence that is unbecoming to Christians. A closer look, however, reveals that in this Psalm David turns to his enemies in a spiritual way. He decides not to defend himself, but he appeals to God to defend him. That is the only form of revenge allowed to a Christian.

The shield and buckler, the spear and javelin are no human weapon in David's hand, but the weapons God uses. They are symbols of the power of the Holy Spirit. "Not by might nor by power, but by my Spirit" (Zechariah 4:6). That David does not intend violence is clear from his surrender of the matter into the hands of God. He sees God armed with the same weapons as his enemies, but the intent is quite opposite. The difference is as great as between the flesh and the spirit, as between earth and heaven.

When David leaves his defense to God, he implies that he is not going to defend himself. That is an important decision, and it is difficult to stick to it. If a person, who is accused of a criminal act, constantly interrupts his lawyer during his court case, he will surely lose through his own fault.

We may not be in a situation as David was; our life may not be in danger in the physical sense of the word. But we all have been at the place where we would like to get back at people who harm us. God told the people of Israel: "It is mine to avenge; I will repay" (Deuteronomy 32:35). The apostle Paul picks up this theme saying: "Do not take revenge, my friends, but leave room for God's wrath, for it is written: 'It is mine to avenge; I will repay,' says the Lord. On the contrary: 'If your enemy is hungry, feed him; if he is thirsty, give him something to drink. In doing this, you will heap burning coals on his head' " (Romans 12:19,20). If we have come to the place where we are able to do this to people who try to harm us, we demonstrate the love of God. Only the realization of God's love for us will allow us to love our enemies.

Psalm 35:4^b-10

"Then my soul will rejoice in the LORD and delight in his salvation. My whole being will exclaim, 'Who is like you, O LORD? You rescue the poor from those too strong for them, the poor and needy from those who rob them'."

Having asked God to contend with his enemies and having turned over his defense to God, David doesn't ask for his enemies' destruction. He prays that God will put them to shame. Shame is an emotion that defies definition. Adam and Eve felt ashamed before God and before each other after they committed their sin (Genesis 3:7,10). Shame is related to a loss of honor and dignity. Shame presupposes a moral awareness that there are certain ethical norms, and that those were not adhered to. A depreciation of self-worth, which is what shame basically amounts to, may be the first step on the road to conversion. If David prayed that his adversaries might be put to shame, he implied that he entertained hope for them. Shame will reach its climax for the human race when Jesus returns, and "every eye will see him, even those who pierced him; and all the peoples of the earth will mourn because of him" (Revelation 1:7).

David may have been speaking about more than King Saul who tried to kill him, or about other human beings who were after his life. The whole of life is a struggle for survival. We live in a "dog-eat-dog" world and Satan and his demons plot our destruction. The grim reaper "Death" stands at the end of our life. We don't have the strength in ourselves to resist and keep our heads above the water. Even if we amass a fortune and build a wall of financial security around us, we are unprotected as far as the finale of life is concerned. In a sense, we are all robbed and poor.

In the middle of all this David saw God and he cried out: "Who is like you, O LORD?" This God, whom he asked to be his lawyer, turns out to be his Savior. Even before he experienced any change in his circumstances, this joy of the Lord and the assurance of his salvation got a hold on David and he burst out in song. "Faith is the substance of things hoped for, the evidence of things not seen" (Hebrews 11:1 KJV).

Psalm 36:1-4

"An oracle is within my heart concerning the sinfulness of the wicked."

One question that comes to mind when reading this Psalm is about whom David is speaking when he mentions "the wicked." If we look at it as a picture of the contrast between the sinners and the righteous, it seems that David wrote two different Psalms and that someone, somehow, glued them together. The word that throws us off is "oracle," which usually means something God says to human beings. The King James Version makes it a little clearer with: "The transgression of the wicked saith within my heart, that there is no fear of God before his eyes." It seems that David speaks about himself; he is the wicked one.

The conviction of his own wickedness came to him when he caught a glimpse of the greatness of God's love. Sin tends to blind our eyes to the reality of our own condition. It is when we are confronted with the glory of God that we realize the evil condition of our own heart. We are all created in the image of God. It is when we see God's image in us placed next to the original that we realize how much we have deviated. The image of God in us has turned into a caricature. The discovery of our iniquity and of God's holiness is always a simultaneous process.

When the prophet Isaiah saw God in the temple seated on a throne, high and exalted and he heard the seraphs singing: "Holy, holy, holy is the LORD Almighty; the whole earth is full of his glory," he cried out: "Woe to me! I am ruined! For I am a man of unclean lips" (Isaiah 6:1-5). When we see something of God's love and righteousness the Holy Spirit will convict us of sin, not for the purpose of condemning us and making us feel miserable, but so that we would confess and cry out for forgiveness.

It is God's love that reaches to the heavens to convict and saves us. What David says is not that there are saints and sinners in this world, but that the dividing line between death and life runs through every human being. Sin is not merely something others do; it is in me. The poison is in my veins, wickedness is in my heart. The watershed between good and evil is in my own life and I need forgiveness, grace, and salvation.

Psalm 36:5-7

"Your love, O LORD, reaches to the heavens, your faithfulness to the skies. Your righteousness is like the mighty mountains, your justice like the great deep. O LORD, you preserve both man and beast. How priceless is your unfailing love! Both high and low among men find refuge in the shadow of your wings."

This is an amazing Psalm! It seems as if David speaks about the sins of others, but a closer look indicates that David looks in his own heart. We could call this Psalm the Analysis of a Conversion. David is conscious of his own sinful nature. Such a discovery can only be made in the presence of God where the Holy Spirit convicts of sin. David speaks here about the exposure of his own unrighteousness.

The root of sin is within us all and the poison is in our veins. We all tend to live our lives outside fellowship with God, and make our plans without consulting our Creator. With our inflated ego we think the world revolves around us.

The actual miracle of conversion is not mentioned in this Psalm, but the sudden change in tone suggests it. There has been a transformation as from death into life.

David describes God's lovingkindness, which brings about conviction of sin, in a grandiose way by stating: "Your love, O LORD, reaches to the heavens, your faithfulness to the skies."

David expresses himself rather primitively by saying that God's love reaches "to the clouds" (KJV). In our age of space travel such a comparison does not amount to much. Translating what David wanted to convey, we could say that God's love fills the universe, outer space and beyond. As the horizon of our conception of reality is enlarged, so is the love of God.

God's lovingkindness is a description of His character. The words "the clouds," "the mountains of God," "the great deep," describe the eternal aspects of God's being. The use of these rather primitive images conveys a better picture than if he had used extraterrestrial terms.

There is in the St. Bavo Cathedral in the Belgian city of Ghent an altar piece by the brothers van Eyck, called *The Adoration of the Lamb*. The painting places this heavenly scene from the book of Revelation in the earthly surrounding of an altar in a Roman Catholic Church of that time. The altar stands in a meadow with flowers that can be found all over Belgium. Heavenly reality is translated in images of every day life in a way that fills this world with the glory of God.

We have to learn to see God's glory in the world in which we live now. If we cannot see it now, we will not be able to see it when we get to heaven either. If we have passed from death into life, glory will fill our soul. We need a sense of glory within to see the glory around us.

Psalm 36:8-12

"For with you is the fountain of life; in your light we see light."

This is one of the great sayings of the Old Testament. The Bible has a lot to say about light. Light is the essence of God's being. John writes: "God is light" (I John 1:5). We all know from experience what light is; yet science has never been able to come up with a formula that defines light. The light we know is natural light; God's light is spiritual. That which we call "light" is, actually, the image of a spiritual reality. Our knowledge of light is mainly limited to sunlight. In the creation story in Genesis, the heavenly bodies make their appearance on the fourth day of creation. This means that God had already finished half of His creation before the sun is even mentioned. The light God created on the first day, therefore, cannot have been the light of the sun. In the book of Revelation the sun is discharged of her duties, and God takes over her task. We read: "There will be no more night. They will not need the light of a lamp or the light of the sun, for the Lord God will give them light" (Revelation 22:5).

All this sounds rather strange to us and it is hard to understand. The first lesson we learn is that the sun is not our only source of light, and not even the most important one. The real source of light is God Himself. That is why Jesus calls Himself "The Light of the World." And He says: "Whoever follows me will never walk in darkness, but will have the light of life" (John 8:12). David uses light and life as poetical parallels. Sin steeps us in darkness, because sin cuts us off from the source of all light. Fellowship with God places us in the light.

How do we interpret the words: "In your light we see light?" We owe our capacity to observe natural light to the fact that God is light, but that is a superficial implication of this statement. Our fellowship with God changes the whole perspective of our life. Natural light provides sight; spiritual light gives us insight. "In your light..." stands, therefore, for fellowship with God. TLB gives the paraphrase: "Our light is from your light." If we walk in the light, we will see the light, and we obtain insight into the spiritual reality of God. It has been suggested that light stands for the glory of God. It is also true that, if we live in fellowship with God, we will know where we are going in our everyday life. Walking in the light is a growing experience. The Book of Proverbs states: "The path of the righteous is like the first gleam of dawn, shining ever brighter till the full light of day" (Proverbs 4:18).

Psalm 37:1-15

"Trust in the LORD and do good; dwell in the land and enjoy safe pasture."

The Israelites had conquered Canaan approximately 300 years before David wrote this Psalm, and they had dwelt in the land ever since.

When Jacob and his family of seventy moved to Egypt they were not a nation but just a large family (Genesis 46:26,27). For several centuries Jacob's descendants lived in Egypt and became slaves of the Egyptians. It was only as they left Egypt that the nation of Israel was born. God sent them to Canaan to conquer and occupy it. There was a sense in which Canaan was the piece of real estate God had given them to live in as a nation. It was an integral part of their freedom and dignity. But it was more.

During the desert crossing the Israelites constructed the tabernacle and all its furniture. The Ark of the Covenant was part of that. God said about it: "There, above the cover between the two cherubim that are over the ark of the Testimony, I will meet with you and give you all my commands for the Israelites" (Exodus 25:22). It was the ark, symbol of God's presence, that lead Israel into the Promised Land. We read: "Whenever the ark set out, Moses said, 'Rise up, O LORD! May your enemies be scattered; may your foes flee before you.' Whenever it came to rest, he said, 'Return, O LORD, to the countless thousands of Israel' " (Numbers 10:35,36). So Canaan became the place of God's rest, the place where God revealed Himself in this world. Israel could only dwell in the land because God dwelled there. It was the only place in the world where God revealed Himself at that time, the only place where He could be worshipped. Dwelling in the land meant dwelling at the place of God's revelation.

The coming of Jesus Christ changed all this. Jesus said to the Samaritan woman: "A time is coming when you will worship the Father neither on this mountain nor in Jerusalem. Yet a time is coming and has now come when the true worshipers will worship the Father in spirit and truth, for they are the kind of worshipers the Father seeks. God is spirit, and his worshipers must worship in spirit and in truth" (John 4:21-24).

Nowadays we dwell in the Promised Land if our sins have been forgiven because of the death of Jesus, and we have become a new creation because of His resurrection. As with Israel it is important to know where to live and how to live in the land. Where we live determines our lifestyle. If we live in the presence of the Lord our lives must demonstrate it.

Psalm 37:1-15

"Delight yourself in the LORD and he will give you the desires of your heart. Commit your way to the LORD; trust in him and he will do this: He will make your righteousness shine like the dawn, the justice of your cause like the noonday sun."

The theme of this Psalm is "dwell in the land." The words "inherit the land" are found at least seven times in this Psalm.

In David's days, the conquest of Canaan was an accomplished fact. Possession of the land is used in Scripture as a rich symbol for the heritage God has given us in a hostile world. Jesus says: "Blessed are the meek, for they will inherit the earth" (Matthew 5:5).

In the ancient world "meekness" was not considered a desirable quality. Even now the definition is not always positive. *The Merriam-Webster Dictionary* defines "meek" as "characterized by patience and long-suffering," but also as, "deficient in spirit and courage." In the Biblical sense the word has acquired the meaning of inner tenderness.

When David says: "Delight yourself in the LORD and he will give you the desires of your heart," he does not mean that we should delight ourselves in the Lord in order to obtain the desires of our heart. If we enter into fellowship with God merely for the purpose of getting out of it what we can, we, obviously, have no idea what it is all about. Our fellowship with God cannot be driven by ulterior motives. Our attitude should be the one the prophet Habakkuk had, who wrote: "Though the fig tree does not bud and there are no grapes on the vines, though the olive crop fails and the fields produce no food, though there are no sheep in the pen and no cattle in the stalls, yet I will rejoice in the LORD, I will be joyful in God my Savior"(Habakkuk 3:17,19). The fact that God gives us the desires of our heart is a byproduct.

It is clear that if God is to give us the desires of our heart some drastic changes will first have to take place within us. It would be unsafe for us to obtain our heart's desires without thorough cleansing and sanctification. Fellowship with God will purify our motives, because we learn to subject our will to His will. James says that God cannot hear some of our prayers, because our motives are not pure. We read, "When you ask, you do not receive, because you ask with wrong motives, that you may spend what you get on your pleasures" (James 4:3). We do not really know what our true desires are. We hardly know ourselves. Fellowship with God will give us self-knowledge. In that way, we will learn to distinguish our vague desires from our real needs.

Psalm 37:16-24
"Those the LORD blesses will inherit the land."

We find in this Psalm two kinds of people, those who trust in the Lord and those who do not take God seriously. It seems that the one who does not take God into account in his life comes out better in this world than the believer. This is true only as long as we look at a section of life without putting things in their perspective. Man's problem is that his field of vision is limited to life on earth; our five senses cannot observe what happens after death. Faith in God helps us to see over the boundaries, but our physical eye cannot see that far. As far as our everyday life is concerned we live in this world alone, not in the one to come. This fact distorts reality for us; unless we can see the perspective, we cannot see things as they really are. This faulty image of reality is the cause of the fretting, or jealousy the Psalmist speaks about.

We all know that our life on earth is limited; yet, many people act as if they are here to stay. If we would spend eternity on this planet, it would make sense to accumulate wealth and build up comfort. But if we know we will have to move on and we spend all our time and energy with the present, hoarding things we will not be able to take with us, we are foolish. We live in a world of sin, sickness, and death. Even if we raise our standards of living, we cannot escape the pollution of sin. We breathe in corruption and breathe out wretchedness. But God promises us a better world to come. Being upset because others are successful and affluent demonstrates that we do not take God's promise seriously. Israel had entered Canaan; when David wrote this Psalm they did possess the land. Yet, David writes: "Those who hope in the LORD will inherit the land." The writer of the Epistle to the Hebrews puts it in the right perspective when he states: "If Joshua had given them rest, God would not have spoken later about another day. There remains, then, a Sabbath-rest for the people of God; for anyone who enters God's rest also rests from his own work, just as God did from his. Let us, therefore, make every effort to enter that rest, so that no one will fall by following their example of disobedience" (Hebrews 4:8-11). So there is more involved here than the physical occupation of a geographical area. It pertains to an attitude towards life, to a claiming of God's promises, to an acceptance of the logical results of salvation. We are no fools if we give up what we cannot keep in order to obtain what we cannot lose.

Psalm 37:25-40

"I was young and now I am old, yet I have never seen the righteous forsaken or their children begging bread. They are always generous and lend freely; their children will be blessed."

In v. 25 we find one of the great promises of the Bible: "I was young and now I am old, yet I have never seen the righteous forsaken or their children begging bread." It appears from those words that David wrote this Psalm at the end of his life. God promises to bless our families, and He serves as the collateral of our existence on earth. If a parent puts his or her trust in the Lord for the sustenance of the family, the children will be blessed. What a profound truth! Our dwelling in the land is demonstrated in our generosity. We can always afford to help others. Again, Paul says: "Remember this: Whoever sows sparingly will also reap sparingly, and whoever sows generously will also reap generously"(II Corinthians 9:6). Our lives should be characterized by compassion with the suffering of others. Our inheriting the land is related to the condition of our heart. Generosity is the result of our confidence that God takes care of us. Avarice is often an indication of fear that we will not be able to make ends meet. We use money to build walls and fortresses around us, as a substitute for a sense of security. The author of the epistle to the Hebrews admonishes: "Keep your lives free from the love of money and be content with what you have, because God has said, 'Never will I leave you; never will I forsake you.' So we say with confidence, 'The Lord is my helper; I will not be afraid. What can man do to me?' " (Hebrews 13:5,6). Dwelling in the land means that we lean on the Lord for our financial security. If we do this, our children will learn the lesson also and become a blessing to other people.

It is true that salvation cannot be expressed in dollars. Our soul is worth more than all of the world's wealth. Jesus said: "What good will it be for a man if he gains the whole world, yet forfeits his soul? Or what can a man give in exchange for his soul?" (Matthew 16:26). Yet, the way we handle our finances is a good thermometer of our spiritual health. Speaking about his contributions to the building of the temple, David said: "But who am I, and who are my people, that we should be able to give as generously as this? Everything comes from you, and we have given you only what comes from your hand. It comes from your hand, and all of it belongs to you" (I Chronicles 29:14,16). If we belong to the Lord, so does our money.

Psalm 38:1-10

"O LORD, do not rebuke me in your anger or discipline me in your wrath. For your arrows have pierced me, and your hand has come down upon me. My guilt has overwhelmed me like a burden too heavy to bear."

David was obviously ill when he wrote this Psalm. He was also burdened by a sense of guilt for a sin he had committed. We do not learn what this sin was. His sickness gives urgency to the matter of his guilt. God, evidently, took David's struggle seriously, otherwise this poem would never have been incorporated in the Book of Psalms.

It is a known fact that our physical condition influences our spiritual life, and it certainly has its bearing upon our emotions. In general, we function better on a social and spiritual level if we feel fit in body. We seldom realize that this in itself is a symptom of the topsy-turvy world in which we live. If sin had never entered our world, our spirit would rule supremely over our body; now, the influence of our spirit upon our physical condition is very limited, even in the best instances. It is important that we are aware of this problem. What God tells us in our suffering is always related to the fact that our body rules over our spirit, and that this situation is abnormal. This is an important feature in the matter of faith healing.

We don't know what David's ailment was. He called his sickness "God's arrows." As missionaries in Indonesia, my wife and I worked among very primitive tribes people who were just emerging from the Stone Age. Some would come to us for medicine to cure a back ache or sore muscles. They called their symptoms "the devil's arrows." David also makes the connection between his physical suffering and a spiritual reality, but he ascribes it to God not to Satan.

David's sickness got him involved in a tremendous struggle. He wrestled with the Lord, not only to experience physical healing, but a complete restoration of his human dignity. His sin and sickness had isolated him from God and society.

The title of this Psalm tells us that it is meant to be a "petition." The Hebrew word literally means "to remember." The word is also used in connection with the burning of incense. There is no note of victory in David's plea. But victory is understood in the fact that David put his complaint on God's altar and lets it burn there. That is what we ought to do with our guilt and our pains. The medium is the message!

Psalm 38:11-22

"My friends and companions avoid me because of my wounds; my neighbors stay far away."

Just as riches and poverty influence human relations, so do sickness and health. In a germ-free society like ours material possessions may exercise a stronger power than the condition of our body. But we do tend to look away when we notice a handicap in someone and we find it difficult to relate to a person who is terminally ill. Even if we feel compassion in our heart, we may find ourselves unable to communicate this to others. This instinctive shyness and reluctance increases the suffering of the shut-ins and physically challenged persons.

This problem varies from one culture to another. In a more primitive society than ours, a sick person is ostracized. Ignorance about the source of sickness makes societies isolate their weak and invalid members. We see in the animal world that the stronger animals kill off the weak and sick among them. This cruel tendency is not completely absent in our Western world either, certainly not in our capitalistic society. Beyond treatment of the physically handicapped, it is considered to be "good business" to drown your competitors. A socialist government will try to avert this, at least outwardly. But under the cover of equality it appears that "some are more equal than others," to borrow George Orwell's great indictment.

It is only in the fellowship of Christ, where the members of the body love one another, that there is place for the sick, and healing is offered. Natural man is always repulsed by sickness. Only a child of God can demonstrate pure compassion, because the love of Christ compels him. God is a God of compassion. He knows what suffering, rejection and isolation are all about. "We do not have a high priest who is unable to sympathize with our weaknesses" (Hebrews 4:15). "He himself bore our sins [and sicknesses] in his body on the tree…by his wounds we are healed" (I Peter 2:24).

It may take determination to demonstrate compassion to those who are suffering. If natural shyness or other inhibitions prevent us from demonstrating the love of Christ to those who need it most, it may help to remind ourselves that one day we may be on the receiving end. Jesus says: "So in everything, do to others what you would have them do to you, for this sums up the Law and the Prophets" (Matthew 7:12). And "Give, and it will be given to you. A good measure, pressed down, shaken together and running over, will be poured into your lap. For with the measure you use, it will be measured to you" (Luke 6:38).

Psalm 38:11-22

"I wait for you, O LORD; you will answer, O Lord my God. For I said, 'Do not let them gloat or exalt themselves over me when my foot slips'."

David expected an answer from God, not only an answer to his own questions, but also that God would answer his enemies. God's answers are often quite different from what we expect. God is always full of surprises. In the Book of Job, Job puts a series of questions to God, to which he receives no direct answer. When God appears to Job, He speaks about things that were quite different from the questions that occupied Job's mind. Yet, we get the impression that Job considered that all his questions were answered.

It appears that God answers the questions we ought to have asked, which are not always the ones we do ask. We often ask the wrong questions, or we don't know what to ask. Seeing God and walking with Him will make most of our questions melt away. As the hymn states: "The things of earth will grow strangely dim, in the light of His glory and grace."

God answers us in Jesus Christ. He does not give an answer; He is the answer. Once we have learned to ask the right questions, we have become mature. C. S. Lewis in his book *Till We Have Faces* tells the story of a Greek queen who tries to come to grips with the questions of life by bringing them before the gods. She wants to meet the gods face to face. She ends up with the profound question "How can we meet the gods face to face till we have faces?"

One of the main purposes of our being on earth is that we learn to ask the right questions. The problem is never that God does not know the answers to our questions. It is never a matter of what is being said, either by God or by us. God's answers to David stopped the mouths of his enemies. God's answer is always creative; to David it came in the form of salvation, healing, and rehabilitation. God's answer to David would completely change the relationship between him and his enemies.

Jesus leaves us with this paradox: "In that day you will no longer ask me anything. I tell you the truth, my Father will give you whatever you ask in my name" (John 16:23).

Psalm 39:1-6

"Show me, O LORD, my life's end and the number of my days; let me know how fleeting is my life. You have made my days a mere handbreadth; the span of my years is as nothing before you. Each man's life is but a breath."

This Psalm deals with death. Some Bible versions entitle it "A Prayer of Acceptance." The question is acceptance of what? One Dutch poet has written the lines: "The heart that does not resist joins those who have become passive. One begins by accepting life, and finally, one accepts death." This Psalm, however, seems to open with a protest. The protest is never put in words, but the inner rebellion comes through clearly. David wrestles with the reality of death. He knows that he will succumb to death's power in the end because he faces a force that he can never vanquish, but he rebels against this with all his strength and energy. We ought to join David in his protest. God did not create man so that man would die. Dying is the most degrading experience a human being can undergo. Everyone who accepts death without any protest, ought to be ashamed.

Jesus protested against death. At Lazarus' grave we read: "He was deeply moved in spirit and troubled" (John 11:33). The Greek word for "troubled" actually means "indignant." Jesus' indignation over death culminated in His resurrection in which He took the key of death away from the devil.

It is true that death is the result of sin, and since we have all sinned, we are all facing death. David's initial silence was caused by a sense of guilt. He wanted to voice a protest against death, but the realization that there was a connection between his sins and his death forced him to keep his mouth shut. The devil knows how to manipulate such feelings with great dexterity. He tries to make us believe that we ought to accept death because we have sinned against God. This is a clever but demonic device. He who is the author of sin and death, tries to tell us that we have to die because we are guilty.

Just as much as Jesus died for our sins, so He rose for our victory over death.

There is, however, a positive feature in death that forces us to face our limitations and arrange our life accordingly. It is of the utmost importance to remember that our days are numbered, that we will not live on earth forever and ever. God will call each of us home and we will appear before Him to give an account. The thought of death may help us to keep a clear conscience by confessing our sins and committing each day to the Lord. One day we will breathe our last. That "one day" could be today.

Psalm 39:7-13

"Hear my prayer, O LORD, listen to my cry for help; be not deaf to my weeping. For I dwell with you as an alien, a stranger, as all my fathers were."

The Living Bible offers an interesting paraphrase of this verse: "Hear my prayer, O Lord; listen to my cry! Don't sit back, unmindful of my tears. For I am your guest. I am a traveler passing through the earth, as all my fathers were."

David's cry for help is still in the context of his struggle with death. The fact that we will not eternally remain on earth makes us strangers. We live here as in a foreign country. For those of us who have never moved very far from the place where we were born, the image may not speak to us so clearly. People who have lived overseas in foreign countries who had to adapt themselves to foreign cultures understand what David means.

We may live here but we don't belong here. God will rehabilitate us after our scornful experience with death. The decomposition of our bodies is painful and shameful, but God will clothe us with our heavenly dwelling. The Apostle Paul writes to the Corinthians: "Now we know that if the earthly tent we live in is destroyed, we have a building from God, an eternal house in heaven, not built by human hands. Meanwhile we groan, longing to be clothed with our heavenly dwelling, because when we are clothed, we will not be found naked. For while we are in this tent, we groan and are burdened, because we do not wish to be unclothed but to be clothed with our heavenly dwelling, so that what is mortal may be swallowed up by life. Now it is God who has made us for this very purpose and has given us the Spirit as a deposit, guaranteeing what is to come" (II Corinthians 5:1-5).

Paul also writes: "Our citizenship is in heaven. And we eagerly await a Savior from there, the Lord Jesus Christ, who, by the power that enables him to bring everything under his control, will transform our lowly bodies so that they will be like his glorious body" (Philippians 3:20,21). We do have a home and, as foreigners on earth, we suffer from homesickness. It is important that we are registered in the place where we want to go. Heaven does not issue any visas; only proofs of citizenship are required.

Psalm 40:1-5

"I waited patiently for the LORD; he turned to me and heard my cry. He lifted me out of the slimy pit, out of the mud and mire; he set my feet on a rock and gave me a firm place to stand. He put a new song in my mouth, a hymn of praise to our God."

These verses describe in a wonderful way the testimony of one who was found by the Lord. The first words are "I waited patiently." The Hebrew reads literally "Waiting, I waited." The repetition of these words does not necessarily express patience. "I waited and waited" states more about our impatience than about our patience. A better rendering would be: "Passionately, I waited for the LORD." People who are sinking in slime and mud cannot be expected to exercise much patience.

There is, probably, no clearer picture of sin than that of falling in a pit we cannot climb out of. For a hygienically disposed person, slime and mud are repulsive substances. In the same way, sin should be repugnant to a child of God. Most of the bacteria that live in mud are bad for our health. If we cry out to God, He will save us from the power of sin that pulls us down, and that will, eventually, kill us. Most of our problems stem from the fact that we refuse to recognize our condition. We tend to live in our pit, as if that is a normal condition. We have to come to the point that we call mud mud, and confess our sin as sin.

It is good to be passionate about our salvation. Blessings often escape us, because we do not long for them with our whole being. God's desire to bless us is immense, but it is often hindered by our indifference. Once we are delivered from apathy, there is little to obstruct the flow of God's blessing and the fullness of His presence in our lives. Only God Himself can kindle such passionate desire in our hearts. Jesus says: "No one can come to me unless the Father who sent me draws him" (John 6:44). It is the pull of the Holy Spirit that will change our indifference into a passionate desire.

David tells us in a nutshell what God does for us when He saves us. First, we are saved from sin and lifted out of the slimy pit. Then there is rehabilitation, under the image of our feet being placed on a rock and being given a firm place to stand. Then follows praise, and finally, the witness of what happened. Those four points are closely related to each other; they all pertain to the life of a child of God.

If this does not describe our experience with God, we had better get passionate about our desperate condition. He will hear our cry.

Psalm 40:6-17

"Sacrifice and offering you did not desire, but my ears you have pierced; burnt offerings and sin offerings you did not require. Then I said, 'Here I am, I have come--it is written about me in the scroll. I desire to do your will, O my God; your law is within my heart'."

The writer of the Epistle to the Hebrews quotes these verses in connection with Jesus' death on the cross as a sacrifice for our sin (Hebrews 10:5-7). David was a prophet whom the Holy Spirit used at several occasions to proclaim a truth that he, himself, could not understand.

We recognize that Jesus died on the cross as our substitute. We ought to have died for our sin but He took our place. David did not know that this would happen, but he understood that God's ultimate purpose could not be to see an animal die as a payment for human sin. David knew that law required animal sacrifices. "Sacrifice and offering you did not desire" does not deny that fact. He understood that the sacrifice of an animal has moral consequences for him. He understood that what happened on the altar gave God a legal basis to come to his aid, to lift him out of the slimy pit, out of the mud and mire, and to set his feet on a rock and give him a firm place to stand. If a person, for whom the sacrifice is brought, continues in his sin, then all shedding of blood is in vain. The essence of a conversion is the discovery that if Jesus died for me I can no longer keep on living for myself. Without an act of unconditional surrender to the will of God, the sacrifice is senseless.

That is the meaning of the phrase: "my ears you have pierced." The words refer to the law, given in Exodus regarding the Hebrew slave. An Israelite who was bankrupt could get out of debt by selling himself to an employer for a period of seven years in order to get his life back together. If after those years the slave decided that he loved his master and the family he had raised while in slavery, he had the option of staying in service as a bond slave. As a token of this kind of slavery out of love, his master would pierce his ear (See Exodus 21:2-6).

In Jesus Christ, God has purchased our freedom. We have the option to tell Him: "I love my master and my wife and children and do not want to go free." Paradoxically, serving God out of love and enslaving ourselves to Him will bring us into a freedom that cannot be found anywhere else.

Psalm 41:1-3

"Blessed is he who has regard for the weak; the LORD delivers him in times of trouble. The LORD will protect him and preserve his life; he will bless him in the land and not surrender him to the desire of his foes."

With these words David pronounced a blessing upon those who love their neighbor as themselves. Our relationship with our fellowmen has a direct bearing upon our relationship with God and vice versa. Jesus puts the love for our neighbor on the same line as our love for God. He says: "Love the Lord your God with all your heart and with all your soul and with all your mind. This is the first and greatest commandment. And the second is like it: 'Love your neighbor as yourself. All the Law and the Prophets hang on these two commandments' " (Matthew 22:37-40). The Apostle John makes it clear that our love for God cannot be separated from our love for our brother: "If anyone says, 'I love God,' yet hates his brother, he is a liar. For anyone who does not love his brother, whom he has seen, cannot love God, whom he has not seen" (I John 4:20).

David didn't merely speak about a fellow human being in general, but about "the weak." The Lord wants us to associate particularly with "the underdog." Jesus identified Himself with the hungry, the thirsty, the foreigners, the naked, the sick, and the prisoners. He says to us: "I was hungry and you gave me something to eat, I was thirsty and you gave me something to drink, I was a stranger and you invited me in, I needed clothes and you clothed me, I was sick and you looked after me, I was in prison and you came to visit me'" (Matthew 25:35,36). To Saul of Tarsus, He introduced Himself with the words: "I am Jesus, whom you are persecuting" (Acts 9:5).

Why do we so often fail to recognize Christ in our fellowmen, especially in the weak ones? Our standards of judgment, evidently, do not correspond to the way God looks at people. We don't look for the eternal values in the life of our neighbor; we fix our eyes upon the physical features. God said to Samuel: "The LORD does not look at the things man looks at. Man looks at the outward appearance, but the LORD looks at the heart" (I Samuel 16:7).

In Jesus Christ God turns our standards and measurements upside-down. He demonstrates that our thoughts and evaluations are wrong. God's beatitude pertains to all who have come to the conclusion that they owe their salvation to the death of Jesus Christ on the cross. If we see in the opening statement of this Psalm only a wish of blessing for those who demonstrate social concern, we miss the point. Love for our neighbor has value only if it is based upon the love of Christ.

Psalm 41:4-12

"Even my close friend, whom I trusted, he who shared my bread, has lifted up his heel against me."

Friendship is a wonderful thing. To be able to share joy and sorrow with a fellowman, one who understands and reciprocates, can make all the difference in the way we face hardship. The Book of Proverbs states: "A friend loves at all times, and a brother is born for adversity" (Proverbs 17:17). But betrayal by a friend causes the deepest emotional wounds. Satan can use friendships to bring us down spiritually, physically, and emotionally. He did this in the case of Job. With friends like Job had, he didn't need any enemies.

David wrote this Psalm after having been seriously ill. He had used the time of his illness to take an inventory of his life and he had identified sin, which he confessed to God. After that God had begun to heal him. During the process David's enemies had shown a heightened interest in his physical condition. They gloated over the expectation that he would die soon. This could be expected from enemies. But the real hurt was what David's friend did to him.

David didn't know that in this hurtful experience he portrayed prophetically a detail of Jesus' intense emotional suffering about Judas. After having washed the disciples' feet, including Judas' feet, and saying to Peter: "Unless I wash you, you have no part with me," Jesus said: "I am not referring to all of you; I know those I have chosen. But this is to fulfill the scripture: 'He who shares my bread has lifted up his heel against me' " (John 13: 8,18).

We often don't know how the pieces of life's puzzle fit together. David certainly couldn't have known that he foreshadowed the greatest emotional hurt of his greatest grandson. He didn't understand that his pain had meaning for God.

We don't know the meaning of our own pain either, do we? On the day God wipes away our tears He will also show us the completed jigsaw puzzle. At present we may find comfort in the fact that Jesus knows the meaning of betrayal and of the pain that goes with it. "For we do not have a high priest who is unable to sympathize with our weaknesses, but we have one who has been tempted in every way, just as we are-yet was without sin. Let us then approach the throne of grace with confidence, so that we may receive mercy and find grace to help us in our time of need" (Hebrews 4:15,16).

Psalm 41:13

"Praise be to the LORD, the God of Israel, from everlasting to everlasting. Amen and Amen."

This doxology not only concludes this Psalm, but the whole first book of the Book of Psalms. Each of the five books into which the Book of Psalms is divided ends with a doxology, Psalm One Hundred Fifty being one great doxology that closes the whole Book of Psalms.

God is addressed here as "the LORD, the God of Israel," that is "Yahweh, Elohim of Israel." Yahweh or Jehovah is the name with which God revealed Himself to Moses, as "I AM WHO I AM" (Exodus 3:14). God calls Himself there: "The LORD, the God of your fathers-- the God of Abraham, the God of Isaac and the God of Jacob" (Exodus 3:15). God reveals Himself to man for the purpose of redeeming him. If we would try to say everything about this subject that can be said, "I suppose that even the whole world would not have room for the books that would be written," to quote the Apostle John (John 21:25).

In the name Elohim, we find an expression of the triune God, the Creator of heaven and earth. God's revelation of Himself means that eternity penetrates the time and space in which we live. Initially, that is before man's fall into sin, there was no contrast between eternity and time. Death made the relationship of the two a paradox. God's revelation builds a bridge that unites time and eternity again. That is the reason it has become possible for man on earth to send praises up to heaven, which will resound eternally above. It is a great miracle that a mortal man on earth can open his mouth and say: "Praise be to the LORD, the God of Israel, from everlasting to everlasting. Amen and Amen." And that he can confirm this with the highest oath of "Amen and Amen!"

There is also in these words the acknowledgment that God reveals Himself in this world through the people of Israel, particularly through Israel's greatest Son. Jehovah, Elohim is the Father of our Lord Jesus Christ. We have infinitely more reason to eternally praise the LORD, God of Israel than David ever had. The praise we intone on earth is a rehearsal for what we will do eternally in heaven. Let us not forget our practice!

Psalm 42:1-4

"As the deer pants for streams of water, so my soul pants for you, O God. My soul thirsts for God, for the living God. When can I go and meet with God?"

The image shows us a hunted deer dying of thirst. The Hebrew text conveys the idea of a stag, the leader of the herd, whose death would leave the other animals in disarray. It is a picture of someone who would leave a trail of sorrow behind if he were to perish spiritually.

In our fellowship with God, we never feed upon Him for our own sake alone. If we go thirsty, others will suffer the consequences also. Our prayer ought always to be: "Lord, bless me, so I can be a blessing." He who only thirsts after God for his own fulfillment does not understand what is at stake. When God blessed Abraham, He had the salvation of the whole world on His mind. "I will make you into a great nation and I will bless you; I will make your name great, *and you will be a blessing*" (Genesis 12:2). And when Jesus invited the thirsty souls to come and drink, He said: "If anyone is thirsty, let him come to me and drink. Whoever believes in me, as the Scripture has said, *streams of living water will flow from within him*" (John 7:37,38). The greatest satisfaction consists of the flowing through of the blessing.

Our foremost problem often is that our thirst is not intense enough. What causes thirst? Physical thirst signals our body that it needs water more than food. A person can live for days without food. Hunger will even disappear after a few days, but thirst only increases. Panting for God, for most people, is not a daily experience. Longing for God is, usually, not the passion of our lives, because of the presence of sin. Profound longing for fellowship with God can only exist on the basis of atonement for sin. A person who never confessed his sin, and who has never received forgiveness, can never pant for God in the way described in this Psalm.

A. W. Tozer, in his book *The Pursuit of God*, concludes one of the chapters with the prayer: "O God, I have tasted Thy goodness, and it has both satisfied me and made me thirsty for more. I am painfully conscious of my need of further grace. I am ashamed of my lack of desire. O God, the Triune God, I want to want Thee; I long to be filled with longing; I thirst to be made more thirsty."

Psalm 42:3-4

"My tears have been my food day and night, while men say to me all day long, 'Where is your God?' "

Where is God when it hurts? is the title of a book by Philip Yancey. It is also the question many of us ask when we hurt. We may have the promises that God keeps record of our tears and puts them in His bottle (Psalm 56:8, NKJV) and we may believe that "God will wipe away every tear from [our] eyes" (Revelation 7:17), but at the moment grief hits us this is of little comfort. We may find some relief when we even cry out to God and say, "God where are you?" At least we believe that He ought to be there, even though we cannot see Him. After Lazarus died, Martha said to Jesus, "if you had been here, my brother would not have died" (John 11:21). But Jesus wasn't there at the crucial moment. Not only that, but Jesus had been absent on purpose. We read: "Now Jesus loved Martha and her sister and Lazarus. So, when He heard that he was sick, He stayed two more days in the place where He was" (John 11:5,6 - NKJV). It was Jesus' love that kept Him away! However incomprehensible this may sound, God may leave us alone in our grief because He loves us.

For what purpose? Note that the Psalmist doesn't himself cry out to God, "God where are you?" It is the people around him that looked at him to see how he reacted to his loss. Their question was not a sympathetic but a cynical one. Their attitude was, "look at that guy who preached to us about this God of comfort! Now as it hits home, he can't handle it." It is one thing to ask. "God where are you?" It is another one when other people ask us, "Where is your God?" God loves us and leaves us alone for a purpose. How we react in times of trouble depends on whether we allow God to put His arms around us when we hurt. If we are in the habit of sharing all the details of daily life with Him, we will turn to Him as by reflex when we hurt. "For in the day of trouble he will keep me safe in his dwelling; he will hide me in the shelter of his tabernacle and set me high upon a rock" (Psalm 27:5). If God does that for us, other people will know it.

Psalm 42:5-11

"My soul is downcast within me; therefore I will remember you from the land of the Jordan, the heights of Hermon--from Mount Mizar."

This Psalm is composed by the Sons of Korah. They are, probably, the descendants of the Levite Korah who perished in the rebellion against Moses (See Numbers 16:1-35). In the days of David they had become gatekeepers at the temple (I Chronicles 26:1,2). The Holy Spirit had given them gifts that far surpassed what they needed to fulfill their daily tasks. They had not become professional musicians, like the sons of Asaph, Heman, and Jeduthun (See I Chronicles 25:1-8), but as good amateurs, they had mastered the art of praising God with their poetical gifts. Their duties took them to the gates of the temple, but this Psalm speaks about a person who is banished from the temple, and who finds himself in "the land of the Jordan, the heights of Hermon... Mount Mizar." One can be physically standing at the gate of God's temple and spiritually removed from it by many miles. The son of Korah recognized the danger that one could get so used to the presence of God that his thirst would dry up. Thirst for God originates with God.

If our fellowship with God has dried up and all that is left is a memory, people around us will know it. The people of the world have a fine intuition that tells them that lives of individual Christians, and the fellowship of the saints ought to be a manifestation of God's presence. The Christian life is impossible on a natural level. Thirst for God, therefore, is a cry for help; it is an acknowledgment that, without the miracle of Jesus' resurrection from the dead, we will not be able to live as we should. When Elisha stood at the border of the Jordan River, with Elijah's cloak in his hands, he cried: "Where now is the LORD, the God of Elijah?" (II Kings 2:14). If we profess to be Christian, people have a right to demand that we live a life that cannot be explained apart from the power of God. If that power is not visible we will make no impression on the world around us. We have a lot to be thirsty for!

Our thirst for God will never be completely satisfied in this life on earth. Our thirst is for the coming of our Lord Jesus Christ. We thirst for the fulfillment of our hope. Every fulfillment and refreshment on earth is a down payment on the eternal returns that await us. There is only one thing that is worse than being thirsty and that is not to be thirsty.

Psalm 43:1-4

"Send forth your light and your truth, let them guide me; let them bring me to your holy mountain, to the place where you dwell. Then will I go to the altar of God, to God, my joy and my delight. I will praise you with the harp, O God, my God."

As a young boy, I lived through Nazi occupation during World War II. The radio only broadcasted Nazi propaganda. A filter of objectivity was needed to sift truth from lies. People who listened to the broadcasts of the British radio went to jail. Aiding British pilots who were shot down over Western Europe was punishable by death. The brother of a friend of mine in Holland was caught helping a pilot to escape. He was sentenced to death. Going to the firing squad he sang a hymn based on these verses: "O Lord, send your light and truth and bring me, guided by their radiance to your sacred tabernacles. Then I will go up to the altar of the Lord, to God, the source of my joy. I will tune my voice and chords to His honor and goodness, to Him who, after a brief time of misery will give me everlasting joy." The presence of death can become a clear wakeup call, as it was for the brother of my friend.

For the sons of Korah, separation from God may have been a physical experience. But if light and truth are the elements that lead us to the place of God's revelation, it is not a physical but a spiritual distance that separates us from God. The separation is not caused by deportation but by darkness and lies. God's truth and light will bring us to that place where His presence becomes a reality in our lives.

For us who have come to know God, the altar is not only the place where the Lord of glory was crucified for our sins, but also the place where we were crucified with Him. It is the place where we give ourselves to Him, spirit, soul, and body, the place where we burst out in unrestrained praise. At the altar we acknowledge God as "God my exceeding joy." The cross of our Lord Jesus Christ is, at the same time, the awful abyss of human depravity, of demonic activity, and of unselfish abandon, and victorious love. Our song of praise contains both the discord, and the harmony of this mystery. There is nothing cheap in going to the altar of God. Our song of praise will cost us almost as much as it cost Him. The place of worship is full of blood, and death, and life, and joy. The altar is the place of victory. In the shooting of my friend's brother, the Nazis who shot him were the losers.

Psalm 43:5

"Why are you downcast, O my soul? Why so disturbed within me? Put your hope in God, for I will yet praise him, my Savior and my God."

These same words are found twice in the previous Psalm. In the Hebrew Bible Psalms Forty-two and Forty-three constitute one Psalm. So these words are a refrain that runs through the whole poem. The repetition of these words by the Psalmist are not signs of old age, as of a person who has gotten in the habit of talking to himself. They indicate that our souls need to be talked to from time to time.

When God created man He made him a well-balanced human being in whom body, soul, and spirit were in perfect alignment. Adam communed with God in his spirit which controlled his thoughts, his emotions, and his bodily desires. Sin has turned this control mechanism upside-down. Most of the time our bodies dictate what we want and our spirit is no longer linked to God in a direct way. We go through life topsy-turvy.

These two Psalms started out with physical thirst, which reminded the Psalmist of the time when he would go up to the temple with other worshippers and experience the quenching of his spiritual thirst for fellowship with God. The memory of blessings past became an encouragement to the Psalmist. He figured that if God met his spiritual and emotional needs before, He would again lead him to another oasis in the desert of life.

Toward the end of this Psalm, the Psalmist sees himself again before God's altar. He remembered the sacrifice that was made for him. Another creature had died in his place, atoning for his sins and allowing him to live. In putting the sacrificial animal on the altar, he had put himself on the fiery coals to be consumed by the fire of God. Then he looked in the mirror and he asked, "Why are you downcast, O my soul?" God had accepted his sacrifice and here he was alive!

The fact that someone else died in our place needs a daily application. A coal from the altar touched Isaiah's lips. We read: "Then one of the seraphs flew to me with a live coal in his hand, which he had taken with tongs from the altar. With it he touched my mouth and said, 'See, this has touched your lips; your guilt is taken away and your sin atoned for' " (Isaiah 6:6,7). Our struggle will always be in applying the truth of the cross to the present time of our life. The coal of the altar has to touch our lips, or any other part of our life that is in need of being touched. That will lift up our soul so we can praise God and serve Him.

Psalm 44

"We have heard with our ears, O God; our fathers have told us what you did in their days, in days long ago. Yet for your sake we face death all day long; we are considered as sheep to be slaughtered. Rise up and help us; redeem us because of your unfailing love."

Remembrance of history is important for our understanding of the present. If we don't know from where we came, we don't know where we're going in life either. Israel's history is an image of the history of our salvation. The sons of Korah, who composed this Psalm, knew that they lived in the Promised Land, because of the Exodus from slavery in Egypt. The miracles of the Egyptian plagues, the desert crossing, and the conquest of Canaan were part of their national heritage.

Yet, the condition of Israel was not what it ought to be in the light of this glorious heritage. We don't know under what circumstances the composer stated: "We are considered as sheep to be slaughtered." He felt that living in the Promised Land ought to mean the fulfillment of God's promises, but the opposite turned out to be true. Actually, it was precisely because of God's salvation that life had become miserable. When Israel faced death all day long, it was for God's sake!

Our heart tells us that when we surrender to God, life should become easier, not unbearable. If God leads us into the Land of His Promises, we feel we ought not to live there as foreigners but as possessors. But Paul states: "In fact, everyone who wants to live a godly life in Christ Jesus will be persecuted" (II Timothy 3:12). And Peter writes: "Dear friends, do not be surprised at the painful trial you are suffering, as though something strange were happening to you" (I Peter 4:12,13).

We understand little of what God is doing with and through us. God performed great miracles for Israel. He did much more than liberate a group of people from slavery, and give them a country to live in. He set up the people of Israel as a monument of His righteousness in this world, which meant both judgment, and glorification. Egypt and Canaan fell under God's judgment; Israel was redeemed and rehabilitated. But the ultimate goal was the coming of the Messiah, the salvation of the world, and the renewal of the whole of creation. Who can ever understand the cosmic proportions of the acts of salvation God performs in the lives of His people? The apostle Paul quotes our verse in his Epistle to the Romans. After stating: "For your sake we face death all day long; we are considered as sheep to be slaughtered," he adds: "No, in all these things we are more than conquerors through him who loved us" (Romans 8:36,37).

Psalm 44

"With your hand you drove out the nations and planted our fathers; you crushed the peoples and made our fathers flourish. It was not by their sword that they won the land, nor did their arm bring them victory; it was your right hand, your arm, and the light of your face, for you loved them. But now you have rejected and humbled us; you no longer go out with our armies. You made us retreat before the enemy, and our adversaries have plundered us."

Although understanding of history is important and we should cherish our heritage, the most important thing in life is not inheritable. Even if our parents and grandparents knew God and served Him, we will not enter into a personal relationship with God and experience the forgiveness of our sin if we do not personally repent and make a commitment of our life to Him. It has been said that God has no grandchildren. We need a second birth to enter into the family of God.

This does not make a spiritual heritage unimportant. We all set an example to our children, as our parents did to us. Growing up in a loving home where relationships are affirmed affectionately will make it easier to surrender ourselves to God. If our father was a faithful image of the Father in heaven, our understanding of God's love for us will come to us in a natural way. If we can remember fondly the warmth of our mother's cuddling and soothing words, it will be easier for us to feel loved by God also. But very few of us, if any, have a perfect pattern to fall back on. Some may unconsciously connect the fatherhood of God to an abusive and choleric father. Alcohol or drugs may have ruined our home life. Maybe we get the wrong picture when we think of God. It may be difficult to understand that God is what our parents were not and that He wants to give us in abundance what they withheld.

But the ultimate obstacle is not the baggage we carry into life; it is the difficulty to surrender the right to ourselves into the hand of God. Conversion is a revolutionary experience. It means the overthrow of a government, of our self-rule. Regardless of our heritage, it means giving up our right to choose what to do with our life and ask God to show what He had in mind when He allowed us to be born in this world. It is a matter of survival. If we live for ourselves, we will ultimately perish, but "the man who does the will of God lives forever" (I John 2:17).

Psalm 45

"You are the most excellent of men and your lips have been anointed with grace, since God has blessed you forever. All glorious is the princess within [her chamber]; her gown is interwoven with gold."

This is one of the most joyful hymns in the hymnal. The heading states: "To the tune of 'Lilies.' " The sons of Korah could not have chosen a more suitable flower to match the tone of this Psalm. The lily surpasses any human garb in beauty. Jesus said: "And why do you worry about clothes? See how the lilies of the field grow. They do not labor or spin. Yet I tell you that not even Solomon in all his splendor was dressed like one of these" (Matthew 6:28,29).

The subject of the Psalm is a royal wedding with all the pomp of a fairytale. Weddings are still highlights in our human experience. In the exchange of vows and the fusing of two human lives, male and female, we come closest to what God wants us to be as human beings. "God created man in his own image, in the image of God he created him; male and female he created them" (Genesis 1:27).

But the intimacy of a married couple is not a goal in itself. In our marriage we enact a higher and eternal relationship of which the apostle Paul states: "This is a profound mystery-- but I am talking about Christ and the church" (Ephesians 5:32). The symbolism of the Psalm suggests more than a human wedding, even a royal wedding. The real topic of this Psalm is about the Lord Jesus and us. We are the bride.

The Psalmist depicts a man who knows no sin. In doing this, he draws our attention immediately to our Lord Jesus Christ. No Greek god can be compared to Him. We don't know what Jesus looked like when He walked on this earth. When John saw Him as He is now, he wrote: "His face was like the sun shining in all its brilliance" (Revelation 1:16).

If we have surrendered our lives to this glorious human being, this perfect Man, this God, we share in His glory. We have little idea what this will be like. But the apostle John saw a glimpse of this and he shares his vision with us in Revelation. An angel says to him: "Come, I will show you the bride, the wife of the Lamb." John says: "And he carried me away in the Spirit to a mountain great and high, and showed me the Holy City, Jerusalem, coming down out of heaven from God. It shone with the glory of God" (Revelation 21:9-11). All wedding ceremonies will pale in the light of that event, when we will be eternally joined to Him who loves us more than anyone can do on earth.

Psalm 46:1-3

"God is our refuge and strength, an ever-present help in trouble. Therefore we will not fear, though the earth give way and the mountains fall into the heart of the sea."

We do not know exactly what the Hebrew word alamoth means. Some Bible scholars believe it is a musical term, indicating that it was to be sung by sopranos, by virgins. There may be more to the title than meets the eye and it may be connected to the previous wedding Psalm. The theme of this Psalm, however, speaks of violence, earthquakes, floods, and revolutions. It deals with a violation of the virgin beauty of God's creation. In the midst of this uproar stands, in undefiled rest and peace of God's Shekinah, the city of God, which is His bride.

This earth is no longer what God intended it to be when He first created it. We hear of natural disasters, storms and earthquakes, fires and floods that kill thousands. Added to this, wars claim millions of victims, as did the two World Wars that marred the Twentieth Century. Some disasters are manmade, others are called "Acts of God." There is enough in this life to scare us and to make us want to hide.

The Psalmist sings: "God is our refuge and strength, an ever-present help in trouble." Martin Luther based his hymn "A mighty fortress is our God" upon this Psalm. He who does not flee disasters, and who thinks he can hold his own in the chaos, is a fool. We do better if we fear the manifestations of the powers of darkness, and run from them. God sometimes even uses fright to save our lives. He is our refuge, which means that we have to flee towards Him. This theme of salvation through fleeing toward God is repeated often in the Book of Psalms.

There was no place for fear in God's original plan for man. When God created Adam and Eve, He stimulated Adam's natural desire for fellowship by causing male and female to be attracted to each other, and, ultimately, to draw man into fellowship with Himself. After the fall, fear began to dominate man's life, and now God uses our fears and feelings of insecurity, to woo us unto His rest and protection. Our natural desires for satisfaction are always agreeable to us. The panic, caused by the menaces of life, is highly unpleasant. We cannot blame God for this. The world in which we are born is the world that is distorted by sin. In the midst of this chaos and corruption stands God's salvation as a fortress, a stronghold, a bunker, and a shelter. As Noah's ark was at the time of the flood, so Jesus Christ is for us the ark of salvation. We are only safe when we are saved by Jesus Christ. "Fear not!" is an integral part of the message of the Gospel.

Psalm 46:4-7

"There is a river whose streams make glad the city of God, the holy place where the Most High dwells. God is within her, she will not fall; God will help her at break of day."

The historical background of the river in this Psalm is probably the water supply of the city of Jerusalem, which was already in existence in the times of the Jebusites. We may assume that this aqueduct was functioning when the sons of Korah wrote this Psalm. We live on earth with many images of heaven. This water supply line is seen as symbolic of the heavenly reality. Ezekiel picks up the image in his vision of the temple brook (Ezekiel 47:1-12) and in Revelation John describes the completion of these prophecies with the words: "Then the angel showed me the river of the water of life, as clear as crystal, flowing from the throne of God and of the Lamb" (Revelation 22:1). Water symbolizes a spiritual reality. The chaotic waters of the previous verses represented the powers of evil, and the river of the water of life stands for the Holy Spirit.

God had chosen Jerusalem as the place of His revelation on earth. The Holy Spirit testifies to this truth in an uninterrupted stream of refreshment and renewal. It is marvelous to realize that the sons of Korah could walk the streets of Jerusalem and drink water from the wells that were fed by the river, knowing all the time that they performed more than a mere physical act of drinking. They had insight in the spiritual significance of things on earth.

Only in Jerusalem God's glory was present above the atonement cover of the ark. All this is fulfilled in the New Jerusalem, the bride of the Lamb, which is filled with the glory of God. The city of the Korahites is an image of the church. This world is in uproar, and the nations are like a raging sea, but this prophecy states that the church of Jesus Christ will not fall victim to any onslaught. The dawn of God's salvation will break upon her. This will be at dawn on the first day of the week, on the day of resurrection. The image expresses the position of those who live in fellowship with God in the midst of the oppression of the world. If we are members of the body of Jesus Christ, we are moving toward the light in the darkness of this world. As the Book of Proverbs states: "The path of the righteous is like the first gleam of dawn, shining ever brighter till the full light of day" (Proverbs 4:18). We have no reason to be afraid of the dark.

Psalm 46:8-11

"Be still, and know that I am God; I will be exalted among the nations, I will be exalted in the earth." The LORD Almighty is with us; the God of Jacob is our fortress."

"Be still!" Silence is a rare commodity in our noisy world and in our busy lives. Most people cannot hear God because they make too much noise themselves.

The words "Be still" acquire a new meaning when we see the context in which they appear. We read in Verse Eight: "Come and see the works of the LORD, the desolations he has brought on the earth." The silence here is not the quietness of wonder and intimate fellowship with God; it is the silence of terror and horror. After his son committed suicide, Ronald Dunn wrote a book When Heaven is Silent. He wrestled with the fact that God had taken his son away from him and that he received no answer to his question why this had happened. He comes to the profound conclusion that God rarely answers our "why?" because it is the wrong question. God only answers us when we ask Him what we must do in the situation in which the desolations on this earth place us.

God often does not answer us and He leaves us in the dark to make us silent. There is a side of God that makes us realize that we cannot call Him to account. He is our Creator and He owes us no explanations of His dealings with us. That is a hard pill to swallow for us as mere human beings.

If we allow ourselves to come to the place where we accept God for who He is without asking questions, we will discover that we can trust Him even when He is silent, especially when He is silent.

Jacob wrestled with this at Peniel, where he asked God for His Name and did not let go till He blessed him (Genesis 32:24-31). The encounter changed Jacob, the one who tripped up people, into Israel, the one who wrestled with God and was victorious. If we accept God's silence by being silent ourselves, God reveals Himself to us as "the God of Jacob, our fortress." Our silence will change us from cheats into conquerors, because of His protection over us. In allowing God to be silent, He becomes the strength of our life.

Psalm 47:1-4

"Clap your hands, all you nations; shout to God with cries of joy."

This Psalm has a strong international flavor. It is hard for us to imagine that a solemn assembly of the United Nations, for instance, would take up this theme at one of its sessions and burst out in spontaneous applause for God. This is especially unlikely if we look at the following verses of this hymn, where the reason for the exuberance is that all the nations of the world have become subject to the nation of Israel. This amounts to a political impossibility.

Israel, as we know it in its present condition, is as far removed from what God intended it to be as man, who has fallen in sin, has strayed from the image and likeness of God into which he was created.

This Psalm, therefore, cannot be seen as intending to sing the praises of Israel's position as a world power, but rather to open the eyes of all peoples on earth to the reality of God's presence and majesty.

God had chosen Israel as the nation through which He would reveal Himself to the whole world. The fact that Israel did a poor job in carrying out this mandate does in no way diminish the marvel of God's revelation. Greater than God's revelation of Himself through Israel is His Incarnation. "The Word became flesh and made his dwelling among us" (John 1:14). It is up to us as Christians to testify to this. Our failure never affects the glory of God. God does not depend on the way we represent Him in this world. He is not the loser; we are!

The invitation contained in this Psalm is primarily meant for the redeemed, that is, for the church of Jesus Christ. The church's present condition, however, seems to be no better suited for the realization of the invitation than Israel was when this Psalm was first composed. But all the elements that are necessary for the fulfillment are present today. The atonement of sin has been achieved, and the Holy Spirit has been poured out upon the church. Yet, we cannot say that praise and worship of God on earth has reached universal proportions. We ought, therefore, to continue to pray: "Our Father in heaven, hallowed be your name, your kingdom come" (Matthew 6:9,10).

The fact remains that, if all the nations of the world recognize God as the One who reveals Himself to mankind, they will burst out in spontaneous praise.

What will happen at one point of time is what the apostle John describes in Revelation: "Look, he is coming with the clouds, and every eye will see him, even those who pierced him; and all the peoples of the earth will mourn because of him. So shall it be! Amen" (Revelation 1:7). Until that day, there is still hope for our planet.

Psalm 47:5-6

"God has ascended amid shouts of joy, the LORD amid the sounding of trumpets. Sing praises to God, sing praises; sing praises to our King, sing praises."

This Psalm is really written about our Lord Jesus Christ. We witness here His ascension to the throne. Before this moment in history took place, He told His disciples: "All authority in heaven and on earth has been given to me..." (Matthew 28:18). The disciples, who heard those words on earth, saw only Jesus' departure; they could not see His arrival in glory. If they could have seen that, they would have sung His praises together with the angels. After the Holy Spirit came upon them, on the day of Pentecost, this Psalm surely acquired a deeper meaning for them.

For us, the ascension is a link in the chain of the facts in the history of salvation. It began with the Incarnation. We tend to see the Lord's crucifixion as the most important link in the chain, but in this Psalm the emphasis is on the ascension. The other links in the chain are not even mentioned. This omission produces a special effect. Without the birth of Christ, His death, and His resurrection, there would be no ascension. We have this advantage over the Korahites that we can see the complete chain, and that we know the significance of each of its links. They looked at one link of the chain with great amazement, without understanding where it came from or where it was leading.

In His exalted position, our Lord Jesus' intercession on our behalf secures our safety as we travel on our way on earth. As the author of Hebrews states: "Therefore he is able to save completely those who come to God through him, because he always lives to intercede for them" (Hebrews 7:25). And David foretold the process by which all rebellion is being squashed when he wrote: "The LORD says to my Lord: 'Sit at my right hand until I make your enemies a footstool for your feet' "(Psalm 110:1). Great things are happening above!

Psalm 47:7-9

"God reigns over the nations; God is seated on his holy throne. The nobles of the nations assemble as the people of the God of Abraham, for the kings of the earth belong to God; he is greatly exalted."

When we look at the world in its present condition, we must admit that God's power over the governments of this world is not yet visible. God has raised some people to high positions in government, but most of those who govern do not understand the source of their power. What the sons of Korah express here is music of a new age. This does not mean that God does not reign over the nations or that He is not seated on His holy throne, but mankind fails to recognize it.

Satan claims to possess the power to rule this earth. In his temptation of our Lord, we read: "Again, the devil took him to a very high mountain and showed him all the kingdoms of the world and their splendor. 'All this I will give you' he said, 'if you will bow down and worship me' "(Matthew 4:8,9). But his claim is illegal. The shields, the banners, the heraldry, and all the other symbols of human power and dignity belong to God, and they are derived from His glory. He is the Lord of lords, and the King of kings. Those who run for a political career in this world should never forget this. The real command of power becomes clear only when they are seen in relation to Jesus Christ. Most people running for offices do not know what they are doing, because they do not realize the source of the power they strive for. When Pilate said to Jesus: "Don't you realize I have power either to free you or to crucify you?' Jesus answered, 'You would have no power over me if it were not given to you from above' " (John 19:10,11). Pilate never understood this.

God's supreme reign over all creation will become evident when every individual has surrendered the authority over his or her life to Him to whom it belongs. We can set an example for a world that goes through history aimlessly. We can help the process by an act of personal surrender and demonstrate in our personal life what it means that God reigns.

Psalm 48:1-3

"Great is the LORD, and most worthy of praise, in the city of our God, his holy mountain."

This Psalm is, originally, about a place on earth, called Zion. It was part of the city of Jerusalem, the first bridgehead captured by David in his siege of the city. David later made it his personal residence. The name Zion was later used for the place where the temple was erected on Mount Moriah, and ultimately for the whole city of Jerusalem. It was the beauty of Zion that, even in David's days, it was a symbol of something greater than itself. In C. S. Lewis' book *The Last Battle*, there is a barn that is bigger inside than outside, which expresses well the principle we see here. The Israelites of old realized that the world in which they lived was an image of a heavenly reality. They understood that the presence of God in Jerusalem expressed in earthly forms and images something of that which surpasses all description, and which will be fully understood only in heaven. Such insight gives a special hue to the things on earth.

As far as cities go, Zion may have been a beautiful location. The temple King Solomon built there was, undoubtedly, a marvel of architecture. But what made Mount Zion the center of the earth was not the way human beings embellished it; it was the presence of God.

The sons of Korah attributed much more to the Mount Zion on earth than meets the eye. In that way they did not see what is visible, but they saw the real meaning of the visible things. Only those who know the Lord are able to see such things; they see Him everywhere because their communion with God is uninterrupted. It is the knowledge that He is everywhere where we are, because we only want to be where He is. That is why Zion is part of heaven on earth, and this is the essence of worship and adoration.

It is the presence of God that makes our barns bigger inside than out. It is God's presence in our home and family that makes us a lighthouse in this dark world. God pledges to reveal Himself in and through us if we make His righteousness and His Kingdom the priority of our life (See Matthew 6:33). We have it within us to make our residence a place of heaven on earth.

This does not mean that we become so heavenly inclined that we will be of no earthly good. Earthly objects tend to become more earthly as they express more clearly the heavenly reality. There are no greater realists than those who see Him who is invisible, as Moses did (See Hebrews 11:27).

Psalm 48:4-7

"When the kings joined forces, when they advanced together, they saw [her] and were astounded; they fled in terror. Trembling seized them there, pain like that of a woman in labor. You destroyed them like ships of Tarshish shattered by an east wind."

These verses describe what it means to be protected by God when the enemy attacks. God protects His church, as well as our personal lives. Both world history and the history of the church are full of examples of kings who joined forces, and who left with their "tails between their legs" when they hit the wall with which God protects His own.

Yet, in many instances it seems as if the devil has the upper hand. Throughout the centuries, Christians have been persecuted and martyrs have been killed by the thousands. But thus far, the gates of hell have not yet prevailed against the church of Christ, and the blood of the martyrs always turns out to be the seed of the church. If we look at that which is visible, it often seems that all is lost. But in this psalm, the psalmist sees demons bent over in pain like a woman in labor.

This picture is full of irony. Men, who are very proud of their masculinity, fall victim to a specifically female form of suffering, which makes their fate the more embarrassing. They suffer labor pains but they do not give birth. They flee, actually, for themselves.

There is a suggestion of economic power in the mention of the ships of Tarshish. The east wind that demolishes the ships depicts God destroying strong men psychologically, as well as materially.

When we take a closer look at this picture, we may not like what we see. In our Western world, we live in an affluent society. We are being bombarded by advertisements that tell us that we owe it to ourselves to raise our standard of living to the highest height. We are told how much we can save by spending our money on cars or furniture. This makes it harder for us to identify with Him who said: "Foxes have holes and birds of the air have nests, but the Son of Man has no place to lay his head" (Matthew 8:20). As we approach the place where God reveals Himself to us, we may have to reassess our lifestyle. Successful living can be dangerous to our spiritual health. Jesus warns us: "Do not store up for yourselves treasures on earth, where moth and rust destroy, and where thieves break in and steal. But store up for yourselves treasures in heaven, where moth and rust do not destroy, and where thieves do not break in and steal. For where your treasure is, there your heart will be also" (Matthew 6:19-21). Let us not be as those who saw Zion and "were astounded; they fled in terror."

Psalm 48:8-11

"Within your temple, O God, we meditate on your unfailing love."

Let's try to catch the ecstasy of the sons of Korah who wrote these words. Their feet stood in Jerusalem; they played the role of a pilgrim who had come from afar, and they said: "This is the way it will be when we arrive at the real city with foundations, whose architect and builder is God, of which this city is an image" (Hebrews 11:10). It is obvious from the tone of the whole psalm that the topic is the real Zion, the mountain that will fill the whole world. Daniel saw this vision when he explained the dream to King Nebuchadnezzar. The rock that was cut out, but not by human hands, became a huge mountain that filled the whole earth (Daniel 2:31-35). Jerusalem on earth is only secure inasmuch as she clearly reflects the real city. It is about the New Jerusalem, the bride of the Lamb, that the psalmist says: "God makes her secure forever."

We differ from the sons of Korah and all the Israelites of their time only in that we don't have to go to Jerusalem to seek God. Jesus replied to the question of the Samaritan woman regarding where to worship God: "The true worshipers will worship the Father in spirit and truth, for they are the kind of worshipers the Father seeks. God is spirit, and his worshipers must worship in spirit and in truth" (John 4:23,24).

We don't need a temple to meditate on God's unfailing love, but we must meditate on it during our life on earth. We will only know God in heaven if we have known Him on earth. If we have never stopped long enough to marvel about the fact that God loves us, we don't know what life is all about.

The meaning of the Hebrew word, which is translated "unfailing love" or "lovingkindness," is "a covenant of love." We express this in the exchange of our marriage vows. Whether we are married or single, we must each have this kind of relationship with God, in which we say "yes" to Him, because He says "yes" to us.

Psalm 48:12-14

"This God is our God for ever and ever; he will be our guide even to the end."

In the last three verses of this Psalm we are invited to walk around Zion and to allow the image to be imprinted on our mind so we can pass it on to the next generation. It is obvious that, if this is meant to be interpreted literally, the next generation could do its own walking and make its own observations. What is meant is the passing on of a vision of that which is not visible with the natural eye.

Zion was the place of God's revelation on earth. But God reveals Himself, not in buildings of brick and mortar, He makes Himself known in human lives. That is what Jesus meant when He said: "Destroy this temple, and I will raise it again in three days." The apostle John adds: "The temple he had spoken of was his body. After he was raised from the dead, his disciples recalled what he had said" (John 2:19,22).

We are called to be monuments of God's grace on earth. The foundations, the walls and the streets of the New Jerusalem are not made out of dead materials, but out of human lives. The city is the bride of the Lamb. God wants us to survey His acts of grace. Every new generation has to rediscover and experience this. But it is the task of the parents to model this for their children. Young people ought to be able to see in the lives of the generation that goes before them that God is a reality. How else would He become a reality to them?

We, obviously, need God's guidance if we want to exhibit the grace of God in our life. God promises us that guidance as long as we live on earth and beyond. The Hebrew word, translated "to the end" also means "to death." But, the Psalm also uses the words "for ever and ever," which means beyond death. People in this world desperately need to see monuments of God's grace, people who are like towers of truth and love. By the grace of God, I want to be such a testimony of the Gospel!

Psalm 49:1-9

"No man can redeem the life of another or give to God a ransom for him-- the ransom for a life is costly, no payment is ever enough-- that he should live on forever and not see decay."

This psalm is the last in this series of three psalms, beginning with Psalm 42, which carry the name of the Sons of Korah. It forms a profound coda to this song cycle. The subject is death. It is particularly important to see these Psalms as one cycle, otherwise we could miss the link between this poem and the preceding one, which ended with the statement: "For this God is our God for ever and ever: he will be our guide even unto death."

We all face death as the end of our existence on earth. Even the promise of eternal life and the hope of the resurrection cannot diminish the grim fact that, one day, my heart will beat its last beat and I will breathe my last breath.

It doesn't help us much that this prospect is presented to us in this Psalm as a song with accompanying harp music, does it? The Living Bible paraphrases Verse Four beautifully: "I will tell in song accompanied by harps the answer to one of life's most perplexing problems."

Our text speaks of a ransom, a pay-off that would buy us out of our predicament of facing death. The question is: "How much would it cost?" and the answer given is: "Too much!" Jesus asks the question: "What good will it be for a man if he gains the whole world, yet forfeits his soul? Or what can a man give in exchange for his soul?" (Matthew 16:26). The surprising implication of this question is that our human soul has more value to God than all the riches of the world. There are things in life that cannot be expressed in money because they are too precious. One of those is your soul and mine. We may not be aware of our own value. The world seems to be full of proofs that human life has little or no value. Maybe our evaluations are completely wrong! The Psalmist states: "Precious in the sight of the LORD is the death of his saints" (Psalm 116:15).

God is willing to pay all He has for our soul. He already paid a price that cannot be calculated by any standards. In Jesus' words: "The Son of Man did not come to be served, but to serve, and to give his life as a ransom for many" (Matthew 20:28). The apostle Paul writes: "[God] did not spare his own Son, but gave him up for us all" (Romans 8:32)."

Since we are worth that much, let us live up to God's evaluation.

Psalm 49:10-20

"But God will redeem my life from the grave; he will surely take me to himself."

If the sons of Korah thought that they would escape death, they were wrong. The authors of this poem died centuries ago. Death made no exception for them. Their statement, therefore, must be considered as one that goes beyond the grave. Their voice comes from "the undiscover'd country from which bourn no traveller returns," to quote Shakespeare's Hamlet.

Our natural eye cannot see beyond the grave. People tend to draw the wrong conclusion from the fact that God has drawn a line on earth beyond which we cannot see until we pass it. King Solomon mused about this as he said: "As for men, God tests them so that they may see that they are like the animals. Man's fate is like that of the animals; the same fate awaits them both: As one dies, so dies the other. All have the same breath; man has no advantage over the animal. Everything is meaningless. All go to the same place; all come from dust, and to dust all return. Who knows if the spirit of man rises upward and if the spirit of the animal goes down into the earth?" (Ecclesiastes 3:18-21).

Yet, we know that a human being is more than an animal. Death does not make us equal with them and everything is not meaningless.

In the first part of this Psalm, we spoke about a ransom that one could not pay for a brother to save him from death. Yet, our hope is based on the fact that our Brother has paid the ransom for us. Peter states this so beautifully in his First Epistle: "For you know that it was not with perishable things such as silver or gold that you were redeemed from the empty way of life handed down to you from your forefathers, but with the precious blood of Christ, a lamb without blemish or defect" (I Peter 1:18,19).

This body of ours may be laid in a grave but God will bring it back to life and make us complete. "For the trumpet will sound, the dead will be raised imperishable, and we will be changed" (I Corinthians 15:52). "We ourselves, who have the firstfruits of the Spirit, groan inwardly as we wait eagerly for our adoption as sons, the redemption of our bodies. For in this hope we were saved" (Romans 8:23,24). The door of death has a crack in it and we may peek through it to give us hope and dignity here below.

Psalm 50:1-6

"The Mighty one, God, the LORD, speaks and summons the earth from the rising of the sun to the place where it sets. From Zion, perfect in beauty, God shines forth. Our God comes and will not be silent."

In this Psalm, we are introduced to a man called Asaph. David appointed Asaph as the head of the Levites who were in charge of the music at the place where the Ark of the Covenant was in Jerusalem (I Chronicles 16:4,5). He was, evidently, an outstanding poet and musician, as were his sons. We find several of his poems in the Book of Psalms.

In this Psalm, Asaph states that God speaks to us from Zion, the place of His revelation. He addresses the whole world, from east to west. God is not silent, yet most people never hear His voice.

The Bible tells us that God spoke the universe, including our planet with all its life, into being. David says: "For he spoke, and it came to be; he commanded, and it stood firm" (Psalm 33:9).

God not only speaks, He also summons the earth. In the first two chapters of Genesis, God speaks to His creation; in the third chapter, God calls man. In between the two is the fall into sin. The implication of the sequence of speaking and summoning here is the same. God calls the earth as He called Adam: "Where are you?" (Genesis 3:9). The omniscient God knew, of course, where man was, but Adam himself did not know where he was. God calls His creation so that His creation might know where he is. "Where am I? Where do I come from? Where am I going?" Those questions are of vital importance for every person who wants to live a conscious life. Those questions show the way to the salvation of the world. God's revelation of Himself in Zion is closely connected to His calling, and His saving of the world.

In order to hear God's voice, we must confess our sin and accept God's forgiveness. When the prophet Isaiah was confronted with God's holiness, he cried: "Woe to me! I am ruined! For I am a man of unclean lips" An angel touched his lips with a coal from the altar, after which we read: "Then I heard the voice of the Lord" (Isaiah 6:5,8). It is important to hear the voice of God so that we know where we are. God calls us out of darkness into His light.

Psalm 50:7-15

"Sacrifice thank offerings to God, fulfill your vows to the Most High, and call upon me in the day of trouble; I will deliver you, and you will honor me."

God did not reproach Israel that they were unfaithful in the bringing of sacrifices. They were, actually, very punctual in the fulfillment of their obligations. But they made it seem as if they were doing God a favor by bringing their sacrifices. They gave the impression that they themselves could do without those sacrifices but they brought them because otherwise God would be shortchanged. The essence of idol worship is that man pacifies the gods by giving them what they want. God ridicules the idea that people on earth would have to feed Him. He is the Creator of all the animals, and of life itself. Everything that breathes is dependent upon Him. Paul explained to the philosophers in Athens: "The God who made the world and everything in it is the Lord of heaven and earth and does not live in temples built by hands. And he is not served by human hands, as if he needed anything, because he himself gives all men life and breath and everything else" (Acts 17:24,25). Sacrifices are brought for our sake, not for His.

The Israelites brought as sacrifice an animal, a fellow-creature, in exchange for their lives to the Lord. If we thoughtlessly bring sacrifices, we do not only fail to understand who God is but also who we are ourselves: sinners who have forfeited their lives. Sacrifices are never meant to still God's hunger but ours. God is not bloodthirsty. We hardly understand what it means that God's holiness is being compromised by our sin. It is terrible if a person thinks he can stand before God in his natural, filthy condition. It is even worse if this person brings the prescribed sacrifices that atone for his sins without knowing what he does, or in an effort to cover up the sins he is not willing to give up. In our blind stupidity, we think that we can deceive God. If we bring a sacrifice, which presupposes contrition and confession of sin, not for the purpose of receiving forgiveness and rehabilitation but as a decoy, we deceive ourselves.

We need no longer kill an animal to receive forgiveness. God sent Jesus to die for our sins. The recognition that He died in our place provides us with all the pardon we need. The sacrifice we must bring now is our praise to God for our salvation. He saved our life, He will save us also in our circumstances.

Psalm 50:16-23

"He who sacrifices thank offerings honors me, and he prepares the way so that I may show him the salvation of God."

The idea that praise is a sacrifice is a revolutionary thought. It means that it does not cost us a thing to praise God; on the other hand it costs us everything. Another life died in our stead, but this also means that we die ourselves, although not in the physical sense of the word.

A friend of mine gave his testimony after the sudden death of his wife. He said he had come to understand the term "sacrifice of praise." Whether he was in the mood for praise or not made no difference. The act of praising God had a therapeutic effect upon him.

Under the pressure of circumstances, praise may not come easily or spontaneously to us. We may have to set ourselves to praise God by an act of the will. It is when we praise God under adverse conditions that we honor Him particularly.

Hardship tends to blur our vision of God. We ask ourselves why God allows us to be sick or to lose the one we love. To praise God, not only in times of trouble, but because of trouble makes no sense. Yet, if we do, we acknowledge that God permitted our problem and that He has a purpose in it.

Paul and Silas had obeyed the call to come to Macedonia to preach the Gospel. They ended up in jail. With bleeding backs because of severe beatings and with their feet in a stock, they decided to praise God. We read: "About midnight Paul and Silas were praying and singing hymns to God, and the other prisoners were listening to them. Suddenly there was such a violent earthquake that the foundations of the prison were shaken. At once all the prison doors flew open, and everybody's chains came loose" (Acts 16:25-27). Praise has a way to loosen chains!

There is nothing unreasonable in the fact that, if we trust, on the basis of the known facts of salvation, we trust that all things work together for good, even if we see no light at the end of the tunnel, or if we do not understand the reason we pass through certain experiences. God says that He is honored if we thank Him under all circumstances. In doing this, we open a way for the Holy Spirit to show us the reality of God's salvation.

Psalm 51:1-6

"Against you, you only, have I sinned and done what is evil in your sight."

This Psalm is David's confession of sin after he had committed adultery with Bathsheba and murdered her husband. The heinous character of David's sin has not lost any of its horror even after some thirty centuries.

We usually do not consider somebody who commits adultery as a criminal, not in the same way we do a murderer. David stood guilty on both counts; one sin led to another. Most human beings know what it is to be sexually tempted, as David was. We tend to accept the fact that "Boys will be boys." But we do not believe that adultery would lead to murder. We seldom see that if we open the door to one sin, that door can remain open to other sins. David did not close the door immediately through confession. He got himself entangled in the spider web of sin to the point where he could not free himself.

We ought never to take any sin lightly. God said to Cain: "Sin is crouching at your door; it desires to have you, but you must master it" (Genesis 4:7).

The question is, against whom did David sin? He violated the sanctity of Bathsheba's marriage and he murdered Uriah, her husband. But in his confession, David says to God: "Against you, you only, have I sinned." Do we really sin against God if we play with sexual temptations? The matter of sin may seem so trivial to us. The apostle Paul defines sin as "falling short of the glory of God" (See Romans 3:23). Does it make any difference how short we fall of God's glory? Does it make any difference if an airplane crashes fifty miles or fifty inches from the runway? God wants us to partake in His glory. Anything less than His glorious perfection for us will not do. If that goal seems beyond our reach, let's remember that He promises to get us there, not on our own strength but on His. That is what confession of sin is all about.

The meaning of the word "sin" in Greek is "to miss the mark." God wants us to become part of His glory; for that reason we were born and live in this world. How tragic it is when we miss that which is the main reason for our existence!

Psalm 51:7-12

"Create in me a pure heart, O God, and renew a steadfast spirit within me."

In praying for a pure heart, David penetrates to the core of his problem. The human heart is the wellspring of everything that pollutes the world in which we live. Jeremiah stated: "The heart is deceitful above all things and beyond cure. Who can understand it?" (Jeremiah 17:9). And Jesus says: "The things that come out of the mouth come from the heart, and these make a man 'unclean.' For out of the heart come evil thoughts, murder, adultery, sexual immorality, theft, false testimony, slander. These are what make a man 'unclean' " (Matthew 15:18-20).

In asking for a pure heart, David prayed that God does for him what He did for the people of Israel in the night they were liberated from their slavery in Egypt. Every family had to kill a lamb and apply its blood with a bunch of hyssop to the doorposts of the house. God said to them: "The blood will be a sign for you on the houses where you are; and when I see the blood, I will pass over you" (Exodus 12:13). The Israelites, who celebrated the first Passover, did not experience a purification of their heart; they were only protected from the judgment that killed the firstborn sons of the Egyptians. But David went beyond that by stating that if God applies the blood of a sacrifice to the door of his heart, it will cleanse him on the inside.

We seldom believe in the absolute wickedness of our own soul. We hope that, when the balance of our life is drawn up, we will have enough credit points to get us into heaven. To accept the fact that our heart is "deceitful above all things and beyond cure" is the first step toward rehabilitation. If we ask God to apply the blood of Jesus Christ to the door of our heart, we will be cleansed and we will know it. Jesus says: "I tell you the truth, whoever hears my word and believes him who sent me has eternal life and will not be condemned; he has crossed over from death to life" (John 5:24). The ultimate reward of being cleansed inwardly is stated in the Sermon on the Mount: "Blessed are the pure in heart, for they will see God" (Matthew 5:8). Seeing God is the purpose for which we were made.

Psalm 51:13-19

"The sacrifices of God are a broken spirit; a broken and contrite heart, O God, you will not despise."

David touches upon the dilemma human sin places on God by stating: "You do not delight in sacrifice." God does not enjoy the killing of animals. We live in a world in which animals are killed daily by the millions and the thought usually does not bother us. I remember, as a little boy, seeing a man killing a chicken and I was horrified. I admit that I have lost this sense of horror over the years. I eat chicken and beef, usually without giving it a thought. Yet, my being shocked, as a sensitive little boy, better reflects the revulsion God must feel when any of His creatures die. God only allows for sacrifices to be made because His loathing of our sin is greater than His abhorrence of the death of an animal.

If we could only see our sins against this background! It would heal us quickly of all arrogance and pride. It would break our spirit and give us a contrite heart. A clear understanding of what God does for us when He forgives our sins in Jesus Christ will bring us to the point where we sing: "Amazing grace! how sweet the sound that saves a wretch like me!"

God wants us to understand that He is justified to condemn us to death. If we really understand that we merit capital punishment, the result in us will be a broken spirit and a contrite heart. The miracle consists in the fact that God accepts this brokenness as a sacrifice that is a sweet aroma to Him. There is nothing beautiful in the spiritual brokenness of a person, nor was there any beauty in the tortured body of our crucified Lord. The marvel is that we may put the brokenness of our lives, the rubble of our spirit, that which nauseates us, on God's altar, and that God says: "I do not despise it." God sees in the bleeding animal that goes up in smoke on the altar, the symbol of a human being who rebelled against Him, and who has put down his arms. If, in that way, we return to dust, the wonder of creation is repeated. God takes this dust, these ashes, and forms us into a new creation by imparting His Holy Spirit into us. This is called: The Crisis of the Deeper Life, which is nothing more or less than God's act of recreating us.

Psalm 52

"But I am like an olive tree flourishing in the house of God; I trust in God's unfailing love for ever and ever."

David wrote this Psalm when he heard what happened to the priests of Nob who had, unwittingly, helped him escape from King Saul when Saul tried to kill him. This Psalm is about a certain Doeg, a descendant of Esau, one of Saul's advisers. He reported to Saul that David had visited the priests and that they had provided him with food. In his rage, Saul ordered all the priests and their families to be killed. Doeg carried out these orders without any qualms. He committed this crime by simply obeying the orders of the king.

After Nazi Germany was defeated and the war criminals were brought to justice, many tried to justify their atrocities by claiming that they were merely following orders. Committing sin because we are ordered to do so does not clear us of guilt. God holds us personally responsible for our actions, whether they are our own initiative or that of our superiors.

David compares himself with Doeg. He had not been completely blameless in the matter that brought about the death of the priests. He had not disclosed that he was fleeing from Saul. The priests thought they were helping the commander-in-chief of Saul's army, not a desperate fugitive. David's deception that led to their death must have plagued his conscience. He did not realize that his brief visit to Nob would have such far-reaching and disastrous consequences for the whole family of priests there. But this did not justify Doeg's crime.

David's negligence can hardly be compared to Doeg's crime. Next to Doeg's act of brute slaughter, David sees himself as "an olive tree flourishing in the house of God." Evidently, David had come to terms with his guilt feelings and, after confessing his failure and dishonesty to God, he felt himself in God's presence blessed and fruitful. Olive trees do not grow in God's house, but if we keep our record clean before the Lord, we will be like a tree planted by streams of water, yielding fruit in season and our leaf will not wither. Whatever we do will prosper (Psalm 1:3).

God will hold us responsible for crimes we commit, but if we fellowship with Him, He will be responsible for the fruit we bear. There is pardon for the foulest of sins that are confessed. Jesus told the murderer on the cross: "I tell you the truth, today you will be with me in paradise" (Luke 23:43).

Psalm 53
"The fool says in his heart, 'There is no God'."

This Psalm is identical to Psalm 14, with one exception. In Psalm 14, we read: "There they are, overwhelmed with dread, for God is present in the company of the righteous." Here: "There they were, overwhelmed with dread, where there was nothing to dread. God scattered the bones of those who attacked you; you put them to shame, for God despised them."

This Psalm is not about atheists, but about a lifestyle that doesn't acknowledge God's standards, which is evinced in the persecution of fellowmen. The result for the unrighteous is panic on the Day of Judgment. The man who lives without God will be confronted with the record of his own life. His prayer will be for the mountains and the rocks to fall on him and hide him. It is the prayer we read about in Revelation: "Then the kings of the earth, the princes, the generals, the rich, the mighty, and every slave and every free man hid in caves and among the rocks of the mountains. They called to the mountain and the rocks, 'Fall on us and hide us from the face of him who sits on the throne and from the wrath of the Lamb! For the great day of their wrath has come, and who can stand?'" (Revelation 6:15-17). This panic is caused by the condition of man's own soul. He will condemn himself before the throne of God. The redeemed will stand before the same throne unafraid, and will not fall under God's judgment. There is no panic when there is no evil conscience.

The scattering of the bones is not only symbolic of death itself but also of the worthlessness of the life that was lived. There will be no monuments for the man who has lived his life without God, at least no monuments that God erects. If fellowship with Him is the only valid reason of our existence, how terrible it will be to be rejected by God!

The foolishness of an atheistic lifestyle results in that man is being put to shame. He who feels ashamed condemns himself. Judgment consists in the drawing of a comparison between God and man who was created in His image. The foolishness of man is demonstrated in the fact that man tries to evade judgment by saying: "There is no God." The righteous is the person who has already passed through God's judgment, and who has received forgiveness for his sins.

Anyone, who professes to believe in God but does not demonstrate this faith in daily living does not differ from an atheist. "If anyone says, 'I love God,' yet hates his brother, he is a liar. For anyone who does not love his brother, whom he has seen, cannot love God, whom he has not seen. And he has given us this command: Whoever loves God must also love his brother" (I John 4:20,21).

Psalm 54

"I will sacrifice a freewill offering to you; I will praise your name, O LORD, for it is good. For he has delivered me from all my troubles, and my eyes have looked in triumph on my foes."

When we do good to people and they repay us with evil, it is hard to accept. David had liberated the town of Keilah when the Philistines had raided it (See I Samuel 23:1-28).

They answered by betraying him to King Saul. Keilah was close to Bethlehem and David's traitors were, probably, his own relatives.

It is hard to accept rejection by family members when we become a Christian. In some cultures, conversion to Christianity means certain death. But under milder circumstances, rejection by the ones we love causes deep hurt.

Sometimes we have to choose between our loved ones and the Lord. Jesus says: "Anyone who loves his father or mother more than me is not worthy of me; anyone who loves his son or daughter more than me is not worthy of me; and anyone who does not take his cross and follow me is not worthy of me" (Matthew 10:37,38).

We do not become less because we follow Christ, even if other people look down upon us.

David prayed: "Save me, O God, by your name; vindicate me by your might." "Vindicate me" means, "exonerate me." He asked that God give him back his worth and dignity that others denied him. The name of God is our honor and worth. People who have dedicated themselves to Christ have the right to call themselves "Christian."

God heard David and David in response offered himself to God in a freewill offering. In order to vindicate David, God distracted Saul from his pursuit by bringing back the Philistines. The people David had liberated saw their old enemy return when they repaid good with evil. There is a lesson in this for all of us!

Psalm 55:1-15

"If an enemy were insulting me, I could endure it; if a foe were raising himself against me, I could hide from him. But it is you, a man like myself, my companion, my close friend, with whom I once enjoyed sweet fellowship as we walked with the throng at the house of God."

This Psalm is probably closely connected to the previous one, in which David reacted to the betrayal by members of his own family to King Saul. In this Psalm, David speaks about "a man like myself, my companion, my close friend, with whom I once enjoyed sweet fellowship as we walked with the throng at the house of God." It must have been one of David's closest friends who reported him. This was what hit him hardest. His confidence in mankind had been deeply shocked, and his soul was profoundly wounded.

David's disappointment became a prophecy of what Jesus experienced when Judas betrayed Him. In another Psalm David wrote a thought which is parallel to this one, and which Jesus quoted in connection with Judas' betrayal: "Even my close friend, whom I trusted, he who shared my bread, has lifted up his heel against me" (Psalm 41:9; John 13:18).

People usually become traitors for the sake of money as if money has more value than human relationships, power more than love!

We all need fellowship with other people. A human being cannot live and function without some form of human interaction, fellowship, and mutual love. David may have been afraid that God would treat him in the same way as his friend treated him; that He would abandon him and hide from him.

Human relationships are meant to be a reflection of God's relationship with us. God wants us to learn about the love of our heavenly Father through the affection our earthly father and mother show us. But the images that surround us are often distorted, and we receive the wrong signals. In some cases this leads to the impression that God's reality is like the human shadows of it that surround us. We tend to think that God is unreliable, and that He would leave us, as men do, at the critical moments when we need Him most.

If we have been wounded by betrayal, by family members, spouses, or colleagues it may help us to remember that no one was ever betrayed like our Lord Jesus Christ. Judas betrayed Jesus with a kiss (Matthew 26:48,49). That kiss became the kiss of death for Judas, not for Jesus. Our Lord has the most wonderful and warm embrace for those who are betrayed by their fellowman. "He will remain faithful, for he cannot disown himself" (II Timothy 2:13).

Psalm 55:16-23

"Cast your cares on the LORD and he will sustain you; he will never let the righteous fall."

The apostle Peter quotes this verse in his first epistle (I Peter 5:7). Peter speaks about humility, as opposed to pride in human relationships, about our fellowship with God, and alertness toward our real enemy, the devil. In connection with this threefold relationship, he uses the word "cares" or "anxiety." It is anxiety that comes from the fact that we lose sight of the factual relations.

The word "cast" is a strong expression; it says more than "let go." It takes an effort to fling down the load we have been carrying. It is an act that requires our full involvement. We have to make up our minds that we do not want to have anything to do anymore with our anxiety and distress. It also requires confidence that God will indeed care for us. If we surrender to Him, we leave the consequences up to Him. If we keep on feeling anxious after our surrender, we indicate that we revoke our initial act of surrender. This amounts to a motion of non-confidence in God. In being anxious, we indicate that we consider the God who created the universe, and who upholds all things by the word of His power, not to be reliable enough to take care of the details of our lives. It helps to see how ridiculous such a notion is.

We have to learn to trust God and cast our burdens upon Him. When, as a child, we first learn to walk, we are afraid to fall. After we have been walking for years, we are not even conscious of the fact that we walk. It is the same with real faith; we trust God without being aware of the fact.

God not only takes care of us, but He picks up our burden and carries it with us. Jesus invites us: "Take my yoke upon you and learn from me, for I am gentle and humble in heart, and you will find rest for your souls. For my yoke is easy and my burden is light" (Matthew 11:29,30). The yoke of Christ is light because, in His humility, He has become lower than we are. He picks up the yoke at its lowest, that is, its heaviest point. When we learn to walk with Him, our steps will be light.

Psalm 56:1-8

"When I am afraid, I will trust in you. In God, whose word I praise, in God I trust; I will not be afraid. What can mortal man do to me?"

This Psalm is related to Psalm Thirty-Four, as it refers to the time when David sought asylum at the court of the Philistine King Achish of Gath. When David was recognized as the one who had killed their national hero, Goliath, who was from Gath, he panicked. In a sense, all David's problems were the result of God's call and anointing, but the fact that he was trampled on as he was at that point, he owed to himself. He fled in panic, and panic is sin.

Panic does not create the right atmosphere to act responsibly or make the right decisions. David, obviously, sinned when he faked insanity at the court of Achish. The fact that God saved him out of his predicament was pure grace; it wasn't because of David's faith. Fear can choke us if we begin to doubt God's promises. The fear of men is always the result of the fact that we lose sight of the value of God's Word.

The words written above: "When I am afraid, I will trust in you. In God, whose word I praise, in God I trust; I will not be afraid. What can mortal man do to me?" therefore, must have been written in retrospect. David recognized that he had failed the Lord and he promises to trust God and His Word from then on.

When panic overtakes us, it shuts down our defense system. It cuts the lifeline with God. Panic is stronger than we are; we lose control over ourselves. We can only lose control if we are trying to keep control in our own hands. The only way to avoid panic when we are overwhelmed by threats to our life is to hand over the reins of our life to God. He is the only One who can keep us from stumbling. God's Word assures us that God "is able to keep [us] from falling and to present [us] before his glorious presence without fault and with great joy" (Jude, verses 24,25). The antidote to all fear is the fear of God.

Jesus puts our position in the right perspective when, speaking about persecution, He says: "Do not be afraid of those who kill the body but cannot kill the soul. Rather, be afraid of the one who can destroy both soul and body in hell. Are not two sparrows sold for a penny? Yet not one of them will fall to the ground apart from the will of your Father. And even the very hairs of your head are all numbered. So don't be afraid; you are worth more than many sparrows" (Matthew 10:28-31).

Psalm 56:9-13

"I am under vows to you, O God; I will present my thank offerings to you."

David had every reason to thank God for his deliverance from the predicament he had got himself into when he went to the Philistine King Achish to ask for asylum. We read that when he realized his life was in danger, he pretended to be insane and was thus expelled from the palace instead of being killed (I Samuel 21:10-15). God delivered David, not because of his clever act, but in spite of it.

After David realized what he had done and how God had pulled him out of a potentially fatal situation, he wrote this Psalm of praise. He also pledged himself to God with a vow.

Vows are not very common among Christians anymore. We thank the Lord for saving our soul, but few people draw the conclusion that their salvation ought to result in an act of dedication of their life to God. Nobody will say so out loud, but we express in our acts that we believe it is nice to obey God but it is not really necessary.

When God saves us, He will never force us into a life of obedience. The choice is ours because obedience must be based upon our love for God, not upon fear.

The apostle Paul advises us: "Do you not know that your body is a temple of the Holy Spirit, who is in you, whom you have received from God? You are not your own; you were bought at a price. Therefore honor God with your body" (I Corinthians 6:19,20).

God saved David in spite of himself because He had destined him to be the king of Israel. God wants to make us kings and priests in His Kingdom. The way to the throne is by dedicating ourselves to God's purpose. The greatest tragedy would be if we would not become what God predestined us to be: to live in this world and never grasp the reason for which we were born! Obedience is the key to our destiny and to a fulfilled life.

Psalm 57:1-6

"Have mercy on me, O God, have mercy on me, for in you my soul takes refuge."

According to the title of this Psalm, David wrote this when he was hiding from Saul in the cave of Adullam. David saw the walls of the cave as symbols of God's security.

Taking refuge in God is more than a physical matter. David says: "In you my soul takes refuge." The inner rest of being sheltered in God's hand is more important than being protected from outward threats.

David prayed: "Have mercy on me, O God, have mercy on me." The Hebrew word, translated "mercy" describes the act of stooping down. God's mercy to us means that He comes down to our level, that He becomes one of us and one with us. God did this when Jesus was born in Bethlehem to live among us to take upon Himself the sins of this world.

How good it is to realize that God protects us, and that this is part of His grace to us!

David's sense of protection is the best indication that he had received pardon for his sins. If we live a life of lying and deceiving, we place ourselves automatically outside the shelter of God's protection, and we expose ourselves to the attacks of the enemy. But if we confess our sins, and ask for forgiveness, as David did, we are immediately safe and protected. That is why it is so dangerous to live with unconfessed sins. Safety, confession, and forgiveness always go hand in hand.

By appealing to God as the Most High, David performs a legal act. He acts as a citizen of the Kingdom–who has the right to appeal to the highest authority. In the Roman Empire, Roman citizens had the right to appeal to Caesar. When the apostle Paul found no justice in the Roman court in which he stood trial, he said: "I appeal to Caesar!" (Acts 25:11). As a Christian, we have legal rights and privileges that far surpass any legal protection a government can give us. On the basis of the pardon of our sins provided for us in the sacrifice of Jesus Christ, we have the right to appeal to God. He promises to hear us.

It is obvious that our appeal cannot pertain to futile and self-serving matters. As citizens of God's Kingdom, we make the matters of the Kingdom our priority. Jesus promises us regarding our own interests: "All these things will be given to you as well" (Matthew 6:33).

Psalm 57:7-11

"I will praise you, O Lord, among the nations; I will sing of you among the peoples."

David wrote this Psalm before he was king of Israel. He made the same statement: "I will praise you, O Lord, among the nations" in the Psalm he composed at the end of his life. In Psalm 18, verse 49, we read: "Therefore I will praise you among the nations, O LORD; I will sing praises to your name." Evidently, he never lost sight of Israel's call to be the bearer of God's revelation. God wanted to win the world for Himself through the people of Israel. God has His eye on the nations, on the peoples of this earth. In Jesus' words: "The field is the world" (Matthew 13:38).

In God's plan for the world salvation is the means, not the final goal. The purpose is that people in the whole world, all the people who are created in God's image and likeness, will praise God and sing Psalms to Him. The greatest tragedy is not that people are lost, as tragic as that is, but that God is not being exalted and praised by all.

God wants to win the world through us. We must realize that our salvation is not an end in itself; it is a means to the end. We are saved for a purpose. God "wants all men to be saved and to come to a knowledge of the truth" (I Timothy 2:4). But the ultimate goal is that "the earth will be filled with the knowledge of the glory of the LORD, as the waters cover the sea" (Habakkuk 2:14). God wants us to be "world Christians," that is, people who consider the whole world and all its inhabitants to be their mission field. For some this may mean going to the end of the world; for all of us it ought to mean that we cover the globe with our prayers. That is why we pray: "Our Father in heaven, hallowed be your name, your kingdom come, your will be done on earth as it is in heaven" (Matthew 6:9-10). Let us not fail to recognize the goal of our salvation by limiting our vision. God wants us to be priests, as well as kings.

Psalm 58:1-9
"Do you rulers indeed speak justly? Do you judge uprightly among men?"

This is a difficult Psalm to read and come to terms with. It seems to go completely against the grain of what God wants our Christian testimony to be. It is a call for revenge, which is incompatible with the message of the New Testament. Or is it? We will look at that tomorrow.

Let us look first at the setting of this Psalm. David addresses the judges. The Hebrew word, translated "judges" means literally, "silent ones." The suggestion is that those who ought to speak up keep their mouths shut.

The topic is the application of justice. There is a parallel thought in a Psalm written by Asaph, which reads: "God presides in the great assembly; he gives judgment among the 'gods': 'How long will you defend the unjust and show partiality to the wicked?' " (Psalm 82:1,2). There the judges are addressed as "gods."

It amazes us that the term "gods" would be used for mortal men. It means that man is lifted above himself, and above the level of his earthly limitations that usually hem him in. The term "gods" establishes a relationship between man and the only true God, the Almighty. This proves that even fallen man is more than an animal. The fact that God's Name is given to man indicates a bond with the character of God. In our being related to God, there are characteristics we have in common with God, such as: knowledge, wisdom, love, fidelity, and many others. Pronouncing judgment is not an every-day activity of man. Yet, this authority is an important part of the mandate God gave to man at his creation. The Apostle Paul writes to the Corinthians: "Do you not know that the saints will judge the world? ... Do you not know that we will judge angels?" (I Corinthians 6:2,3).

In this Psalm, man is addressed as if the fall never took place. God denies us the opportunity to excuse our weaknesses by saying: "That's the way I am. I cannot help myself." This shows us how we ought to be. It implies a judgment upon our lives, but it also addresses us from a position of victory over sin. As man is promoted in life to a higher position, he often believes that he becomes less accountable. This is why corruption always reaches the top. This is true, not only on a secular level but also in the church. Very often, we seek more our own interests than the Kingdom of God and its righteousness. It is important that we keep our focus on God's image, and that we exercise our spiritual authority in a way that is in accordance with this image.

Psalm 58:10-11

"The righteous will be glad when they are avenged, when they bathe their feet in the blood of the wicked."

The end of this Psalm makes one recoil in horror. "The righteous will be glad when they are avenged, when they bathe their feet in the blood of the wicked." What satisfaction can a righteous person get from a bloodbath? In some cases the Holy Spirit uses pictures that are repulsive to us in order to evoke repulsion about the horror of sin, and in order to bring us to repentance. The picture David paints here has the same effect on us as the one we find in Revelation, where the birds of prey are invited to eat the flesh of Christ's victims. We read: "And I saw an angel standing in the sun, who cried in a loud voice to all the birds flying in midair, 'Come, gather together for the great supper of God, so that you may eat the flesh of kings, generals, and mighty men, of horses and their riders, and the flesh of all people, free and slave, small and great.' ... The rest of them were killed with the sword that came out of the mouth of the rider on the horse, and all the birds gorged themselves on their flesh" (Revelation 19:17,18,21).

This is not a celebration of sadism. God does not cause bloodbaths, that is the work of human hands and it is horrible. Putting the picture before us the way David does makes us realize how horrible and inhumane our human race has become.

The picture David paints speaks of God's judgment and of the victory of righteousness over unrighteousness. Evil must be punished in order for God's righteousness to prevail. Leaving sin untouched would be similar to letting an infection fester in the human body. This does not mean that we should personally take revenge upon those who persecute us. Vengeance is God's business. In everyday practical life the best effort we can make is to conquer our enemies by making them our friends. We can be victorious by praying for those who persecute us. Jesus says: "Love your enemies and pray for those who persecute you, that you may be sons of your Father in heaven" (Matthew 5:44-45). Some victims of the Nazi concentration camps went back to their tormentors after the end of World War Two and preached the Gospel to them. They avenged themselves by getting some of them saved.

Psalm 59:1-5

"Deliver me from my enemies, O God; protect me from those who rise up against me. Deliver me from evildoers and save me from bloodthirsty men."

David wrote this Psalm when he first fled from Saul. We read: "An evil spirit from the LORD came upon Saul as he was sitting in his house with his spear in his hand. While David was playing the harp, Saul tried to pin him to the wall with his spear, but David eluded him as Saul drove the spear into the wall. That night David made good his escape" (I Samuel 19:9,10). Samuel had anointed David as king; "and from that day on the Spirit of the LORD came upon David in power" (I Samuel 16:13). Little would David have expected that he would immediately become the target of Satan. From that time on, he found himself going through life surrounded by evil powers that wanted to destroy him.

We rarely anticipate this kind of opposition when we surrender ourselves to the Lord. It is of great importance that we put ourselves under the protection of the Most High. David knew this from the moment Saul's spear missed his heart by a few inches and stuck into the wall of the palace; he realized that he looked into the eyes of a bloodthirsty madman.

Even the feeling of tension when the noose is pulled a little tighter around one's neck can become common. But first experiences, with the fright and panic that accompany them, tend to engrave themselves on our memory more deeply.

It was this shock, the panic that followed his narrow escape that made David cry out to God for revenge. Later, during his efforts to evade Saul's madness, David would tone down his reaction and be less avenging.

He finds relief for his panic in a prayer in which he calls God, "LORD God Almighty, the God of Israel." The Hebrew text reads literally "LORD God of hosts," that is the supreme commander of the heavenly armies. The realization that God has a huge army to protect David from Saul's single spear has a soothing effect upon him. Would God who called him not protect him and bring him to the place where He wanted him to be? The thought is ludicrous.

We may go through experiences in life that evoke fear and panic. The Bible calls Jesus the author of our salvation who leads us to glory (See Hebrews 2:10). We can be assured that we will arrive at our appointed destination if we allow ourselves to be led. Keeping our eye on our destination will help us to traverse moments of intense pain and suffering. The LORD, the God of hosts, has His eye on us. He will protect us from any fiery dart the enemy of our souls will aim at us.

Psalm 59:6-17

"O my Strength, I watch for you; you, O God, are my fortress, my loving God. O my Strength, I sing praise to you; you, O God, are my fortress, my loving God."

In the midst of this Psalm that deals with deadly hatred, panic, and vengeance, these words are like flowers in a desert. David had panicked when Saul had sent his police force to David's house to arrest and kill him. His wife, Michal, helped him escape through a window and deceived Saul's men (See I Samuel 19:11-17). David cannot have had much time for poetry at that moment. He probably did not write this Psalm until he was safely hidden in the cave of Adullam. Then he asked himself what God in heaven would think of his harrowing experience and, in his mind, he saw a smile on the face of the Almighty.

It is salutary to imagine how things on earth look from above; it helps to diminish the tension. It made David resolve that from then on he would no longer stare at circumstances surrounding him, but look up to God above. The house which had become unsafe to him and from which he escaped through a window was exchanged for God's fortress, that invincible bunker, where he was completely safe.

Faith needs to be exercised. David received glimpses of God's reality that surrounded him. His prayer to see God's love and mercy and lovingkindness for victory over his enemies would be answered, little by little, in his own heart. After all, God's lovingkindness had always been with David, and his enemies had already been overcome before they surrounded the house. David was invincible under God's protection, but he had to learn to stand in this victory by exercising daily fellowship with God.

There is no safer place on earth to hide than in the bunker of God's love. If we learn to hide in Him, we feel the warmth of His affection and we can truly say: "If God is for us, who can be against us?" (Romans 8:31).

Psalm 60:1-5

"But for those who fear you, you have raised a banner to be unfurled against the bow."

This Psalm explains things that are not found in the historical records of the Bible. While David's army carried out successful campaigns on the battlefield, his enemies came and raided his hometown, causing extensive damage. David was victorious but he paid a high price for it. One *Bible Commentary* observes: "But for this Psalm and its title we should have no inkling of the resilience of David's hostile neighbors at the peak of his power. His very success brought its dangers of alliances among his enemies, and of battles far from home. At such a moment, when his main force was with him near the Euphrates, Edom evidently took its chance to fall upon Judah from the South." David won the victory on the battlefield, but he lost the battle at home. That is the reason this Psalm is not a song of victory, but the cry of a saddened heart.

The lesson is that, in our spiritual struggles, no position should be left undefended, and God's priorities should always be kept in clear focus. Many of the workers in the Kingdom of Heaven who won great victories on the front line, lost out in their marriages, and in their family life.

In Churchill's *History of the Second World War*, the author describes Hitler's strategy, as that of a spider in a web. The reason Germany lost the war, he says, was that the spider left the center of the web. We have to be careful in the spiritual battle that our ministry does not grow any faster than we ourselves grow. It is possible for the devil to draw us out too far. He will even go so far as to show us visions of lost souls in order to make us stretch ourselves beyond the limit. There is a fine line between reaching out in faith to that which actually lies beyond our reach, and recklessly stretching farther than the Lord wants us to reach, thus playing into the devil's hand. We always have to ask ourselves to what degree our ministry hinders our fellowship with God. If we are watchful in this, everything will be all right.

If we make God the central focus of our life, our home ought to be filled with His presence and our spouse and children ought to experience the safety and peace that are only found in Him. The banner of God's love must be unfurled at the porch of our house first. If it is, we may go as far away from home as God allows us. For some of us this may be to the uttermost parts of the world, for others no farther than the immediate neighborhood.

Psalm 60:6-12

"God has spoken from his sanctuary ... With God we will gain the victory, and he will trample down our enemies."

The picture David paints for us in verses 6-8 of this Psalm will not have much meaning for us if we are not familiar with the geography and history of the places he mentions. Shechem and Sukkoth were the first parts of the Promised Land Jacob appropriated for himself when he returned from his Uncle Laban. Gilead is the territory on the other side of the Jordan River. Manasseh occupied the area on both sides of the River Jordan; this tribe formed a bridge between the two parts. Ephraim and Judah were the most important tribes, respectively in the north and in the south of the country. So these verses give us a picture as to how the occupation of Canaan took place historically. In other words, God reminds David of his heritage.

David may have lost a battle, but God had not lost the war. The Promised Land was still there and God promised to mend what the enemy has broken. "Judah my scepter" are words referring to the reign of Jesus Christ. David can hardly have understood what God was saying to him in those words he penned himself.

There is even playfulness in the reference to Moab, Edom, and Philistia. God pokes fun at David's enemies because He knows their future. They were gloating over the damage they had caused to David's home, but God knew that the roles would be reversed.

It may be terrible when our home is in shambles and our family is ruined. It is even worse if we are partly to be blamed for the catastrophe. Sickness and death can cause terrible havoc in our lives. It is often impossible for us to see beyond our loss and sorrows. But God promises that He will wipe away the tears from our eyes. The day will come when our fiercest enemy, death, will be defeated and we will enter into the reality of God's Promised Land. Jesus says: "A woman giving birth to a child has pain because her time has come; but when her baby is born she forgets the anguish because of her joy that a child is born into the world. So with you: Now is your time of grief, but I will see you again and you will rejoice, and no one will take away your joy" (John 16:21,22).

Psalm 61:1-3

"Lead me to the rock that is higher than I. For you have been my refuge, a strong tower against the foe."

When David wrote this Psalm he had lost the sense of God's presence. He saw himself at the ends of the earth, far away from God who lived in Jerusalem. The distance of separation was more spiritual than topographical. People can live in the shadow of the temple and still be miles away from God in their spiritual experience. In asking God to lead him to "the rock that is higher than I," David prays for God to lift him out above himself. David had lost sight of the horizon; his world had become too small, and he lacked perspective.

Our fellowship with God is indispensable for an evaluation of ourselves, and of the situation in which we are. Jesus would stop from time to time to draw a line from the place where He stood to the throne of God, and then judge His circumstances in the light of eternity. Such a panoramic vision cannot be a daily experience, and it does not have to be; however, if we never find an answer to the two questions who we are, and what the importance of our acts is in the great frame of God's design, we are not the human beings God wants us to be. The rock is too high for us. We cannot lift ourselves up above our own level; God will have to do that for us.

In the light of the New Testament, David's picture opens even greater perspectives. We can see in it an image of the sinful "I" that hinders the man who is born again. The Apostle Paul expresses this in the words: "I no longer live, but Christ lives in me" (Galatians 2:20). A. B. Simpson wrote: "O, to be free from myself, dear Lord…" A person who is full of himself is at the ends of the earth, far from fellowship with God. "The rock that is higher than I" is Christ. Standing on that rock means to be crucified, to be dead, and buried with Him, and to live in the power of His resurrection. For David this was an unreachable goal; for us, who are in Christ, this elevation to the top of the rock has already taken place.

The image of the rock is an expression of three aspects of spiritual life. The rock is the foundation on which we stand, and upon which we are built up. Secondly, the rock is the cleft rock, which symbolizes the body of Christ that was struck and broken on the cross, by which we receive forgiveness and renewal. And thirdly the rock is the stronghold, which is our position in Christ in which we stand against the attacks of the enemy, who wants to undo the victory of the risen Lord in our lives.

Psalm 61:4-8

"I long to dwell in your tent forever and take refuge in the shelter of your wings."

David was thinking of the tabernacle where the Ark of the Covenant stood with the two cherubs that spread their wings above the cover. It was the place where only the high priest was allowed to enter. In his wish to live in God's tent forever, he reached beyond the picture into the spiritual reality itself.

David had made a vow to God, pledging his life to God's service. He speaks of the heritage God had given him. All this is expressed in earthly terms and in the form of material blessings. But the fact that he repeatedly uses the word "forever" means that he envisioned eternity. David realized that what he experienced on earth was merely a picture of the reality to come. David fully planned to spend eternity with God in His glory and he planned his life accordingly.

Our real heritage is God Himself. God spoke to Abraham: "I am your shield, your very great reward" (Genesis 15:1). And to Aaron He said: "I am your share and your inheritance among the Israelites" (Numbers 18:20). Peter connects this inheritance to the resurrection of Christ when he says: "Praise be to the God and Father of our Lord Jesus Christ! In his great mercy he has given us new birth into a living hope through the resurrection of Jesus Christ from the dead, and into an inheritance that can never perish, spoil or fade-- kept in heaven for you" (I Peter 1:3,4). Everything we own at present is borrowed goods that we will have to leave behind when we leave this world. Our real possessions will be given to us when we arrive at the other side. The surety of these possessions is the Holy Spirit, who is given to us now. The Apostle Paul said: "Now it is God who has made us for this very purpose and has given us the Spirit as a deposit, guaranteeing what is to come" (II Corinthians 5:5). This truth is mind-boggling. Some years ago, a lady in Florida won fifty-five million dollars in a lottery. Anyone who has received the Holy Spirit as a deposit, and who would be willing to trade places with that lady is a fool. As an immortal child of God, I do not want to be swallowed up by mortality. Standing on the rock that is higher than I, I can see this horizon--under the shelter of His wing. And the Lord whispers to me what is awaiting me on the other side. We have to think of Jim Elliot's words: "He is no fool who gives up what he cannot keep, in order to obtain what he cannot lose."

Psalm 62:1-8

"My soul finds rest in God alone; my salvation comes from him … Find rest, O my soul, in God alone; my hope comes from him."

The keyword in this Psalm is "silence." Another translation for "My soul finds rest in God alone" is "For God alone my soul waits in silence." The Hebrew text reads literally "Only to God (in) silence (is) my soul."

Silence is a rare commodity in life. Most people are afraid of silence. We are afraid that, when the noise stops, we will hear things we don't want to hear. Actually, silence is never a complete absence of sounds. Only in death there is absolute silence; where there is life, there is vibration. People have done experiments by placing persons in a one hundred percent soundproof place. The result was that those people began to hear their own heartbeat, and the swishing of their blood amplified like a thundering noise.

Silence before God is not a soundless experience, but it is a shutting out of all the cacophony that bombards us from all sides, in order to listen to the sounds of life in fellowship with the living God. It is the quieting of our soul. It is what we hear when we go into our room and close the door to be alone with God. We close the door to the noises of sin in our lives.

As our body recovers from sickness in rest, so our soul is restored in the quietude of the presence of God. Becoming quiet and being alone with God requires practice. The fact that it is one of the soul's natural abilities to be silent does not mean that our souls will automatically become silent. Walking, for instance, is a natural function of the body, but we all had to learn to walk; so it is with the silence of our souls.

We can only be silent, quiet, and peaceful before God if we have had the experience of salvation. Silence without the atonement for our sins by the sacrifice of Jesus Christ can be a terrifying experience. But if the realization of God's love that sent Jesus to die in our place dawns upon us, moments of silence in God's presence can restore our soul. Praise and love can find their richest expression in moments of silence.

Psalm 62:9-12

"One thing God has spoken, two things have I heard: that you, O God, are strong, and that you, O Lord, are loving. Surely you will reward each person according to what he has done."

The expression "One thing … two things" in the verse "One thing God has spoken, two things have I heard" is probably a Hebrew idiom that conveys the idea of something excellent. If we take this statement in a literal sense, we see that David sees unity between God's speaking in the physical world and in the spiritual realm. The Apostle Paul applies this principle when he says: "For God, who said, 'Let light shine out of darkness,' made his light shine in our hearts to give us the light of the knowledge of the glory of God in the face of Christ" (II Corinthians 4:6). As God created all things by simply speaking His Word, so He makes us a new creation by speaking to us. When we hear the Word of God and allow it to enter our life, light and life will begin to fill our existence. One difference between God's creation, as we read it in the first chapters of Genesis and in our life is that the universe had no choice in being created. The water could not refuse to separate or to produce fish; we can refuse to let the Word of God do its creative work in us. No one becomes a new creation in Christ against his will. God is strong, but He also loves. In His love He respects us more than we respect ourselves. His strength guarantees that He can fulfill what He promises and His love draws us out of the quagmire of sin in which we are lost.

Once we are brought to life, God's Word will continue to create. When Jesus said: "Blessed are the poor in spirit, Blessed are those who mourn, Blessed are the meek, Blessed are those who hunger and thirst for righteousness, Blessed are the merciful, Blessed are the pure in heart, Blessed are the peacemakers, Blessed are those who are persecuted because of righteousness" (Matthew 5:3-10), His Word creates the blessing. In fact, "Blessed rather are those who hear the word of God and obey it" (Luke 11:28).

Psalm 63:1-5

"Because your love is better than life, my lips will glorify you."

David realized, in the Desert of Judah, that he was about to perish because of thirst, both physically and spiritually. It was probably this danger of dying of thirst that opened his eyes to what was about to happen to him. He realized that he would soon stand before the throne of God, and in that light he began to take an inventory of his spiritual condition. He understood that fellowship with God, at that moment, was more important than drinking water. The lesson David had to learn from his thirst was that there were more important things than water.

The verse "Because your love is better than life, my lips will glorify you" is one of the golden verses in the Bible. One of the most important discoveries we can make is that there are more important things than our personal life. We tend to think that our life on earth has top priority; yet everyone knows that all humans have to die. In spite of this fact, people are often willing to steal and to commit murder in order to stay alive. Jesus emphasizes that the key to eternal life is the willingness to die.

God does not demand of us that we give up life without anything in return, but that we exchange it for something better: His love, His lovingkindness. If a man is ready to die for God's lovingkindness, he will live by that lovingkindness. D. L. Moody used an illustration about a toddler playing with a pair of scissors. The older sister tried to take that dangerous toy away from him, but the child began to scream. But when the girl came with a nice big orange and showed that to her little brother, the kid's hands opened, the scissors dropped, and he took the orange. In the same way God shows us His lovingkindness. If we open our hands and reach for it, we will not be able to hold on to our own life at the same time.

Whether we want to or not, life will slip away from us. This does not happen all at once, of course; it is a developing process that will take a lifetime. It begins with the recognition that God's lovingkindness is better than life, and it is followed by a choice. As we progress in life, we will understand how good our choice has been. God's lovingkindness, His goodness, and His character harbor a treasure of hope for us. When we think of His strength and glory, we can still ask ourselves if we will profit from it, but God's lovingkindness makes us understand that He wraps us in the embrace of His loving arms. This realization will make our talking about "giving our life for the Lord" rather insignificant.

Psalm 63:6-11

"On my bed I remember you; I think of you through the watches of the night. Because you are my help, I sing in the shadow of your wings. My soul clings to you; your right hand upholds me."

When people get older, sleep can become elusive. It is not uncommon for the elderly to wake up in the middle of the night and not be able to go back to sleep again. David turned this insomnia into a blessing by directing his thoughts toward God. Better than counting sheep, he imagines himself as a baby chick under the wing of his mother hen and the emotional warmth and comfort this gave him made him begin to sing. We may not want to follow David in this literally and wake up others, but turning our thoughts to the Lord in the middle of the night may be advice that is worth considering. If we prepare ourselves for such spells of wakefulness by committing some Bible verses to memory, we may find that very helpful for the purpose.

"My soul clings to you" suggests a unity and intimacy similar to a marriage relationship. The same Hebrew word that is translated "to cling" is the same that is used in the verse "For this reason a man will leave his father and mother and be united to his wife, and they will become one flesh" (Genesis 2:24). It may sound strange to us that David uses a word that has a sexual connotation to describe his relationship with God. We tend to draw a sharp line between sexuality and spirituality, mainly because the devil has caused so much havoc in the domain of human sexual behavior. The Holy Spirit, though, shows us that the physical unity between husband and wife is a shadow of the real unity between God and man. How wonderful it is to see God in the sanctuary, and then enter into a love relationship with Him. This goes beyond our wildest dreams. We usually think of adoration and praise of God as something that creates a distance between Him and us. David speaks about God in terms of the tenderest caressing, stroking, and intimacy known to man. Very few people know this kind of relationship with God. This may also be the reason that so few also are able to enjoy married life to the full. It is a two-way street. Intimacy with God creates the basis for a good and healthy relationship between spouses, and on the other hand a sound marriage will reinforce our love of God. All this requires an effort.

Psalm 64:1-8

"Hear me, O God, as I voice my complaint; protect my life from the threat of the enemy."

The tone of this Psalm is quite different from the previous one. In Psalm 63 God was in the center and the enemies stood on the side; in this Psalm the enemies take the limelight, but the final result is the same. The main part of the Psalm is taken up by the conspiracy of the enemy. God's revenge is rapid and swift. One single arrow puts an end to all the threats. The Psalm begins and ends with David's reaction, first to the threats of the enemy and then to God's retribution. This reprisal is an answer to David's prayer. When the answer comes, it has far-reaching consequences that go well beyond the horizon of David's own life.

It is a liberating experience to place the threats in this Psalm in a larger context. It cuts the ground from under the enemy's feet. We realize how cleverly this Psalm is composed.

We all need protection from the enemy of our souls. Unless we are covered by the righteousness of Jesus Christ, the devil will have a handle on us. As a snake hypnotizes his victim before swallowing it, so could we fall under the spell of the Evil One. Unless God protects us, the enemy would surely impair our ability to think and act logically. The only remedy against the enemy frightening us is reconciliation with God, receiving pardon for sin, and putting on the whole armor of God. Sometimes healing of anxiety will be instantaneous, but often it is a growing process of increasing spiritual health.

A man once prayed the following prayer: "Lord, let my name be known in hell." When he was questioned about this, he explained that he had read the story in Acts about the sons of Sceva, who tried to cast out a demon, with the words "In the name of Jesus, whom Paul preaches, I command you to come out." The evil spirit answered them, "Jesus I know, and I know about Paul, but who are you?" (Acts 19:13-16). "I want the devil to know who I am," the man said.

If we are armed with God's righteousness, He has given us authority over the enemy and he knows us. God does much more than protect us from the enemy. As Paul promises: "The God of peace will soon crush Satan under your feet" (Romans 16:20). If we meet the devil, which one ought to flee? Think about it.

Psalm 64:9-10

"All mankind will fear; they will proclaim the works of God and ponder what he has done."

It is amazing to see how easily David takes a personal experience and elevates it to a universal principle. He demonstrates that what happened to him-- God extinguished the fiery darts of slander and evil talk that were meant to ruin his life-- will have its effect upon all of mankind.

This Psalm deals with slander. David said about his enemies: "They sharpen their tongues like swords and aim their words like deadly arrows." God countered this by shooting them down with their own arrows. We read: "But God will shoot them with arrows; suddenly they will be struck down. He will turn their own tongues against them and bring them to ruin; all who see them will shake their heads in scorn." This, David says, is what will install fear in all of mankind. The general principle is that we will be judged by our own words. Our gossip will testify against us.

Jesus lashed out against the pious people of His time, calling them a "brood of vipers." He said: "For out of the overflow of the heart the mouth speaks. The good man brings good things out of the good stored up in him, and the evil man brings evil things out of the evil stored up in him. But I tell you that men will have to give account on the day of judgment for every careless word they have spoken. For by your words you will be acquitted, and by your words you will be condemned" (Matthew 12:34-37).

Let me illustrate this. Let's say that you are a faithful churchgoer. Saturday evening, sitting around the coffee table, the talk veers toward some people in church you don't particularly appreciate. Some unkind words are spoken about a certain person. Your rebellious teenage boy, without your knowledge, tapes this conversation and he somehow manages to take the tape to church the next morning where he succeeds having it played over the sound system. The person who was the subject of your gossip sits next to you and hears your voice. Nothing can cover your shame and embarrassment!

On the day of judgment God will push a playback button on His recorder and we will hear our words come back to us to condemn us. That is what makes all mankind fear! We are all like Isaiah in need of a coal from the altar to touch our lips, because we are all people of unclean lips. (see Isaiah 6:5-7). Our prayer ought to be: "Set a guard over my mouth, O LORD; keep watch over the door of my lips" (Psalm 141:3).

Psalm 65:1-4

"Praise awaits you, O God, in Zion; to you our vows will be fulfilled."

There is something in the Hebrew text that is difficult to render in English. A literal translation would be "To you, silence–praise, O God, in Zion, and to you is a vow completed." As in Psalm Sixty-Two, in this Psalm also there is silence, a silence that praises God. In Psalm Sixty-Two, David became silent to shut out all the noises that disrupt fellowship with God. There, silence was a preparation for intimacy with the Lord; here it is a form of worship. Silence, as a form of worship, can be very effective. It can be the climax of adoration.

After all, our words can only partially express our experiences. If we can say all we feel, our feelings do not amount to much. Our stillness before God fills in what is lacking in our words. It is like the silence of a smile exchanged between lovers. Without love and openness, such a silence cannot exist. Wordless communication requires growing together; it is a mutual experience. God smiles upon us in silence, and we smile back. And we both understand what is meant.

The fulfillment of vows can also be seen as part of the silence, as a confirmation. As every silent smile exchanged between loving spouses is a confirmation of their wedding vows, so is the silence of our worship. We say to God that the previous surrender of ourselves to Him is still valid.

If we learn to be silent in the presence of God, we have entered into an intimacy that cannot be expressed in words and God's silence will become the most eloquent expression of His love for us. This is not the silence that gives no answer to our questions; it is the silence of all answers. It is not the silence of the grave but the silence of life at the highest plane.

This silence may seem to be beyond our reach, but our lives will be enriched when we practice it. When God no longer speaks to us because He doesn't have to, we have entered into the fullness of His fellowship and love.

The Old Testament prophet, Zephaniah, corroborates the above saying: "The LORD your God is with you, he is mighty to save. He will take great delight in you, he will quiet you with his love... (Zephaniah 3:17). Then the fulfillment of our vows and promises to Him will also be a matter of quiet and loving obedience.

Psalm 65:5-8

"You answer us with awesome deeds of righteousness, O God our Savior, the hope of all the ends of the earth and of the farthest seas."

Answers require questions. God's answers presuppose our prayers. In calling God "the hope of all the ends of the earth," David demonstrates a tremendous missionary vision. We cannot exaggerate the universality of this. God is not a local deity, He is the Creator of the universe and He wants to be the Savior of all mankind.

If we have accepted the Gospel of Jesus Christ and have experienced the application of His righteousness to our lives, we must dedicate ourselves to intercessory prayer for the whole human race, spread out over the whole of our globe. Christians can never be isolationists.

When God chose the nation of Israel, He wanted them to become a kingdom of priests. After God led them out of the slavery of Egypt, He said to them "Now if you obey me fully and keep my covenant, then out of all nations you will be my treasured possession. Although the whole earth is mine, you will be for me a kingdom of priests and a holy nation" (Exodus 19:5,6). As for us, He washed us from our sins in His own blood, and has made us kings and priests (Revelation 1:5,6). Priests build bridges between God and man. For some of us this may mean going to the ends of the earth and crossing the farthest seas. For all of us, it means to cover the globe with our prayers.

Some Christians tend to cling together like people in a ghetto. Some churches attract only people of one particular social class or race. The real church of Jesus Christ, which is the body of our Lord, consists of people from all strata of society, of all countries. God wants us to think internationally. Since God is the hope of all the ends of the earth, He wants us to work on fulfilling that hope.

Some Stone Age tribes in New Guinea knew that centuries ago man enjoyed eternal life, but that it was taken away from them. They believed that one day God would give it back to them. From generation to generation they would cherish the hope that it would happen in their lifetime. When missionaries finally came with the Gospel, they were told "We have waited for this for centuries!" Some have not yet heard. God wants us to do something about that.

Psalm 65:9-13

"You crown the year with your bounty, and your carts overflow with abundance."

This beautiful picture is of a field, which a farmer ploughs, and plants, and which produces an abundant harvest. As one Bible Commentary states: "There is no harvest thanksgiving hymn that equals this Psalm." The New King James Version reads: "You visit the earth and water it." We think of springtime. After the death of nature during the long winter months, the ground bursts open with new life. In our part of the world, we rightfully celebrate Easter in the spring, when nature that surrounds us reflects the resurrection from the dead. We could place Jesus' words above this Psalm: "I have come that they may have life, and have it to the full" (John 10:10).

David describes an ideal world. We could almost say that such conditions cannot be found on earth. There is no mention of "the sweat of your brow" to which Adam was condemned to eat his food after he sinned. This is a new earth. It is also a picture of the personal experience of the new man in Christ.

When David sings: "You visit the earth," he describes a subjective experience, not an objective reality. God is always here, because He is omnipresent. But after our conversion we look at nature with different eyes. This is a common reaction of many who have received new life in Christ. David's discovery that God is present in nature corresponds with his awareness of God's presence in his own heart. In all of this he reaches forward to the time when "the earth will be full of the knowledge of the LORD as the waters cover the sea" (Isaiah 11:9; Habakkuk 2:14).

"You crown the year with your bounty," or as another translation reads: "You crown the year with Your goodness." The year of God's goodness is the Year of Jubilee. The Year of Jubilee was the year the Israelites had to celebrate every fifty years. In it all debts were cancelled and all slaves were set free.

The bountiful harvest of the farmer, which is described here, is a picture of another blessing, much greater than anything the earth can produce. It is a picture of God's harvest of souls that will be brought into His barns, of a thanksgiving celebration that will last throughout eternity and fill us with greater joy than any enjoyment on earth can provide.

Psalm 66:1-7

"Come and see what God has done, how awesome his works in man's behalf!"

In the preceding Psalm, God the Creator occupied the central place; in this Psalm it is man who lets his adoration rise toward his Redeemer. The reason given is that God "turned the sea into dry land, they passed through the waters on foot." This is a reference to the exodus of Israel from Egypt and the conquest of Canaan. The whole earth is called upon to participate in shouting with joy to God. In this way Israel's redemption from slavery in Egypt, and her entrance into the Promised Land is put forth as a paradigm of the redemption of the whole earth. The events are elevated above the realm of historical facts with only national significance to the redemption of the whole of creation.

Israel was the most important nation in the world, because God had chosen her to be the vehicle of His revelation. The real subject of this Psalm, therefore, is God's revelation of Himself in Jesus Christ. As God liberates Israel from Egyptian slavery so He frees man from the power of darkness through a supernatural intervention, and He provides him with a new life in a similarly miraculous way. Our becoming a new creation in Jesus Christ is the result of God's involvement in our lives.

For many people in this world the Gospel of Jesus Christ is not the most important part of their lives. The statement "All the earth bows down to you," can, therefore, hardly be seen as a statement of fact. Present reality does not corroborate this; the phrase should be seen as a wish. It is similar to the prayer: "Your kingdom come, your will be done on earth as it is in heaven" (Matthew 6:10). The Psalmist lets the mystery of man's disobedience lie. God will, eventually, act upon this Himself. It is good for us to long intensely for the time when all mankind will glorify God. The brotherhood of men can only be realized in a common worship of the Father, the Son, and the Holy Spirit.

There are two reasons given for praising God, the first is who God is, and the second what He does. Those two truths are the greatest in the entire universe. These truths will either keep us occupied throughout eternity, or they will crush us.

If we have experienced God's acts in our own life, we will praise God and we will want the whole earth to be involved in this.

Psalm 66:8-12

"We went through fire and water, but you brought us to a place of abundance."

The second part of Psalm Sixty-Six no longer deals with deliverance from an outside enemy but with salvation from self. The subject is a process of cleansing which is known as sanctification. The means employed are not always pleasant to experience. Verses 11 and 12 describe the process as: "You brought us into prison and laid burdens on our backs. You let men ride over our heads; we went through fire and water." Those are terrible things to undergo for people who have only recently been freed from the slavery of Egypt. This refining of the silver, as it is called, is described by the Apostle Peter as a proof of the genuineness of our faith. Peter writes: "In this you greatly rejoice, though now for a little while you may have had to suffer grief in all kinds of trials. These have come so that your faith-- of greater worth than gold, which perishes even though refined by fire-- may be proved genuine and may result in praise, glory and honor when Jesus Christ is revealed" (I Peter 1:6,7). The Old Testament prophet Malachi speaks about the same subject: "He will sit as a refiner and purifier of silver; he will purify the Levites and refine them like gold and silver" (Malachi 3:3). In every instance such painful experiences are placed against the background of praise.

One of the hardest things in the life of a Christian is to thank God for trials at the moment he goes through them. But praise in times of testing helps us to keep things in perspective. James writes: "Consider it pure joy, my brothers, whenever you face trials of many kinds, because you know that the testing of your faith develops perseverance" (James 1:2,3). We should begin to praise God as soon as we see the difficulties approach, even before our mind can grasp that it is reasonable to do so. Praise is the key to the solution of most of the problems we encounter.

God puts us to the test, not because He does not know who we are and what is inside us, but because we do not know. Most people do not readily accept the fact that they are rotten to the core of their being. We usually assume that there is something redeemable in us. Unless we acknowledge that our condition is one of total depravity, we will not allow the Holy Spirit to do His sanctifying work in us. It is of the greatest importance that we become holy because "without holiness no one will see the Lord" (Hebrews 12:14).

Psalm 66:13-20

"If I had cherished sin in my heart, the Lord would not have listened."

Verses 16-20 of Psalm Sixty-six are the testimony of a person who sees his prayers answered. It has been said that God always answers prayer, either with "yes," "no," or "wait." The Psalmist, however, suggests that there are prayers God does not hear. They are prayers with mixed motives. That statement ought to shake us up since rarely, if ever our motives are completely pure. There are traces of sin and impurity in the heart of even the greatest saints on earth.

The only chance we have to receive an answer to our prayers, therefore, is to accompany them with a confession of sin. This does not mean that we always have to present God with an inventory of things we have done wrong. It does mean that every time we approach God, we place ourselves on the basis of the sacrifice of our Lord Jesus Christ, whose blood cleanses us from all sin. This makes our petition a prayer in Jesus' Name in the truest sense of the word.

Although praying is, in a way, as natural and easy as breathing, there is a sense in which prayer must be learned and exercised. Some people are better at prayer than others. This does not mean that the best prayers are the most eloquent ones. There are people who have entered into such a close and intimate fellowship with God that they know, as by intuition, what the will of God is in a certain matter. And knowing the will of God is the key to answered prayer. The apostle John writes: "This is the confidence we have in approaching God: that if we ask anything according to his will, he hears us" (I John 5:14). George Mueller, who founded several orphanages in Bristol, England in the Eighteenth Century, was a man of prayer. He confessed that he often spent more time trying to find out what the will of God was in a certain matter than he spent in actual prayer. Once he was certain of God's will, the answers to his prayers would sometimes come instantaneously.

Our prayers can be greatly hindered by making our own wishes and needs the priority before God. If we seek first God's Kingdom and its righteousness, God will give priority to our prayers and we will avoid cherishing sin in our heart.

Psalm 67

"May God be gracious to us and bless us and make his face shine upon us ... that your ways may be known on earth, your salvation among all nations."

This is another Psalm with a strong international flavor. It expresses the purpose of God's blessing on our personal lives. God blesses us to make us a blessing. God had said to Abraham: "I will make you into a great nation and I will bless you; I will make your name great, and you will be a blessing. I will bless those who bless you, and whoever curses you I will curse; and all peoples on earth will be blessed through you" (Genesis 12:2,3).

Because of the words in Verse Six "Then the land will yield its harvest, and God, our God, will bless us" some Bible scholars believe that this Psalm may have been a Thanksgiving hymn, written to celebrate the harvest.

Nowhere is the vision of Israel's task in this world formulated as clearly as in this Psalm. God blessed Israel so that she would be a kingdom of priests in this world. This was the original mandate given to Israel at Mount Sinai, after the people had left Egypt (Exodus 19:5,6). This promise was ultimately fulfilled in the death of Jesus Christ on the cross. Paul wrote about this: "Christ redeemed us from the curse of the law by becoming a curse for us, for it is written: 'Cursed is everyone who is hung on a tree.' He redeemed us in order that the blessing given to Abraham might come to the Gentiles through Christ Jesus, so that by faith we might receive the promise of the Spirit" (Galatians 3:13,14). The secret which "No eye has seen, no ear has heard, no mind has conceived" (I Corinthians 2:9) forms the basis of this Psalm. It *is* a hymn of thanksgiving for the harvest. Some harvest!

It begins with God's grace, the unmerited favor by which we receive pardon and cleansing of sin. God rehabilitates us, and the shining of His face upon us means that we become partakers in His glory and holiness.

God's goal for Israel was not that they would smugly and comfortably enjoy God's presence in their midst but that in this dark world they would be a light unto other nations. For us personally it means that, in Paul's words, "None of us lives to himself alone and none of us dies to himself alone. If we live, we live to the Lord; and if we die, we die to the Lord. So, whether we live or die, we belong to the Lord" (Romans 14:7,8). And living for Jesus means giving our life for our fellowmen. If we show compassion to our fellow human beings, Jesus will say to us on the Day of Judgment: "Whatever you did for one of the least of these brothers of mine, you did for me" (Matthew 25:40).

Psalm 68:1-6

"A father to the fatherless, a defender of widows, is God in his holy dwelling. God sets the lonely in families, he leads forth the prisoners with singing; but the rebellious live in a sun-scorched land."

This Psalm is a celebration of victory in the widest sense of the word. We don't know what triggered this praise, but it must have been a particular battle in which the enemy was defeated. From that occasion David draws lines of personal application.

It is a terrible experience for a child to lose his father early in life and for a woman to lose her husband. Children need the strong protection of a father's love to become well-balanced human beings in adulthood. Widows who are left to fend for themselves are at a great disadvantage in life. They not only have to cope with grief and experience the pain of an emotional amputation, but they also have to deal with opposition that their male partner would have taken upon himself with lesser damage.

In this Psalm, God offers Himself to us if we are orphans or widows. If we draw close to Him in the experience of a terrible loss, we will come to realize that fathers and husbands are shadows of another reality. God is the original Father of all children. He is *The Father.* He is also the original husband in all human relations. If our earthly father dies, it does not mean the end of strong loving protection. The experience may ultimately draw us to the One who is the source of all strong fatherly love. And the love, intimacy, tenderness, and safety a married woman can experience in marriage are also a shadow of a heavenly reality. The realization of this may not take away the pain of separation, but it will certainly promote healing if we allow God's Spirit to minister to us.

God also opens the door of our prisons, even if we have received a life sentence. The hardest prisons are not the ones with iron bars and steel doors. Some prisoners who have accepted Jesus Christ in their lives are freer than their jailors. Ultimately there is no circumstance that can separate us from God's love. Our suffering due to loss and freedom is temporary. If we know the real Father, the real Husband, and the real Liberator, we are headed for the ultimate restoration of all love and freedom. In the words of the apostle Paul, "Our present sufferings are not worth comparing with the glory that will be revealed in us (Romans 8:18). And "Neither death nor life, neither angels nor demons, neither the present nor the future, nor any powers, neither height nor depth, nor anything else in all creation, will be able to separate us from the love of God that is in Christ Jesus our Lord" (Romans 8:38,39).

Psalm 68:7-10

"When you went out before your people, O God, when you marched through the wasteland, the earth shook, the heavens poured down rain, before God, the one of Sinai, before God, the God of Israel."

The original picture is of Israel trekking through the desert on their way to the Promised Land, with the Ark of the Covenant going before them. God marched with them "through the wasteland" and transformed the desert into a lush habitat.

When God created our planet, He made it a pleasant and fitting place for man to live. Human sin, the breaking of the lifeline with God transformed our world into a wasteland, a place without the fruits of fellowship and joy. It is through such a place that God marches ahead of us if we care enough to follow Him.

One of such a wasteland was the Nazi concentration camp of Ravensbrück. A Dutch lady, Corrie ten Boom, and her sister were imprisoned there because they had helped Jews in Holland to stay out of the places where Hitler and his minions exterminated them. She writes in her book, The Hiding Place: "More than conquerors... It was not a wish. It was a fact. We knew it, we experienced it minute by minute—poor, hated, hungry. We are more than conquerors. Not 'we shall be.' We are! Life in Ravensbrück took place on two different levels, mutually impossible. One, the observable, external life, grew every day more horrible. The other, the life we lived with God, grew daily better, truth upon truth, glory upon glory."

Few of us may have to live through such a hell as the one Corrie experienced. But even if we do, we may discover the reality that "neither death nor life, neither angels nor demons, neither the present nor the future, nor any powers, neither height nor depth, nor anything else in all creation, will be able to separate us from the love of God that is in Christ Jesus our Lord" (Romans 8:38,39). God marches with us through every wasteland, however dreary and miserable the place may be. He may even use us to influence our surrounding and make the desert a place of springs, where the autumn rains cover it with pools (See Psalm 84:6).

Psalm 68:11-19

"The mountains of Bashan are majestic mountains; rugged are the mountains of Bashan. Why gaze in envy, O rugged mountains, at the mountain where God chooses to reign, where the LORD himself will dwell forever?"

David, probably, wrote this Psalm on the occasion of the bringing of the Ark of the Covenant from the place where it had been kept to Jerusalem, to a tent prepared for it on Mount Zion.

This Psalm celebrates God's power and greatness. Compared to God's heavenly army, the military power of the strongest nations on earth amounts to nothing. The difference is like an army of toy soldiers and a tank brigade in modern warfare.

But there is another side to God's revelation of Himself that looks like the opposite of might and strength. David looks at the mountains of other nations, and compares them to the tiny hill of Zion.

He states an eternal principle in vs. 16: "Why gaze in envy, O rugged mountains, at the mountain where God chooses to reign, where the LORD himself will dwell forever?" God's identification with that which is weak shows, of course, no inherent weakness in God. If God conquers the world with His weakness, what will happen when He reveals His omnipotence? David proclaims that, in terms of weaponry, God has millions of tanks and missiles at His disposal. During a summit meeting in World War II Stalin, speaking about the pope, posed the question to Churchill: "How many divisions does he have?" The question was absurd unless Stalin wanted to voice his doubt about the spiritual status of the Roman Catholic Church, which is unlikely.

There is no contradiction between God's unbelievably superior might and His election of Mount Zion. The choosing of that which is weak places the common belief about that which is strong and wise in the right light. What God chooses is not really weak; it only seems to be so. And that which the world calls strong is not really strong either.

We owe our salvation to the fact that God became a weak human being in Jesus Christ who took our sins upon Himself and died. In rising from the dead, He displayed a power over death that has never been equaled. Human military might is used to kill; God's power brings life. Since the rise of terrorism, there are no longer any safe places on this earth. There is little or no defense against people who are willing to commit suicide in order to kill others. We do well to put our hope for protection in Him who became weak for our sake that we might be strong in Him.

Psalm 68:20-27

"Praise be to the Lord, to God our Savior, who daily bears our burdens. Our God is a God who saves; from the Sovereign LORD comes escape from death."

In Hebrew, the words "Our God is a God who saves" are given as a name for God, "God our salvation." Salvation cannot be separated from the person of God. He not merely *gives* salvation; He *is* our salvation. We will experience salvation to the measure in which we have fellowship with Him.

God carries us through life. Moses says: "The eternal God is your refuge, and underneath are the everlasting arms" (Deuteronomy 33:27). God does more than carry our burdens, He carries *us*. This realization ought to alleviate much needless tension in our lives.

There are instances in which God intervened and saved people from a certain physical death. But even those who are saved from dying prematurely do die one day. The fact that "from the Sovereign LORD comes escape from death" does not mean that we will never die. But for those who have surrendered their bodies to God, death does not have the last word. The apostle John states: "The man who does the will of God lives forever" (I John 2:17). And the writer of the Hebrew Epistle tells us that Christ "shared in [our] humanity so that by his death he might destroy him who holds the power of death-that is, the devil–and free those who all their lives were held in slavery by their fear of death" (Hebrews 2:14,15). God's salvation consists of our deliverance from the fear of death. For those who belong to Jesus Christ, death is a gateway into a life of eternal blessing.

This fact ought to change the way we live. For example, when we enter an elevator carrying a heavy suitcase, we can put our burden down on the floor of the elevator; it will carry both our load and us. If God carries our burdens daily, we better take a deep breath, relax in Him, and praise Him for it. We should not keep on carrying what God wants us to put down. This assurance ought to affect the way we live our daily lives.

Psalm 68:20-27

"Surely God will crush the heads of his enemies, the hairy crowns of those who go on in their sins...I will bring them from the depths of the sea, that you may plunge your feet in the blood of your foes, while the tongues of your dogs have their share."

Verses 21-23 are not the kind of poetry that is easily appreciated: God crushing the heads of His enemies, feet plunged in the blood of foes, and blood being licked up by dogs! We must remember that the enemies are, first of all, demonic powers. In the first prophecy of the Bible, God said to the serpent: "He will crush your head, and you will strike his heel" (Genesis 3:15). But here the picture is less appealing. On purpose it is painted in colors that are repulsive to us, so that we would feel aversion. The intent is not that we would find sadistic enjoyment in the death of others. We saw the same principle in connection with Psalm Fifty-eight, where we read "The righteous will be glad when they are avenged, when they bathe their feet in the blood of the wicked" (Psalm 58:10). Revulsion will have the wholesome effect on us that we will not identify with wickedness.

God is not bloodthirsty. War is a human invention. Hatred and murder come from the devil and his demons. In verses 21-23 of this Psalm, we see the end result of the actions of man who has removed himself from God's protection and has opened himself to Satan.

We want to identify with Him who said, "I have told you these things, so that in me you may have peace. In this world you will have trouble. But take heart! I have overcome the world" (John 16:33).

Ever since sin entered this world, our planet has been a bloody mess. It began with Cain's murder of his brother Abel. Following this, trillions of gallons of blood have soaked the earth. Looking down from heaven God is horrified at what we have done to His creation and He holds us responsible, even if we have never shed human blood ourselves. Jesus said to the people of His time, "Upon you will come all the righteous blood that has been shed on earth, from the blood of righteous Abel to the blood of Zechariah son of Berekiah, whom you murdered between the temple and the altar. I tell you the truth, all this will come upon this generation" (Matthew 23:35,36). The only way to escape from responsibility for all crimes against humanity is by being covered by the blood of Jesus Christ, who died for our sins. The author of the Hebrew Epistle puts it this way: "You have come to Jesus, the one who mediates the new covenant between God and people, and to the sprinkled blood, which graciously forgives instead of crying out for vengeance as the blood of Abel did" (Hebrews 12:24 NLT). God shocks us into reality so that we will hide in Him. If we do, we will join Israel in this universal praise.

Psalm 68:28-36

"You are awesome, O God, in your sanctuary; the God of Israel gives power and strength to his people."

Our God is an awesome God. Modern use of the word "awesome" has devalued its meaning. God is awesome in the sense that He commands awe and fear. People who speak about God in terms of "the old man upstairs" have no concept of the fear God's glory will trigger in them when they stand before Him. The apostle John describes the scene in his vision: "Then I saw a great white throne and him who was seated on it. Earth and sky fled from his presence, and there was no place for them" (Revelation 20:11). The magnificence of the glory of God will be so overwhelming that even the greatest saint will fall flat on his face when he sees it. If we would see the full reality of God's glory on earth, our bodies would not be able to endure it. God said to Moses: "You cannot see my face, for no one may see me and live" (Exodus 33:20). That is the reason God mercifully hides His glory from us. To believe that God's glory is non-existent because we cannot see it, would be the most foolish and dangerous thing we can do.

We do well to remember what the writer of the Hebrew Epistle states: "It is a dreadful thing to fall into the hands of the living God" (Hebrews 10:31). Unless our intimate relationship with God stands against this background it has little or no value. An example of a reverse situation is the fact that the name of Eva Braun has become known in world history because she was Adolph Hitler's mistress. If Eva had carried on an affair with someone else, the world would never have known her name. The fact that God is the Almighty One, and that it is a dreadful thing to fall into His hands if we oppose Him, gives such a deep glow and beauty to His love for us. Intimate fellowship with the Almighty makes us more than conquerors. The fact that His power becomes manifest in our weakness does not change the essence of this. It is this awesome power of God's glory that gives power and strength to His people.

Psalm 69:1-4

"Save me, O God, for the waters have come up to my neck."

The Psalm opens with the prayer of a drowning man: "Save me, O God, for the waters have come up to my neck" (literally, "up to my soul"). David had lost his footing and was sinking away in the mud. There is, probably, no more poignant image of man's desperate condition. The words depict the opposite of David's testimony in another Psalm: "He lifted me out of the slimy pit, out of the mud and mire; he set my feet on a rock and gave me a firm place to stand" (Psalm 40:2).

Not everyone who thinks he is drowning is in reality losing his life. Our feelings do not always correctly represent the reality of our situation. Depression has often little connection with reality. If we feel as if we are sinking and our cry to God seems to remain unanswered, we do well to ask ourselves if we really are where we think we are.

We don't know what caused David's cry for help. In verse 5 he states: "You know my folly, O God; my guilt is not hidden from you." So the cause of his despair was probably a moral failure.

If before David could state that God had lifted him out of the slimy pit and here he finds himself drowning in his despair, we get a picture of what sin can do in the life of a child of God.

Whatever David's sin may have been, he knew that he had failed God. Becoming a king with absolute power had brought corruption to his soul. It has been said that "power corrupts and absolute power corrupts absolutely." That needs, however, not to be the case. If we think that we have come to the point in our relationship with God where we have become immune to temptation, we enter a danger zone. Peter thought this and he said to Jesus: "Even if all fall away on account of you, I never will." Jesus answered, "I tell you the truth, this very night, before the rooster crows, you will disown me three times." But Peter declared, "Even if I have to die with you, I will never disown you (Matthew 26:33-35). After that he denied his Lord. We must not trust ourselves in the matter of temptation. We must be thoroughly convinced that only God "is able to keep [us] from falling and to present [us] before his glorious presence without fault and with great joy" (Jude 24).

152

Psalm 69:5-12

"Zeal for your house consumes me, and the insults of those who insult you fall on me."

It seems a quantum leap from David's confession of guilt to his becoming the scapegoat for the scorn of people who insult God. The bridge between those two extremes is in the forgiveness of sin. David must have confessed his sin publicly and stated that he had received forgiveness. The people probably reacted by suggesting that if God let him get off the hook that easily, it reflected adversely on God's integrity.

Is it true that God forgives glibly and easily? Can we just sin, say "sorry" and shake off the consequences as a duck shakes water off its back? Yes and no! It is true that "Everyone who calls on the name of the Lord will be saved" (Joel 2:32; Romans 10:13). But this doesn't mean that grace is cheap. Forgiving man's sin cost God more than we can ever imagine. Grace is a deep and complicated matter that we will never be able to fully understand. But the application of God's grace to our life is simple, almost too simple. It is like electricity. I don't understand what electricity really is and where it comes from but I can flip a light switch and use that which I cannot understand. Sensing the enormity of God's love that saved me will caution me not to talk glibly about forgiveness.

When David got a glimpse of God's grace that rehabilitated him, he conceived the vision for the building of a temple where the Ark of the Covenant could be placed. That vision consumed him. He was not allowed to begin the actual construction but had to delegate that to his son Solomon. But he gave all he had for the preparation.

David's zeal became a prophecy about Jesus' cleansing of the temple centuries later. When Jesus chased out the sellers and overturned their tables, His disciples remembered that it is written: "Zeal for your house will consume me" (John 2: 17).

If we realize what God has done for us in forgiving and restoring us, it is natural to respond to Him with a zeal that will consume us and make us burn up for Him. The missionary C. T. Studd once said: "If Jesus Christ is the Son of God and if He died for me, nothing is too much to do for Him." May that be our attitude!

Psalm 69:13-18

"But I pray to you, O LORD, in the time of your favor; in your great love, O God, answer me with your sure salvation."

God answers prayer but we cannot boss God around and tell Him to hurry up. God reveals Himself to us in His own time, not in ours. That is why we are given the advice in the Bible to wait for God.

David realizes that there is a time of God's favor. He, purposely, leaves the moment of salvation in God's hands. "The time of your favor" means literally "the time of your delight." In using these words, David expresses a deep confidence in God's goodness. This Psalm is interlaced with words like "great love," or "mercy," "sure salvation," "great mercy."

Actually, David felt in need of an immediate response. In the first verse of this Psalm he believed he was drowning. Yet, he chooses to wait till God is ready to act on his behalf.

Patience is one of the most difficult things to exercise in life. We are often too much in a hurry to wait, either for men or for God. But what God is preparing for us in His love is something so glorious and precious, that hurrying into it would make us miss the full enjoyment. God's favor is like a wedding in which everything is organized with precision and abundant glory. He does not want us to elope, but to celebrate the ceremony to the full.

People who elope or hurry into married life miss out on the beauty of it. The slogan "real love waits" not only serves as warning against premarital sex; it is also a wise advice to enter a relationship with deliberation and care. God wants us to wait because He loves us too much to become negligent and dull in our relationship with Him.

God did not let David drown. He saved him at exactly the right moment. He does the same for us and we will understand that our waiting was more than worthwhile. "Wait for the LORD; be strong and take heart and wait for the LORD" (Psalm 27:14). Waiting requires courage.

Psalm 69:19-28

"Scorn has broken my heart and has left me helpless; I looked for sympathy, but there was none, for comforters, but I found none."

The statement "scorn has broken my heart and has left me helpless" is deeply moving. David expected sympathy but he found none. Not only did no one show compassion, but onlookers found sadistic pleasure in seeing him suffer.

God created us with an ability to love Him and to love our fellowmen. When we do not develop our capacity for love, we not only become miserable but we are prone to turn to hatred. Thus our world has become a breeding ground of hatred, suffering, and killing.

Nowhere was this better demonstrated than in what happened to the Son of God. God demonstrated His love for us in sending His Son to save us from the sin of hatred. But the people of His time, His own people, rejected Him and subjected Him to the most cruel death. As He was suffering while hanging on a Roman cross, the bystanders jeered and mocked Him, clearly enjoying the scene. We read: "Those who passed by hurled insults at him, shaking their heads and saying, 'You who are going to destroy the temple and build it in three days, save yourself! Come down from the cross, if you are the Son of God!' In the same way the chief priests, the teachers of the law and the elders mocked him. 'He saved others,' they said, 'but he can't save himself! He's the King of Israel! Let him come down now from the cross, and we will believe in him. He trusts in God. Let God rescue him now if he wants him, for he said, 'I am the Son of God.' In the same way the robbers who were crucified with him also heaped insults on him" (Matthew 27:39-44). This nauseating scene is horrible beyond imagination. If human beings did this to the Lord of glory, how deeply fallen is our human race!

David's complaint is a prophecy of this event, the darkest in world history. But David's reaction to it is different from Jesus' own response. David prayed: "May they be blotted out of the book of life and not be listed with the righteous." Jesus prayed for those who tortured Him.

Corrie ten Boom tells the story of a guard in a Nazi concentration camp, where her sister died and she suffered. She met the man years later during an evangelistic meeting in which she had spoken about God's love and forgiveness. The man came to her and told her that God had forgiven him and made him new in Jesus Christ.

If God forgives those who crucified Jesus and Nazi sadistic camp guards, we ought to forgive those who withhold sympathy to us. God's love for sinners must flow through us to others. Didn't He forgive us first?

Psalm 69:29-36

"I am in pain and distress; may your salvation, O God, protect me."

There is a connection between the malediction David uttered in the preceding verses and his pain and distress. Evidently, the fate of those who hated him did not leave him untouched. He realized that his own pain could not be compared to the suffering of people in hell, and the thought deeply affected him.

If we hate others for what they have done to us, it hurts us more than it hurts them. God's salvation protects us and our emotions against the dangers and pitfalls of hatred. The apostle Paul testifies: "For Christ's love compels us, because we are convinced that one died for all... We are therefore Christ's ambassadors, as though God were making his appeal through us. We implore you on Christ's behalf: Be reconciled to God" (II Corinthians 5:14,20).

The protection of salvation God gives us will lead to praise. When David realized what God had done for him in delivering him from his hate feelings, he burst out in songs of praise. He understood that praise is the best sacrifice that we can give to God. If praise is a sacrifice, it means that it will cost us something. Praise does not come easily, unless we comprehend the extent of God's salvation in our lives.

Our praise will also affect other people. "The poor will see and be glad." Those poor are, probably, the ones that David had earlier wanted to be blotted out of the Book of Life. Jesus says to us: "Love your enemies and pray for those who persecute you, that you may be sons of your Father in heaven" (Matthew 5:44,45). If people are saved because we turn the other cheek, it is worth doing so.

Our praise to God will have cosmic result. "Let heaven and earth praise him, the seas and all that move in them." And ultimately it will restore our planet to what God intended it to be: a paradise where people live in peace and happiness. "The earth will be full of the knowledge of the LORD as the waters cover the sea" (Isaiah 11:9). If praise has such an effect in our personal life, in the lives of those who perish, and in our planet, we ought to practice it more often!

Psalm 70

"I am poor and needy; come quickly to me, O God. You are my help and my deliverer; O LORD, do not delay."

David cried out for help because there were people and powers who intended to kill him, and others who mocked him. Mockery is also a form of murder. David needed both life and respect. Man cannot live without some honor and respect, as he cannot live without oxygen David cried for help: "Hasten, O God, to save me; O LORD, come quickly to help me."

The words "make haste" occur twice in this Psalm. Haste is a typical human concept; it is related to time and the use we make of it. We feel that unpleasant situations last longer than pleasant ones. Enjoyable experiences seem to take up less time. Haste presupposes a shortening of time, especially in connection with bad conditions. But time cannot be long or short for God. What David wanted to say is that he was eager to experience God's presence. The call for God to make haste means that David said to God: "Show me that you are with me." God is omnipresent; we cannot, therefore, interpret this request as an objective statement, as if there would be a moment when God were not there, although such may seem to be the case.

This Psalm, therefore, speaks about a change in human experience, not in God's behavior. There never was a moment when God was not there and when He did not protect David. There was also never a time when God was not exalted. This prayer was answered the moment David's eyes were opened for the reality of God.

The realization: "Surely the LORD is in this place, and I was not aware of it," as Jacob experienced at Bethel (Genesis 28:16) may not always be a salutary experience for everybody. Paul says that our spreading of the aroma of Christ may be for some "a smell of death" (II Corinthians 2:16).

In this Psalm, David does not ask for the condemnation and destruction of enemies, as he did in other Psalms, but that they will feel ashamed. A feeling of shame presupposes an awareness of moral standards and requirements. Shame occurs when we become convicted that we have not measured up to moral demands. Shame is the first step on the way to salvation. Without conviction of sin, forgiveness of sin has little effect upon our lives. In asking for his enemies to be put to shame, David, actually, asked for their salvation.

The two lessons we may draw from this are, first of all, that our being ashamed of our moral failures and of ourselves is wholesome and salutary. Conviction of sin can lead to repentance and salvation.

The second lesson is that the best way to deal with our enemies is to pray for their salvation. We eliminate our enemies by making them our friends.

Psalm 71:1-4

"In you, O LORD, I have taken refuge; let me never be put to shame."

There is no title above this Psalm, but the first three verses are a duplicate of the opening verses of Psalm Thirty-one so we may conclude that David is the author of this Psalm also. It was obviously written by an old man whose earthly tent was being destroyed, as the Apostle Paul puts it in Second Corinthians 5:1. The conversational tone of the Psalm reminds me of Elsie McKay's book *Green Winter*, in which the author describes a series of conversations an elderly lady carries on with God. These monologues before God are very refreshing to read.

Older people often fall into the habit of talking to themselves. Oswald Chambers in *My Utmost for His Highest* states that older people tend to address those who are mature which makes people talk to themselves! Some people who have lost loved ones have taken on the habit of talking to them, as if they were still there to listen. They believe it helps them to conquer their sense of loss and loneliness. I am not advising that we do this. Better to share our thoughts with the Living God than with the dead. Taking God as a sounding board in our monologues can be a healing experience. After all, what is prayer but talking to oneself in front of God.

This raises the question what is prayer? Prayer is a conversation in which we commune with God. But very rarely do we hear God answer us in an audible voice. Jesus, who prayed more than any other human being on earth, only received two audible answers. When we pray we do so in faith that God hears us and when the answers come they often come in the form of actions, not words.

It may be good for all of us, regardless of age, to talk to ourselves before the throne of God. We are under constant attack by the devil, especially in our thoughts and emotions. When impure or harmful ideas pop up in our head, a good way of getting rid of them is to say out loud, "Lord, you see what I am thinking!"

David knew that God was his refuge, his rock of protection and safety against all the attacks that were launched against him. Saying this out loud to God helped him to not only know that he was safe, but also to feel safe in God's presence. It may be a good way to go through our day, talking to ourselves, knowing that God listens.

Psalm 71:5-13

"You have been my hope, O Sovereign LORD, my confidence since my youth. Do not cast me away when I am old; do not forsake me when my strength is gone."

David was afraid that God would abandon him as he was getting older. He had served the Lord since his youth. When he killed the Philistine giant, Goliath, he single-handedly defeated a whole Philistine army. That was a remarkable feat, to say the least. As he was getting older, he realized that if ever such a situation would recur he would not be able to meet the challenge. The strength of his youth was gone.

Getting older is not a pleasant experience. As our bodies break down and we feel our energy sapping, we tend to feel discouraged and depressed. People are still seeking frantically for the fountain of youth, without ever getting any closer to finding it.

There was a fatal flaw in David's reasoning that we do well to be aware of. David did not kill Goliath because he was physically stronger than the giant. David's strength was not physical energy but faith in God's power. The fact that the stone from David's slingshot killed the giant was God's doing, not David's.

Getting older and losing the energy of one's youth does not, necessarily, affect our effectiveness for the Lord. If the Holy Spirit resides in our heart, we are connected to a power that will withstand all attacks upon our life. The power of the Holy Spirit is far greater than any nuclear weapon.

As David grew older, he worried that he might deteriorate to the point that he became an easy prey to the enemy of his soul. We should be careful that we do not become sour in old age and hard to live with. George Mueller, the founder of the orphanages in Bristol who is considered a man of prayer, prayed that God would keep him from turning into a sour old man at the end of his life. The painful part of aging is not that we are unable to do all we used to do but that we become less able to defend ourselves and we cannot keep ourselves under control any longer. What comes out is, of course, what has always been within. We can trust ourselves even less when we get older than in our younger years. It becomes, therefore, more urgent to trust the Lord in old age than when we were young.

In old age, God want us to turn into spiritually mature Christians who exhibit wisdom, love, and tenderness that can become a model for the younger generation.

As we grow older, our prayer ought not to be "God keep me healthy," but "let the beauty of Jesus be seen in me in my old age."

Psalm 71:14-18

"Even when I am old and gray, do not forsake me, O God, till I declare your power to the next generation, your might to all who are to come."

One more meditation about Senior Citizens! Actually, David probably did not pray this prayer when he was old and gray, but earlier in life. He prepared himself for his old age, as people nowadays prepare throughout their lives for their years of retirement.

Few people prepare for old age. I don't mean that we do not try to make arrangements for being financially independent later in life. But what David looked forward to was a spiritual and emotional condition that would make him an influence for good for the younger generation. Many people believe that as far as our spiritual influence is concerned the younger generation doesn't show any evidence that they need us, so we feel we are no longer needed.

How do we prepare for old age? Like David, we ought to pray about it. Some people pray that the Lord will spare them prolonged illness. They prefer a sudden death to a slow one. Some pray that God will keep them mentally alert. There is ample evidence that God hears such prayers.

David prayed that the Lord would keep him spiritually healthy so that he could be an influence for good for the next generation. He had come to the conclusion that it was the power of God that had kept him throughout his life. It was God who took him from behind his father's sheep and made him king of Israel. He had not campaigned for the job; it was given to him. He wanted the testimony of the power of God in his life to be read by his children and grandchildren. David was, obviously, not overly concerned about the "generation gap." That gap usually occurs when serving God is being reduced to a meaningless ritual. Older people who have a living relationship with the Lord frequently have a strong attraction for the younger generation. The fact that David himself began living with the Lord when he was still young makes a strong point.

We can only pray David's prayer for our offspring and ourselves if the power of God is indeed the strength by which we live. Ultimately, it is not what we will be in later years, but what we are in the present that counts.

Psalm 71:19-24

"Though you have made me see troubles, many and bitter, you will restore my life again; from the depths of the earth you will again bring me up. You will increase my honor and comfort me once again."

The Psalmist does not use the word "resurrection," but that is what he describes in these verses. He looks beyond the grave to a renewal of his life that he could not really imagine. He sums up his life's experiences as "you have made me see troubles." And he longs for the time when "God will wipe away every tear from [his] eyes" (Revelation 7:17). That is a realistic expectation.

It may seem strange to us that we would enter heaven weeping. We know, though, that a release of deep emotions can bring tears to our eyes. Weeping gives relief and comfort. God will take us in His arms when we come home and wipe away the tears that are the quintessence of all the pains we endured on earth.

But that is not all. God will restore us to the fullness of our humanity. Our deceased bodies will come back to life. Even if our remains had been buried for centuries and the process of decomposition was complete, God, the Creator of all atoms and molecules, will reconstruct and renew us in the twinkling of an eye. We will stand before Him, renewed in spirit, soul, and body.

We will realize how denigrating sin and death that governed our existence had been and we will be restored to the full honor and dignity God had intended for us when He created the first human couple. God will crown us with a crown that would make every monarch on earth jealous.

We understand that our crowns are given to us so that we will give them back. The apostle John shows us in Revelation: "The twenty-four elders fall down before him who sits on the throne, and worship him who lives for ever and ever. They lay their crowns before the throne" (Revelation 4:10). God will not force us to give up the crown He gave us, but we will want it no other way. The honor that is given to us belongs to God alone. To do such a thing proves genuine nobility. It proves that we have royal blood in our veins. Bringing us from a life of pain and suffering, from the valley of tears into God's eternal palace and setting us upon the throne, next to Jesus Christ, is God's doing. We want to thank Him for that with the best that we have, with our crown and with our life.

But we will only be able to do so if we learn the principle of sacrifice in our life on earth. So, let's rehearse!

Psalm 72:1-7

"Endow the king with your justice, O God, the royal son with your righteousness."

The heading of this Psalm states "Of Solomon," but in the last verse we read: "This concludes the prayers of David son of Jesse." Some Bible scholars, therefore, believe that David wrote this Psalm for his son, Solomon, after he had placed him on the throne of Israel.

In reality, this Psalm pertains to Jesus Christ, the one who is the "one greater than Solomon" (Matthew 12:42). Most of what is written here applies to the Kingdom of Heaven and its King. David and Solomon only reigned over Israel by the grace of God. God had given them their royal dignity and power.

It is a tragic truth that so few of Israel's monarchs saw themselves as God's representatives on earth, as kings by the grace of God. They acted as if they had ascended the throne by their own power and that their authority was theirs to use as they pleased. That made some of them tyrants and evil men who sacrificed their own children to heathen idols.

No one on earth has absolute power, even those who think they do. If we have risen to the top in society, as some of us may have (this author excluded), we tend to believe that we got there on our own steam. Only people who know that their power and authority are borrowed and that they will have to give account of their acts are those who exercise real power in life.

As a matter of fact, the principle applies to us all, regardless of our status in society. None of us has life in himself. If the very life we live and the air we breathe is not our own, why do we think anything else would be. We will have to leave behind whatever we possess in life. Speaking about money, we say "You can't take it with you." It is not just money but everything we have borrowed and used must be returned to its rightful owner, our Creator. The apostle Paul advises us: "What I mean, brothers, is that the time is short. From now on those who have wives should live as if they had none; those who mourn, as if they did not; those who are happy, as if they were not; those who buy something, as if it were not theirs to keep; those who use the things of the world, as if not engrossed in them. For this world in its present form is passing away" (I Corinthians 7:29-31).

Psalm 72:1-7

"Endow the king with your justice, O God, the royal son with your righteousness"

This Psalm is written about or by a king. That is the reason we can see the image of our Lord Jesus Christ in it. It is about Jesus that we read: "On his robe and on his thigh he has this name written: KING OF KINGS AND LORD OF LORDS" (Revelation 19:16). All justice and righteousness on earth is derived from Him. If there is any righteousness in our lives, it is His.

When Solomon ascended the throne of Israel he prayed for wisdom. God said to Solomon in a dream: "Ask for whatever you want me to give you." Solomon answered: "Give your servant a discerning heart to govern your people and to distinguish between right and wrong" (I Kings 3:4-12). God was pleased with Solomon's request and gave him a wisdom that has become proverbial.

In a sense, we are like King Solomon. The difference is that Solomon became first king and then asked for wisdom. In our case, we begin with wisdom and ascend to royalty because of it. Paul, the apostle, states: "It is because of him that you are in Christ Jesus, who has become for us wisdom from God-that is, our righteousness, holiness and redemption" (I Corinthians 1:30). It is the wisdom, righteousness and holiness of our Lord Jesus Christ that was imparted to us in our redemption which makes us kings. We are "kings or queens by the grace of God," or rather "kings or queens through the grace of God." Again, in Paul's words: "For if, by the trespass of the one man, death reigned through that one man, how much more will those who receive God's abundant provision of grace and of the gift of righteousness reign in life through the one man, Jesus Christ" (Romans 5:17).

The governments of this world may not recognize our royalty, but that does not change the reality in which we live. God has provided us with His righteousness, which allows us to live a life "fit for a king." Our righteousness ought to set us apart. Let's not defile the crown we are wearing!

In a world that is torn apart with strife and injustice, we must model what God's righteousness looks like. Righteousness always precedes peace; it is the foundation of it. The writer of Hebrew, speaking about Melchizedek in the Old Testament, states: "First, his name means 'king of righteousness'; then also, 'king of Salem' means 'king of peace'" (Hebrews 7:2). God wants our righteousness to bring peace on earth.

Psalm 72:1-7

"The mountains will bring prosperity to the people, the hills the fruit of righteousness."

The Psalmist paints a beautiful picture of the results in nature of the reign of the righteous king: "The mountains will bring prosperity to the people, the hills the fruit of righteousness." The Hebrew text reads literally: "The mountains shall bring peace to the people and the hills by righteousness." The Hebrew word, translated "prosperity" is *shalom.*

In the previous meditation, we saw how God made us kings by imputing to us the righteousness of Jesus Christ. Here we see the fruit of God's work in and through us.

Obviously, the mountains that bring peace represent a figure of speech. That is how a poet expresses it. Mountains never fail to impress us. Their towering heights and snow-topped ridges can take our breath away. God wants indeed to overwhelm us and make us stand in awe because of His righteousness and peace.

God's righteousness makes us ambassadors of peace in this world. Although world peace has been elusive ever since sin entered this world and governed human relationships, God's peace on earth will, eventually, prevail. The angels did sing at the announcement of Jesus' birth: "Glory to God in the highest, and on earth peace to men on whom his favor rests" (Luke 2:14). And God wants to use us in the process. World peace begins in our own heart and it will, eventually, conquer this world. Jesus confirms this with the words He spoke to His disciples on the night before His crucifixion: "I have told you these things, so that in me you may have peace. In this world you will have trouble. But take heart! I have overcome the world" (John 16:33).

We know that the world, as it is at present, will never know God's peace. The Bible speaks about an increase of iniquity and persecution that will lead to the world's last night. But the new morning will bring a reign of peace by the Prince of peace that will put an end to sin and darkness. That world will be inhabited by people in whose heart the transformation has already taken place; those who know peace with God because of the application of God's righteousness to their lives. "Blessed are the peacemakers, for they will be called sons of God" (Matthew 5:9).

Psalm 72:8-11

"All kings will bow down to him and all nations will serve him."

Although this Psalm was probably written on the occasion of Solomon's ascension to the throne, the details that depict his reign go, obviously, far beyond anything any king, even a king like Solomon, could achieve. The scope of the king's reign is given as "from sea to sea and from the River to the ends of the earth." This is a reference to the conquest of Canaan. God said to the Israelites who were still in the desert on their way to the Promised Land: "I will establish your borders from the Red Sea to the Sea of the Philistines, and from the desert to the River" (Exodus 23:31).

What seems to be hyperbolic in connection with Solomon's reign is a reality as far as the reign of Jesus Christ is concerned.

We have seen, in the last few centuries of world history, how western nations have tried to establish world hegemony through colonialism and conquests. Actually, the phenomenon is almost as old as the human race. In early history, Nimrod established his empires (see Genesis 10:8-12), and many emperors followed in his footsteps.

The empire of Jesus Christ is not like the colonialism or conquests we know from history. Jesus did not rise to the top over the dead bodies of His opponents, like this world's emperors and dictators. It is because, in Paul's words, "He humbled himself and became obedient to death- even death on a cross! [that] God exalted him to the highest place and gave him the name that is above every name, that at the name of Jesus every knee should bow, in heaven and on earth and under the earth, and every tongue confess that Jesus Christ is Lord, to the glory of God the Father" (Philippians 2:8-11).

The dominion of our Lord Jesus Christ is based upon His humility. There will be a time in world history, when the rulers of this world will recognize that the basis of their rule has crumbled. Real power does not come from the barrel of a gun, as the Chinese leader Mao Dze Dung once said. All kings will bow down to Jesus Christ because they will recognize that the foolishness of the cross is stronger than their might. We will be kings with Christ when we understand that He became weak for our sake in order to deliver us from our power, which destroyed us. "Blessed are the meek, for they will inherit the earth" (Matthew 5:5).

Psalm 72:12-20

"He will rescue them from oppression and violence, for precious is their blood in his sight."

Continuing the ode to Solomon's reign as an image of the reign of the Messiah, the Psalmist depicts the salvation of those who submit to the authority of the Savior. If the world in which Solomon ascended the throne of Israel had been a perfect one, there would have been no need for salvation. But Israel's most magnificent king took power in a world of misery and woe. Not that his father David had mismanaged his mandate. But, from the very beginning, ever since sin and death entered our planet, people have been needy and afflicted. Neither Solomon nor David was able to "save the needy from death" as this Psalm suggests. The most any king or potentate can do in this world is make life livable. Even when the grain abounds throughout the land and sways on the tops of the hills and its fruit flourishes like Lebanon and thrives like the grass of the field, death still awaits every citizen.

Only the King, who has entered death and has broken its power by resurrecting from it, can save the needy from death and all its consequences. He is the one who literally lives forever and who gives eternal life to all who bow to His authority.

The Psalmist must have had some understanding of a bodily resurrection because he mentions salvation from death. No one reading this Psalm in Solomon's day would have understood it to mean that people would no longer die during that king's reign. The very words "precious is their blood in his sight," suggests martyrdom. Blood only becomes precious when it is shed.

This prayer of blessing for the reign of King Solomon is a picture of the glory of the real King, the one who allowed His own blood to be shed for our salvation and who opened the gates of eternal life for us by His own death and resurrection. His Name endures forever. It outlives the sun. "All nations will be blessed through him, and they will call him blessed." Long live the King!

Psalm 73:1-3

"Surely God is good to Israel, to those who are pure in heart."

Asaph begins this Psalm with a conclusion. He has experienced an inward struggle from which he emerged victoriously, but not because of his own moral superiority but because of an encounter with God. If we are honest with ourselves, we will be able to identify with the Psalmist and come to the same conclusion that God is good to us, not because our heart is so pure, but because it is not. The cleansing of our heart and mind is God's doing, not ours.

The sin that spoiled Asaph's purity of heart was jealousy. He compared himself to other people who were successful in life because they were unscrupulous. He had come to the conclusion that crime *does* pay. In pursuing the high moral standards he had set for himself, he found himself holding the shorter end of the stick.

Comparing ourselves with other people can be very hazardous to our spiritual health. This comparison can be done in two ways; we can conclude that we are better than they are and believe that God owes us a greater recompense because of our holier living, or we can feel that God is cheating us because He withholds from us what He gives in such abundance to others. He who uses the life of other people as a mirror always gets a good self-portrait. The only valid standard of comparison, however, is not the character of our neighbor, but the character of God. We will be judged by God's absolute standards and not by the ever-changing values of the society in which we live sets for itself.

If we feel we are missing out on the good things in life because we are following Christ, we suffer from myopia. Compared to the glory God has prepared for those who love Him, the rewards of this life, the success, affluence, and fame that some people experience here below, are mere trinkets. If we prefer the temporary ease and rewards of the present to the eternal glory that awaits us, we are poorer than the poorest. There *is* a pot of gold at the bottom of the rainbow that encircles the throne of God. It is for those whose heart is purified by the blood of Jesus Christ and by the ministry of the Holy Spirit. Why then keep up with the Joneses?

Psalm 73:4-14

"Surely in vain have I kept my heart pure; in vain have I washed my hands in innocence."

The picture Asaph paints of the wicked is not only shortsighted, it is also false. It is not true that there is more sickness among believers than among unbelievers. Atheists are not healthier or happier than Christians. Rich people do not experience more satisfaction in life than the poor. As a matter of fact, according to the testimony of some movie stars, the opposite seems to be the case more often than not.

I remember a story I read in elementary school about a certain king of France, who was particularly unhappy and asked his wise counselor for advice. He was told that he would have to find a happy man and wear his shirt. The king searched the corners of his land without finding anyone who confessed being truly happy. One day, however, he found a farmhand working in the field who answered "yes" to the king's question whether he was happy. The king asked for the man's shirt, but the poor laborer didn't own a shirt!

Asaph could have known, as we all do, that the storms of life hit everyone with equal force. The difference is not in the pressures we all encounter but in the strength we find in facing and bearing them. In that respect, those without God have no one to fall back on. Compare the grief of a man without God who loses his spouse in a car accident with those who can turn to the Lord for comfort. Where do the wicked find hope when they are diagnosed with cancer?

The wicked are like dumb animals that don't realize that they are destined to be slaughtered. As they approach the Day of Judgment, they brag about the things that will be used as evidence against them and bring about their condemnation. Would anyone who has received God's pardon for sin want to trade places with those who are going to hell?

How can we say that it is in vain that we keep our heart pure, if we know that only the pure in heart will see God? A little temporary inconvenience of poor health and tight economy is a small price to pay for the eternal heritage that awaits us.

Paul's answer to Asaph is "I consider that our present sufferings are not worth comparing with the glory that will be revealed in us" (Romans 8:18).

Psalm 73:15-22
"... till I entered the sanctuary of God; then I understood their final destiny."

As a Levite, Asaph was freer to enter the sanctuary than the average Israelite. We read in Chronicles that he was allowed to stand before the ark: "He [king David] appointed some of the Levites to minister before the ark of the LORD, to make petition, to give thanks, and to praise the LORD, the God of Israel: Asaph was the chief" (I Chronicles 16:4,5). The presence of the Shechinah (God's glory) was a phenomenon that was observable by the human senses. Yet, the ark stood in the tabernacle and in the temple without exercising any influence upon the moral conduct of the Israelites. We can dull our conscience, even in the presence of God. Thus, it was possible that Judas could embezzle money while being in the company of the Lord Jesus. Unless the Holy Spirit dwells in our heart, the presence of God will not operate any change in us. This is why the spiritual reality in which we live and our "confidence to enter the Most Holy Place by the blood of Jesus" (Hebrews 10:19) is more glorious than anything Asaph could do. He could not go through the veil as we do. He could stand at the altar of incense with longing and rapture, but he could not go beyond that. If such a partial and incomplete approach had such a dramatic effect upon Asaph, what about us who can stand before the very throne of God?

The awareness of God's presence immediately placed Asaph's problems in the right perspective. He thought of the end of his own life and compared that with what was in store for the wicked. We will all be judged according to the measure of God's glory. "All have sinned and fall short of the glory of God" (Romans 3:23). If the righteous fall short, how much more the wicked! This must have been part of Asaph's meditation in the presence of God.

The glory of God puts everything in the right perspective. If a person goes through life without God, he has nothing left at the moment of death. The end will be hopelessness and despair when all else in life falls away. But the Book of Proverbs states: "The path of the righteous is like the first gleam of dawn, shining ever brighter till the full light of day" (Proverbs 4:18). For the man without God darkness will increase. Over against the fading away into nothingness of the wicked stands Paul's flamboyant testimony: "I have fought the good fight, I have finished the race, I have kept the faith. Now there is in store for me the crown of righteousness, which the Lord, the righteous Judge, will award to me on that day-- and not only to me, but also to all who have longed for his appearing" (II Timothy 4:7,8).

Psalm 73:21-22

"When my heart was grieved and my spirit embittered, I was senseless and ignorant; I was a brute beast before you."

Asaph confesses his guilt before God. Coming to his senses, he wondered how he could possibly have been so foolish as to feel grieved, embittered, and senseless. Only animals are jealous of each other like this!

Comparing himself with an animal the Psalmist realizes the basic difference between a human being and all the other creatures God created on the earth. We read in Genesis that when God created the animals He said: " 'Let the land produce living creatures according to their kinds: livestock, creatures that move along the ground, and wild animals, each according to its kind.' And it was so. God made the wild animals according to their kinds, the livestock according to their kinds, and all the creatures that move along the ground according to their kinds. And God saw that it was good" (Genesis 1:24,25). We understand this to mean that God formed the animals in the same way He created Adam-- from the dust of the earth. There is in fact an amazing similarity between the human body and the body of some animals. We're all made of the same stuff. The great difference is that God "breathed into [Adam's] nostrils the breath of life" (Genesis 2:7), which made him into a being created in the image of God. It is the Spirit of God in us that distinguishes us from all other creatures on earth.

Giving way to feelings of jealousy impairs that glorious distinction. In the animal world the most gorgeous creatures chase and devour each other without knowing what they are doing. The beautiful humming birds that come to the feeder outside our house don't even allow one another the joy of drinking together. That is only a mild manifestation of how much creation has deviated from God's original concept. If we are jealous of other people's success in life, whether they are good or bad people, we demonstrate the same bitter spirit as brute beasts.

If we have fellowship with God the Holy Spirit will convict us of the sin of jealousy. In the presence of God our bitterness will change into love and compassion for others. Bitterness is the predecessor of hatred, and hatred leads to murder. If we have seen God's love for us in Jesus, we will be willing to give our lives for others. The Apostle John says: "This is how we know what love is: Jesus Christ laid down his life for us. And we ought to lay down our lives for our brothers" (I John 3:16). A sense of the presence of God should make us into people who are moved with compassion for the condition of other people. The rich and arrogant are also in need of God. When God's love flows through us it will give us emotional equilibrium.

Psalm 73:23-28

"Whom have I in heaven but you? And earth has nothing I desire besides you."

These words are among the most precious statements in the whole Bible. They reveal that the essence of heavenly glory is the person of God Himself. We often think of heaven as the place where we will be reunited with our loved ones who preceded us in death. Asaph's ecstatic exclamation: "Whom have I in heaven but you?" does, of course, not mean that such a reunion will not take place. But it is good to remember that, unless God occupies the central place in our lives, all human relationships are without value. And we will not give this top priority to God in heaven if we have never done that on earth.

In reading Asaph's description of the wicked, we learned more about Asaph than about the godless. Asaph, also, learned more about himself than about the fate of the wicked. This was, evidently, God's intention in allowing this temptation to come to him. We always tend to think of ourselves as being reliable, and we want God to think the same about us. We ought to pray: "God, please do not leave me to my own thoughts, because I will go wrong!"

After weathering the storm of temptation, Asaph may have thought that God would reject him. He found instead love and forgiveness. God's love for us is constant and unwavering. We do not always appreciate this stability. The father of the prodigal son said to his older boy: "My son, ... you are always with me, and everything I have is yours" (Luke 15:31). The younger son, who had lost everything and then found it again, knew how rich he was. His older brother never realized what he possessed. Asaph understood the wonder of what he had, and he knew that he would never have to be separated from God again. This was the outcome of the temptation he had gone through. If the devil understood how useful he sometimes is, he would probably be less busy tempting us!

Asaph's conclusion of the temptation that upset him so much is: "But as for me, it is good to be near God." This speaks about the intimacy of a love relationship in which two people who love each other long to be together. There is the same mutual longing between God and the person who loves Him.

The Psalm ends as it began with the testimony of God's goodness. Goodness is the essence of all God does. All His acts are motivated by love and goodness. A pure heart is needed to see this.

Psalm 74:1-3

"Why have you rejected us forever, O God? Why does your anger smolder against the sheep of your pasture?"

This Psalm opens with the question "Why?" Although we are not told what actually happened, we will find no difficulty in identifying with Asaph's question and despair. The description of the disaster sounds like the destruction of Jerusalem by King Nebuchadnezzar when Israel was led into captivity. But since Asaph, who lived centuries before that happened, wrote these words, that cannot be the case.

One of Israel's enemies, evidently, attacked Jerusalem and desecrated the place where David had put the Ark of the Covenant. Asaph's conclusion is that this could only have happened because God was angry at Israel.

Asaph's premise was, obviously, that there was no reason for God to do this to His own people. This was not a punishment for some specific sin they had committed. Yet, it seemed that the bond with God was broken forever.

Worse than what happened to Asaph and his compatriots is what happened to the tabernacle and the Ark of the Covenant, and to God Himself. One would have thought that almighty God would not allow foreigners to desecrate His sanctuary, but He did.

The event brought home to Asaph in a forceful manner how horrible the destruction of sin in this world is. The devastation of war in itself is terrible enough, but if it affects man's fellowship with God, if it destroys the place of God's revelation of Himself, what hope is then left for man?

Actually, God's way of dealing with man's sin is to submit to it and suffer under it. God knew that the only way to redeem mankind was to become one with man and suffer with him. He not only allowed His tabernacle to be desecrated and His body to be broken; the Good Shepherd became one with His sheep and allowed Himself to be slaughtered.

Asaph cried to God, "Why have you forsaken us?" When Jesus died on the cross, God cried to God "Why have you forsaken Me?" Sin that cleft the human heart and separated man from himself, also cleft the heart of God.

Asaph could not have known that in this way God would create a solution to the problem of our sin. Had someone told him in his day, he would have called it foolishness. Jesus' death on the cross, the ultimate desecration of God's tabernacle, is not foolishness. It is God's supreme wisdom, ordained for our salvation. John Wesley understood this when he wrote: "Amazing love! how can it be that Thou, my God, shouldst die for me!"

Psalm 74:4-11

"We are given no miraculous signs; no prophets are left, and none of us knows how long this will be."

With the desecration and destruction of the sanctuary there was no place left on earth people could point to and say, "God is here." Asaph knew that the God of Israel was a supernatural Being and that He had revealed Himself to His people with great miracles of deliverance. God had brought Israel out of Egypt by defeating the most powerful nation on earth of that time. The Red Sea has split open to let Israel pass and the Jordan River had done the same. The sun had stood still at Joshua's command to bring about a complete victory over the kings of Canaan who resisted God's people. Moses and the other prophets had spoken God's Word to them, saying: "Thus says the Lord." Now all was dead and silent. Asaph knew that "Where there is no revelation, the people cast off restraint" (Proverbs 29:18).

When God spoke His ultimate Word to the world in the Incarnation of Jesus Christ, the scene repeated itself in an even worse manner. Those who believed that Jesus was the Messiah, the Savior of the world, and who witnessed His crucifixion and His death, found no words to express their despair. Mary Magdalene, from whom Jesus had cast out seven demons, found herself in danger of being repossessed by those powers of darkness again when Jesus died. The two men who walked to Emmaus said to the stranger who accompanied them: "[Jesus] was a prophet, powerful in word and deed before God and all the people. The chief priests and our rulers handed him over to be sentenced to death, and they crucified him; but we had hoped that he was the one who was going to redeem Israel. And what is more, it is the third day since all this took place" (Luke 24:19-21).

Asaph said about this desperate situation: "None of us knows how long this will be." It took God three days to rebuild the sanctuary in the resurrection of our Lord Jesus Christ. And because of this our bodies, those temples of the Holy Spirit, will be rebuilt after death destroys them. When our Lord returns, He "will transform our lowly bodies so that they will be like his glorious body" (Philippians 3:21).

Psalm 74:12-23
"But you, O God, are my king from of old; you bring salvation upon the earth."

As we saw in previous meditations about this Psalm, the conditions in Jerusalem, the place where the ark stood, where God had revealed Himself and where people worshipped, were such that worship was no longer possible. It seemed as if God were dead. We don't know when this could have happened, but Asaph must have been looking at a situation that was incongruent with what he knew about God. The persistent question throughout this Psalm is "How could God permit this to happen?" How could the God who saved Israel from slavery and led them in a miraculous way to the land of promise, allow this?

This Psalm deals with an absurdity: God is the shepherd of the sheep; He is the good shepherd, who lays down His life for the sheep, but the situation Asaph faced was as the one of the hired hand who abandoned the sheep and ran away (see John 10:10-15). This is exactly what Jesus said could not happen. The Church, the Bride, instead of being given in marriage, is being dragged away as an outcast and abandoned to a gang of rapists. At the place of God's revelation, where He spoke to Moses, stands the enemy who roars out his blasphemous speech. It is as if the Antichrist had come already and set himself up in God's temple, proclaiming himself to be God, challenging God (II Thessalonians 2:3,4; Revelation 13:5). The lunacy of this world had reached its peak, and God didn't do anything against it. In the mockery of Jesus, hanging on a cross, world history reached its deepest point. But "the foolishness of God is wiser than man's wisdom, and the weakness of God is stronger than man's strength" (I Corinthians 1:25). It is at this point that the powers and authorities were disarmed and made a public spectacle (Colossians 2:15). The axe that cut down the green wood also brought about Satan's ultimate defeat; Satan cut off his own feet.

It is easy to be fooled by what we see. No one completely escapes this optical illusion. The martyrs in heaven cry out to God, "How long, Sovereign Lord, holy and true, until you judge the inhabitants of the earth and avenge our blood?" (Revelation 6:10). And God answers them that things will get worse before they get better!

When we find ourselves in an emergency like Asaph's we do well to remember what God has done for us in the past. We have the assurance that "neither death nor life, nor anything else in all creation, will be able to separate us from the love of God that is in Christ Jesus our Lord" (Romans 8:38,39).

Psalm 75:1

"We give thanks to you, O God, we give thanks, for your Name is near; men tell of your wonderful deeds."

The subscript of this beautiful Psalm of Asaph reads "To the tune of Do Not Destroy." Some Bible scholars believe this title may be a reference to a popular tune that was sung at grape harvest time about a miserable little bunch of grapes. We find a reference to this in Isaiah: "This is what the LORD says: 'As when juice is still found in a cluster of grapes and men say, 'Don't destroy it, there is yet some good in it,' so will I do in behalf of my servants; I will not destroy them all' " (Isaiah 65:8).

Since there is mention in this Psalm about some people who are promoted and others demoted, it could be that the Psalm was written for someone who was passed up by someone else in his promotion, and who brought his disappointment about this to God.

Asaph sets this personal disappointment against a larger, more cosmic background of God's judgment. He states: "But it is God who judges: He brings one down, he exalts another."

When we face smaller or larger disappointments in life, it is good to look at the big picture. If we could, so to speak, compare our problem with God's problem, we place things in their right perspective. After all, creating a planet and preparing it for population by man and beast, providing vegetation and oxygen, and then seeing how that world is ruined by sin, would that not be a problem for God? Even if we think of God in terms of being omniscient and almighty, we know that God doesn't fix our human woes as by magic. God chooses individuals to lead His people who are like sheep without a shepherd. What if some of those leaders turn out to be a Nero, a Hitler, or a Mao? If we think God cannot grieve over human misery, we don't understand who God is.

It is part of His greatness that He shows compassion for our suffering, our frustration, and our woe.

And what are our little setbacks in comparison with His blessings? Even in the midst of disaster, God's love and grace are there. Contemplating the destruction of his country, his city, and God's temple, Jeremiah said: "Because of the LORD's great love we are not consumed, for his compassions never fail. They are new every morning; great is your faithfulness" (Lamentations 3:22,23).

Psalm 75:2-5

"As for me, I will declare this forever; I will sing praise to the God of Jacob. I will cut off the horns of all the wicked, but the horns of the righteous will be lifted up."

The word "horn" in this Psalm is a strange word. We know that certain animals grow horns and that some can use them in a powerful way. The Hebrew word, translated "horn" has a wide variety of meaning. It means any kind of projection, not only on animals but also on objects. People used animal horns as drinking vessels or to store oil. A mountain peak was called a horn. Horns became symbols of power, which is the way in which the word is used in this Psalm.

The prophet Daniel saw in his visions some great political events played out in images of goats and rams that came charging with their horns, goring one another to death.

Asaph sees man's rebellion against God as a charging bull, trying to run through his opponent.

Can we really say that our revolt against God presents any danger to Him? Would God have to get out of His way in order to avoid being injured by our charge? The thought is ridiculous. Yet, when David prophetically described the crucifixion of our Lord Jesus Christ, he wrote: "Many bulls surround me; strong bulls of Bashan encircle me. A band of evil men has encircled me, they have pierced my hands and my feet" (Psalm 22:12,16). The Son of God allowed Himself to be gored by man's horns. The horns of our arrogance and human power went straight through Him. That is how He broke them off! God breaks our power, not by crushing us, but by being crushed Himself. The horns of our pride snap off like matchsticks when they hit the cushion of His love.

The amazing truth is that the meekness of Jesus Christ is more dangerous for us than the wrath of God. We read in Revelation: "Then the kings of the earth, the princes, the generals, the rich, the mighty, and every slave and every free man hid in caves and among the rocks of the mountains. They called to the mountains and the rocks, 'Fall on us and hide us from the face of him who sits on the throne and from the wrath of the Lamb! For the great day of their wrath has come, and who can stand?' " (Revelation 6:15-17). The kings of the earth cried for the mountains to fall on them, not because they saw a lion, but because they were afraid of a Lamb!

Psalm 75:6-8

"No one from the east or the west or from the desert can exalt a man. But it is God who judges: He brings one down, he exalts another. In the hand of the LORD is a cup full of foaming wine mixed with spices; he pours it out, and all the wicked of the earth drink it down to its very dregs."

These verses speak about people who have risen to the top in society and who occupy places of leadership. They are the ones in power. I don't flatter myself with the thought that some of the present world leaders will read this meditation. I may be preaching to the choir. But there is a general thought in these verses that merits the attention of all of us. God brings us to the place where we are at present, whether this is at the bottom of the ladder or at the top echelon. We may have power over other people or we may be subjected to other people's decision making. The problem usually begins when we climb up and begin to be aware of our own importance. We tend to credit ourselves for our achievements more than for our failures. Power can be a heady thing; it tends to impose itself on those who use it. Lord Acton is credited with the dictum: "Power corrupts and absolute power corrupts absolutely."

The Psalmist issues a warning to those who are in positions of power. He compares power to a cupful of wine that inebriates the one who drinks it. The only safeguard against abuse of power is the recognition that God is at the origin. It is His business whether we are low or high. We do well to remember this at either stage. We need pride to accept a low position in life, and we need humility to bear exaltation. God gives both to those who ask. To those who don't ask He serves His heady wine, with all the awful consequences.

Not only presidents, senators and CEOs are tempted to misuse power; fathers and mothers can misuse it toward their children, children can bully one another. Hardly anyone is immune to its temptations. We all need God's grace in the position in which He places us in this world. The realization that none of us are placed haphazardly in this world, that God knew what He was doing when He placed us where we are, will help us to see life in its right perspective.

Psalm 76:1-3

"His tent is in Salem, his dwelling place in Zion."

The words "In Judah God is known" sounds like an understatement; as if God were merely a local hero. Asaph speaks about the Creator of heaven and earth, the almighty God. He is the God who is known throughout the universe.

The tragedy, however, is that on our planet the opposite is often true. In our time, God is not known in many places. Large sections of Europe, Asia, and South America fall into this category. Some countries boast about being officially atheist. John's pronouncement is, unfortunately, still all too true: "He was in the world, and though the world was made through him, the world did not recognize him. He came to that which was his own, but his own did not receive him" (John 1:10,11). It is a terrible thing if the world does not know its maker and redeemer, but it is wonderful if a people and a nation do know God. David exclaims: "Blessed are the people whose God is the LORD" (Psalm 144:15).

It is a miracle that the infinite God limited Himself to a specific period of world history, to a small location on earth, and to a small nation. Even more miraculous is the fact that He took upon Himself the limited form of a human being, and that the Word that created everything became flesh. The Almighty became, indeed, a national entity on a small and provincial scale, outwardly indistinguishable from any other little citizen. Solomon rightfully cried out: "But will God really dwell on earth? The heavens, even the highest heaven, cannot contain you!" (I Kings 8:27). But Solomon was also, in a way, wrong--even very wrong. God not only became a human being but "being in very nature God, [he] did not consider equality with God something to be grasped, but made himself nothing, taking the very nature of a servant, being made in human likeness. And being found in appearance as a man, he humbled himself and became obedient to death-- even death on a cross!" (Philippians2:6-8). "He was led like a lamb to the slaughter..." (Isaiah 53:7).

Verse 2 adds another dimension to the truth Asaph proclaims: "His tent is in Salem." "Salem" means "peace." God annihilates man's arms of destruction because He is the Prince of Peace. In Revelation, we see the Lion of Judah as the Lamb that breaks the seals of God's scroll (Revelation 5:5,6). The sword that ends all wars is the Word of God, the sword that comes out of the mouth of the Lord Jesus Christ. No human power can stand against this weapon, through which all is created and which sustains all. God's Revelation means the end of all display of human power. Satan himself is powerless against the glory of the Lord, our Lord Jesus Christ.

Psalm 76:4-9

"You are resplendent with light, more majestic than mountains rich with game."

This Psalm contrasts the glory of God with the rebellion of man. Asaph depicts God's glory as a chain of mountain peaks that are set aglow by the rising sun. Another possible translation of "mountains rich with game" is "the everlasting mountains." The majesty of a snow-covered mountain and the sun shining upon a glacier can be breathtaking. While my wife and I worked as missionaries in Indonesia, on the island of New Guinea, we often saw that glorious sight when the sun came up over a 16,000 feet high peak. Asaph says that God is far more glorious.

It is that glory that will be the measuring stick on the Day of Judgment. The apostle Paul writes: "All have sinned and fall short of the glory of God" (Romans 3:23). If sin means falling short of the glory of God, it means that we stand in danger of being condemned because we are not as glorious as God is. We are desperately in need of glory!

The scene Asaph describes at the foot of God's mountain is of an army that has come to rebel against God. A greater contrast than between God's majesty and a bunch of angry human beings who shake their fists at God can hardly be imagined. They come with their bows and arrows, their horses and riders to declare war on God. In modern terms, they come with nuclear weapons. What effect could our atomic bombs have on God who created a universe of stars in which nuclear explosions occur every second? How effective are our rockets for Him who controls heavenly bodies that are millions of light years away from us?

Who in his right mind would consider declaring war on a King who can cut off, not only our supply lines, but even the oxygen we breath?

We are desperately in need of glory! God gives His glory to us if we consent to become His children. The good news is that "to all who received [Jesus], to those who believed in his name, he gave the right to become children of God" (John 1:12). The apostle Paul adds: "Now if we are children, then we are heirs-heirs of God and co-heirs with Christ, if indeed we share in his sufferings in order that we may also share in his glory" (Romans 8:17). No need for anyone to fall short.

Psalm 76:10-12

"Surely your wrath against men brings you praise, and the survivors of your wrath are restrained."

The above stated verse has been translated differently: "Surely the wrath of man shall praise thee: the remainder of wrath shalt thou restrain," (KJV) or "Man's futile wrath will bring you glory. You will use it as an ornament!" (TLB). Whosever's wrath it is, we understand that God can use evil and negative things and turn them around so that He receives praise. Joseph's slavery in Egypt and Paul's imprisonment are examples. Joseph said to his brothers who sold him into slavery: "You intended to harm me, but God intended it for good to accomplish what is now being done, the saving of many lives" (Genesis 50:20). And, speaking from a prison cell, Paul states: "Now I want you to know, brothers, that what has happened to me has really served to advance the gospel. As a result, it has become clear throughout the whole palace guard and to everyone else that I am in chains for Christ. Because of my chains, most of the brothers in the Lord have been encouraged to speak the word of God more courageously and fearlessly" (Philippians 1:12-14). The greatest example of all is, of course, the crucifixion of Jesus Christ. Human wrath and rebellion constitute no threat whatsoever to God. Human wrath not only ricochets off God's glory, it even increases the Revelation of that glory. Pharaoh's resistance against the exodus of the people of Israel is a clear illustration of this. God wraps man around His finger. A Dutch poet once wrote a poem about another deceased poet and described him as a flame that for one single moment scorched the face of God. The thought is as ridiculous as wanting to fly to the sun to light a match! It is true, however, that man being created in the image of God can demonstrate wrath which is a reflection of the wrath of God. In fellowship with God, wrath can be a mighty weapon; but human wrath that is directed against God reduces man to the level of the ridiculous.

This does not mean that a child of God cannot be injured in a deep and painful way by the wrath and anger of man. Joseph, for instance, must have suffered immensely in his slavery and imprisonment in Egypt. The suffering of our Lord Jesus Christ has become a symbol of all suffering in this world. But the end for God's children is glory and not perdition.

Psalm 77:1-9

"I remembered you, O God, and I groaned; I mused, and my spirit grew faint."

It is stated that Asaph wrote this Psalm for Jeduthun. Jeduthun was Asaph's colleague who, like Asaph, had been appointed by David as responsible for the music in the tabernacle or the temple (See I Chronicles 16:41,42; 25:1-3). Asaph composed this hymn as an act of kindness to help a colleague who was suffering from a depression.

The mood of the Psalm is gloomy and sad. Jeduthun was a professional musician. He was paid for praising the Lord. But the routine of his daily performance had robbed him of the sense of God's presence and of the joy and peace that flow from this fellowship.

It is good to be aware of the danger of routine. It can cause dryness in relationship. This is true on a human level as well as in our fellowship with God. In human friendships, in a marriage, love can grow stale. This is the reason that some couples break up after having been married for twenty or thirty years.

How do we keep our relationships fresh? How do we keep love flowing? First of all, it is good to differentiate between loving and being in love. The emotional high of the latter is actually the least important part of it. Floating away on cloud nine may make us lose our firm footing on earth. Secondly, we must remember that the source of our love for others is the love of God for us. "We love because he first loved us" (I John 4:19). God is not the one who changes in the relationship we have with Him; He is not subject to mood swings; the attention He pays to us never diminishes. The change and fickleness is on our side. "[God's] compassions never fail. They are new every morning; great is [His] faithfulness" (Lamentations 3:22,23).

As human beings, we are subject to mood changes. This is not bad in itself. Accepting the fact that we cannot always be euphoric and that dry spells and wet seasons are part of our humanity is a step in the right direction. We keep our balance, if we understand that God is the only constant one, the real reference point of our direction in life.

Asaph showed Jeduthun what to do about his depression. He brings his gloom before the Lord, which makes him realize that God's unfailing love cannot be a thing of the past; it is new every morning. We may begin every morning reminding ourselves of this truth. It will take the dryness out of our routine.

Psalm 77:10-20

"I will remember the deeds of the LORD; yes, I will remember your miracles of long ago. I will meditate on all your works and consider all your mighty deeds."

Still being in a mode of depression, Asaph says: "To this I will appeal" The Hebrew text is difficult to translate. Some versions read: "This is my anguish" (NKJV), or "This is my infirmity" (KJV). A plausible although rather modern translation might be to use the idiom "this rubs me the wrong way." After all, if in fact His character had changed, what is stated goes against all we are and all God would want us to be. We all know intuitively what God ought to be like. There are enough traces of His image left in us to know this; otherwise we would not possess any concept of morality. A change in God's character would, therefore, take away all ground from under our feet. It would not only go against the very fiber of our existence and make us sick, but it would mean death for us.

There is an anecdote about Martin Luther that tells that he felt depressed. His wife entered his study and proceeded to draw the curtains. When Luther asked her why she did this she answered: "Because God is dead." The realization that God cannot die is the best remedy against depression.

Sometimes the future seems dim and gloomy to us because we do not remember the past. If we do not bother to look at history, we don't know where we came from and we lose our identity. This is even more important in connection with the history of salvation. It is of the utmost importance for us to remember the deeds of the LORD and His miracles of long ago, to meditate on all His works, and consider all His mighty deeds.

In other words, we should read our Bible and remember that "Jesus Christ is the same yesterday and today and forever" (Hebrews 13:8).

Psalm 78:1-8

"I will open my mouth in parables, I will utter hidden things, things from of old…"

This Psalm will gain considerable depth for us if we place it beside Matthew's Gospel where the evangelist quotes verse 2 as a prophecy about Christ's parables regarding the kingdom of heaven. We read there: "Jesus spoke all these things to the crowd in parables; he did not say anything to them without using a parable. So was fulfilled what was spoken through the prophet: 'I will open my mouth in parables, I will utter things hidden since the creation of the world' " (Matthew 13:34,35). Asaph never reached the point Christ reached, but we could say that in this Psalm he laid the foundation for the revelation of our Lord Jesus Christ.

Both Asaph and Christ speak about things since the creation of the world. Before there ever was any creation, God had worked out the plan of redemption in which man would play such an important part. Asaph also speaks about the coming of the kingdom of heaven and about an earlier stage of the kingdom. Jesus deals with the last phase of the coming of the kingdom.

Israel's history is one vast illustration of the history of salvation. A nation loses its identity when it forgets its history. In the same way an individual will not know where he is going if he forgets where he came from. The problem with most people is that they do not know their own history, let alone learn from it.

This is one of man's great problems caused by the theory of evolution: if man descended from the apes, he has a very bleak future. But a person who knows that God created him and redeemed him also knows that he is headed for glory. This knowledge is an important part of our identity. Knowledge of our past and of our future not only helps us to know where we are, but also who we are. That is why Jesus could say: "Even if I testify on my own behalf, my testimony is valid, for I know where I came from and where I am going. But you have no idea where I come from or where I am going" (John 8:14).

It is important for us to know the history of the Bible. Our experience of God's grace will be deepened by our understanding of how God dealt with the people of Israel, in their redemption from slavery, in the restoration of their human dignity, as well as in the punishment they received when they chose not to live up to the standards God had set for them. "For everything that was written in the past was written to teach us, so that through endurance and the encouragement of the Scriptures we might have hope" (Romans 15:4).

Psalm 78:1-8

"What we have heard and known, what our fathers have told us. We will not hide them from their children; we will tell the next generation."

There is a tendency among young people to assert their independence by cutting their ties with previous generations. Some young people act as if they have to invent life by themselves, as if their knowledge is superior to the wisdom of their elders. Sometimes the elders are just as much to be blamed for the creation of a generation gap as the youth are. Someone once stated that we should never trust anyone over thirty years of age. The speaker may have changed his tune as he grew older himself.

The obvious truth is, of course, that there would be no young people if there were no older generation. If my grandfather had died at the age of 6, I would not be here, writing this today.

Asaph realized that he not only owed his very existence to his ancestors, but that they had given him a heritage that was worth passing on to his own children and grandchildren. Once I spoke with a lady who admitted that she hardly ever darkened the door of a church, but she wanted her children to attend Sunday school in order to give them some direction in life. I challenged her that she could not give to her children what she did not have herself. In order to give to our children what they need in life, we have to model for them a life of fellowship with God. God said about Abraham: "I have chosen him, so that he will direct his children and his household after him to keep the way of the LORD by doing what is right and just, so that the LORD will bring about for Abraham what he has promised him" (Genesis 18:19). We can only steer our children in the right direction if we are going that way ourselves.

In writing this, Asaph thought of the miraculous way God had delivered Israel from slavery in Egypt and brought them into the Promised Land. We have an even greater heritage to pass on to our children and grandchildren if we can prove to them that God has saved us in the forgiveness of our sins and the renewal of our lives. They will want to follow the Lord if they can see in us how attractive the Gospel is.

Psalm 78:9-16

"They forgot what he had done, the wonders he had shown them."

There were two sides to Israel's great heritage. There were God's miraculous interventions that led to Israel's redemption and there was the people's reaction to those miracles with unbelief and disobedience. Why would young people want to follow a Gospel that their parents and ancestors did not adhere to? Young people are very sensitive to hypocrisy. And, unfortunately, Israel's history was not one glorious account of victorious and holy living. Of all the people who left Egypt where they had been slaves, only two made it to the Promised Land. Out of the several million that crossed the desert, only Caleb and Joshua kept the vision and lived to see it fulfilled.

We tend to color history and speak in glowing terms about our founding fathers. The story of slavery and Indian wars is not a popular lesson to be taught in schools. In order to set the record straight, Asaph gives us both sides of the story. He speaks about the wonderful things God did for His people and of the horrible way they repaid Him for His love.

The keywords in Asaph's record are "they forgot." We must be cautious not to have a selective memory regarding the past. The good old days were not so good if we take a closer look at them. If we could only remember our history and learn from the mistakes that were made! Reality shows that we don't learn from history. And even that truth we do not take to heart. Maybe our forefathers paved the way for us to an empty way of life. History will only repeat itself if we do not learn from it. God has a solution for us that helps us to overcome the past, however dismal it may have been, and keep our eye on a glorious future. In the words of the apostle Peter: "For you know that it was not with perishable things such as silver or gold that you were redeemed from the empty way of life handed down to you from your forefathers, but with the precious blood of Christ, a lamb without blemish or defect" (I Peter 1:18-20). If we remember how much God paid for us in the past, our future will be bright.

Psalm 78:17-64

"Men ate the bread of angels; he sent them all the food they could eat."

From a human viewpoint, the logistics of Israel's desert crossing from Egypt to Canaan was an absolute impossibility. Several million people traveling for forty years in one of the most uninhabitable regions of our planet is a sheer miracle. The scarcity of water makes even a one- or two-day trip a serious health hazard. Yet God gave His people plenty of food and fluid. They ate not just food; God served them "manna," "the bread of angels."

But the people did not like the food from the celestial cuisine; they preferred their prison rations in Egypt, in spite of the fact that the Egyptians had murdered their infant sons. As the proverb states, "there is no accounting for tastes."

Moses interpreted the bread of heaven as a pointer to the Word of God. He told the Israelites: "[God] humbled you, causing you to hunger and then feeding you with manna, which neither you nor your fathers had known, to teach you that man does not live on bread alone but on every word that comes from the mouth of the LORD" (Deuteronomy 8:3).

Jesus takes us a step further by pointing out that food for the stomach is a shadow of the soul food we need. He says: "Do not work for food that spoils, but for food that endures to eternal life, which the Son of Man will give you" (John 6:27). He declares: "I am the bread of life. He who comes to me will never go hungry, and he who believes in me will never be thirsty" (John 6:35). And finally, He stated: "I am the bread of life. Your forefathers ate the manna in the desert, yet they died. But here is the bread that comes down from heaven, which a man may eat and not die. I am the living bread that came down from heaven. If anyone eats of this bread, he will live forever. This bread is my flesh, which I will give for the life of the world" (John 6:48-51). This is not an invitation to practice cannibalism, although Jesus' hearers may have interpreted it that way. Jesus referred to His death on the cross, which provides eternal life for our souls. That is the bread that angels are not given to eat. Our feasting upon that which is our life must make them extremely jealous. God treats us better than He treats the angels!

Psalm 78:65-72

"Then the Lord awoke as from sleep, as a man wakes from the stupor of wine. He beat back his enemies; he put them to everlasting shame."

These verses contain one of the most amazing prophecies in the Bible. At first glance, it seems as if Asaph gives exaggerated praise to David at his ascension to the throne. The coming of David meant the birth of a vision. David was the only man in Old Testament history who clearly understood that he was king in a theocracy. The bringing over of the ark to Jerusalem symbolizes this. With David, respect for God's revelation was restored. Asaph represents this spiritual revival as a waking up by God from His sleep. God intervened in the history of Israel. Once again there came a supernatural element into the daily life of the nation. But the Holy Spirit shows us here a picture of the coming of the Messiah, our Lord Jesus Christ.

The way Asaph describes this revival is rather humorous. He reverses the roles, as if God woke up, whilst, in reality, it was an awakening of men. God had not been drunk and awoke "as a man wakes from the stupor of wine," but human beings came to a new awareness of reality. The object of God's enthusiasm is His Son Jesus Christ and His incarnation. This is the topic in these last verses: the birth and ascension to the throne of Jesus.

The coming of Jesus means the defeat of the enemy. The Hebrew text, rendered "He beat back his enemies" is actually more graphic. It reads literally, "He smote his adversaries in the hinder part." We can visualize this as God spanking Satan's bare bottom. The enemy is being put to shame, and a rear-end spanking may be a good way to express the embarrassment. More is intended than a war between humans and national pride as the result of victory. When Jesus died on the cross, He embarrassed His opponent. In Paul's words: "And having disarmed the powers and authorities, he made a public spectacle of them, triumphing over them by the cross" (Colossians 2:15). Satan's shame was exposed in the nakedness of Jesus on the cross. For this reason we will never have to feel ashamed again before God. The apostle Paul assures us that "the one who trusts in him will never be put to shame" (Romans 9:33). God will never embarrass us because He loves us.

Psalm 79:1-4

"We are objects of reproach to our neighbors, of scorn and derision to those around us."

The Psalm bemoans the destruction of that which is the best and the rape of that which is most intimate: God's revelation of Himself to man, and His fellowship with us. The pigs are trampling the pearls under their feet. World history is full of examples of devastation of that which gives purpose and meaning to human life. The Babylonians and the Nazis murdered Jewish babies, but the deepest point of world history was when He, of whom the temple was a shadow, was destroyed. This Psalm, therefore, is a prophecy of the crucifixion of our Lord Jesus Christ.

The place where the living God revealed Himself in Asaph's day was defiled, and people who served and loved God were killed. Such things happened countless times in world history. The climax was Golgotha, but ever since that day, persecution and violation of that which is holy has not ceased. Most of the Lord's Apostles met with a violent death. In Revelation, John sees the souls of those who had been slain because of the Word of God under the altar and they are told that they are not the last ones to be killed in persecution (Revelation 6:9-11).

It is difficult for us to understand why God allows those He loves to suffer and to be martyred. We tend to think that the Almighty would be able to assure the safe keeping of those who have put their trust in Him. But world history is full of instances in which "bad things happen to good people." Cain killed Abel and Herod massacred the children in Bethlehem at the birth of Jesus. It seems that God stands by and doesn't act.

We only know that when Jesus died on the cross, and God's temple was desecrated and destroyed, this deepest point in world history became a turning point that led to our salvation.

If bad things happen to us or to our loved ones, we may take the apostle Paul as an example, who, before being decapitated by Nero wrote: "But even if I am being poured out like a drink offering on the sacrifice and service coming from your faith, I am glad and rejoice with all of you. So you too should be glad and rejoice with me" (Philippians 2:17,18). And "For I am already being poured out like a drink offering, and the time has come for my departure. I have fought the good fight, I have finished the race, I have kept the faith. Now there is in store for me the crown of righteousness, which the Lord, the righteous Judge, will award to me on that day-and not only to me, but also to all who have longed for his appearing" (II Timothy 4:6-8).

Psalm 79:5-8

"Do not hold against us the sins of the fathers; may your mercy come quickly to meet us, for we are in desperate need."

There is an undeniable link between the previous generations and us. This applies not only to our physical presence but also to the cultural and spiritual inheritance we possess in this world. The United States of America consists mainly of immigrants of other parts of the world. Even "Native" Americans came from somewhere else, as most African Americans. We all bring some cultural and spiritual baggage with us of which we can be proud or ashamed or both.

Asaph spoke with shame of his cultural heritage. He mentions "the sins of the fathers." In a way this can be seen as a confession of sin. The prophet Daniel identified himself with the sins of the preceding generations (Daniel 9:1-19), but Asaph seems to keep his distance from the ancestors. He may have thought of what God said in the Ten Commandments: "I, the LORD your God, am a jealous God, punishing the children for the sin of the fathers to the third and fourth generation of those who hate me, but showing love to a thousand [generations] of those who love me and keep my commandments" (Exodus 20:5,6). Peter also speaks about "the empty way of life handed down to you from your forefathers" (I Peter 1:18,19).

The dilemma for most of us is that we have a history, part of which we can be proud of, part of which we must bow our head in shame about. Being of Dutch ancestry, I can probably trace my roots back to a Dutch sea captain who transported slaves from Africa to the Americas. However proud I may be of being Dutch, I must take my stand against what my forefather did and acknowledge before God that I am his offspring.

Jesus told His contemporaries that they would be held responsible for the first murder committed on this earth. He said: "And so upon you will come all the righteous blood that has been shed on earth, from the blood of righteous Abel to the blood of Zechariah son of Berekiah, whom you murdered between the temple and the altar" (Matthew 23:35). I didn't kill Abel, yet God will hold me responsible unless I take my stand with the Lord against humanity that commits crimes like these.

The author of Hebrews states: "You have come to God, the judge of all men, to the spirits of righteous men made perfect, to Jesus the mediator of a new covenant, and to the sprinkled blood that speaks a better word than the blood of Abel" (Hebrews 12:23,24). The blood of Jesus protects me from culpability of all the crimes my ancestors committed. I need this protection that cancels out all responsibility for ancestral sins as well as my own.

Psalm 79:9-13

"Help us, O God our Savior, for the glory of your name; deliver us and forgive our sins for your name's sake."

When we pray with the intent to bring glory to God, our prayers will always be heard. Asaph asked for the forgiveness of his own sin and the sins of his people. He bases his prayer upon the character of God. He must have taken Moses' prayer as a model. When Israel refused to enter Canaan, stating that God had left them at the mercy of their enemies and God threatened to destroy them for their lack of faith, Moses appealed to God's glory and said, "If you put these people to death all at one time, the nations who have heard this report about you will say, 'The LORD was not able to bring these people into the land he promised them on oath; so he slaughtered them in the desert' " (Numbers 14:15,16). Moses understood that the perishing of God's people would harm God's testimony among the heathen nations. The purpose of all our prayers ought to be to seek the glory of God's Name. The first words in the Lord's Prayer are "Our Father in heaven, hallowed be your name" (Matthew 6:9). We must test our motives and see if we really seek the holiness of God when we pray, or whether we are after our own gain. Our prayers can condemn us.

The effectiveness of our prayers will increase as we understand more about the character of God. When Moses asked to see God's glory and God revealed Himself to Moses, He called out: "The LORD, the LORD, the compassionate and gracious God, slow to anger, abounding in love and faithfulness, maintaining love to thousands, and forgiving wickedness, rebellion and sin" (Exodus 34:6-7). It was because Moses had heard God call Himself "compassionate and gracious" that he dared to challenge God about His intent to destroy His own children.

The Psalm opens with a city in ruin and ends with a pastoral symphony. Where the sheep are grazing the Good Shepherd cannot be far away. This opens the perspective of love that gives His life for the salvation of the sheep.

God will forgive and restore and bless if we ask Him, not only because we need it, but because we know what He is like. If we know what God is like, we can say with confidence: "He who did not spare his own Son, but gave him up for us all-how will he not also, along with him, graciously give us all things? (Romans 8:32).

Psalm 80:1-11

"Hear us, O Shepherd of Israel, you who lead Joseph like a flock; you who sit enthroned between the cherubim, shine forth before Ephraim, Benjamin and Manasseh. Awaken your might; come and save us."

On his deathbed, Jacob called together his twelve sons. He gave this blessing to his son Joseph. "Joseph is a fruitful vine, a fruitful vine near a spring, whose branches climb over a wall. But his bow remained steady, his strong arms stayed limber, because of the hand of the Mighty One of Jacob, because of the Shepherd" (Genesis 49:22,24). Following Jacob's words, Asaph includes both images of the vine and the shepherd in this Psalm.

He calls God the Shepherd of Israel. This implies a confession of human weakness because sheep have a tendency to go astray. But it also implies a deep trust that God will do for us what we cannot do for ourselves.

The image of the shepherd and the sheep precedes that of the vine. The first image speaks of our salvation and God's care of us; the second of the fruit we must bear. The first could be described as God's responsibility toward us, the second as our responsibility toward God.

God is ready to take responsibility to save us, to keep us from harm and to guide us through life, as a shepherd does with his sheep. Ezekiel states: " 'You my sheep, the sheep of my pasture, are people, and I am your God,' declares the Sovereign LORD" (Ezekiel 34:31).

The image of the vine tells us that God wants us to keep connected with Him in intimate fellowship so that the Holy Spirit can produce in us the fruit that glorifies God. Jesus says: "No branch can bear fruit by itself; it must remain in the vine. Neither can you bear fruit unless you remain in me" and "apart from me you can do nothing" (John 15:4,5). And He adds "This is to my Father's glory, that you bear much fruit, showing yourselves to be my disciples" (John 15:8).

Asaph states how God saves as and allows us to bear fruit. The chorus of this hymn reads: "Restore us, O God; make your face shine upon us, that we may be saved." God makes His face shine upon us. The warmth and glory of God's face awakens us from our sleep of sin and death and makes the grace of God germinate in our lives so that we may bear the fruit that the Holy Spirit sows in our hearts. God's face that shines upon us is His smile, His blessing.

Psalm 80:12-19

"Restore us, O LORD God Almighty; make your face shine upon us, that we may be saved."

In these verses Asaph shows us the other side of the coin of God's grace. The wall that protected the vine is broken down and the beautiful plant is ruined. Boars from the forest trample grapes that were meant to produce choice wine.

Asaph, obviously, spoke of people who were no longer enjoying the safety of God's protection. Actually, one person is singled out. He is called "the branch" or "the son," even "the son of man." This Psalm, therefore, is a prophecy about our Lord Jesus Christ and His suffering on the cross. Jesus repeated the question "Why have you broken down its walls?" when He cried out "Eloi, Eloi, lama sabachthani?" "My God, my God, why have you forsaken me?" (Matthew 27:46).

We all know the answer to this question. The Father forsook His Son because He carried away the burden of our sins. He took away the curse from our lives so that God could come and bless us again. In Paul's words: "Christ redeemed us from the curse of the law by becoming a curse for us, for it is written: 'Cursed is everyone who is hung on a tree.' He redeemed us in order that the blessing given to Abraham might come to the Gentiles through Christ Jesus, so that by faith we might receive the promise of the Spirit. (Galatians 3:13,14).

By taking away the wall of protection from His Son, God builds a wall around our lives that is so strong and solid that nothing can harm us.

The Hebrew words that are translated "Restore us" literally mean, "give us life." Jesus says: "I give them eternal life, and they shall never perish; no one can snatch them out of my hand. My Father, who has given them to me, is greater than all; no one can snatch them out of my Father's hand. I and the Father are one" (John 10:28-30). No one is so safe as he who puts his trust in Jesus Christ.

Psalm 81:1-7

"He says, 'I removed the burden from their shoulders; their hands were set free from the basket. In your distress you called and I rescued you, I answered you out of a thundercloud; I tested you at the waters of Meribah'."

This Psalm may have been written for the celebration of the Feast of Trumpets, which fell in the middle of the month of September. That month was important in Israel because of the ceremonies that were observed. The most important one was the Day of Atonement, Yom Kippur, on which all the sins were atoned for by the sacrifice of a goat and by the scapegoat that carried away the sins of the whole nation. This was followed five days later by the Feast of Tabernacles, when the people commemorated the desert crossing by living for one whole week in huts made with branches and leaves. September was the month of remembrance for God's people.

God wants us to remember from where we came in order to make us realize where we are going. If we cannot remember our point of departure and we don't know where we are heading, we can have no idea either where we are at present. We need points of comparison to get our bearing in life.

For Israel it began with the deliverance from slavery in Egypt, when God lifted the heavy burden from their shoulders. And it ought to have ended with their entry into God's rest and their occupation of the Land of Promise.

We sometimes live under the mistaken impression that our freedom merely consists in getting rid of our burdens in life. Somehow that is not the way it works. Our struggle for survival will last till we take our last breath. God's deliverance consists of exchanging our burdens for His. Jesus invites us to unburden ourselves on Him. He says: "Come to me, all you who are weary and burdened, and I will give you rest. Take my yoke upon you and learn from me, for I am gentle and humble in heart, and you will find rest for your souls. For my yoke is easy and my burden is light. (Matthew 11:28-30). He is our scapegoat, the Lamb of God who carries away our sins. He comes to our side and lifts our burden in order to help us carry it. Since He is gentle and humble in heart, He stoops down lower than we ever can and the heaviest part of the load falls on His shoulder. That makes our burden so light that we can walk erect through life and praise God.

Psalm 81:8-16

"I am the LORD your God, who brought you up out of Egypt. Open wide your mouth and I will fill it."

God promises that He will completely satisfy us if we open ourselves up for Him. The image makes us think of a nest with young birds, waiting with stretched-open beaks for their mother to satisfy their hunger. A lack of happiness is never due to God's unwillingness, but always to our lack of desire. Idolatry, in whatever form or shape it may present itself, always dulls man's appetite.

Every newborn creature knows hunger; it is inherent in each living being that comes into this world. One of the few things a newborn baby can do is drink. God does not ask us to do something we are unable to do. He asks that we do that for which we were made, that we be creatures who hunger for their Creator. God reveals Himself to us as our mother, demonstrating love, tenderness, nourishment and all maternal attributes. He invites us to enter into a life-giving intimacy with Himself. Why are there so few satisfied people in this world? If we know how to get satisfaction on the natural level of this world, why don't we experience it in the spiritual realm?

God said to the Israelites: "I brought you out of Egypt; allow me now to feed you." During the journey through the desert, God fed His people with natural food. But He also made them fast from time to time in order to make them understand that material things were an image of a spiritual reality. Physical hunger points to spiritual hunger. Moses expresses this with the words: "He humbled you, causing you to hunger and then feeding you with manna, which neither you nor your fathers had known, to teach you that man does not live on bread alone but on every word that comes from the mouth of the LORD" (Deuteronomy 8:3).

Our soul will be satisfied if we saturate it with the Word of God. In the words of the apostle Peter: "Like newborn babies, crave pure spiritual milk, so that by it you may grow up in your salvation, now that you have tasted that the Lord is good" (I Peter 2:2,3).

Psalm 82

"I said, 'You are ' 'gods' '; you are all sons of the Most High.' But you will die like mere men; you will fall like every other ruler."

One problem in reading this Psalm is the translation of the word "gods." The Hebrew word *Elohim* can mean "God," "angels," or "magistrates." We take it from the context and from the way in which Jesus quoted this Psalm that the reference is to human judges.

King Jehoshaphat referred indirectly to this Psalm when he gave instructions to the judges in the reorganization of the judicial system in Judah. He said: "Consider carefully what you do, because you are not judging for man but for the LORD, who is with you whenever you give a verdict" (II Chronicles 19:6).

Jesus' quotation of this Psalm throws a clear light on the meaning of it. When the Jews objected to the fact that Jesus called Himself the Son of God, we read: "Jesus answered them, 'Is it not written in your Law, ' 'I have said you are gods' '? If he called them 'gods,' to whom the word of God came-- and the Scripture cannot be broken-- what about the one whom the Father set apart as his very own and sent into the world? Why then do you accuse me of blasphemy because I said, 'I am God's Son'?" (John 10:34-36).

It is important to note the glorious effect the Word of God can have upon us if we take care to listen to it. When God speaks to us things happen in our life. God's Word has creative power. David stated: "By the word of the LORD were the heavens made, their starry host by the breath of his mouth" (Psalm 33:6). God's Word heals and saves, as another Psalmist proclaimed: "He sent forth his word and healed them; he rescued them from the grave" (Psalm 107:20). And the apostle Paul indicates that the Word of God makes us a new creation. We read: "For God, who said, 'Let light shine out of darkness,' made his light shine in our hearts to give us the light of the knowledge of the glory of God in the face of Christ" (II Corinthians 4:6). But not only that; when God speaks to us and we listen, we become God's child. God shares His life with us and we become partakers of His very nature and glory. If we don't listen we will die.

Psalm 83

"O God, do not keep silent; be not quiet, O God, be not still. Let them know that you, whose name is the LORD--that you alone are the Most High over all the earth."

In this last Psalm of Asaph, Israel is portrayed as being attacked by enemies and God, apparently, does nothing. Asaph felt that, since Israel is God's people, those who attack them attack God. Yet, God remained inactive.

Little has changed in world history. Other nations have always considered Israel to be an intruder in the land of Canaan. Even during Israel's captivity there were periods when some tried to exterminate the Jewish people, as is evinced in the story of Esther (See Esther, Chapter Three). The period between Haman and Hitler has been marked by a sad series of pogroms. Central in this is the endeavor to cut off the Anointed One, as we see in Daniel's prophecy (Daniel 9:26), meaning the crucifixion of our Lord Jesus Christ. It is he battle against Him who crushes the head of the serpent (Genesis 3:15). Behind the scene stands the archenemy, of whom all haters of Jews are merely like pawns in a chess game.

God's reaction to this is incomprehensible for man. The Apostle Paul calls this the foolishness of the cross (see I Corinthians 1:18-29). Even Satan did not understand God's strategy, which was his undoing. When God's own Son was mocked and crushed, God kept silent and remained inactive. He did not even answer the cry: "Eloi, Eloi, lama sabachthani?" Israel's experience, as described in this Psalm, is therefore an image of the suffering and death of our Lord Jesus Christ. This Psalm contains a prophecy. God's inactivity is intentional and strategic. This strategy leads to a complete victory over evil. Man's problem is that the process takes too much time. We think that God ought to complete His business within the scope of one human lifetime. We understand very little of the perspective of things from the viewpoint of eternity. God is the enemy's real target, not we who are under God's protection. The issue in the final victory, therefore, is not primarily our salvation, but the manifestation of God's glory. How wonderful this is that the devil cannot attack us because of what we are, but because he hates the glory of God that is within us! How good it is when we understand what is at stake, and why we experience that which befalls us!

Psalm 84:1-4

"How lovely is your dwelling place, O LORD Almighty! My soul yearns, even faints, for the courts of the LORD; my heart and my flesh cry out for the living God."

The sons of Korah composed this beautiful Psalm. They were not professional musicians but gatekeepers, appointed by King David. As amateur musicians they made important contributions to the praise literature.

Working at the gates of the tent where the Ark of the Covenant was kept, they saw a picture of the heavenly reality in which God resides. With intense longing, they looked forward to the time when they would enter the pearly gates and walk the streets of gold.

They called what they saw on earth "lovely." The place was lovely, because of the presence of God. It is love that makes things and places lovely. If we can remember the place where we first asked Jesus to come into our heart and where we experienced the love of the Savior flooding our soul, we will always consider the location sacred.

The sons of Korah saw in the presence of the sparrow and the swallow with a nest full of little ones an illustration of God's tender love. God, the Lord of hosts, the commander-in-chief of the heavenly armies, the Lord Almighty manifests His tender compassion over a nest of little birds.

God is concerned when two sparrows, sold for a penny, fall to the ground (See Matthew 10:29). We live in a world where, not only birds are sold, but where their necks are wrung, and where bodies and souls of men are bought and sold (See Revelation 18:13). God's revelation of Himself gives back value, honor, and rights to every living thing.

Yet, one can dwell in Jerusalem and be far from the loveliness of God. It is the contrast between what we believe to be a disparity between the might of the Lord of hosts and the loveliness of His dwelling place that gives to the image that is used here such a wonderful radiance. And the place the Psalmist describes is in itself only an image of the heavenly reality. If the picture is that glorious, what will the reality be? A certain poet, speaking about the beauty of the autumn leaves, wrote: "If the portals are made of gold, what will the halls be like?" Look at the picture of the place where we will spend eternity.

Psalm 84:5-7

"Blessed are those whose strength is in you, who have set their hearts on pilgrimage."

Blessing consists in the realization of the source of our strength. A person who thinks he is strong apart from God deceives himself. The Book of Proverbs interprets this verse well by saying: "Trust in the LORD with all your heart and lean not on your own understanding" (Proverbs 3:5). Awareness of the source of strength is of little value if there is no application of this in daily life. If we know that God is the source of our strength and we do not draw from that source, our faith has little merit. Isaiah describes how it works: "He gives strength to the weary and increases the power of the weak. Even youths grow tired and weary, and young men stumble and fall; but those who hope in the LORD will renew their strength. They will soar on wings like eagles; they will run and not grow weary, they will walk and not be faint" (Isaiah 40:29-31). Often people fail to avail themselves of the riches and abundance God has put at their disposal.

People who know God as the source of their strength become pilgrims. They are on their way to Zion; they are goal-oriented, purpose driven people. This does not make them unfit for human interaction. As a matter of fact, they bring about changes for good as they pass through life. The valley of Baca is the valley of tears. People who are invigorated by God provide consolation and blessing for those who weep. They bring showers of blessing down upon those whose lives are arid and fruitless. Goodness and mercy follow them all the days of their life. Being strong in God's strength means giving strength to those who are falling. Being on our way to Zion means showing the way to those who have lost their way in life. And those who give strength to other will be strengthened in the process.

Psalm 84:8-12

"I would rather be a doorkeeper in the house of my God than dwell in the tents of the wicked."

The sons of Korah were doorkeepers at the temple. Theirs was a menial task; they were merely porters or janitors. This was their calling in life but it was also a matter of choice. They could serve God and the people who came to the tabernacle of the temple or they could associate with the important people in the land and, forgetting moral scruples, live more comfortably and respectably. They chose to be humble and stay close to God.

Even if we have chosen to serve God, we are not automatically exempt from ambition. There are higher and lower places in the Kingdom, why not climb up and go after the better places where we are more visible and receive more recognition?

Jesus' disciples, James and John asked: "Let one of us sit at your right and the other at your left in your glory" (Mark 10:37).

Peter states that we "like living stones, are being built into a spiritual house to be a holy priesthood, offering spiritual sacrifices acceptable to God through Jesus Christ" (I Peter 2:5). What kind of stone would I like to be? At least one that is placed at an important junction, where I uphold the structure, where the building would collapse if it weren't for me? Close to where I grew up in Europe, was a medieval ruined castle. The crumbling walls were of red small bricks and six or more feet thick. When I read Peter's words about being a living stone, I ask myself if I would agree if God placed me as a brick in the middle of that wall, where no one could see me and only God knew I was there. I have come to the conclusion that it is better to be anywhere in God's building than in a position of power and visibility outside. Being blessed means to choose the place where God placed us.

Psalm 85:1-7

"You showed favor to your land, O LORD; you restored the fortunes of Jacob. You forgave the iniquity of your people and covered all their sins."

The basis of this Psalm is the relationship between the land of Israel and the people of Israel. Such a relationship is established elsewhere in Scripture also. In Leviticus, we read: "Keep all my decrees and laws and follow them, so that the land where I am bringing you to live may not vomit you out" (Leviticus 20:22). There is a mystical tie between land and people. We develop a historical consciousness about the place in which we live. Like a tree, we put our roots down in the ground where our ancestors lived. In the case of Israel, this consciousness was particularly strong because God had pledged Himself to the land through His promise to Abraham, and He had chosen the place where His Son would be born and live as a human being.

This relationship between man and soil goes back to the time of the creation of man. The Genesis account states: "The LORD God formed the man from the dust of the ground" (Genesis 2:7). Man's first task was to take care of the garden from which soil he had been taken. The punishment for Adam's sin affected, first of all, the ground. God said to Adam: "Cursed is the ground because of you" (Genesis 3:17). When God took away Adam's crown, the earth suffered. Consequently, when God shows favor to the land, it is because He restored His relationship with the people who inhabit the land.

God shows favor to the land and He is satisfied because the human debt is paid. This refers to the atonement for the sins of the people. It is not a matter of God switching from a bad mood to a good one, but of expiation of the iniquity of the land through the sacrifice of Jesus Christ. The death of our Lord Jesus Christ will result in that: "The wolf will live with the lamb, the leopard will lie down with the goat, the calf and the lion and the yearling together; and a little child will lead them." And "The earth will be full of the knowledge of the LORD as the waters cover the sea" (Isaiah 11:6,9). "The wilderness and the solitary place shall be glad for them; and the desert shall rejoice, and blossom as the rose" (Isaiah 35:1, KJV).

If the atonement of our sins has such a bearing upon the place of our residence, we better take it seriously. If we are reconciled with God, our country will have peace and blessing. It will make a difference whether we are the salt of the earth and a light in the darkness or not. God had more than our own salvation in mind when He forgave our sins.

Psalm 85:8-13

"The LORD will indeed give what is good, and our land will yield its harvest."

The last part of this Psalm is a beautiful pastoral symphony. The harvest the Psalmist describes is a crop of love, faithfulness, righteousness, and peace. Adam's curse is lifted and the thorns and thistles of sickness and death no longer spoil the field.

But we know that this symphony is music of the future. We are saved from perdition but we still live in a world that is lost. Yet, there are notes of music that can be heard now, even before our salvation has become perfection and God's plan has found its consummation.

Love and faithfulness meet together; righteousness and peace kiss each other. This marriage is made in heaven but expressed on earth. The fruit of the land grows in the lives of human beings. The order in which they are given is not haphazard. Throughout the Bible, this order is maintained: first righteousness, then peace. There can be no peace where righteousness doesn't come first. Here the two embrace. Peace at any price is no peace. "Love and faithfulness meet together; righteousness and peace kiss each other." What a wonderful meeting this is! The four meet on earth, and they perform the most perfect square dance ever seen.

Heaven and earth connect with each other. This representation is a reference to the incarnation. When Jesus was born and lived on our planet, when He ministered, died and rose from the dead, the Father looked on and showed His approval. In the field of Ephrata, the angels sang. When Jesus was baptized in the River Jordan the Father spoke. In Revelation Jesus is called "Faithful and True" (Revelation 19:11).

Faithfulness means perseverance in love. We use the word faithful in connection with a marriage relationship. Jesus was faithful to the Father and to His righteousness. Faithfulness is linked with righteousness. Peace is realized through the faithfulness of our Lord Jesus Christ through whom we are made righteous.

God has saved us and planted us in this world so that we would bear fruit that glorifies Him. That fruit is called "the fruit of the Spirit." The apostle Paul specifies: "The fruit of the Spirit is love, joy, peace, patience, kindness, goodness, faithfulness, gentleness and self-control" (Galatians 5:22,23). This is the crop that will grow in our life if we allow the Word of God, that is sown in our heart, to develop and come to fruition.

Psalm 86:1-10

"Among the gods there is none like you, O Lord; no deeds can compare with yours. All the nations you have made will come and worship before you, O Lord; they will bring glory to your name."

Who were these gods David was trying to compare with God? He was probably thinking of the idols of the nations that surrounded Israel.

From ancient times, people have had a concept of a Creator, the source of life and of all that is visible. My wife and I lived as missionaries among tribal Stone Age people, who knew the Name of the Creator. But God was not a living presence to them. He had created the world, but something went wrong and the Creator went back to heaven, taking eternal life with Him. The vacuum created by His absence was immediately filled by evil spirits, hiding in trees and rocks, that made humans sick and caused death. Eternal life became a memory of the past and a vague hope for the future.

How could such gods be compared with the living God, who created life? David comes to the conclusion that the God of Israel is not only superior, but that He is, in fact, incomparable.

The kind of idols David knew are no longer popular in our day. But we have also lost the sense of God being incomparable to anything else. We cannot manipulate God as we try to manipulate any other power that influences our lives.

David had never seen God with his physical eyes. But when Samuel had anointed him with oil to make him the future king of Israel, we read: "From that day on the Spirit of the LORD came upon David in power" (I Samuel 16:13). David was changed overnight. After this overpowering experience with God, David realized that there is no comparison between God and all the other gods.

The overwhelming sense of God's greatness made David look around to the people who inhabited the world. He came to the conclusion that they could not continue to live eternally in the vacuum of God's absence. He not only expressed the wish that they would know what he knew, but he foresaw the time that this would actually happen. When the Stone Age people, mentioned above, heard the Gospel, they said: "That is it! That is the eternal life we had lost and had hoped God would give back to us one day."

If we realize who God is, we can say: "You alone are God," and surrender to Him. If we experience God's incomparable greatness in our own life, God wants us to tell others.

Psalm 86:11-13

"Give me an undivided heart, that I may fear your name."

It has been observed that almost every line in this Psalm is a quote from another Psalm or from a verse in the Pentateuch. It is the way David brought the various strands of truth and beauty together in this Psalm that makes it an original creation.

David had experienced salvation in that God saved him from a certain death. He experienced God's love for him and he states, "You have delivered me from the depths of the grave." For him this probably meant that he was ill and God healed him, or that he was kept from being killed by King Saul or in battle. For us it is a perfect picture of what God has done for us in saving us from going to hell.

The experience did not automatically align David with the will of God. He prayed that God would teach him the way. But even when God did this, David discovered that he was prone to deviate from the way he knew he had to go. He found that he was not ready to follow the Lord wholeheartedly. Hence his prayer: "Give me an undivided heart, that I may fear your name." It is an awful discovery to make that our heart is divided. There is a constant battle raging between our will to be good and the part of us that enjoys being bad. David relates this to the fact that he doesn't fear God's Name.

I have caught myself making pious promises to God that I would rid myself of sinful habits, only to come to the discovery that part of me enjoyed those habits too much to let go. I identify with Paul's desperate cry: "What a wretched man I am! Who will rescue me from this body of death?" (Romans 7:24).

Our deliverance is in honestly owning up to our hypocrisy and confessing to God what He knew all the time. It helps to realize whom we are talking to when we confess our sins. If we fear God we understand that He is not the kind of person we can make deals with. He saved us from hell; we must ask Him to save us from ourselves also.

Without the ministry of the Holy Spirit there can be no walking in God's truth. Obedience brings forth understanding and understanding leads to freedom. This is the result of our communion with the Son.

Psalm 86:14-17

"Give me a sign of your goodness, that my enemies may see it and be put to shame, for you, O LORD, have helped me and comforted me."

David sees himself surrounded by enemies. He doesn't ask for a complete change of circumstances but for "a sign of your goodness." The point is not that David finds himself so much surrounded by darkness that he sees no light at the end of the tunnel, but that his enemies don't see a way out. David does not ask God to change his circumstances but to open the eyes of the ones who are attacking him so that they will be put to shame. David's prayer is, in fact, a prayer of intercession for his enemies for the purpose of their conversion. In doing so, he anticipated Jesus' advice: "Love your enemies, do good to those who hate you, bless those who curse you, pray for those who mistreat you" (Luke 6:27,28). David understood that the hateful attitude of his enemies was the result of their wrong vision of God. They never understood that God is "a compassionate and gracious God, slow to anger, abounding in love and faithfulness." His prayer was that God would put David as an example to them.

Circumstances can easily overwhelm us. If our hardship is caused by others who purposely want to make life difficult for us, we tend to react in a manner that would not qualify as "sanctified." We rarely accept that God might allow adversity in our daily life for the purpose of seeing how we react. Moses said to the people of Israel: "Remember how the LORD your God led you all the way in the desert these forty years, to humble you and to test you in order to know what was in your heart, whether or not you would keep his commands" (Deuteronomy 8:2).

But God is not the only one who is interested in our reaction to adversity. When we make it known to people around us that we are Christians, we will become the object of their intense scrutiny. Unbelievers, usually, have a clear concept of what the behavior of a Christian ought to be. Our verbal testimony will only carry weight if it is backed up by a daily life that exudes love and compassion for those without God. We may ask God for signs of His goodness, so we can emulate His goodness before others.

Psalm 87:1-3

"The LORD loves the gates of Zion more than all the dwellings of Jacob."

Zion is a relatively small section of the city of Jerusalem. God's reason for choosing Zion was that it was the dwelling place of David. The fact that David was "a man after God's own heart" is probably the main reason that Zion occupies such an important place in Scripture. God's love for the place cannot be detached from the love He has for His Son. David captured Zion from the Jebusites and made it his home. Having conquered the fortress, David proceeded to capture the city of Jerusalem. David's choice of the place, eventually, gave it significance that went far beyond its own. David's residence became God's residence. Because David was the man of God's choice, David's choice became God's choice. Since God moved in with David, Zion became a piece of heaven on earth.

Choice is the essence of human liberty. Life is made up of choices. We all go through life making small and big decisions. We choose our partners, our vocation, and our destiny. Very often we make wrong choices. The most important choice we can make is our choice for God. Moses told the people of Israel: "This day I call heaven and earth as witnesses against you that I have set before you life and death, blessings and curses. Now choose life, so that you and your children may live and that you may love the LORD your God, listen to his voice, and hold fast to him. For the LORD is your life" (Deuteronomy 30:19,20).

If we choose God, we will discover that God had chosen us long before. If we learn to involve God in our daily choices, we will always make the right choices. God will love what we do. God will love our home and make it His.

The object of God's love was, ultimately, not David, but Jesus. God loves us because of His Son, and He sets us apart and calls us by His grace in order to reveal His Son in us.

Psalm 87:4-7

"Indeed, of Zion it will be said, "This one and that one were born in her, and the Most High himself will establish her." The LORD will write in the register of the peoples: 'This one was born in Zion'."

One of the salutary effects of the Diaspora and of the Babylonian captivity was that the Egyptians and Babylonians came in touch with the Gospel of the Old Testament. Daniel's testimony to Nebuchadnezzar and to Darius was probably not an exception. Among the Philistines--Israel's archenemies, in Tyre--the land of Israel's business relations, and in Ethiopia-- for Israel the end of the earth, people were born again because of the testimony of pious Jews. They testified to their jailers (in Egypt and Babylon) and to everyone who wanted to hear. Those are the "glorious thing" that can be said of Zion. This shows the other side of the coin from Jonah's story; it is the lesser-known side of the coin. The encounter with God in Zion makes the Babylonian, the Philistine, and the other foreigner into a new man. In most cases, those people did not go to Zion, but Zion came to them.

The new birth, which is mentioned here, is in the first place a prophecy about the time when people would be renewed by looking at the cross of Jesus Christ and by the coming of the Holy Spirit. One becomes a citizen of the Kingdom of Heaven--of which Zion is the capital--through conversion, confession of sin, and forgiveness by the blood of Jesus, and the baptism of the Holy Spirit. All men become brothers in Christ in the brotherhood of heaven. And we eagerly await a Savior from there, the Lord Jesus Christ (Philippians 3:20).

As long as Zion on earth is the center of world evangelism: "the Most High himself will establish her." When the church of Jesus Christ ceases to love and obey her Lord, the candlestick will be removed from its place, as was the case in the church of Ephesus (Revelation 2:5). At that point the church ceases to be church. Let's not allow that to happen!

"As they make music they will sing, 'All my fountains are in you.' " This excludes the possibility of finding our full satisfaction elsewhere. The only place to meet the Lord is in Zion. Only there can we have fellowship with God and with one another, and only there will all our needs be met, and will we be fully satisfied. This will never be experienced perfectly as long as we are on this earth. This Psalm, therefore, is a prophetic pointer to the time when we shall see His face and He will wipe away all tears from our eyes (Revelation 21:4).

Psalm 88:1-9

"My soul is full of trouble and my life draws near the grave. I am counted among those who go down to the pit; I am like a man without strength. I am set apart with the dead, like the slain who lie in the grave, whom you remember no more, who are cut off from your care."

This is saddest Psalm in the hymnbook. The author is Heman. The sadness of this Psalm purposes to teach the reader humility, in showing how Heman's painful experiences led him to humility.

The Psalm is written in a minor key. No light shows at the end of the tunnel. The only positive feature is the fact that Heman calls upon God in his time of need. This calling upon God is the result of suffering. Maybe we can better say that God calls Heman in the midst of his pain. In the words of C. S. Lewis "God shouts to us in our pain."

Heman states: "I am counted among those who go down to the pit." The Apostle Paul uses the same words but in a completely different way, when he says: "We always carry around in our body the death of Jesus, so that the life of Jesus may also be revealed in our body" (II Corinthians 4:10). Heman and Paul use the same words to say completely opposite things. Paul sees himself as counted among the dead as a way that leads to resurrection; Heman utters a cry of despair. Yet, the Holy Spirit inspired both!

When we surrender to God's will, God wants us to completely accept the consequences of our death. The only possibility to really die inwardly is if we die without hope of a resurrection. This may be the deepest lesson of this Psalm: it shows us the way to true humility. When we put ourselves on God's altar, the fire will keep burning till all that is left is ashes. We read in Leviticus 6.9, "The burnt offering is to remain on the altar hearth throughout the night, till morning, and the fire must be kept burning on the altar."

Strangely enough, the Psalm opens with the words: "O LORD, the God who saves me," calling upon YHWH as "the God of my salvation" (NKJV). That is the real breakthrough of light in this Psalm. It is the guarantee of hope God is not the God of the dead but of the living (Matthew 22:32). However hopeless the contents of this Psalm may be, it is framed in hope.

All of this points prophetically toward the suffering of Christ. Or better, these elements of human suffering culminated in Jesus' loneliness and isolation. Our Lord looked in vain for human fellowship and sympathy and at the deepest point He cried out: "Eloi, Eloi, lama sabachthani?" (Matthew 27:46). As Jesus took up Heman's cry, it became the turning point of history.

Psalm 88:10-18

"Do you show your wonders to the dead? Do those who are dead rise up and praise you? ... Is your love declared in the grave, your faithfulness in Destruction? Are your wonders known in the place of darkness, or your righteous deeds in the land of oblivion?"

Obviously, Heman's own answer to these questions is "No!" His problem with death was that it looked like a closed door. One passes through it and the door closes, never to open again. The door doesn't have the word "HOPE" written on it.

Yet, Heman knew that death was not the last word. He may not have known what we know, but as a member of God's people, he knew with David: "And I-- in righteousness I will see your face; when I awake, I will be satisfied with seeing your likeness" (Psalm 17:15). He knew that God called Himself "the God of Abraham, the God of Isaac, and the God of Jacob." And that, consequently, "He is not the God of the dead but of the living" (Matthew 22:32).

Therefore, the death Heman speaks about is not physical death but the ultimate separation from God, "the Second Death." That is the reason for Heman's cry of despair in this Psalm. We don't know why this poor man felt that way. He may have suffered, what we would call nowadays, "a clinical depression." That sickness is often accompanied by feelings of hopelessness. He saw himself in the pit of hell, where God could not reach him and where he was unable to reach God.

The fact that Heman cries out to God is the answer to his own question. As long as he can cry out to heaven, the way of communication is still open. As a young Christian, I was often tossed to and fro, riding an emotional roller coaster. Once I thought I had become an atheist. So I went down on my knees and cried: "God, I don't believe anymore that you exist!" When it dawned on me what I was doing, I got up, shook my head and laughed at my own inconsistency.

In writing this Psalm Heman knew that God still showed His wonders in the darkness in which he found himself. Heman could not hide from God in the darkness, and God doesn't hide Himself from us in the darkness either.

Psalm 89:1-4

"I will sing of the LORD's great love forever; with my mouth I will make your faithfulness known through all generations."

The main theme of the Psalm revolves about one person with whom Israel as a nation was closely connected in everything he experienced. Ethan, who wrote this, spoke about King David. God had made a covenant with David in which He promised to establish his throne in Israel forever.

We understand that the Holy Spirit speaks here about our Lord Jesus Christ. As the fortunes of Israel were wrapped up in what happened to their king, so our destiny depends on what happened to Jesus Christ. If we call ourselves Christian, God considers us to be *in* Jesus Christ. What happened to Jesus, happened to us.

In the Old Testament, people who wanted to come to God had to bring a sacrificial animal to the tabernacle or the temple. They had to lay their hands on its head to identify with the animal. What happened to the animal was, in a way, happening to the person who brought it to be sacrificed. In the Book of Leviticus there are five different kinds of sacrifices, most of which involve the death of a sacrificial animal as a means of communication with God.

The meaning of this was that the person who came to God confessed that he had forfeited his life and God could no longer accept him. But instead of dying himself, another creature took his place in death, so that he could stand before God's throne.

This substitution is proof of God's eternal love. Ethan calls it God's "great love." The KJV renders the Hebrew word "lovingkindness" or "mercy." If we are in Christ, we are the recipients of this love. This gives us an eternal reason to praise God.

The apostle Paul writes about this: "Praise be to the God and Father of our Lord Jesus Christ, who has blessed us in the heavenly realms with every spiritual blessing in Christ. For he chose us in him before the creation of the world to be holy and blameless in his sight. In love he predestined us to be adopted as his sons through Jesus Christ, in accordance with his pleasure and will- to the praise of his glorious grace, which he has freely given us in the One he loves. In him we have redemption through his blood, the forgiveness of sins, in accordance with the riches of God's grace" (Ephesians 1:3-7).

Psalm 89:5-18

"O LORD God Almighty, who is like you? You are mighty, O LORD, and your faithfulness surrounds you."

The main theme of this Psalm is God's faithfulness. God is utterly reliable; He can be trusted one hundred percent. It is important to cling to this assurance, because, as we will see later in this Psalm, circumstances change and, to all outward appearance, God abandons the ones He promised to save and protect.

Things happen in the life of each of us that would make us question the reliability of God's promises. Unless we are deeply convinced that God is faithful, our faith could suffer irreparable damage.

The Psalmist, therefore, takes us up into heaven to show us briefly the overwhelming glory of God's reality. The apostle John had a vision of this reality. He saw a door open in heaven and was invited into the very presence of God. He states: "There before me was a throne in heaven with someone sitting on it. And the one who sat there had the appearance of jasper and carnelian. A rainbow, resembling an emerald, encircled the throne. From the throne came flashes of lightning, rumblings and peals of thunder. Before the throne, seven lamps were blazing. These are the seven spirits of God. Also before the throne there was what looked like a sea of glass, clear as crystal" (Revelation 4:2,3,5,6). Ethan, upon seeing this kind of vision, concludes: "You are mighty, O LORD, and your faithfulness surrounds you."

God's faithfulness in heaven translates itself in His faithfulness on earth. Looking at the awesome beauty of God's creation, at the precision of its operation, the moving of the sun and the stars, the tides of the oceans, the succession of seasons, all testify to the fact that He is the God who is "sustaining all things by his powerful word" (Hebrews 1:3). The faithfulness of the clockwork of God's creation gives us to understand that He is faithful toward us also, however hard our circumstances may contradict this. This conviction must take a powerful hold of us before we come to the point where we say: "But you have rejected!"

It takes the eyes of faith to see through the obstacles. The enemy of our souls launches a powerful campaign of propaganda to unsettle us. Unless we are thoroughly convinced that nothing can separate us from the love of Christ, we may not reach the goal.

Psalm 89:19-37

"I have exalted a young man from among the people. I have found David my servant; with my sacred oil I have anointed him. I will also appoint him my firstborn, the most exalted of the kings of the earth."

Ethan, who wrote this Psalm, clearly had the coronation of David as king of Israel in mind when he penned these words. As far as he was concerned, God's choice of David was the best thing that had ever happened to Israel. His words may sound to us like nationalistic pride gotten out of hand. We must remember though that God had chosen Israel to be "out of all nations [God's] treasured possession" and "a kingdom of priests and a holy nation" (Exodus 19:5,6). In revealing Himself to Israel, God revealed Himself to the whole world.

David did more than any other king of Israel to realize God's vision. He restored the Ark of the Covenant, symbol of God's presence, to its place of importance. He prepared all for the building of the temple in Jerusalem and he reigned as king by the grace of God. But the Holy Spirit thought of someone else besides David when He inspired Ethan to write these words. David reminded Him of Jesus Christ, God's ultimate revelation in this world.

When I was a teenager, growing up in the Netherlands, I met an American pastor who treated me with extreme kindness. Initially, I didn't understand why he paid such attention to me until I heard that he had a boy my age, whom he had left behind in the United States. I reminded him of his son.

God still treats us with love and tenderness when we remind Him of His Son. After all, He predestined [us] to be conformed to the likeness of his Son, that he might be the firstborn among many brothers" (Romans 8:29). It is important that the beauty of Jesus be seen in us. The apostle Paul writes, "For we are to God the aroma of Christ among those who are being saved and those who are perishing (II Corinthians 2:15). If God smells Jesus in us, people around us will also.

We cannot work ourselves up to this. What made David so special to God and to Israel was that the Holy Spirit had anointed him with sacred oil. Without the Spirit's unction, we won't get anywhere.

Psalm 89:38-52

"But you have rejected, you have spurned, you have been very angry with your anointed one. You have renounced the covenant with your servant and have defiled his crown in the dust. You have broken through all his walls and reduced his strongholds to ruins."

Ethan was like a man who had made a beautiful trip abroad and, coming home with the sweet memories of his experiences, he finds his house in ruin and his loved ones killed. A greater contrast than between heaven's glory and earth's misery can hardly be imagined. In heaven he had seen God and he had been overwhelmed with the sense of God's faithfulness, but coming back on earth and standing before the smoking ruins of God's covenant, he gropes for answers. His faith is now stretched to the limit and beyond. How could a loving and faithful God do this to him or to us? He cries out: "O Lord, where is your former great love, which in your faithfulness you swore to David?"

For some of us it is not difficult to identify with Ethan's crisis of faith. Where is God "When bad things happen to good people?" as the author Harold Kushner entitled the book he wrote at the death of his fourteen-year-old son.

Ethan did not understand that God gave him a prophecy about what would happened to God's own son, Jesus, who came to earth and was rejected, despised, and defiled by men. We know, what Ethan could not know, that the covenant God revoked was the contract with His own Son. The wall that was broken down, the crown that was defiled was God's own. It was done for our sake. We did this to Him. Ethan's cry foreshadowed Jesus' cry: "My God, my God, why have you forsaken me?" (Matthew 27:46). Ethan couldn't understand this. Can we?

God demonstrates His eternal faithfulness to us in this breaking of His covenant with His beloved Son. He provides healing for our broken hearts in the breaking of His own heart. The ocean of His faithfulness is too deep for us to measure. We must never doubt it.

Psalm 90:1-2

"Lord, you have been our dwelling place throughout all generations. Before the mountains were born or you brought forth the earth and the world, from everlasting to everlasting you are God."

This is the only Psalm in the hymnal that bears the name of Moses. As we will see, its content fits well in the ministry of Moses as the one who led Israel out of Egypt to the Promised Land.

The Psalm draws a vivid picture of God's eternal character and the brevity of human life on earth.

We cannot really understand eternity. Living within the confines of time, we tend to see it as an endless continuation of time, going from the present into the past and into the future. How can we understand that God is not bound by time as we are? He is eternal; He created time but He is not subject to it. The only way we come close to understanding eternity is by comparison.

Moses does this for us by showing us the mountains. I was born in the Netherlands, one of the flattest places on earth. I was about twenty-seven when I first saw a real mountain and the sight took away my breath. There is nothing that makes you feel smaller than to have several thousand feet of granite looking down upon you. When you face a massive cliff that has been there for thousands of years, it makes you realize that you are not more than an ephemeral creature.

God made that mountain that makes me look so small. And He invites me to hide myself in Him.

Not only does the mountain reduce me to size, but also forces me to take another look at my own place in the sea of humanity and at my own importance. Moses speaks of "all generations." Where do I find myself as a member of the human race? Am I more than one grain of sand on the beach of life's ocean?

But then, I remember that this God, who created the highest mountain peaks, and the billions of humanity, who is God from everlasting to everlasting, came down to my level. He who created the universe by His Word became a human being Himself, so I could hide myself in Him. I don't know what takes away my breath more, the greatness of God or the fact that He became so small. It is God's smallness that saves me and allows me to hide in Him.

Psalm 90:3-12

"Teach us to number our days aright, that we may gain a heart of wisdom."

Moses was probably inspired (if that is the correct word in this context) to write this Psalm during the forty years that Israel trekked around in the desert. They had been liberated from slavery and had set out to enter the land of God's promise but they never reached their goal.

It is a blessing that no one knows how long he or she will live. God wants us to live our lives to the full without being weighed down with worry about matters that cannot be changed. Some people who live with the shadow of death upon them try to drown out their fear with "Let us eat and drink, for tomorrow we die" (Isaiah 22:13; 1 Corinthians 15:32). But if we don't know how long we will live, how then can we number our days and gain a heart of wisdom?

The people of Israel who had crossed the desert on their way to the Promised Land, who refused to take God's promise seriously, knew how long they would live. God said to them: "As surely as I live... I will do to you the very things I heard you say: In this desert your bodies will fall--every one of you twenty years old or more who was counted in the census and who has grumbled against me. Not one of you will enter the land I swore with uplifted hand to make your home, except Caleb son of Jephunneh and Joshua son of Nun. As for your children that you said would be taken as plunder, I will bring them in to enjoy the land you have rejected. But you--your bodies will fall in this desert" (Numbers 14:28-32). For thirty-eight years they wandered around in the wilderness, waiting till the last person reached the age of fifty-eight. Theirs was the saddest form of arithmetic imaginable. The wisdom they acquired from their count was that they could have entered into God's promise if they had obeyed.

That is the kind of wisdom God wants us to acquire also. He does not want us to fear death to the point where we store up as much of pleasure and fun as we can into today, but to concentrate upon our obedience to the Word of His promise. God wants us counting when He calls us home, counting on Him alone.

Psalm 90:13-17

"May the favor of the Lord our God rest upon us; establish the work of our hands for us-- yes, establish the work of our hands."

A certain tool of evangelism introduces the Gospel to people with the statement: "God has a wonderful plan for your life!" God had a wonderful plan for Israel but instead of accepting that plan and acting upon it, they ended up going around in circles for forty years.

Many of us resemble Israel in the desert, going through life like a dog chasing its own tail--but then in slow motion. We rob life of its meaning because we do not begin by asking what God had in mind when He brought us into this world. The only way to do something with our lives that has lasting value and makes it meaningful is to turn over the reins of our life to God and let Him direct us. Telling God that we want to conform to His plan for us and allowing Him to use us where and how He wants, will make us the happiest creatures on earth. How tragic it is when we come to the end of our days and we must admit that they don't add up to anything.

If we believe that God's favor rests upon us, our lives will count in this world and God will establish us and the works of our hands.

God had promised Israel that He would give them rest in the Promised Land. They refused to believe this promise and chose their own plan for their life. Every single one of them perished. The author of the Epistle to the Hebrews declares: "There remains, then, a Sabbath-rest for the people of God; for anyone who enters God's rest also rests from his own work, just as God did from his. Let us, therefore, make every effort to enter that rest, so that no one will fall by following their example of disobedience" (Hebrews 4:9-11). If we put our trust in God, we must obey Him.

Psalm 91:1-8

"He who dwells in the shelter of the Most High will rest in the shadow of the Almighty...
He will cover you with his feathers, and under his wings you will find refuge; his faithfulness
will be your shield and rampart."

One cannot read this Psalm without being overwhelmed by the beauty of its poetry. The image is one of total powerful protection and at the same time warmth and love. The One who is portrayed here as the ultimate shelter and the "mother hen" is the Most High, the Almighty God. No power can ever match the one that protects and cherishes us.

We live in a dangerous world in which the one that directs human affairs is Satan himself. A person who has no protection is doomed.

Placing oneself under God's protection is like entering into a marriage relationship. It presupposes the giving up of one's independence and it involves an act of surrender. Without these conditions, the majestic opening words of this Psalm will be nothing but an empty phrase for us.

If we enter into a marriage relationship with God, we sleep in His arms. As in a marriage, protection cannot be separated from love, intimacy, and fidelity which are the marks of a good marriage.

Actually, if we compare our relationship with God to marital love, we turn things around. Our marriages are pictures of God's love for us and our response to it, not the other way around. The apostle Paul writes: "Husbands, love your wives, just as Christ loved the church and gave himself up for her to make her holy, cleansing her by the washing with water through the word, and to present her to himself as a radiant church, without stain or wrinkle or any other blemish, but holy and blameless. In this same way, husbands ought to love their wives as their own bodies. He who loves his wife loves himself. After all, no one ever hated his own body, but he feeds and cares for it, just as Christ does the church-for we are members of his body. 'For this reason a man will leave his father and mother and be united to his wife, and the two will become one flesh.' This is a profound mystery-but I am talking about Christ and the church" (Ephesians 5:25-32).

In acting out our love for our spouses, we demonstrate what the real divine love relationship is like. Without that reality conjugal love would be impossible.

Single people do not miss out on this reality. They may not have the experience of the earthly expression of this heavenly reality, but the real thing can be as much theirs as everybody's who chooses God's love over anything else.

Psalm 91:9-16

"Because he loves me," says the LORD, "I will rescue him; I will protect him, for he acknowledges my name. He will call upon me, and I will answer him; I will be with him in trouble, I will deliver him and honor him."

"If you make the Most High your dwelling" speaks of an act of faith, of an initiative we take. God does not protect us against our will. Nor is our role in this merely passive. We are actively involved in this act of being protected. As a bride gives herself willingly and consciously into marriage, not passively letting herself be married, so we establish our position in God.

We are responsible for putting on our spiritual armor. It is up to us to practice truth, righteousness, readiness, and faith, to think clearly and to pray. Putting on the helmet of salvation means that we think in terms of salvation. Our brain needs to be protected. The thrust of Ephesians Chapter Six is not that we have to win certain battles but that we stand in the victory Jesus has won for us and that we maintain our position. This is all implied in the fact that we make the Most High our dwelling and our refuge. It is about His truth and righteousness, not about ours.

The result of such an act of surrender is absolute and overwhelming. There are no accidents. We no longer stumble; victory over the enemy is guaranteed. God guarantees angel protection to us. David says: "The angel of the LORD encamps around those who fear him, and he delivers them" (Psalm 34:7). How this must enrage the enemy that, although we are weak human beings, he cannot even come close enough to us to inflict lasting harm upon us! If, however, we withdraw from God's protection, we are defenseless. If God is our refuge, we "will tread upon the lion and the cobra; [we] will trample the great lion and the serpent." Paul says in Romans: "The God of peace will soon crush Satan under your feet" (Romans 16:20).

The most amazing part in God's promise of deliverance is that God will honor us. Jesus confirmed this when He said, "Whoever serves me must follow me; and where I am, my servant also will be. My Father will honor the one who serves me" (John 12:26). Serving Jesus Christ will elevate us above ourselves to the level where we become genuinely honorable. I cannot imagine this, but when I go the heaven, God will stand up from His throne and greet me. God knows me because I love Him.

Psalm 92:1-8

"How great are your works, O LORD, how profound your thoughts!"

This lovely Psalm is the only one in the book that was especially written for the Sabbath day. The Genesis account states: "By the seventh day God had finished the work he had been doing; so on the seventh day he rested from all his work. And God blessed the seventh day and made it holy, because on it he rested from all the work of creating that he had done" (Genesis 2:2,3). Before that statement we read: "God saw all that he had made, and it was very good" (Genesis 1:31). The Sabbath, therefore, was a celebration of beauty and an enjoyment of rest. It is the rest that God intends to share with us. The writer of Hebrews tells us that "the promise of entering his rest still stands" (Hebrews 4:1). And Jesus invites us "Come to me, all you who are weary and burdened, and I will give you rest" (Matthew 11:28).

The Sabbath originates in the time before man's fall into sin, but in the celebration of the day in Israel sin stamped its mark upon it. From a day of rest and celebration the Sabbath became a day on which man was forbidden to work on threat of death. The beauty of the Sabbath was broken by sin. As soon as Adam fell in sin, God began to work again. Jesus Himself broke the Sabbath, and in doing so He made the Sabbath for us a symbol of redemption from sin, a day of resurrection from the dead. He said about the Sabbath: "My Father is always at his work to this very day, and I, too, am working" (John 5:17).

There is still a lot of beauty to be seen in God's creation. God's blessings break through the curse at many points. But the overall picture is marred and spoiled. The apostle Paul states: "The creation waits in eager expectation for the sons of God to be revealed. For the creation was subjected to frustration, not by its own choice, but by the will of the one who subjected it, in hope that the creation itself will be liberated from its bondage to decay and brought into the glorious freedom of the children of God" (Romans 8:19-21). We can hasten the process by accepting Christ's invitation of rest and take His yoke upon our shoulders. He said: "Take my yoke upon you and learn from me, for I am gentle and humble in heart, and you will find rest for your souls. For my yoke is easy and my burden is light" (Matthew 11:29,30).

Psalm 92:9-15

"The righteous will flourish like a palm tree, they will grow like a cedar of Lebanon; planted in the house of the LORD, they will flourish in the courts of our God. They will still bear fruit in old age, they will stay fresh and green."

The Psalmist obviously mixes his metaphors as he compares the righteous to trees planted in the house of the LORD. Trees don't grow inside churches. Also palm trees and cedars are quite different species. The image suggests greatness like the beauty of a large piece of real estate surrounded by giants of the forest that increase the majesty of the property. The righteous are factors that enhance the glory of the house of the Lord. On the other hand, the presence of the Lord is the essence of our glory.

The place where the trees are planted suggests fellowship with God. The images describe what happens to a man who knows fellowship with God; there is life and growth. The words "flourish" and "grow" speak of the vitality of the fellowship. Growth also implies progress. Our relationship with God is never static; there is an increase of love and intimacy. Fruit bearing is also mentioned. Psalm One states that the righteous will "yield its fruit in season" (Psalm 1:3).

It seems that the Psalmist had senior citizens in mind when he wrote these words. He assures us that God wants us to keep on bearing fruit and to stay "fresh and green" as old age creeps up upon us.

Many people prepare for retirement by making financial arrangements. Few of us make spiritual preparations for our sunset years. As with all future planning, it pays to start early. We don't know what our physical or mental condition will be as we grow older, but we can tell God what we would like them to be. I have told the Lord that He may do with my body as He thinks good, but that I would like to remain mentally and spiritually alert till He calls me home. So far so good! We may ask the Lord that we produce a much-needed fruit of mature wisdom as our lives mature in fellowship with Him. Even if our mental capacity diminishes we can shine and proclaim God's uprightness. People who suffer from Alzheimer's disease can still light up at the mention of the Name of Jesus.

Let's start early and plan ahead!

Psalm 93

"The LORD reigns, he is robed in majesty; the LORD is robed in majesty and is armed with strength."

This Psalm celebrates God's omnipotence. It opens with the statement that God wears His majesty as a robe and it concludes by stating that His statutes stand firm. The actual meaning of the Hebrew word of "statutes" is "testimonies." The word is sometimes used in the Bible to identify the testimony of a witness.

This Psalm depicts God's majesty as He reigns supremely over a world that is in uproar. The pounding waves of the roaring ocean symbolize man's rebellion against God's reign.

It would be easy for an omnipotent God to crush our revolt in a display of overpowering glory, but the Bible reveals that this is not the way in which God establishes His kingdom. He does it by entering into the insurgence and conquering it from the inside out. God did this by becoming one of us. When God became a human being in Jesus Christ, He entered into the core of our resistance against Him by surrendering to us and allowing us to reject and kill Him. The apostle Paul describes this with the words: "[Jesus] being in very nature God, did not consider equality with God something to be grasped, but made himself nothing, taking the very nature of a servant, being made in human likeness. And being found in appearance as a man, he humbled himself and became obedient to death- even death on a cross!" (Philippians 2:6-8).

God laid aside His robe of glory when Jesus died naked on the cross. In the resurrection of Christ, He took it up again and He told us to give our testimony as a witness to the fact, saying: "All authority in heaven and on earth has been given to me. Therefore go and make disciples of all nations, baptizing them in the name of the Father and of the Son and of the Holy Spirit, and teaching them to obey everything I have commanded you. And surely I am with you always, to the very end of the age" (Matthew 28:18-20).

God is mightier than the breakers of the sea. Jesus' death on the cross seemed to be an utter defeat and the ultimate victory of evil over good. We ought not to let the roaring of the sea make us believe that our testimony will not be heard. Even the softest whisper of God's truth will speak louder than any shouts of evil. The weakest light is always stronger than the thickest darkness.

Psalm 94:1-7

"O LORD, the God who avenges, O God who avenges, shine forth. Rise up, O Judge of the earth; pay back to the proud what they deserve."

We are taught that it is wrong for us to take revenge when we are wronged. We tend to draw the wrong conclusion from this that revenge in itself is wrong. But God is called the "God of vengeance." It is wrong for us to revenge ourselves because revenge is God's prerogative.

God is called "God of vengeance" because He is the source and measure of all justice. Justice without punishment of sin would be a farce. God's vengeance is the exercise of His office as judge of the whole earth. His vengeance is one of the elements of His glory. This is implied in the words "shine forth."

There are things that belong exclusively to God. It will be our undoing if we take that which belongs solely to God and use it for ourselves. For instance, God says emphatically: "I will not give my glory to another," and "I will not yield my glory to another." (Isaiah 42:8; 48:11). Similarly, He does not allow us to take revenge upon a fellow human being.

Our problem is that God seems to be so slow in setting things right. From our perspective, what doesn't get done today is done too late. Living within the framework of time, we cannot imagine what our world looks like from God's viewpoint in eternity. This gives rise to the question how God can allow certain things to go on. We may as well begin to question God's love as well as His righteousness!

God told Abraham: "Know for certain that your descendants will be strangers in a country not their own, and they will be enslaved and mistreated four hundred years. But I will punish the nation they serve as slaves, and afterward they will come out with great possessions. You, however, will go to your fathers in peace and be buried at a good old age. In the fourth generation your descendants will come back here, for the sin of the Amorites has not yet reached its full measure" (Genesis 15:13-16). Who can afford to wait four hundred years for God to act!

The fact that God's Name is "God, LORD of vengeance" ought to give us enough assurance that evil will be punished and things will be put right. We will live to see it since we will share eternity with Him.

Psalm 94:8-23

"Blessed is the man you discipline, O LORD, the man you teach from your law."

We all have an inborn tendency to stray away from God. Even if we have decided to follow Jesus and to subject our will to His, there is always a pull to the side, an aberration from the path to follow. This is one of the reasons God allows difficulties in our lives. The Psalmist uses a Hebrew word translated "discipline" which means "to chastise," either as a corporal punishment or with words. We are not told what form this chastising takes here but it is sufficient to know that in disciplining us God is treating us as sons. The writer of Hebrews states: "Endure hardship as discipline; God is treating you as sons. For what son is not disciplined by his father? If you are not disciplined (and everyone undergoes discipline), then you are illegitimate children and not true sons. Moreover, we have all had human fathers who disciplined us and we respected them for it. How much more should we submit to the Father of our spirits and live! Our fathers disciplined us for a little while as they thought best; but God disciplines us for our good, that we may share in his holiness. No discipline seems pleasant at the time, but painful. Later on, however, it produces a harvest of righteousness and peace for those who have been trained by it" (Hebrews 12:7-11).

Chastisement implies healing. In this Psalm, chastisement is used in a beatitude: "Blessed is the man you discipline, O LORD, the man you teach from your law." This kind of thinking means a reversal of our value system. James follows the same line of thought when he writes: "Consider it pure joy, my brothers, whenever you face trials of many kinds..." (James 1:2). God's chastisement keeps us from God's wrath. When God chastises us it means that He thinks it worth the effort to discipline us. As the writer of Hebrews points out, God wants us to share in His holiness. And "without holiness no one will see the Lord!" (Hebrews 12:14).

God's discipline cannot be separated from the study of His Word. God disciplines, or *disciples* us in teaching us His law, which is an expression of His will and character. In a sense we discipline ourselves by constantly comparing ourselves with God's character. In comparing ourselves as bearers of the image of God with the original, we become aware of our deviations. It is this realization and subsequent confession of sin that makes us realize who we are before God. This confession will lead us into the rest of fellowship with the Father. In the words of the Epistle to the Hebrews: "Anyone who enters God's rest also rests from his own work, just as God did from his" (Hebrews 4:10).

Psalm 95:1-7[a]

"Come, let us bow down in worship, let us kneel before the LORD our Maker; for he is our God and we are the people of his pasture, the flock under his care."

The invitation "Come, let us…" suggests that we are not at the place where we ought to be. We should be kneeling before the Lord, our Creator, and we obviously aren't. We should recognize that He is our shepherd, but we don't.

Praising God does not come naturally to us; we need exhortation. Even if we have received forgiveness we do not easily come to the point of spontaneous adoration.

We cannot really worship God without understanding who He is and what He has done for us.

He is, first of all, the Creator of heaven and earth. He made the highest mountain peaks and the deepest depths of the oceans. People have climbed Mount Everest but no one has gone down deep enough to explore the lowest ocean floor.

Somewhere between those two extremities we live as human beings like sheep grazing in a pasture.

The comparison with sheep is not very flattering to our human dignity. Sheep are known for their ability to go astray and without the oversight and care of a shepherd they do not fare well. This makes the resemblance between us and them embarrassingly appropriate. The difference between us and them is that we can know our shortcomings but sheep do not. Living between the limits of the highest height and the deepest depth we can be lost. But it is there that God pledges His love and care for us and provides us with salvation. If we understand who we are and where we are, we ought to come before our Creator and fall on our knees with thanksgiving and worship. Those who don't do this show by their behavior that they have no idea who and where they are. The comparison with sheep becomes for them the more appropriate and embarrassing.

Praise and worship make us more human and they enhance our dignity. God does not improve with our worship, we do!

Psalm 95:7^b-11

"Today, if you hear his voice, do not harden your hearts…"

We not have only the freedom to come or not to come to worship God, but also the doubtful privilege to harden our hearts. It is not merely a matter of praising and thanking God, or not to do so. If we do not recognize God as our Creator and our Savior, we miss what life on earth is all about and we live our life in vain.

The people of Israel had arrived at the border of the Promised Land. They had sent spies into the land and decided on the basis of their negative report that entering and conquering what God had promised to them was too hazardous to consider. They preferred returning to slavery and going back to Egypt. The question whether Egypt would take them back was never contemplated. They ended up wandering through the desert for the remainder of forty years till all the men who refused to enter Canaan had died.

It was at that point that they incurred the wrath of God at a place called *Massah and Meribah*, "proving and strife."

Twice they said that they would have been better off if they had remained in Egypt, or if they had all died in the desert (Numbers 14:1-4; 20:2-5).

God told them that entering the Promised Land was no longer an option.

If we resist God's grace by not recognizing who He is and what He has done for us, our life will fizzle out. God created us to enjoy eternity with Him. By hardening our hearts we will defeat God's goal and at the end it will prove that we have lived in vain. Gratitude toward God is more than an expression of appreciation; it is the essence of fulfillment in life.

The Psalmist wrote this Psalm after Israel had lived in the Promised Land for centuries. He reminded them of their history and the failure of their ancestors. And he gave them the warning: "Today, if you hear his voice, do not harden your hearts as you did at Meribah." The people he addressed were not the ones who were at Meribah; they had entered the land and conquered it. But obviously, living at the place of God's rest they had not entered into His rest. We can live where God wants us to live and not be what He wants us to be. Peace of mind, rest of the soul is not a matter of circumstances but of the condition of our heart. A restless heart is a heart that is hardening itself against hearing the voice of God. We ought to learn at least that much from history.

Psalm 96:1-6

"Sing to the LORD a new song; sing to the LORD, all the earth."

A new song, sung twice, is no longer new. How can we sing a new song to God without repeating ourselves? Evidently, "new" in this context does not mean that it has never been done before but that what has been done acquires a new meaning. If praise to God becomes *déjà vu*, or boring, there is something basically wrong with our perception of reality. The writer of Ecclesiastes had this problem when he stated: "Meaningless! Meaningless! ... Utterly meaningless! Everything is meaningless. Is there anything of which one can say, 'Look! This is something new'? It was here already, long ago; it was here before our time" (Ecclesiastes 1:2, 10).

The new song in the Bible is always connected to the experience of salvation. The apostle Paul states: "If anyone is in Christ, he is a new creation; the old has gone, the new has come!" (II Corinthians 5:17). Only those who have been made new can sing new songs to God. About the redeemed who are sealed by the Holy Spirit, we read in Revelation: "And they sang a new song before the throne and before the four living creatures and the elders. No one could learn the song except the 144,000 who had been redeemed from the earth." (Revelation 14:3). It is our redemption that makes new our singing.

We can categorize life as follows: Sin is old (no one ever invents new sins); salvation is new! Death is old; resurrection from the dead is new! If we want to be original and do something that has never been done before, we must stay away from sin and death. Holiness and eternal life are not old and dull; they provide the newness and meaning the writer of Ecclesiastes was trying to find so desperately.

We can even experience this newness when everything around us falls apart. Looking at the ruins of the temple and the burned out remains of what was once the holy city of Jerusalem, the prophet Jeremiah exclaimed: "Because of the LORD's great love we are not consumed, for his compassions never fail. They are new every morning; great is your faithfulness" (Lamentations 3:22, 23).

We can sing something new every day to God, because we will experience His faithfulness as something new every morning. The eternal God is new to us every day.

Psalm 96:7-13

"Say among the nations, 'The LORD reigns.' The world is firmly established, it cannot be moved; he will judge the peoples with equity."

The wide scope of this Psalm catches our attention. The whole earth is involved. In Jesus' words: "The field is the world" (Matthew 13:38). This Psalm gives us a powerful stimulus to world evangelism.

Sin has limited our horizon and has steeped us in a "village" mentality. The builders of the tower of Babel did not want to be scattered over the face of the whole earth. We read in the Genesis account: "Now the whole world had one language and a common speech. As men moved eastward, they found a plain in Shinar and settled there. They said to each other, 'Come, let's make bricks and bake them thoroughly.' They used brick instead of stone, and tar for mortar. Then they said, 'Come, let us build ourselves a city, with a tower that reaches to the heavens, so that we may make a name for ourselves and not be scattered over the face of the whole earth'" (Genesis 11:1-4).

The Holy Spirit opens our eyes for the fields that surround us and gives us a realistic vision. When our eyes are opened and we begin to see who God is, we will also know what our task on earth involves.

The people in Babel had turned things around. They wanted to build a tower that reached to the heavens because they did not realize that God would come down to earth. We read, however, "but the LORD came down to see the city and the tower that the men were building" (Genesis 11:5).

We have a message to people all over the world who are trying to climb up to God and reach heaven, that heaven came down to earth when God became one of us in order to save us. Jesus Christ came, first of all, as the Savior of the world. He will be coming again as judge.

The apostle Paul traveled to Athens to tell the philosophers that God "has set a day when he will judge the world with justice by the man he has appointed. He has given proof of this to all men by raising him from the dead" (Acts 17:31). This link between Jesus' victory over sin and death and His coming as judge is the core of the message people need to hear. If we keep silent, the stones will cry out against us.

Psalm 97:1-9

"The LORD reigns, let the earth be glad; let the distant shores rejoice."

In the previous Psalm, the return of the Lord is seen as the homecoming of the beloved master; here the emphasis is more upon the triumphant entry of a victorious hero.

The Lord's coming to judge the earth means the end of all unrighteousness. This great event is also sung about in the opening verses of Revelation: "Look, he is coming with the clouds, and every eye will see him, even those who pierced him; and all the peoples of the earth will mourn because of him. So shall it be! Amen" (Revelation 1:7).

The resistance against God's rule melts away as wax in the sun. Human unrighteousness is the result of that which forms the core of secular life: idolatry, in whatever form it is demonstrated. Only the person who loves God will be able to display righteousness and justice in his life. Serving God implies surrender of self. The motive for idolatry is self-preservation. We think, deep in our hearts, that we will be able to manipulate the gods we serve. We live under the illusion that we serve ourselves, but often too late we discover that behind our idol hides a dark power that is out to exterminate us. It is not true that we have three options to choose from: God, the devil, or self. Choices are limited to the first two, whether we like it or not.

Our reaction to the announcement of Jesus' return depends on our attitude toward Him. To those who are performing their deeds in the dark, "clouds and thick darkness surround Him" because "righteousness and justice are the foundation of His throne." The Bible states: "God is light; in him there is no darkness at all" (I John 1:5). But God is only light for those who live in His light. If we live self-centered and self-serving lives, the Second Coming will not be a joy to be anticipated. Only those who love Jesus will be able to say: "Amen. Come, Lord Jesus" (Revelation 22:20).

Psalm 97:10-12

"Let those who love the LORD hate evil, for he guards the lives of his faithful ones and delivers them from the hand of the wicked."

The essence of our relationship with God is love. This love is the response of our entire being to God's love for us. The apostle John writes: "We love because he first loved us" (I John 4:19).

Our love for God does not bring about an automatic protection against temptations. We have to consciously take a stand against evil. No perfect love for God is possible without an absolute hatred for all that is not in accordance with God's holiness. We cannot say a strong "Yes" without also saying a strong "No!"

It is painful to realize that we need this kind of admonition. We tend to compromise. Our natural tendency is soften the consequences of our choice for God. We may think that Jesus is unreasonable and inflexible when He says: "If anyone comes to me and does not hate his father and mother, his wife and children, his brothers and sisters — yes, even his own life — he cannot be my disciple" (Luke 14:26). We want to soften the blow by thinking that Jesus speaks comparatively about love and hate. But the Lord's demands are extremely radical to the point of scaring us off. He says, "If your right eye causes you to sin, gouge it out and throw it away. It is better for you to lose one part of your body than for your whole body to be thrown into hell. And if your right hand causes you to sin, cut it off and throw it away. It is better for you to lose one part of your body than for your whole body to go into hell" (Matthew 5:29,30). This means amputation of that which hinders our total fellowship with God. A person who consents to have his leg amputated will only do so when he hates the cancer that threatens his life.

We need God's protection against ourselves and we will only ask for this if we hate the evil within us sufficiently. This protection is also a guarantee against the power of the enemy. We know that our fellowmen can kill us or can make life bitter for us. Our Lord Jesus Himself was not spared, and there is no promise that we will be spared suffering. But the almighty God puts Himself as a surety for our soul. Men and demons can only incur temporary damage to our lives; our eternal salvation is guaranteed.

Psalm 98

"Let the sea resound, and everything in it, the world, and all who live in it. Let the rivers clap their hands, let the mountains sing together for joy; let them sing before the LORD, for he comes to judge the earth. He will judge the world in righteousness and the peoples with equity."

This Psalm gives us three reasons to praise God. There are three Hebrew words that express what God has done for us, which are translated in our Bible as "marvelous things" and "salvation." Actually the translation "salvation" stands for two different words, one meaning "victory" and the other "salvation." Unfortunately, "salvation" is not the only word that lost something of its original flavor in the translation. In Hebrew, "victory" is linked to salvation and "salvation" is the translation of the word *yeshuw`ah*, which is the proper name for Jesus.

God has done "marvelous things" or supernatural things in order to save us. He invaded the laws of nature and overruled them in impregnating the virgin Mary and causing the Word to become flesh.

He saved us by overcoming death and the power of death in the resurrection of our Lord Jesus Christ.

And He provided us with salvation to the uttermost in giving us a High Priest who intercedes for us in heaven. The writer of the Hebrew Epistle states: "[Jesus] is able to save completely those who come to God through him, because he always lives to intercede for them" (Hebrews 7:25).

We have only a limited understanding of the damage sin caused in the world. There are things we consider to be natural which are in direct opposition to God's original intent with creation. Sickness and death are unnatural, and yet we have to admit that there are laws of nature involved when a human body decomposes at death. When Jesus, by the power of the Holy Spirit, healed people, and raised some from the dead, and rose from the dead Himself, nothing supernatural happened; He merely rehabilitated the laws of nature that God intended to be originally. Yet, these are miracles, because when God performs miracles, He makes that which had become sub-natural natural again. That which is sick becomes healthy, and that which was dead comes alive, justice replaces injustice. God performs such miracles all the time.

We have also little understanding about the effect our salvation has upon creation as a whole. The apostle Paul writes: "The creation itself will be liberated from its bondage to decay and brought into the glorious freedom of the children of God" (Romans 8:21). That is why the sea roars and the rivers clap their hands in celebration of the Gospel. We must follow suit!

Psalm 99

"Exalt the LORD our God and worship at his holy mountain, for the LORD our God is holy."

This Psalm continues the theme of God's reign which runs like a thread of gold through this series of Psalms (96-100). Each Psalm highlights a different aspect of God's reign. In Psalm 96 the accent is upon the worldwide extent of the kingdom. In Psalm 97 the difference between God and the idols is accentuated. Psalm 98 celebrates God's reign in tones of pure jubilance, and in this Psalm God's holiness is emphasized.

The word "holy" is repeated three times in this Psalm. We find this three-fold repetition several times in the Bible. The cherubs in Isaiah's vision sing: "Holy, holy, holy is the LORD Almighty; the whole earth is full of his glory" (Isaiah 6:3). And the four living creatures before the throne of God cry out continuously: "Holy, holy, holy is the Lord God Almighty, who was, and is, and is to come" (Revelation 4:8).

The concept "holy" is a great mystery to us. It draws us to God in a way that surpasses our comprehension. We can relate to most of God's attributes because we find traces of them in our own being. Knowledge, power, and love, for instance, are characteristics we can understand, although we cannot imagine what it means that God possesses those in an eternal and infinite measure. But holiness overwhelms and perplexes us. We can grasp intuitively that God's holiness represents all that we are not. It is God's holiness that makes us understand that God is infinitely more than we are. God is not merely like us only greater and better; God is holy and we are not. Holiness is more than the sum of God's attributes; it is the essence of His being. God can add to the knowledge we already possess, and He can increase the love that is already there, but when He makes us share in His holiness (which is what He does), He imparts something to us that was not there before: He gives us Himself.

The theme of the Book of Leviticus is "Be holy for I am holy" (Leviticus 11:44). This indicates not only that God's holiness is meant for us but also that holiness must be expressed in our moral conduct. The fact that we seldom take this seriously causes us to stand before God with fear and trembling. The most frightening verse in the Bible is Revelation 20:11 where the Apostle John says: "Then I saw a great white throne and him who was seated on it. Earth and sky fled from his presence, and there was no place for them." If we have never trembled before God in this manner, we do not live in a real world.

Psalm 100

"Know that the LORD is God. It is he who made us, and we are his; we are his people, the sheep of his pasture."

In this Psalm, our relationship with God is reduced to its most elementary factors. He is our Creator and we are His creatures.

This fact requires of us a threefold response: Shout, worship, and come! In Hebrew the words are more expressive than in English. "Shout" is the translation of a Hebrew word that means, "to split the ears." The Hebrew word translated "worship" can also be rendered "to become a slave." Shouting and serving as a slave are used as parallel expressions in this Psalm. This means that our praise is not to be a senseless ecstasy but a practical form of joyful obedience to the will of God. God has created us so that we would obey Him with great joy. Joy is a byproduct of obedience. Our word "worship-service" would be a good way to emphasize this double aspect of our relationship with God.

This kind of fellowship is also expressed in the phrase "Come before him with joyful songs." Obedience and fellowship go together as much as do obedience and joy. When Jesus chose His disciples, we read that His primary consideration was "that they might be with Him." Mark's Gospel reports: "He appointed twelve-designating them apostles-that they might be with him and that he might send them out to preach" (Mark 3:14). This aspect will also be the culmination of all our spiritual experiences; as we read in Revelation: "His servants will serve him. They will see his face, and his name will be on their foreheads" (Revelation 22:3,4).

This Psalm demands a two-fold acknowledgment from us in that it uses the two names for God: Yahweh (or Jehovah) and Elohim. Elohim is the Creator and Jehovah is the Redeemer of His people. Acknowledgment of God as our Creator implies that He has a right to our lives and also that we believe He is willing to take the responsibility for our lives if we entrust ourselves to Him.

In our experience, acknowledgment usually precedes shouting for joy. Joy is an emotional reaction; acknowledgment is the result of a rational process. Our intelligence has to be a guide to our emotions, especially in spiritual things. In the practice of daily life, however, this is often turned around. We are more easily convinced by our feelings than by our understanding of the truth.

This Psalm is particularly a celebration of God's goodness. For us, sinful human beings, God's goodness is just as incomprehensible as His love and His holiness. Only when we receive forgiveness of our sins do we understand what it means that God is good.

Psalm 101

"I will be careful to lead a blameless life--when will you come to me?"

If, as some Bible scholars believe, David wrote this Psalm when he became king of Israel, it describes what the life ought to be of a person who holds a public office. We could extend this by saying that, as Christians, we are all in the public eye and our lifestyle and actions are a testimony to unbelievers. What we do and are becomes the criterion by which people will judge the Gospel.

Mahatma Gandhi, the man who led India in its efforts to shake of British colonial rule, is reported to have said that he would have considered the claims of Christianity if it hadn't been for the lives of people who professed to be Christians.

If our profession of faith does not translate itself into acts of love and righteousness, we become a hindrance to the salvation of others.

We read about Daniel, who was a minister at the Persian court, that his colleagues, "the administrators and the satraps tried to find grounds for charges against Daniel in his conduct of government affairs, but they were unable to do so. They could find no corruption in him, because he was trustworthy and neither corrupt nor negligent" (Daniel 6:4).

Holiness begins at home. "No king is great to his own valet." At the place where we can let our hair down and be ourselves, it turns out that there is something wrong with "self." Corruption and dishonesty begin at home. If the Lord doesn't transform us inside out, our situation is hopeless before we begin. It stinks in our closet. We need a miracle to become "to God the aroma of Christ" (II Corinthians 5:15).

But even after this miracle in our life has taken place, we have to walk cautiously. The devil will whisper unworthy thoughts in our ears and project dirty images on the screen of our mind. Job said: "I made a covenant with my eyes not to look lustfully at a girl" (Job 31:1). Job was, obviously, not immune to sexual temptations. As Christian we must decide that we will only look at those things God wants us to see. We must subject our eyes and our thoughts to the censorship of the Holy Spirit. In Paul's words, "We take captive every thought to make it obedient to Christ" (II Corinthians 10:5). Either we do what David said he did: "I have set the LORD always before me. Because he is at my right hand, I will not be shaken" (Psalm 16:8) or we give Satan a free reign in our lives. The ripple effect of our fellowship with God will reach far beyond the boundaries of our own life.

Psalm 102:1-11

"Hear my prayer, O LORD; let my cry for help come to you. Do not hide your face from me when I am in distress. Turn your ear to me; when I call, answer me quickly."

The Psalmist was obviously sick and at the end of his rope. He saw no help on the horizontal level and, therefore, he turned to the Lord. Turning to God in times of distress is good; it often makes such moments the best in one's life. Writing about the blitz of London, one of the darkest moments during World War II, Winston Churchill called his book *Their Finest Hour.* Although we may not realize this as we are passing through times of crises, we often see in retrospect that it was at such moments that we were closer to the Lord than ever before.

Why is it that sickness often weakens our sense of God's presence? When our bones ache, we feel as if God hides His face from us. We measure the sense of God's presence with the yardstick of our fitness and the amount of energy we feel we have. But faith must be based upon the objective fact of God's omnipresence and not upon our subjective feelings. The Biblical principle is that God's "power is made perfect in weakness" (II Corinthians 12:9).

There is no need for us to delve into the various symptoms of this Psalmist's sickness. We may substitute our own aches and pains for his. Some of us may be able to identify more with this poet than others. Pain is at times also more intense than at other moments. When we enjoy good health and feel fit, we must be careful to thank the Lord for it. If good health hinders us from drawing close to the Lord, we are not as blessed as we may think we are.

On the other hand, pain should not separate us from God either. Our pain will often be relieved considerably when we compare it to the suffering of Jesus on our behalf. Carrying away the sin of the world, including my sin, He suffered excruciating pain against which mine retains little weight. "For we do not have a high priest who is unable to sympathize with our weaknesses, but we have one who has been tempted in every way, just as we are-yet was without sin" (Hebrews 4:15). In that sense also "He took up our infirmities and carried our sorrows" (Isaiah 53:4).

If pain draws us into fellowship with Jesus Christ, we must do more than endure it; we must thank Him for it. God can make our deepest points our "Finest Hour."

Psalm 102:12-24

"The LORD looked down from his sanctuary on high, from heaven he viewed the earth, to hear the groans of the prisoners and release those condemned to death."

Some Bible scholars believe that this Psalm was written during Israel's captivity in Babylon and that the picture of the sick man is actually an image of the condition of a whole nation. Whether this is so, we don't know. What is obvious, though, is that God has compassion on those who are suffering whether individuals or nations.

When circumstances weigh down upon us, we sometimes tend to conclude that God is oblivious to our plight. Since we cannot see God, we may think that He does not really care. Yet, the Bible speaks clearly about God's compassion. David states: "As a father has compassion on his children, so the LORD has compassion on those who fear him; for he knows how we are formed, he remembers that we are dust" (Psalm 103:13,14). And in the Gospels we read: "When [Jesus] saw the crowds, he had compassion on them, because they were harassed and helpless, like sheep without a shepherd" (Matthew 9:36).

In one of C. S. Lewis' book in series *The Chronicles of Narnia*, the boy Eustace meets the lion Aslan, who is the type of Christ. Eustace's mother is sick and dying in England and he asks the lion for help. Looking up at the lion's face, he sees that Aslan has big tears in his eyes, actually bigger than his own. However incomprehensible this may seem to us, our suffering hits God harder than it does us.

To Moses God said: "I have indeed seen the misery of my people in Egypt. I have heard them crying out because of their slave drivers, and I am concerned about their suffering. So I have come down to rescue them from the hand of the Egyptians" (Exodus 3:7,8). We must not underestimate God's love for us and His compassion for our need.

As the word "com-passion" implies, God actually suffers with us and for us. He has identified Himself with our pain and our death. In doing so, He gained the victory and prepared for us the place where there is "no more death or mourning or crying or pain" (Revelation 21:4).

Psalm 102:25-28

"You remain the same, and your years will never end. The children of your servants will live in your presence; their descendants will be established before you."

The Psalmist must have been a young man, since he asked God, 'Do not take me away, O my God, in the midst of my days." As he faced premature death, he looked to God and asked Him to share with him some of His eternity. He felt that it might be natural for old people to pass away but that to die in youth was abnormal and could not be God's will for His creatures. He said, "Here I am dying as a young person, but your years go on through all generations."

The comparison is audacious to say the least. But in a way, this Psalmist was right in his assumption that young people ought not to die. He could have said that human beings ought not to die, period! God did not create us for death but for life. That makes death so frightful and repulsive for us. If sin had not entered God's beautiful creation, we would all still be in the Garden of Eden, enjoying the presence of the Lord together with Adam and Eve. Death is abnormal. It is even more so when we compare it to God's eternity.

Jesus explained to the people who did not believe in the resurrection that God treats death as abnormal and even as non-existent. He said to the Sadducees: "Have you not read what God said to you, 'I am the God of Abraham, the God of Isaac, and the God of Jacob'? He is not the God of the dead but of the living" (Matthew 22:31,32).

This whole planet will eventually fade into oblivion, as will our whole solar system. God will treat them as we treat a change of clothes. He will disregard creation as we throw away the worn clothing.

We may, therefore, compare our short lives to God's eternity and glory in the fact that He will share His eternity with us. In the words of the apostle John: "The world and its desires pass away, but the man who does the will of God lives forever" (I John 2:17). So, let's do the will of God!

Psalm 103:1-5

"Praise the LORD, O my soul; all my inmost being, praise his holy name. Praise the LORD, O my soul, and forget not all his benefits..."

This Psalm is more a song of forgiveness, healing, and renewal than a song of praise. Praise never comes naturally for us. Although the ultimate purpose of creation is that God would be praised, we as human beings have to push ourselves into doing so. Even in the lives of the best Christians, praise is rarely abundant. This is the reason David exhorts himself to praise. "Praise the LORD, O my soul" is more a wake-up call to reality than an actual act of worship. In this respect this Psalm differs from the following ones.

This difference shows implicitly how much damage sin has caused. We have to call ourselves back from a world of unreality to a conscious reality in which we can see who God is. Our actual acts of praise are usually preceded by a mobilization of our senses, of our mind, and of our sense of reality.

David addresses himself more than God in this Psalm. All this proves man's dichotomy as a result of sin. We harbor more than one nature in ourselves. There is no real inner harmony within us. We have become strangers to ourselves because of sin. One part of us wants to worship God and another part puts up resistance. Real worship, therefore, is usually preceded by an inner victory over self. Without the help of the Holy Spirit we would never be able to praise God.

David calls upon his soul and upon his memory to praise the Lord. One commentary renders Verse One, "Bless Yahweh, I tell myself."

Our memory is one of the most extraordinary and complex gifts God has given to us. It may cause trouble, as we grow older. An elderly lady we knew called her memory "the thing I forget with." We can manipulate our memory, especially when certain events are too painful to remember. We can also forget certain things because we want to forget.

David mentions in the list of "benefits" that flow from his relationship with God: forgiveness, healing, redemption from death, experience of God's love, and satisfaction. Some people prefer to accept the "benefits" without expressing gratitude to God for fear that it would cramp their lifestyle. They may be in danger of losing all.

If we are realists, we thank God for our salvation and all it entails and live a life that is worthy of our calling.

Psalm 103:1-5

"Praise the LORD ... who satisfies your desires with good things so that your youth is renewed like the eagle's."

David is careful not to say that God satisfies all our desires. Some of the things we desire are bad for us. As a matter of fact, we rarely know what is good for us. Many people for instance would like to be rich. *Who wants to be a millionaire?* is the title of a TV talk show. Yet for some people the worst that could happen to them spiritually would to become rich. The nineteenth century Scottish writer George MacDonald once asked: "Do you believe that God can punish someone by making him rich?" Most of us believe we could stand a lot of punishment along that line. God satisfies our desires as long as they are the right desires. That may be something we ought to work on.

The result of this satisfaction, David states, is a renewal of our youth "like the eagle's." The eagle as a majestic and powerful bird has always spoken to man's imagination. An observation as to how the eagle deals with its young provides a valuable spiritual lesson. The eagle, first of all, stirs up its nest and throws out its young. The first part of the flying lesson is that the young birds learn to fall. It is the fear of falling that makes them spread their wings. Their fluttering does not resemble flying yet, but it is the first step. Without the fear of falling there is no security of being carried on the pinions of the mother bird.

God's Spirit does not keep fear from our doorstep; He allows it, He introduces it to force us to depend on Him for our security. God does not protect us from the storms of life without letting us experience those storms. His presence does not guarantee clear skies but it gives us the assurance that we will not perish in the storm. Our nests will be stirred up. God Himself will see to that. How else would we learn to fly?

The renewal of the eagle's youth is another object lesson worthy of note. The eagle renews its youth by molting. It sheds its feathers and then grows new feathers, like a tree that sheds its leaves in the fall to bloom again in spring. God's satisfying of our desires results in a complete makeover of our old nature and disposition. As Paul writes: "You were taught, with regard to your former way of life, to put off your old self, which is being corrupted by its deceitful desires; to be made new in the attitude of your minds; and to put on the new self, created to be like God in true righteousness and holiness" (Ephesians 4:22-24).

Psalm 103:6-18

"As a father has compassion on his children, so the LORD has compassion on those who fear him."

David uses two measurements for the love of God. One is the distance from the earth to heaven; the other is the distance from east to west. Both are immeasurable. How far is heaven from earth? If we imagine that the location of heaven is beyond the existing galaxies, we speak in terms of trillions of light years, a distance that is incalculable. If David had used north and south as reference points on earth, he would have given us the measurable distance between the two poles of our globe. But the distance between east and west is infinite and immeasurable.

God's love is expressed in the crossing of an infinite vertical and an infinite horizontal line and the two lines cross on earth. The Holy Spirit uses David's word to paint a picture of a cross. And at the point where the two lines cross, we read the statement, "As a father has compassion on his children, so the LORD has compassion on those who fear him." God's infinite, immeasurable love for us is expressed in this drawing of the cross. In the words of the apostle Paul: "God demonstrates his own love for us in this: While we were still sinners, Christ died for us" (Romans 5: 8).

All this is said in the context of our struggle with sin and guilt feelings. David speaks of God's right to accuse us and to be angry with us, of treating us as our sins deserve and repaying us according to our iniquities. We have all reason to feel guilty, but God answers us by showing us what He has done for us in the death of His Son on the cross.

The comparison with a flower that blooms and then withers away adds to our feeling of guilt a sense of insecurity and futility. God's love for us in Jesus Christ answers to our mortality also. God's compassion that forgives our sins also opens for us the gates of eternity.

And even after we pass away from this world as a flower in the field, God's love will remain with us "from generation to generation," with our children and grandchildren.

Maybe this realization will take us a step closer to praising the Lord as we ought to.

Psalm 103:19-22

"The LORD has established his throne in heaven, and his kingdom rules over all."

In these last verses the Psalmist opens all the stops. Heaven and earth join together in a magnificent, multi-voiced choir which culminates in one single voice that sings the same words as in the opening verse of the Psalm: "Praise the LORD, O my soul."

David sees God enthroned upon the throne of the universe. How much more glorious is this vision than all the personal experiences which he mentioned before! Forgiveness and healing on a personal level are, of course, important and the redemption of Israel from Egypt's slavery was a great event. But what is all of this in comparison with the vision of the apostle John, who testified: "Before me was a throne in heaven with someone sitting on it. And the one who sat there had the appearance of jasper and carnelian. A rainbow, resembling an emerald, encircled the throne" (Revelation 4:2,3). Everything else stands in the shadow of this vision, and everything owes its meaning to this. God reigns over all. That is the basis and content of all praise, also for us who live, in the words of C. S. Lewis, on *"A Silent Planet."* This Psalm is a call to break the silence and to blend our voices with the shouts of joy that fill the universe.

We live in a world that lies under the rule of the Evil One. The enemy tries to forbid us to praise God. David's Psalm is a shout of rebellion against the rule of darkness. David reaches out to the redemption that is coming.

It seems strange and preposterous to us that a puny human would address angels in heaven--those mighty ones, God's servants--and tell them to praise God. Who does David think he is? If David has to exhort himself in order to praise God, why bother with the angels?

But this Psalm shows an ascending line of praise. Angels are already involved in the business of praise in heaven. But, evidently, heavenly praise will not be complete without the "Vox Humana," the human voice. God's plan for us will only be complete when we join the choir.

Psalm 104:1-13

"O LORD my God, you are very great; you are clothed with splendor and majesty. He wraps himself in light as with a garment; he stretches out the heavens like a tent."

In this Psalm, the Psalmist begins to worship and adore; this is not a mobilization of the soul to prepare it for praise. But his intimacy with God is not yet perfect. He tries to imagine God, which is not the same thing as entering into the sanctuary and meeting God face to face.

The images he uses are all borrowed from human experience. He pictures God as getting dressed. God's glory is an inner glory. He doesn't have to clothe Himself with splendor and majesty; He is splendor and majesty. The essence of God's glory becomes evident in Jesus' transfiguration. We read in Mark's Gospel: "After six days Jesus took Peter, James and John with him and led them up a high mountain, where they were all alone. There he was transfigured before them. His clothes became dazzling white, whiter than anyone in the world could bleach them" (Mark 9:2,3). Jesus' inner glory broke out through His clothing.

We can associate splendor and majesty with clothing but not with light. To us, light is not a covering. "God is light; in him there is no darkness at all" (I John 1:5). We hardly understand what physical light is. This makes the existence of spiritual light an even greater mystery for us. Yet, we experience light as pleasant. We realize that light is of vital importance to our existence, both for our body as well as for our mind. David says: "For with you is the fountain of life; in your light we see light" (Psalm 36:9). And, as we saw from the quotation of John's First Epistle, the Psalmist contrasts God's light with the darkness of sin. This makes light an image of holiness and purity. This is why living in fellowship with God is called "walking in the light."

All images used in these verses are borrowed from the space below the stratosphere; they belong to the earth, not to heaven. The Psalmist is on earth, and he looks to God from an earthly perspective. His vision is limited to the blue sky and the clouds. This does in no way diminish God's greatness. The poet speaks about God in the greatest terms that are in man's vocabulary and he makes clear that God is greater than all he can say about Him. As the body is more than clothing so is God more than the light in which He wraps Himself and more than the clouds on which His chariot rides.

This God of light is the one we must worship and adore. We will be able to do so only if we wrap ourselves in His light and do not allow any darkness to block the view.

Psalm 104:14-23

"He makes grass grow for the cattle, and plants for man to cultivate--bringing forth food from the earth: wine that gladdens the heart of man, oil to make his face shine, and bread that sustains his heart."

In painting this beautiful picture of God's creation for us, the Psalmist follows almost literally the account of the first chapter of Genesis. We see the days of creation following each other, each bringing about a new phase in the development of the earth up to the creation of man. We find no reference to evil in this Psalm. This is not a picture of fallen nature as we know it now. This is the earth as God meant it to be.

This is not the ground of which God said to Adam: "Cursed is the ground because of you; through painful toil you will eat of it all the days of your life" (Genesis 3:17). The Psalmist puts the clock back to demonstrate that the earth we know is not the earth God had prepared for man. Corruption is not part of the original design. It is not what God created but what we made of it.

The moon comes up and the sun goes under, but the following darkness is God's darkness. The one who is called "the Prince of Darkness" is not even mentioned here. The inhabitants of this darkness are nocturnal creatures. Both day and night belong to God. The roaring of the lion is directed toward God. That which is hostile to us is not hostile to God. To us the irreconcilable differences in nature all find their solution in the fact that God created them and that they are all in His hand.

The provision of man's needs is expressed in terms of wine, oil, and bread. This clearly refers to more than the satisfaction of our physical needs; it pertains to the heart. "Wine that gladdens the heart of man...and bread that sustains his heart." Before Adam fell into sin, there was no distinction between the feeding of the body and the feeding of the soul. To live "by bread alone" was unknown. Jesus restored the harmony in the institution of the Lord's Supper. Since sin entered the world, we can eat and drink and remain inwardly empty. In the new creation, it will be possible to have an empty stomach and yet to be spiritually fulfilled. At present we have come to the point where eating and drinking are often considered unspiritual activities. This has never been God's intention.

In a way, this Psalm shows us what we have lost. It also draws our gaze to what is ahead of us. In the words of the apostle Peter: "We are looking forward to a new heaven and a new earth, the home of righteousness (II Peter 3:13).

Psalm 104:24-35

"These all look to you to give them their food at the proper time. When you give it to them, they gather it up; when you open your hand, they are satisfied with good things."

It is so easy for us to fall into the trap of believing that we are able to provide for our own needs. The fact that often we have to work hard for it tends to strengthen this misconception. For that reason it is good to remember this example of the animals. Jesus says in Matthew's Gospel: "Look at the birds of the air; they do not sow or reap or store away in barns, and yet your heavenly Father feeds them. Are you not much more valuable than they?" (Matthew 6:26). It sounds as if Jesus advocates a reckless insouciance. Obviously, the Lord does not want us to live irresponsibly, but He wants us to understand who the Father is who opens His hand to satisfy all of creation with good things.

These verses do not take into account the dichotomy of life. Satan will draw our attention to the fact that people perish in famines. We can turn around and ask him whose fault it is that death entered this world. This Psalm draws a picture of the original relationship between the Creator and creation. What Jesus meant was not that we should deny the hard realities of life, but that we can break through the impasse by faith. This faith is expressed in the words: "These all look to you to give them their food at the proper time."

The British preacher, John Stott, once remarked that Jesus' statement that the birds do not sow or reap or store away in barns does not imply that they don't have to make an effort to get their food. They must fly, seek, and scratch the soil, before being satisfied with good things. But effort and exertion by themselves are not sufficient. Solomon said: "Unless the LORD builds the house, its builders labor in vain. Unless the LORD watches over the city, the watchmen stand guard in vain" (Psalm 127:1).

What pertains to the satisfaction of our physical and material needs also extends to our soul and spirit. God takes responsibility for our complete satisfaction. He "satisfies your desires with good things so that your youth is renewed like the eagle's" (Psalm 103:5). But this doesn't mean that God spoon-feeds us. He provides the talents but we must work with them. A musically inclined person will not become a good musician without hours of daily exercise. We must never forget that the talent belongs to God and not to us.

To recognize that hand of God in the work of our hands makes for a happy and satisfied life. Failure to see God's hand will result in our feeling terrified and returning to dust.

Psalm 105:1-4

"Give thanks to the LORD, call on his name; make known among the nations what he has done."

We will see that most of this Psalm deals with what God has done for Israel. This doesn't mean that it has no importance for us. "Salvation is from the Jews," as Jesus said to the Samaritan woman (John 4:22), but that salvation is the salvation of the whole world.

The author of this Psalm gives us all a three-fold task to accomplish in the opening verse. We have to "Give thanks to the LORD," "call on his name," and "make known among the nations what he has done."

Our first task on earth is to praise God and thank Him. That is our reason for being here. People who never learn to thank God live in vain. As The Westminster Catechism states, the purpose of life is "to glorify God, and to enjoy him forever." The whole of this world's misery can be summed up in the words of the apostle Paul about the human race: "For although they knew God, they neither glorified him as God nor gave thanks to him, but their thinking became futile and their foolish hearts were darkened" (Romans 1:21). Whether we praise and thank God-- or not-- will determine where this world is going.

Calling on God's Name means to pray to God. While living on earth as a genuine human being Jesus saturated His life with prayer. We read: "Jesus told his disciples a parable to show them that they should always pray and not give up" (Luke 18:1). Paul adds to this: "Do not be anxious about anything, but in everything, by prayer and petition, with thanksgiving, present your requests to God. And the peace of God, which transcends all understanding, will guard your hearts and your minds in Christ Jesus" (Philippians 4:6,7).

Having experienced salvation by the application of Jesus' blood to our lives, we must spread the word. It has been said that there are only two kinds of people in this world, missionaries and mission fields. We are not really saved until we tell others. This may not sound orthodox, but Paul defines salvation as follows: "If you confess with your mouth, 'Jesus is Lord,' and believe in your heart that God raised him from the dead, you will be saved. For it is with your heart that you believe and are justified, and it is with your mouth that you confess and are saved" (Romans 10:9,10).

Psalm 105:5-13

"He set the earth on its foundations; it can never be moved. You covered it with the deep as with a garment; the waters stood above the mountains."

The Psalmist goes back to the beginning of creation when the earth was covered with water and God brought about the continents on which we live. In the first verses of this Psalm the poet sees God as wrapping himself in light as with a garment; here he sees water as the garment of our planet.

In Greek mythology it was believed that the globe on which we live was carried on the shoulders of the god Atlas. In this Psalm God is seen as placing the earth on its foundations. This sounds as a primitive representation of cosmology. As far as we can understand, our planet is suspended by nothing in an empty space. The magnetic forces of other heavenly bodies keep us maintaining a fixed and preset pattern with other stars and planets in our constellation. In the same manner as the atoms behave inside their molecules, so stars and planets relate to each other within our constellation. Maybe the same law that determines them also regulates the position of one constellation to each other. We are speaking about expanses of trillions of light years and distances that we cannot imagine.

We know, however, that the force that keeps it all together is the Word of God. The author of Hebrews states that Jesus Christ is sustaining all things by his powerful word (Hebrews 1:3). There is one central force, one powerful Word, handled by one Person in this whole universe that keeps everything together. The One who is at the control center is the same person who took care of the problem of our sin. He is God, "the blessed and only Ruler, the King of kings and Lord of lords, who alone is immortal and who lives in unapproachable light, whom no one has seen or can see" (I Timothy 6:15,16). He is also the most approachable human being who has sealed our salvation by dying for us and conquering death for us by rising from the grave. Both the heavenly bodies in outer space and the anchor of our soul are in His hands. As long as the atoms in our body and the planets in space hold together, our salvation holds.

Psalm 105:14-45

"He remembered his holy promise given to his servant Abraham."

This Psalm gives us a historical review of the birth of a nation. The Psalmist begins with Abraham and ends with Israel's entrance into Canaan, covering a period of over four hundred years. Even in the days when people like Abraham and Jacob lived to be over one hundred years old, the period covered in this Psalm spans more than the life of one human being. God had revealed to Abraham what He intended to do, and so Abraham could understand the meaning of his own experiences. He was able to look at life from God's perspective and comprehend his place in it. This kept him from getting bogged down in life.

The same principle is valid for those who are in Christ Jesus. If we know from where we came and where we are going, we can determine our present position. God counts every Christian as being a child of Abraham. The Apostle Paul states: "Consider Abraham: 'He believed God, and it was credited to him as righteousness.' Understand, then, that those who believe are children of Abraham. The Scripture foresaw that God would justify the Gentiles by faith, and announced the gospel in advance to Abraham: 'All nations will be blessed through you.' So those who have faith are blessed along with Abraham, the man of faith. ...Now you, brothers, like Isaac, are children of promise" (Galatians 3:6-10; 4:28).

The history of Israel is, at the same time, the history of God's revelation in this world. We may, therefore, consider this Psalm as being addressed to us.

This Psalm does not mention what Israel did with God's revelation and how they failed to live a life that was worthy of the calling they had received. The emphasis is on God's faithfulness not on theirs.

In this respect also we may draw a parallel between them and us. God will remember what He promised, whether we are faithful to Him or not. But this will not free us from our obligation to live a life that is worthy of God's calling. It opens the door for us to return to God when we fail, to confess, to stand up, and to take God's promises seriously enough to live up to them.

Without confession of our sins and a full surrender to Him, we will never experience the full riches of His strength. The lesson we have to keep on learning all through life is that the strength is His and not ours. We do not become strong. God will, purposely, allow weakness in our lives so that we will not lose sight of the real source of our abilities.

Psalm 106

"Praise the LORD. Give thanks to the LORD, for he is good; his love endures forever. Who can proclaim the mighty acts of the LORD or fully declare his praise? Blessed are they who maintain justice, who constantly do what is right."

This Psalm shows us the other side of the coin that was displayed in the previous Psalm. There the emphasis was upon the miraculous aspect of God's dealings with Israel; here we see how the people reacted to God's acts with a lack of understanding, with a demonstration of egoism, and by sinning against God.

The Psalmist stresses the fact that God's goodness is greater than man's disobedience. In the words of the Apostle Paul: "Where sin increased, grace increased all the more" (Romans 5:20[b]). Man's wanderings and hardness of heart accentuate God's goodness and greatness. The emphasis in this Psalm, therefore, is not on man's failure (although that takes up the greater part of the Psalm) but on praise to God and on an exhortation for us to avoid the incomprehensible foolishness of unbelief.

The author of this Psalm comes before God to confess the sins of his people and his own sin. He acts like the high priest on the Day of Atonement who entered into the holy place, first with a sacrifice for his own sin and then with the sacrifice that atoned for the sins of the people.

We cannot intercede for others if our own heart is not clean. We cannot obtain for others what we are not ready to receive for ourselves. The New King James Version expresses this beautifully: "Remember me, O LORD, with the favor You have toward Your people. Oh, visit me with Your salvation."

Whether we plead before God for our loved ones or for other individuals God has laid upon our hearts, or whether we are concerned for the nation of which we are a member, the best and foremost thing we can do that will bring God's blessing to others is to keep our communication line with God clear. Healing for others cannot be obtained without inner healing of ourselves. This doesn't mean that we have to enjoy good physical health to be a blessing, but a pure heart is mandatory. As King Solomon said to his son: "Above all else, guard your heart, for it is the wellspring of life" (Proverbs 4:23). That is your own life and that of others.

Psalm 107:1-9

"Give thanks to the LORD, for he is good; his love endures forever. Let the redeemed of the LORD say this--those he redeemed from the hand of the foe."

This beautiful Psalm describes an Old Testament testimony meeting in which people who have experienced the grace of God in their lives express what God has done for them in bringing them out of the darkness into His wonderful light. Their stories are different, they come from different backgrounds, but they all have in common that they were hostages, held by the enemy, who were facing certain death but were freed by the power of God.

They all give credit to the LORD for the change in their lives and they all conclude that God's love is eternal.

The first testimony is from a person who was lost in the desert. The physical features of the place depict a spiritual condition. A desert is a place without water without which no human being can live. We may survive periods without food, but not without water. Lack of water spells certain death both for the body and the soul.

Even if we never lost our way in a desert and faced death by dehydration, we all know what thirst of the soul is like. But we do not all realize that God is the only and ultimate thirst-quencher. Jesus Christ invites us all with the words: "If anyone is thirsty, let him come to me and drink. Whoever believes in me, as the Scripture has said, streams of living water will flow from within him" (John 7:37,38). He not only quenches our thirst but he transforms our lives. To a woman in Samaria, He said: "Whoever drinks the water I give him will never thirst. Indeed, the water I give him will become in him a spring of water welling up to eternal life" (John 4:14).

It is the eternal goodness and love of the Lord that satisfies the deepest longing of our soul and makes us people who become a blessing to others. If we are lost in the desert of life, God saves us from death by dehydration and makes us citizens of His city. When we get there, we will have reached our goal and we will know that we are home, where we belong as a human being.

Those who have drunk the water God gives will never want to drink anything else.

Psalm 107:10-16

"Then they cried to the LORD in their trouble, and he saved them from their distress. He brought them out of darkness and the deepest gloom and broke away their chains."

This section deals with people who are bound with iron chains. Their imprisonment is an inner bondage. Sin not only separates man from God and man from man but it also isolates man from himself. Sin breaks our inner harmony. This paranoia is the result of a lack of fellowship with God. Communion with God brings healing on the deepest level.

The chains represent our rebellion to the Word of God. "They had rebelled against the words of God and despised the counsel of the Most High."

The Psalmist's analysis can be applied to the sin of Eve and Adam as well as to any other crime man commits. We harm ourselves when we disobey God's Word. On the other hand, obedience is the key to inner freedom. We read in John's Gospel: "To the Jews who had believed him, Jesus said, 'If you hold to my teaching, you are really my disciples. Then you will know the truth, and the truth will set you free.' They answered him, 'We are Abraham's descendants and have never been slaves of anyone. How can you say that we shall be set free?' Jesus replied, 'I tell you the truth, everyone who sins is a slave to sin. Now a slave has no permanent place in the family, but a son belongs to it forever. So if the Son sets you free, you will be free indeed' " (John 8:31-36). Our inner dichotomy causes us to stumble and the person who stumbles ceases to progress. Progress, therefore, depends on obedience and inner harmony.

The change in our condition occurs when we cry unto the Lord. There is no other helper; we cannot help ourselves. These verses demonstrate that the "suffering in iron chains" and the humiliation to which we are subjected as a result of our rebellion against the Word of God is also an act of God. Suffering is not only an automatic result of man's break with God; it is also a consequence of God's intervention. "So he subjected them to bitter labor." When God does this to a person, He has salvation in mind. It is not an act of revenge on the part of God. God wants us to call upon Him in our low condition so He can save us from our distress. Breaking of our chains, deliverance from despair, and being brought out from darkness and gloom are only possible if we are willing to be saved. The only thing needed is to cry to the Lord in our trouble.

Psalm 107:17-22

"He sent forth his word and healed them; he rescued them from the grave."

This section deals with the sick. There is no reason to interpret these verses as a figure of speech. There is mention of physical suffering, lack of appetite, and being close to death. The cause of this sickness is described as following "rebellious ways" and "iniquities." Although in a general sense, sickness is always a result of sin, this does not mean that every incident of sickness can always be linked to a specific personal sin. That is certainly not the general rule. But even when such is the case, we read in these verses that there is salvation and healing with the Lord. The first result is deliverance from distress. The Hebrew word used here means "narrowness," or figuratively "trouble." The KJV translates it sometimes "anguish." Anguish or fear is the single factor that binds these stanzas together. We read here, as in the other sections, "And he delivered them from their distress." "Anguish" or "angst" is a good modern equivalent of this condition.

God did not create man for "angst" or "narrowness." Narrowness refers to circumstances; fear or panic describes man's reaction to those circumstances. Fear is incapacitating. Man who knows no fellowship with God lives in angst.

A picture of mental depression comes to mind when reading these verses. We must not conclude from this, as from any other illness, that there is always a direct link between sickness and sin. The Bible does not always leave the use of medicine out of the picture either.

"He sent forth his word and healed them," may be seen as a prophecy about the coming of Jesus Christ. "The Word became flesh and made his dwelling among us" (John 1:14). The coming of the Word of God in this world brings healing. Matthew describes this so beautifully in the following scene: "When evening came, many who were demon-possessed were brought to him, and he drove out the spirits with a word and healed all the sick. This was to fulfill what was spoken through the prophet Isaiah: 'He took up our infirmities and carried our diseases' " (Matthew 8:16,17). The Psalmist cannot have understood how much our healing would cost God in that God Himself would carry our diseases. This is the essence of the Gospel message. For this reason it is appropriate that those who are healed bring a thank offering to God. In Leviticus the thank offering as a sacrifice was a tangible form of gratitude, expressing obedience and surrender, which has to be renewed daily. The healing of our whole man also produces "songs of joy." God wants us to personally experience deliverance from sickness and death.

Psalm 107:23-32

"They saw the works of the LORD, his wonderful deeds in the deep."

The Israelites were not known to be seafarers. But seafaring was not completely foreign to Israel either. Some Israelites must have experienced storms at sea, either on their own ships or on those belonging to other nations. The story of Jonah indicates that the Israelites were more involved in seafaring than we know.

The emphasis in these verses is not upon man's sin but on the disturbance of the equilibrium in creation of which man becomes the victim. Man at sea is a toy of the elements.

Strangely enough the storm is represented as "the works of the LORD, his wonderful deeds in the deep." Yet, before the fall, there were, obviously, no hurricanes or other forms of natural disaster. The disturbance of nature's equilibrium is the result of man's break with God. The earth, over which man was set to reign, has become enemy territory to him. We perish in the creation God had prepared for us. Jesus' rebuking of the storm bears this out. We read in Mark's Gospel: "He [Jesus] got up, rebuked the wind and said to the waves, 'Quiet! Be still!' Then the wind died down and it was completely calm" (Mark 4:39).

A Dutch poet wrote a beautiful little poem about some Dutch fishermen. He says that all the fishermen in the little Dutch fishing village of Scheveningen are Christians because they all came to know the Lord during the storms on the North Sea. This seems to be similar to what the poet wants to convey in this stanza. As the writer to the Hebrews says: "It is a dreadful thing to fall into the hands of the living God" (Hebrews 10:31). We live in a hostile world and, unless God stretches out His protecting hand over us, we will all perish.

If we compare this picture with the first one about the traveler in the desert, we see that both are traveling in a hostile environment. In one there is a lack of water, in the other there is too much of it. In the desert, man is alone, but the sailors are all in the same boat. We are no match for either danger, but God demonstrates His love in that He saves us in all circumstances, whether we are about to perish in loneliness or en mass. Individually and together we have reason to praise God for salvation. God has for each of us a city and a safe haven.

Psalm 107:33-48

"He turned rivers into a desert, flowing springs into thirsty ground, and fruitful land into a salt waste, because of the wickedness of those who lived there. He turned the desert into pools of water and the parched ground into flowing springs."

It seems as if God reverses Himself at random by making good things bad and bad things good. That may be the impression God's involvement in our world, or the lack of it, makes upon us. We expect the omniscient, all wise, and omnipotent God to do better than what we can see.

God reverses the roles, both the roles of nature and of men. And we bear responsibility for these reversals. The land dries out "because of the wickedness of those who lived there." Man has demonstrated a lack of ecological responsibility. If we do not look at this world as God's world, we treat nature without respect and end up in a world that is uninhabitable. There are various ways in which a land can spew out its inhabitants.

What do we do with the riches God gives? When God turns the desert of our life into well-watered land, how do we respond?

There are few people who can handle riches responsibly. The amount of our possessions does not determine our value. A person who is said to "be worth one hundred million dollars" may be one of the poorest people on earth. Jesus says: "A man's life does not consist in the abundance of his possessions" (Luke 12:15). Our soul is worth more than all the riches of the world. Jesus also said: "What good is it for a man to gain the whole world, yet forfeit his soul? Or what can a man give in exchange for his soul?" (Mark 8:36,37).

Wealth tends to deceive us into thinking that we are more than others who possess less than we do. We equate wealth with power. Oppression in this world consists of what the rich do to the poor.

That is why God reverses the roles. In Jesus' Parable of the Rich Man and Lazarus, Lazarus ended up rich and the rich man destitute. There may be no instant retribution in this world, but no one gets away with his sins.

"Whoever is wise, let him heed these things and consider the great love of the LORD" (v.43).

Psalm 108

"Give us aid against the enemy, for the help of man is worthless. With God we will gain the victory, and he will trample down our enemies."

This Psalm is a combination of two other Psalms. Part of Psalm Fifty-Seven is joined to part of Psalm Sixty. The heading of Psalm Fifty-Seven states that David wrote it "When he had fled from Saul into the cave." The Sixtieth Psalm, according to the subscript, was written, "When he fought Aram Naharaim and Aram Zobah, and when Joab returned and struck down twelve thousand Edomites in the Valley of Salt." In the first poem David celebrated the fact that God had saved his own life; in the second the victory was gained on a national level.

It is this bi-level victory, as expressed in the combination of those two parts, that constitutes the message of this Psalm.

David had seen earlier in his life the importance of God's intervention in his personal life by which his faith was strengthened to undertake greater acts of valor. Before engaging the giant Goliath and thus saving the whole nation of Israel from defeat, he said to King Saul: "Your servant has been keeping his father's sheep. When a lion or a bear came and carried off a sheep from the flock, I went after it, struck it and rescued the sheep from its mouth. When it turned on me, I seized it by its hair, struck it and killed it. Your servant has killed both the lion and the bear; this uncircumcised Philistine will be like one of them, because he has defied the armies of the living God. The LORD who delivered me from the paw of the lion and the paw of the bear will deliver me from the hand of this Philistine" (I Samuel 17:34-37).

This teaches us a lesson in the way faith can be built up. If we learn to trust God for the smaller things in our life, He strengthens our hands to undertake more for Him.

It also shows that the enemy of our souls will attack us in more than one way, and we have to make sure that we remain under God's protection in every respect. Satan attacked David personally when Saul tried to kill him; he attacked Israel as a whole when David became their king. This Psalm demonstrates David's growing vision: from personal safety to the victory of a whole nation.

What God does in our private lives has its effect upon people around us. God deals with us, not merely as one individual, but as members of the body. Strictly speaking there is no such thing as a purely personal experience. In Paul's words: "None of us lives to himself alone and none of us dies to himself alone" (Romans 14:7). Our failures will affect those we rub shoulders with; so will our victories.

Psalm 109:1-20

"In return for my friendship they accuse me, but I am a man of prayer. They repay me evil for good, and hatred for my friendship."

Our immediate reaction to the reading of this Psalm may be a feeling of dismay and shock. We may ask ourselves how this poem ever found its way into the inspired Word of God? God is love and as His children we ought to love our enemies and not to curse them as David seems to do in this Psalm.

Before we enter any further into this, we must observe that some of the verbal abuse in this Psalm may have been voiced not by David but by David's enemies. David then quoted what they said to him and the text does not state what David wants to be done with those who hate him.

David calls himself "a man of prayer," but the prayer he prays is a prayer of vengeance. How we handle this depends on how we react to evil in general.

If ever we witnessed a brutal murder or have come close to people who carried out genocides, feelings of love and forgiveness are not the first ones to come up. The Allied troops that discovered Hitler's extermination camps were justified in being outraged by what they saw. What do we say about the Nazi soldier who kindly said to a Jewish mother: "May I hold your baby?" and then smashed the infant against the wall, crushing its skull? There are situations in life when outrage is the only legitimate response to cruelty and brutality.

This doesn't mean that we ought to take matters in our own hands. David didn't do this either. He asked God not to remain silent and he asks the Lord to pay back to this depraved person what he did to others. God is love but He is also the God of vengeance. Elsewhere in the Book of Psalms we read: "O LORD, the God who avenges, O God who avenges, shine forth. Rise up, O Judge of the earth; pay back to the proud what they deserve" (Psalm 94:1,2). It is important that we know God, not only as the loving Savior but also as the One who cannot tolerate evil. We do well to remember and remind others: "It is a dreadful thing to fall into the hands of the living God" (Hebrews 10:31).

Psalm 109:21-31

"I am poor and needy, and my heart is wounded within me."

It is difficult to determine who pronounces the curses in this Psalm. We know of no example in David's life in which he cursed his enemies. His attitude toward King Saul, for instance, is a classic illustration of repaying evil with good. No curse is inspired by the Holy Spirit. The only way we can curse others is by taking recourse to demonic powers. If we are kept in the shelter of God's love, no curse can affect us.

The fact that people cursed him affected David deeply. He confessed to being wounded in his soul and it caused him to feel physically ill. David wrestled with the problem that he knew people's opinion about him, but he wasn't sure what God thought of him. In other Psalms he expressed confidence that God is a shield that protected him. In this Psalm, this conviction is absent. This sense of insecurity can be traced to a lack of awareness of cleansing.

As New Testament Christians, we can hardly understand the difference between the cleansing of our conscience by the blood of Jesus and the covering of sin in the Old Testament by the blood of a sacrificial animal. The believing Jew was never quite able to overcome the gnawing of his conscience. Normally, the love of God reaches us via other human beings. It is a miracle in itself that, sometimes, we can experience God's love in spite of what men do to us.

But even if our conscience is clean, our heart can be wounded by what people say to us or by their gossip about us. We may follow David's example and ask that God will put to shame those who attack us. In the last stanza of this Psalm, David prays for more than his own justification. He prays, in a sense, for the conversion of his enemies. Because, if man becomes ashamed of his conduct, it means that he has begun to measure himself with God's measurements. David does not merely ask that God rehabilitates him but that He does it in such a way that his enemies will understand that there has been a divine intervention in his life upon which the curse bounces off. A Christian ought never to be afraid of curses or of magic used against him. No one ever put it more powerfully than the Apostle Paul did when he wrote: "Who will bring any charge against those whom God has chosen? It is God who justifies. Who is he that condemns?" (Romans 8:33,34). David had never read Paul's words but he understood the truth of them intuitively through the Holy Spirit. Peter advises us: "Do not repay evil with evil or insult with insult, but with blessing, because to this you were called so that you may inherit a blessing" (I Peter 3:9).

Psalm 110

"The LORD says to my Lord: 'Sit at my right hand until I make your enemies a footstool for your feet.' The LORD has sworn and will not change his mind: 'You are a priest forever, in the order of Melchizedek'."

This Psalm is one of the most important Psalms in the Bible. In it Christ is presented as both King and Priest, a combination of offices that was impossible in the Old Testament. A king in Israel could not be priest at the same time.

The Psalm is a prophecy about the resurrected Jesus at the right hand of God the Father in heaven. He is the one to whom is given all power in heaven and on earth and also the high priest who intercedes for us. Every coronation on earth and all human authority are a vague replica (in most cases a corrupted one) of this heavenly reality. This is the only real authority that exists.

At the moment of his death, Stephen was given a glimpse of this. We read: "Stephen, full of the Holy Spirit, looked up to heaven and saw the glory of God, and Jesus standing at the right hand of God" (Acts 7:55).

Jesus occupies this place as representative of the whole human race. God is preparing us to share in His glory. He says to us: "To him who overcomes, I will give the right to sit with me on my throne, just as I overcame and sat down with my Father on his throne" (Revelation 3:21). We are destined for the throne.

This Psalm is a Psalm of victory in more than one sense. If the first moon landing meant "a giant leap for mankind," the ascension of the man Jesus to the throne of the universe is greater than anything human ingenuity has ever been able to achieve.

It is also a victory in our personal life as believers in Christ. In the words of the writer of Hebrews: "Therefore, since we have a great high priest who has gone through the heavens, Jesus the Son of God, let us hold firmly to the faith we profess. For we do not have a high priest who is unable to sympathize with our weaknesses, but we have one who has been tempted in every way, just as we are—yet was without sin. Let us then approach the throne of grace with confidence, so that we may receive mercy and find grace to help us in our time of need" (Hebrews 4:14-16). And: "Therefore he is able to save completely those who come to God through him, because he always lives to intercede for them" (Hebrews 7:25). Our salvation and the very life we live on earth depends on what Jesus does for us in heaven today.

Psalm 111:1-9

"He has shown his people the power of his works, giving them the lands of other nations."

This Psalm is the first in a series of three "Hallelujah Psalms." All three have, not only the opening word in common but also, in general terms, the theme. The three Psalms place different emphases on the acts of God, but the main theme in all three is the same. In this Psalm God's greatness is demonstrated in the fact that He gave "them the lands of other nations," the Promised Land for Israel to live in. Or, as the KJV renders: "that he may give them the heritage of the heathen." In the following Psalm, the subject is the moral character of the people who inhabit the Promised Land. And in the last one, God shows His greatness in the restoration of fallen man.

Only one concrete example of God's great acts is mentioned: Israel's entry into Canaan. This does not mean that it is the only illustration available but, rather, that there is such an abundance of proofs that further mention is not necessary. It is left up to the hearer to search further. Unprejudiced investigation will lead to insight into the greatness of God's character, which is the beginning of all human wisdom.

The exodus from Egypt and the occupation of Canaan are the greatest illustrations of salvation documented in the Old Testament. They give us the clearest Old Testament picture of man's salvation through the death and resurrection of Jesus Christ.

For Israel, the exodus was a monument of grace and compassion God erected in this world. This monument is not drawn for us in clear and heavy lines.

As God delivered Israel from slavery and made them into a nation and gave them a place in the Promised Land, so He delivers us from the bondage of sin and addiction to make us people with human dignity. He invites us to enter into the place of emotional and spiritual rest that He wants us to inhabit.

For Israel, it all began in the evening when they killed the Passover Lamb and applied its blood to the doors of their houses. God wants us to celebrate life in fellowship with Him because "Christ, our Passover Lamb, has been sacrificed" (I Corinthians 5:7). He makes us victorious in the Promised Land. As He said to Joshua, He says to us: "I will give you every place where you set your foot," and "I will be with you; I will never leave you nor forsake you" (Joshua 1:3,5). It is appropriate to respond by shouting "Hallelujah!"

Psalm 111:10

"The fear of the LORD is the beginning of wisdom; all who follow his precepts have good understanding. To him belongs eternal praise."

The words "The works of the LORD are great, sought out of all them that have pleasure therein" (verse 2 in the KJV) are written above the entrance of the Cavendish Laboratory in Cambridge, Great Britain. This is the scene of some fundamental scientific discoveries. It is good that those who possess the intellect and brainpower to do scientific research praise God more than anyone else.

It is true that the church of Christ consists mainly of "not many ... wise by human standards; not many ... influential; not many ... of noble birth," (I Corinthians 1:26) but that doesn't mean that such was God's original intent. The royal wedding banquet in Jesus' parable was originally not intended for those who loitered at the street corners either (Matthew 22:1-14). We can say, therefore, that this *Hallelujah* Psalm belongs primarily to the intelligentsia.

The words "The fear of the LORD is the beginning of wisdom" originate in the Book of Job and they summarize the contents of the Book of Proverbs (Job 28:28; Proverbs 1:7). When Adam and Eve ate the fruit from the Tree of the Knowledge of Good and Evil, they separated true knowledge from fellowship with God.

Man is the only "animal" that possesses knowledge and is able to work with it. This ability is connected to our gift of speech. Animals possess some knowledge but they are unable to put it to work and to express it. God has created us and endowed us with the gift of knowledge, thought, expression, and application. One of the most fatal facets of the fall is that knowledge became an independent entity, separated from God and that it began to live a life of its own. It became a form of cancer for mankind. One of my unbelieving relatives told me once that he didn't believe in God because he was "an intellectual!"

Real wisdom has become elusive because "the fear of the Lord," which is the beginning of wisdom, has disappeared. Fear, in this context, has nothing to do with being afraid. It is the awe and reverence we experience when entering into the presence of one who is infinitely greater than we are.

Wisdom is never delivered in a package. We have to apply ourselves to fellowship with God in order to become wise. The real exercise of knowledge consists of "[Loving] the Lord your God with all your heart and with all your soul and with all your mind and with all your strength" (Mark 12:30).

The ultimate source of wisdom is in our Lord Jesus Christ. "It is because of him that you are in Christ Jesus, who has become for us wisdom from God-that is, our righteousness, holiness and redemption" (I Corinthians 1:30). If we have Jesus, we possess wisdom.

Psalm 112:1-4

"Blessed is the man who fears the LORD, who finds great delight in his commands."

As mentioned earlier, this Psalm is connected to the previous Psalm and also to the following one. The emphasis here is on the moral character of the person who lives in fellowship with God.

The word "fear" in Biblical context has nothing to do with being afraid. It means an intensive, passionate respect for God that gives us the desire to obey Him with all our heart. This "fear" produces blessing on the basis of obedience. It is not a forced obedience as of a person who faces an overwhelming force before which he has to bow the head but it is obedience out of love, which begins in the heart. It is the obedience of which Jesus says: "If anyone loves me, he will obey my teaching" (John 14:23). And the Apostle John writes: "This is love for God: to obey his commands" (I John 5:3). This natural, spontaneous, and wholehearted obedience is only possible if the Holy Spirit fills our lives.

The first place where this influence is felt is in the family. Our children are exposed to all kinds of influences. Parents cannot always be blamed when children take the wrong road. And we cannot take much credit either when our children follow the right path. There is a sense in which the conduct of our children is beyond our control. Our influence upon the lives of others is limited. If we try to influence too much, the effect is usually the opposite of what we want to achieve. The Lord promises that, if we obey Him wholeheartedly, He will take care that our children experience the wholesome consequences. This promise ought to release the tension for us and give us a solid basis for our intercessory prayers.

God's promise emphasizes the importance of the family. God considers the family as a unity, not merely as a group of people who are related to each other and who can each go their own way. The authority of the head of the family is a decisive factor in the conduct of its members. The importance of the family is obvious from God's soliloquy: "Shall I hide from Abraham what I am about to do? Abraham will surely become a great and powerful nation, and all nations on earth will be blessed through him. For I have chosen him, so that he will direct his children and his household after him to keep the way of the LORD by doing what is right and just, so that the LORD will bring about for Abraham what he has promised him" (Genesis 18:17-19).

Our fear of the Lord will enable us to take the place in our relationships God wants us to have, so we can be an example and a guide in showing our children the right way by walking in it ourselves.

Psalm 112:5-10

"Good will come to him who is generous and lends freely, who conducts his affairs with justice."

In the Old Testament blessing was often expressed in terms of material prosperity. We know, however, that there are other riches than possession of money. Happiness and wealth are not synonymous, although they seem to be so in the mind of many people. Some millionaires, however, are among the unhappiest people.

This Psalm describes the riches of a person who loves God. The Bible calls us righteous if we love God and demonstrate that love in our relationship with others. The Psalmist states: "A righteous man will be remembered forever."

The word "righteous" in the Bible is interesting. Both in Hebrew and Greek it has the meaning of giving something away. Jesus uses it in connection with giving alms. He says: "Be careful not to do your 'acts of righteousness' before men, to be seen by them. If you do, you will have no reward from your Father in heaven" (Matthew 6:1). God does not make us righteous and generous so that others will appreciate us, but when we fear God and obey Him out of love, He raises up a monument for us.

Sometimes other people will honor us when we honor God, but even if this is not the case, we will receive honor from where it counts.

Generosity will never make us poor. And we do not need much to be generous. As a matter of fact, riches tend to make stingy. God shows a preference for poor widows and He honors them. We read: "Jesus sat down opposite the place where the offerings were put and watched the crowd putting their money into the temple treasury. Many rich people threw in large amounts. But a poor widow came and put in two very small copper coins, worth only a fraction of a penny. Calling his disciples to him, Jesus said, 'I tell you the truth, this poor widow has put more into the treasury than all the others. They all gave out of their wealth; but she, out of her poverty, put in everything-all she had to live on'" (Mark 12:41-44). The greatest riches we can have is when God honors us. It may not be very expensive; it will cost all we have!

Psalm 113

"He raises the poor from the dust and lifts the needy from the ash heap; he seats them with princes, with the princes of their people."

The emphasis in this third *Hallelujah* Psalm is on the fact that God raises up fallen man. In the order of our experience, this Psalm comes first. The editor of The Book of Psalms has reversed the order, beginning with the victory and returning to the basis of God's grace. That is a healthy principle that we ought to apply often in our spiritual life.

God's salvation does more for us than forgiving our sin and keeping us from going to hell. When God saves our souls, He rehabilitates us and gives us the human dignity He intended us to have.

Some of the words in this Psalm remind us of the songs of Hanna and of Mary. Hanna's song of praise after the Lord had heard her prayer and given her Samuel, marked the beginning of a new era in the history of Israel. People began to hear the Word of God again through Samuel and Samuel anointed "the Once and Future King" David. Mary sang her "Magnificat" in connection with the birth of the Son of David, the King of kings, whose birth marked the beginning of a new are in the history of the whole world. The Psalmist emphasizes these new beginnings with the words: "He settles the barren woman in her home as a happy mother of children. Hallelujah!"

The first human being who sinned was a woman. Salvation was born into this world through a woman.

This Psalm is also the first in a series which is called "The Egyptian Hallel," which consists of Psalms 113-118. Jesus sang this Psalm with His disciples after they had celebrated the Last Supper together. Mark states: "When they had sung a hymn, they went out to the Mount of Olives" (Mark 14:26). As He walked the way to the cross, Jesus sang: "He raises the poor from the dust and lifts the needy from the ash heap; he seats them with princes, with the princes of their people."

It was by humbling Himself and becoming obedient to death that He raised us up to a place of royal dignity and glory. God considers us so important that He paid the ultimate price for us. If ever we are being tempted to feel self-important, we ought to remember how unimportant we are in our self, how important we are for God, and how much it cost Him to make us what we are and will be.

Psalm 114

"When Israel came out of Egypt, the house of Jacob from a people of foreign tongue, Judah became God's sanctuary, Israel his dominion."

This Psalm depicts both the humorous and the supernatural elements of the exodus, the birth of Israel as a nation. Both of these aspects are constantly present in the history of God's revelation. They also are characteristic for the normal Christian life.

Israel's journey to freedom and dignity was accompanied by a series of great miracles. The crossing of the Red Sea and the River Jordan, which marked the beginning and the end of the journey, were supernatural events. God's appearance on top of Mount Sinai is compared to an enormous earthquake. Looking at the manifestations that accompanied God's revelation of Himself, the Psalmist laughs and pokes fun at the shocked face of Mother Nature when she saw the face of her Creator.

Laughter is often a byproduct of God's miracles. Sarah first laughed in unbelief at the announcement of Isaac's birth but afterwards she admitted that God had made her laugh (See Genesis 18:12-15). And after Isaac was born: "Sarah said, 'God has brought me laughter, and everyone who hears about this will laugh with me' " (Genesis 21:6). The name Isaac means "One who laughs."

Israel's deliverance from slavery in Egypt and her entrance into the Promised Land was more than the birth of a nation. God chose Israel to reveal Himself in this world. God wanted to live in this world and dwell among us. He ordered Moses to build a tabernacle and an Ark of the Covenant with a cover, called "the Mercy Seat." And God said: "There, above the cover between the two cherubim that are over the ark of the Testimony, I will meet with you and give you all my commands for the Israelites. (Exodus 25:22). This miracle of God's presence was repeated when King Solomon dedicated the temple in Jerusalem. We read: "When the priests withdrew from the Holy Place, the cloud filled the temple of the LORD. And the priests could not perform their service because of the cloud, for the glory of the LORD filled his temple" (1 Kings 8:10-11).

Yet, these manifestations were small in comparison with the Incarnation of the Word of God, which John describes as: "The Word became flesh and made his dwelling among us. We have seen his glory, the glory of the one and Only, who came from the Father, full of grace and truth" (John 1:14). This is the most serious event of all. It will make the whole earth tremble in the presence of the Lord. It will also fill with hilarious laughter all who experience the wonderful salvation that has come to us through Jesus Christ.

Psalm 115:1-8

"Our God is in heaven; he does whatever pleases him. But their idols are silver and gold, made by the hands of men."

God created man in His own image. We read in Genesis: "So God created man in his own image, in the image of God he created him; male and female he created them" (Genesis 1:27). Even when Adam and Eve fell in sin, the image of God in them was never eradicated. It was severely damaged, but it wasn't wiped out. That is why our conscience warns us when we sin and we carry around a sense of guilt for unconfessed sin.

But when we turn to God and ask for forgiveness, the process of restoration of God's image in us begins. This process is called sanctification. It may never be completed while we live on earth, but our fellowship with God will enhance it. It will be completed when we see Jesus, either when we get to heaven or when the Lord returns. The apostle John writes: "Dear friends, now we are children of God, and what we will be has not yet been made known. But we know that when he appears, we shall be like him, for we shall see him as he is" (I John 3:2). And Paul states: "You have taken off your old self with its practices and have put on the new self, which is being renewed in knowledge in the image of its Creator" (Colossians 3:9,10).

The image of God will appear clearly in those who serve God. Everyone bears the image of the god he serves, either the image of God, our Creator, or the image of that which has become our idol. The Psalmist says: "Those who make [idols] will be like them, and so will all who trust in them."

The Psalm opens with the words: "Not to us, O LORD, not to us but to your name be the glory, because of your love and faithfulness." This suggests that we are in danger of claiming for ourselves the honor that belongs only to God.

It ought to be the all-consuming passion of our lives to bring glory to God in everything we do. Paul admonishes us: "Whether you eat or drink or whatever you do, do it all for the glory of God" (I Corinthians 10:31).

If the aim of our life is anything less than God's glory, we aim for something that has no value and our life will become devoid of meaning. Whatever idol we make, we will become like it. Idols are dumb, blind, deaf, and mute. "Those who make them will be like them, and so will all who trust in them." Idolatry, in whatever form it is practiced is demeaning. Our idols will destroy us and we destroy ourselves by making them.

Psalm 115:9-18

"The LORD remembers us and will bless us: He will bless the house of Israel, he will bless the house of Aaron, he will bless those who fear the LORD--small and great alike."

These verses are an appeal for faith that is focused correctly. The appeal is addressed to Israel as a nation, to the priesthood of Israel, and to each individual. Like the church of Jesus Christ, Israel was meant to be a kingdom of priests. A nation consists of individuals. Without individual faith, there is no kingdom of priests.

The Psalmist repeats three times, like a slogan, the phrase: "He is their help and shield." "Shield" depicts the protection God provides. "Help" speaks of the active initiative, the energy that is provided by God's presence with us. Paul expresses how limitless God's help is to everyone who has accepted the payment for his sins in the death of Jesus Christ. He states: "He who did not spare his own Son, but gave him up for us all-how will he not also, along with him, graciously give us all things?" (Romans 8:32).

It is important to note how God's blessings are bestowed upon us. They are meant for the kingdom of priests, that is, for the fellowship of believers who stand between God and the rest of mankind. The house of Israel was blessed because God blessed the house of Aaron. As Aaron passed on the blessing he received from the Lord, it flowed down to the lowest points in society–"small and great alike." We will be blessed in the measure in which we pass it on. God does not pour His blessings into our reservoirs but through our channels. The principle is expressed in God's blessing to Abraham: "I will make you into a great nation and I will bless you; I will make your name great, and you will be a blessing. I will bless those who bless you, and whoever curses you I will curse; and all peoples on earth will be blessed through you" (Genesis 12:2,3). God will pour it on us if we pray: "Make me a blessing!"

Psalm 116:1-11

"Be at rest once more, O my soul, for the LORD has been good to you."

Why would one talk to his own soul? Apparently, our soul sometimes needs to be talked to. We have to come to grips with ourselves, know who we are, where we come from, where we are going, and what we are supposed to do.

This author of this Psalm had experienced a wonderful touch of God in his body. Evidently, he had been sick and close to death and the Lord brought him back to life and healed him. He reacted to this blessing by declaring: "I love the LORD, for he heard my voice; he heard my cry for mercy." He was able to function again and to return to a life of normal activity. His next question was what to do with his newfound blessing. The following step for his soul was to "be at rest."

The fact that God touches us does not always lead us to the place where our soul is able to rest in God. God blesses us not for the purpose of taking that blessing and going home. God's blessings are meant to draw us into fellowship and intimacy with Him. The hymn writer expresses this beautifully in: "Jesus, I am resting, resting in the joy of what Thou art."

It is possible for us to forfeit our blessings if they don't lead us to intimacy with God. We have the example of the people of Israel. God led them out of slavery to the Promised Land, a land flowing with milk and honey. From the moment they left Egypt till they arrived at the border of Canaan, they experienced one miracle after another. But they refused to enter the place of rest God had prepared for them. The apostle Paul comments: "Now these things occurred as examples to keep us from setting our hearts on evil things as they did" (I Corinthians 10:6). Sometimes the blessing of physical healing does not amount to the healing of our souls. Some of us may be drawn into a deeper relationship with God through physical weakness.

We may want to have a good talk with ourselves and consider what we have done with the blessings God poured out over us. I tell my soul: "Be at rest once more, O my soul, for the LORD has been good to you."

Psalm 116:12-17

"How can I repay the LORD for all his goodness to me?"

It is impossible for us to repay God for what He did for us. There is nothing we can give in ransom for our soul. Throughout eternity we will be indebted to God. This should determine our attitude as we stand before God.

In order to fully comprehend how this influences our relationship with God, we have to think back to the damage sin has caused in this relationship. When Eve began to believe Satan's lie, she tarnished the reliability of God's Word and in doing so she tainted God's character. Sin cut us off from the source of life. The restoration of fellowship entails much more than a return to the former conditions. "The cup of salvation" brings us much closer to God than Adam ever was.

The Psalmist gives five answers to his own question, each of which outlines what our response to God's goodness to us ought to be.

- Lifting up "the cup of salvation" means for us that we celebrate our communion with God on the basis of Jesus' death for us. In the words of the apostle Paul: "Whenever you eat this bread and drink this cup, you proclaim the Lord's death until he comes" (I Corinthians 11:26).

- We respond to God's goodness by vowing obedience to His will. The surrender of our will to the will of God is the most reasonable thing we can do.

- Obedience can lead to martyrdom. Some of God's saints paid with their life for their faith in Jesus Christ. But even if that is not what God requires of us, the willingness to give our life for God is the surest way to defeat Satan. "They overcame him by the blood of the Lamb and by the word of their testimony; they did not love their lives so much as to shrink from death" (Revelation 12:11).

- We respond to God's goodness by considering ourselves to be a slave of Jesus Christ. Like the Hebrew bond slave we can declare: "I love my master and my wife and children and do not want to go free" (Exodus 21:5). God will pierce the ear of our heart so we can hear the voice of the Holy Spirit.

- Finally, we respond to God's goodness by simply saying "Thank You!" Gratitude is the highest form of praise.

Our five-fold response will not settle the account with God. We will never be able to pay Him back in full, but by not responding we forfeit all. We cannot afford to give Him less than ourselves.

Psalm 117

"Praise the LORD, all you nations; extol him, all you peoples. For great is his love toward us, and the faithfulness of the LORD endures forever. Praise the LORD."

It is amazing how many surprises are packed into this shortest of all the Psalms in the Bible. The Psalm may be short but it encompasses enormous dimensions. The Psalmist addresses the whole world in calling upon "all you peoples." And about the love and faithfulness of God, he says that it is great and eternal.

The Hebrew word translated "peoples" actually means "Gentiles," or "heathen." They are the people who do not know God or who are revolting against them. We met them in Psalm Two, where they shouted: "Let us break their chains and throw off their fetters" (Psalm 2:3).

The Psalmist doesn't describe what happened to them so that they would come to the place where they would praise the Lord. He leaves it to us to fill in the blanks.

When God revealed Himself to Israel, it was for the purpose that they would be "a kingdom of priests and a holy nation" (Exodus 19:6). God wanted the Israelites to stand between Him and the rest of the world, so that the peoples of this world would know Him. Israel has done a rather poor job in fulfilling their priesthood. But then, the church of Jesus Christ has not been a perfect example either.

Only when we become living demonstrations of God's love and faithfulness, will we bring others to the knowledge of salvation.

We are not at present at the point where all the nations and all the peoples praise the Lord. This Psalm is a prophecy of times to come. The time will come when, what the apostle John saw becomes a reality. In Revelation he states: "There before me was a great multitude that no one could count, from every nation, tribe, people and language, standing before the throne and in front of the Lamb" (Revelation 7:9).

We can hasten the fulfillment of this Psalm's prophecy by demonstrating God's eternal love and faithfulness in our own lives. Our own salvation isn't only meant to get us into heaven, it enables us to become witnesses to a rebellious world and bring them to the place where they praise the Lord as we do.

This short Psalm presents us with a task description. God wants us to take on the whole world as our mission field, as the object of our praying, giving and going.

Psalm 118:1-14

"It is better to take refuge in the LORD than to trust in man. It is better to take refuge in the LORD than to trust in princes."

This beautiful Psalm is the last one in the series of the Egyptian Hallel, which consists of Psalms 113-118. It is the last Psalm Jesus sang with His disciples before going to the cross (See Matthew 26:30).

The Psalm begins with the liturgical call to worship: "Give thanks to the LORD, for he is good; his love endures forever." Those were the words that were sung daily at the beginning of the temple worship service (See I Chronicles 16:41). The fourfold recurrence of this exhortation is very impressive.

There is in the use of liturgy always a danger that words lose their meaning and become an empty formula. We have the ability to rob words of their power.

There is also the difficulty that the Psalmist tries to express the inexpressible. God's eternal goodness and love are beyond description, particularly when all man has at his disposal is weak words that tend to lose their meaning. In a paradoxical way, this realization helps us to keep our amazement alive. As human beings, we are more than can be expressed in words. For this reason God became man Himself when He wanted to demonstrate that His lovingkindness endures forever.

The Psalmist contrasts the goodness and love of God with the hostility of the world of men in which he lives. Evidently, he had burned himself in trusting people who turned themselves against him. He asked the question "What can man do to me?" The answer is that man can and does kill. The two world wars that raged in the twentieth century testify to the damage human beings can inflict upon one another. We really have no reason to trust one another.

The author of Hebrews places the words of the Psalmist in the context of financial security. We read: "Keep your lives free from the love of money and be content with what you have, because God has said, 'Never will I leave you; never will I forsake you.' So we say with confidence, 'The Lord is my helper; I will not be afraid. What can man do to me?' (Hebrews 13:5,6).

God knows that we need money to stay alive and that we need friendship and intimacy with our fellowmen to live a life that is emotionally stable and satisfying. He will provide for us if we trust Him for it. But if we put our trust in anything else but God, we will find out that this world is a hard place to live in.

Psalm 118:15-29

"I will not die but live, and will proclaim what the LORD has done. The LORD has chastened me severely, but he has not given me over to death."

Most of this section of the Psalm contains a prophecy that was, at least partially, fulfilled during the last week of Jesus' life on earth. In Matthew's Gospel, in the chapter that describes the events of Palm Sunday, we find two quotations taken from this Psalm. As Jesus entered Jerusalem, the crowd shouted: "Hosanna to the Son of David! Blessed is he who comes in the name of the Lord! Hosanna in the highest!" (Matthew 21:9). This is a free quotation of the words in this Psalm "O LORD, save us; O LORD, grant us success. Blessed is he who comes in the name of the LORD." The Hebrew word rendered "save us" is *howshiy`aah*, or *hosanna*. And on that same day, Jesus told the priests and people in the temple: "Have you never read in the Scriptures: 'The stone the builders rejected has become the capstone; the Lord has done this, and it is marvelous in our eyes'?" (Matthew 21:42).

Less than one week later Jesus died on the cross to open for us the gates of righteousness. The words "I will not die but live, and will proclaim what the LORD has done. The LORD has chastened me severely, but he has not given me over to death" don't seem to apply to our Lord, because He did die. But death was not the final word for Him. As Jesus entered the prison of death, He overpowered the prison guard and took away his keys. He could say to the apostle John: "I am the Living one; I was dead, and behold I am alive for ever and ever! And I hold the keys of death and Hades" (Revelation 1:18).

"The LORD has done this, and it is marvelous in our eyes. This is the day the LORD has made; let us rejoice and be glad in it." It is marvelous in our eyes. It leaves us dumbfounded. It means that God has destined us to live today. This is the day He made, the day of resurrection. "Let us rejoice and be glad in it!"

Jesus entered Jerusalem to die. The Psalm reads in the New King James Version: "God is the LORD, And He has given us light; Bind the sacrifice with cords to the horns of the altar." How can this be a reason for celebration? We will look at that in our meditation tomorrow.

Psalm 118:15-29

"This is the day the LORD has made; we will rejoice and be glad in it. Bind the sacrifice with cords to the horns of the altar."

Returning to the fact that this Psalm contains a prophecy about the last week of Jesus' life on earth, we ask ourselves the question how we can rejoice in the death of the most wonderful and perfect human being who ever lived on earth?

It took our Lord all His willpower and human determination to go to the place where He knew He would be tortured and killed. We read in Luke's Gospel: "As the time approached for him to be taken up to heaven, Jesus resolutely set out for Jerusalem" (Luke 9:51). It may have been the day that the Lord had made, but how can we rejoice and be glad about what happened and the way it happened?

It seemed that Jesus' triumphal entrance in Jerusalem, riding on a donkey over the cloaks and palm branches people had strewn on the ground–was all one enormous mistake. The people were mistaken because they celebrated the coming of the King they believed would chase out the Roman government. That whole celebration turned out to be a charade on the day the same people shouted: "Crucify Him!" (Matthew 27:22).

Yet, God the Holy Spirit inspired the Psalmist to prophesy about the event centuries before it happened. The same Spirit would inspire the prophet Zechariah to predict the details of Jesus' entry. He wrote: "Rejoice greatly, O Daughter of Zion! Shout, Daughter of Jerusalem! See, your king comes to you, righteous and having salvation, gentle and riding on a donkey, on a colt, the foal of a donkey" (Zechariah 9:9).

What happened at Calvary was horrible; it was the most shameful act our human race ever committed. This was our shame! But God in heaven ordained this to happen for our salvation. Jesus' entry into Jerusalem, His being tied to the horns of the altar was God's doing. The shout of the crowd was the voice of God shouting "Hosanna!" It was God's celebration of the greatest sacrifice of love ever brought on earth. We have all reason to be ashamed of what happened to Jesus on that Friday. We did it to Him. God did it for us. He made that day and He wants us to rejoice in it. He made it "Good Friday."

Psalm 119:1-8

"Blessed are they who keep his statutes and seek him with all their heart."

This Psalm is the best-known example of an acrostic, that is, a poem in which each of the stanzas starts with one of the letters of the Hebrew alphabet.

The Psalm is about the Law of God and man's reaction to it. Few people get enthusiastic about the law. Those who do are usually lawyers who study it in order to find the holes in it that allow their clients to escape the consequences of their acts. For most people the law, even the Law of God, is made to be broken.

The Psalmist realized that the Law was the expression of God's character. His love for the Law was related to his love for God.

Although this is not differentiated in this Psalm, we must remind ourselves that God's Law involves more than the Ten Commandments. The greater part of the Law was ceremonial; it provided atonement for man's sin.

The Law that was engraved on the two tablets and later on the scrolls of the Torah, began as the Word God spoke. As such it had the same power as the Word by which the universe was created. The Psalmist was deeply conscious of the creative power of the Word. He realized that it was the key to life out of death. He knew that he himself lived in the shadow of death and that his nature had been affected to the core by death. We could, therefore, consider this Psalm to be a prayer for immortality.

The Psalmist uses eight different Hebrew words that emphasize the different characteristics of God's Law. The different shades of meaning of the Law of God that are expressed in this Psalm tell us that God wants to teach us through the Law. He reveals in it who He is, that He has authority as the Almighty. And He enriches our lives with the promises of His blessing.

The Psalmist looked to the Law of God with delight, love, and with a sense of awe. He experienced his study of the Law of God as liberating and a means to receive insight in moral values. For him the Law of God became a source of life and stability.

We will see in the next several meditations about this Psalm how struggle, victory and deep emotions accompanied the Psalmist's experiences with the Law of God. He has a lot to teach us in the lengthy but beautiful poem.

We will be blessed if we set our heart upon the knowledge and the practice of the Word of God as we find it in the Bible.

Psalm 119:1-8

"Blessed are they whose ways are blameless, who walk according to the law of the LORD."

This first stanza makes clear that God does not diminish His demand for holiness. We cannot bargain with Him. It remains true that "without holiness no one will see the Lord" (Hebrew 12:14). God intends to share His holiness and His glory with us. We must strive for perfection, as God is perfect.

This thought tends to cause complete discouragement in the soul of every human being. No one is perfect and even if we try to be perfectionists in the details of our daily life, we all know that we fail. There are no perfect people and there are no perfect relationships. We may find satisfaction in doing the best we can, but the best we can is not enough when we compare our lives with the glory of God. And the glory of God is the measure with which we will be judged. The apostle Paul writes: "All have sinned and fall short of the glory of God" (Roman 3:23).

We may not all fall short in the same way. None of us commits all the sins in the book. Some persons who cheat in their marriage may be honest in their financial dealings. Some crooked businessmen can be loving fathers of their children. No one keeps the law perfectly, but no one sins against all the commandments either. But what difference does it make whether an airplane crashes ten feet from the runway or blows apart thirty thousand feet up in the air? God demands perfection and no one is perfect!

The Psalmist realized this; otherwise he would not have said: "I will obey your decrees; do not utterly forsake me." None would make it without God's help. God said to the Israelites in the Old Testament and to us: "I the LORD am holy--I who make you holy" (Leviticus 21:8).

That is why the first word of this Psalm is "blessed." We will never be perfect, however hard we try. But if we allow ourselves to be blessed by the Word of God, He will share His holiness with us. If we occupy ourselves with the Law of God, our real condition will be unveiled; but it is in occupying ourselves with the Word that the creative power of the Word becomes operative in us. When we come to the healthy realization that we haven't arrived yet, we understand that God isn't finished with us yet. Our holiness is God's responsibility and He is quite capable of making us what He wants us to be. We must not resist.

Psalm 119:9-16

"How can a young man keep his way pure? By living according to your word."

The opening words of this stanza suggest that the Psalmist was himself a young man. Since we all begin life with being young, these words pertain to each one of us.

The Psalmist was obviously conscious of the danger of being young and furthermore, he believed that purity should be an integral part of youth.

Purity of character is a choice. The fact that the Psalmist wanted to keep his way pure means that God had made it pure to begin with. God had forgiven his sins and put him on the way he ought to go.

Jesus used the image of the small gate and the narrow path. He said: "Enter through the narrow gate. For wide is the gate and broad is the road that leads to destruction, and many enter through it. But small is the gate and narrow the road that leads to life, and only a few find it" (Matthew 7:13, 14). This young man went through the gate. He had made the decision; he was walking on the path.

Keeping our way pure is a matter of walking in the footprints of a Person. Purity consists in following Jesus. This purity is the blamelessness of verse one. It means that the blood of Jesus Christ purifies our lives, so that every accusation that is brought to us loses its power. This purity is not our own, but it is the purity of Jesus Christ, that is imputed to us.

Our greatest obstacle in walking the Jesus Way is half-heartedness. The Psalmist says: "I seek you with all my heart." He follows this up by asking God to help him to be obedient.

We will be able to seek and love God with all our heart only if Jesus Christ and the Bible become our guide. Fellowship with Him keeps us from straying away. Ever since the cross of Golgotha, there are no more obstacles from God's side. The Father will come running towards us and embrace us if He sees us coming in the distance. Our problem is to get up and go to the Father.

Hiding the Word of God in our hearts is the best antidote against sin. It will give us single-mindedness to walk the path through life which Jesus has traced for us.

If we meditate upon God's Word, we use the critical functions of our intellect. God's commandments appeal equally to our intellect as to our emotions. The key to both the head and the heart is found in the will.

Psalm 119:17-24

"Open my eyes that I may see wonderful things in your law."

The Psalmist prays: "Do good to your servant." In the Hebrew language the words "do good" have a very rich meaning that doesn't convey itself easily in English. It means "to treat a person well," or "to make ripe." On the side it also has the meaning of "to carry a burden." God treats us well by making us mature in letting us carry His burden. This reminds us of the words of Jesus: "Take my yoke upon you and learn from me, for I am gentle and humble in heart, and you will find rest for your souls" (Matthew 11:29).

The depth of God's Word is invisible to the naked eye. Sin makes us blind for God's reality. The Bible will be a closed book for us as long as Jesus does not occupy the central place in our life. When God opens our eyes we will begin to see wonderful things in His Law. This gift of sight is one of the most precious blessings God gives to people who ask for it.

In a way, the Old Testament was written in code. Jesus deciphered this code for us. He was the first human being whose eyes were open to see the wonderful things of the law. In Luke's Gospel we read: "Then he opened their minds so they could understand the Scriptures" (Luke 24:45). And the Apostle Paul says that the veil over our minds is removed in Jesus Christ. "But their minds were made dull, for to this day the same veil remains when the old covenant is read. It has not been removed, because only in Christ is it taken away" (II Corinthians 3:14). The two young men who met Jesus on the road to Emmaus and who listened to Jesus' Bible lessons said: "Were not our hearts burning within us while he talked with us on the road and opened the Scriptures to us?" (Luke 24:32). The Bible becomes a living book only for those who have received pardon of sin by the blood of Christ and who have come to life through the Holy Spirit.

It is easy to get sidetracked and lose the burning sensation in our heart when reading the Word of God. The love of God will make the Word of God a priority in our life. But if we exchange God's love for something else, if there is anything we begin to love more than Jesus, the Bible will lose its grip on us. "Open my eyes that I may see wonderful things in your law" must become part of our daily prayer. We will know what the man experienced whose eyes Jesus touched. He said: "One thing I do know. I was blind but now I see!" (John 9:25).

Psalm 119:17-24

"I am a stranger on earth; do not hide your commands from me."

When God created our planet, He made it a perfect place of habitation for the human race. The earth may be the only heavenly body that can support life. Our first parents lived in a paradise. The word "Paradise" still rings with a sound of sweet promise.

Our globe is no longer the perfect habitat for humanity it was when God first made it. Sin tore apart its perfect harmony. We live no longer in a paradise. When Adam broke off the intimate relation he had enjoyed with God, his palace turned into a slum.

There are still many things of beauty to be enjoyed in this world. The sun still rises and sets in outbursts of gold. The snow-covered mountain peaks still take our breath away. Roses still smell like roses and birds still sing in trees, but this beauty is all set against a background of death and decay. In the words of the apostle Paul "the creation was subjected to frustration" and is in "bondage to decay" (Romans 8:20, 21).

We may feel at home in the slum in which we live, but something inside us tells us that we do not really belong there.

Our home is where our roots are, both physically and emotionally. We may lose the roof of our house by a tornado; as long as our family survives, we still have a home. It is love and fellowship, more than place and structure that determines whether we are at home or not.

If the world around us is no longer a strange place for us, then we no longer see the wonderful things of His law either. If we are touched by God's love, we will not feel at home among the thorns and thistles and the garbage dumps of this world. If we were born in heaven, we do not actually belong on earth.

"Our citizenship is in heaven. And we eagerly await a Savior from there, the Lord Jesus Christ, who, by the power that enables him to bring everything under his control, will transform our lowly bodies so that they will be like his glorious body" (Philippians 3:20, 21).

If we feel too much at home on this earth, we may lose out on the real thing.

Psalm 119:25-32

"I am laid low in the dust; preserve my life according to your word."

"I am laid low in the dust" conveys more than a sense of discouragement. The Hebrew word suggests a being thrown into the dust and clinging to it.

The Psalmist goes back to the day when God first created man out of the dust of the earth and breathed the breath of life into him by which act man became a living soul. We read in Genesis: "The LORD God formed the man from the dust of the ground and breathed into his nostrils the breath of life, and the man became a living being" (Genesis 2:7). The coming of sin into the world brought about a structural change in man so that God saw no more in him than the dust from which he was formed. That is why we read after the fall: "for dust you are and to dust you will return" (Genesis 3:9). Seeing himself thrown back into the dust, the Psalmist realizes how enormous the damage is that sin caused in this world. He prayed for a repetition of the miracle of creation of that day when man first became a partaker of the divine life.

The Psalmist's prayer was answered in the Lord Jesus Christ, who breathed upon His disciples, so they would receive the Holy Spirit. We read in the Gospels: "And with that he breathed on them and said, 'Receive the Holy Spirit' " (John 20:22). At the same time "He opened their minds so they could understand the Scriptures" (Luke 24:45).

We will only recognize the creative and life-giving power of the Word of God if we have been made alive by that Word. The miracle of creation, which we read about in Genesis, is repeated in the spiritual realm in the heart of each child of God. That is why Paul says "For God, who said, 'Let light shine out of darkness,' made his light shine in our hearts to give us the light of the knowledge of the glory of God in the face of Christ" (II Corinthians 4:6). The Psalmist must have gotten a taste of this, but he could as yet not drink his fill of the Holy Spirit as we can now.

God makes us new when we ask Jesus to come into our life. "If anyone is in Christ, he is a new creation; the old has gone, the new has come!" (II Corinthians 5:17).

The fact that God makes us a new creation does not eliminate our choices. The Psalmist states clearly: "I have chosen the way of truth. "I hold fast to your statutes." And "I run in the path of your commands." As a matter of fact the Holy Spirit within us makes us free and enables us to choose.

Psalm 119:33-40

"Turn my eyes away from worthless things; preserve my life according to your word."

One old children's song goes: "Be careful little eyes what you see!" Our eyes can get us into trouble. The eyes of Eve got the whole human race in trouble. Sin entered the world "When the woman saw that the fruit of the tree was good for food and pleasing to the eye, and also desirable for gaining wisdom, [and] she took some and ate it" (Genesis 3:6). Our eyes can trick us and make us attribute non-existent qualities to things we see. The advertising business has capitalized on this and perfected their trade to a science. Experts in the business have put up cameras to record people's reactions to certain colors, shapes, or scents of products they wanted to sell. Some of them were shocked with their findings. They realized that some ways of introducing a product would stop the blinking of the people's eyelids and bring them into a trance in which they would buy without needing or knowing.

Our eyes can deceive us and cause us to lie to ourselves. In spite of what the sellers tell us, we don't owe it to ourselves to buy everything they offer.

The Book of Ecclesiastes provides us with some valuable lessons. King Solomon begins his treatise by stating: "Meaningless! Meaningless! Utterly meaningless! Everything is meaningless" (Ecclesiastes 1:2). No one ever told him that if everything is meaningless, the word "meaningless" has no meaning either! From his following statements, we conclude that the emptiness Solomon saw around him revealed the emptiness of his own soul.

Our eyes deceive us because our heart deceives us. Jeremiah complained: "The heart is deceitful above all things and beyond cure. Who can understand it?" (Jeremiah 17:9).

The cure for our heart and for our eyes is in the Word of God. Even if our words are meaningless, God's Word has meaning, because God is the meaning of all creation. If the Word of God has given us life, it can also preserve our life. It will guide us to the things that are worth looking at and we will learn to look at things in the right way. Some things we see will make us wise, others will not. Those we want to avoid. Jesus says: "I counsel you to buy from me…salve to put on your eyes, so you can see" (Revelation 3:18).

Psalm 119:41-48

"I will speak of your statutes before kings and will not be put to shame, for I delight in your commands because I love them."

Not many of us will move around in palaces and rub shoulders with royalties and heads of states. Most of us would be too impressed by the dignity of a king, a queen, or a president to do more than stammer a few polite words. In most cases court etiquette would not even allow us to open our mouths unless we were asked to do so.

The Psalmist imagines himself in a situation where he would stand before the king. The fact that God had spoken to him, made him realize how unimportant human powers are in comparison to the highest authority of God. If God speaks to us we become the most important person in the world.

Chuck Colson, an aide to President Nixon, says in one of his books that he had always been deeply aware of the importance of his visits at the "Oval Office," but after his conversion, he realized how relatively unimportant human authority was.

The human being who is in authority over us is a person who needs salvation in Jesus Christ as much as everybody else. If we are the one to give him or her the good news, shame or embarrassment must not keep us from it.

Daniel knew that the king of Babylon could order his death at any moment if he would make a slip of the tongue. Yet in his audiences with Nebuchadnezzar he said bravely: "Therefore, O king, be pleased to accept my advice: Renounce your sins by doing what is right, and your wickedness by being kind to the oppressed. It may be that then your prosperity will continue" (Daniel 4:27).

Jesus warned His disciples that they might be arrested and have to appear before a royal court for the specific purpose of giving their testimony of the Gospel of Jesus Christ. He said: "On my account you will be brought before governors and kings as witnesses to them and to the Gentiles. But when they arrest you, do not worry about what to say or how to say it. At that time you will be given what to say, for it will not be you speaking, but the Spirit of your Father speaking through you" (Matthew 10:18-20).

There is no need to be brave now, but we may pray that we will not let our Lord down when we are called upon to do what He predestined us to do. And if we are willing to testify to the king, we may start by doing it to any of the king's subjects.

Psalm 119:49-56

"Your statutes have been my songs in the house of my pilgrimage."

I definitely prefer this verse in the New King James Version to the New International Version's "Your decrees are the theme of my song wherever I lodge." Being a music lover this text speaks deeply to me.

If we have ever traveled abroad and have been submerged in a culture that is foreign to us, we know what it means to feel homesick. Nothing is so much part of a culture than music. To be thousands of miles from home and hear the national anthem of our motherland can stir us to the depths of our souls.

The Psalmist considered himself to be a foreigner on earth. His native country is heaven. God's statutes are to him like his native music. We can almost see him, spending the night somewhere in a motel far away from home, grabbing his guitar and playing a tune from home.

The Psalmist was more than a foreigner far away from home; he called himself a pilgrim. According to *The Merriam-Webster Dictionary*, a pilgrim is "one who travels to a holy place as an act of devotion." This man is a tramp on his way to heaven. God's statutes are like heavenly music to him.

If we feel too much at home in the world in which we live, God's music will not stir our souls. But if we know that this earth is only a temporary abode, that our life here is like a place we pass through on our way home, the tunes from heaven will have a deep and beautiful meaning for us.

If earth has lost its culture shock for us, we are in danger of losing our vision of the world to come. God's statutes ought to be the tunes we hum when we travel along life's road. If we are to join the choir of angels we better get some practice on earth.

What the Psalmist is saying is that obedience to the will of God made him sing.

The apostle Paul says some beautiful things about our homecoming. He says about our life on earth "We know that as long as we are at home in the body we are away from the Lord." And about life to come, he writes: "Now we know that if the earthly tent we live in is destroyed, we have a building from God, an eternal house in heaven." And "Now it is God who has made us for this very purpose and has given us the Spirit as a deposit, guaranteeing what is to come" (II Corinthians 5:1,5,6).

Psalm 119:57-64

"You are my portion, O LORD; I have promised to obey your words."

God made arrangements for Aaron and the priests, that they would inherit no land in Canaan. We read in Numbers: "The LORD said to Aaron, 'You will have no inheritance in their land, nor will you have any share among them; I am your share and your inheritance among the Israelites'" (Numbers 18:20).

The Psalmist may have been a priest or a Levite, or he understood that God had made the Levites an example of what was actually true for every Israelite.

Even as God's children, if we have earthly possessions, we should deal with the world as though we had no dealings with it. Paul writes: "And those who deal with the world as though they had no dealings with it. For the form of this world is passing away" (I Corinthians 7:31 – RSV). If God is our portion, we are unbelievably rich. To enjoy things on earth and leave God out is sheer stupidity. Making the Lord our portion does not narrow things down; it enlarges them infinitely. It means the summit of positivism; it is all encompassing.

The priests and Levites were richer than the other Israelites, not poorer. The other people possessed only images of the real riches; the priests had the original. For us "The Lord is my portion" means: "Christ in you, the hope of glory" (Colossians 1:27).

The most important thing we can do is study the Word of God It is a catastrophe if we start concentrating on things of secondary importance. We are rarely able to see things sharply. Sin has spread a thick blanket of fog over our awareness so all contrasts disappear in the mist. It takes an act of the will, the binding effect of a promise to God, to make us keep the exact course.

There is a direct connection between the knowledge that God is our portion and our being occupied with the Word of God. Jesus makes this clear when He says: "Whoever has my commands and obeys them, he is the one who loves me. He who loves me will be loved by my Father, and I too will love him and show myself to him" (John 14:21). Obeying the will of God is a prerequisite of God's revelation to us. There has to be a climate of obedience and love for us to become conscious of God's presence. If we do not remind ourselves of the Word of God in this corrupt world, we lose our direction. We need two promises: God's and ours. It is my experience that if we promise God to have our quiet time with Him, God will wake us up in time in the morning. If God is our portion, we will make Him our priority.

Psalm 119:57-64

"The earth is filled with your love, O LORD; teach me your decrees."

When Isaiah saw God in a vision, the angels that surrounded the throne of God sang: "Holy, holy, holy is the LORD Almighty; the whole earth is full of his glory" (Isaiah 6:3). Here the Psalmist states, "The earth is filled with your love, O LORD." From our perspective, that is on the basis of the things we can see, we tend to react strongly to this statement. We see with our own eyes how one animal tears another one apart and how this world is full of cruelty. But the little voice inside us tells us that this is not the way things ought to be. Very rarely we are aware of the fact that the visible things that threaten us are not natural; they are not part of what God meant our world to be. What the devil tries to accomplish goes against the grain of God's creation. Yet there is enough left of the original glory of creation, even after the fall, to conclude that "The earth is filled with [God's] love."

What we can see in the beauty that surrounds us are traces of God's love, glory, and holiness. It may be better if we say that these are seeds. Human sin may have marred the original glory and God's love may be hard to detect in the behavior of man and beast, but that which is dormant in the soil will one day sprout and bear fruit again. "For the earth will be filled with the knowledge of the glory of the LORD, as the waters cover the sea" (Habakkuk 2:14).

When the Psalmist exclaims that the earth is filled with God's love, he utters a profession of faith. It is a protest against the present condition of our planet and a proclamation of a coming renewal.

We may have adapted too well to a world that is filled with evil and corruption. But if, in the words of the apostle Peter "we are looking forward to a new heaven and a new earth, the home of righteousness" (II Peter 3:13), we must prepare ourselves for the change. That is why the Psalmist concludes his statement of faith with the prayer "teach me your decrees." While living on earth now, we must rebel against what we see and prepare ourselves for the new earth to come by obeying God's decrees.

Psalm 119:65-72

"Before I was afflicted I went astray, but now I obey your word. It was good for me to be afflicted so that I might learn your decrees."

In these verses the Psalmist shows deep insight in the purpose of suffering. This doesn't mean that pain and suffering do not remain difficult to endure and that we can always see the reason for what we have to endure. The Psalmist came to the conclusion that the goal God wants to reach in human life is ripeness and that hardship is often the only route to achieve this purpose. It is because of his affliction, not in spite of it, that he says: "You are good, and what you do is good."

This is a true confession of faith. It shows that we, humans, don't know ourselves what is good for us. We think affliction is harmful. If we are left alone, we tend to go astray. Only when God begins to put pressure upon our life, do we start to understand what is good and bad. It is bad for us to be at ease. Maturity is shown in our ability to distinguish between good and evil, both objectively as well as subjectively.

Obeying the commandments is not something we do automatically without knowing what we do. God wants us to understand what we obey and why we obey it. This is even more important for us, in whose heart the Holy Spirit has written the law.

It is the Word of God that creates ripeness and maturity in us through affliction. The Psalmist states: "Do good...according to your word, O LORD." But this is not an automatic process. An Indian evangelist, Sadu Sundar Singh once gave the illustration of a butterfly he saw that wrestled to work itself out of a cocoon. When Singh tried to help it by cutting open the cocoon, the butterfly got out without any problem, but after that it was unable to fly. Its struggle to work its way out of the cocoon would have forced the juices of its body into its wings, but now they hung down paralyzed.

It is in times of affliction that we flee toward God. Our moral conscience is awakened and strengthened to the point where we reach spiritual maturity. So it is good that we come under so much pressure that we flee to God. Without the famine, the prodigal son would never have come to himself in the foreign country and returned home.

We don't have to seek suffering, but when it comes upon us, we may find solace in the thought that God intends it, not for our punishment, but for our growing in grace.

Psalm 119:73-80

"Your hands made me and formed me; give me understanding to learn your commands."

The Psalmist does not merely refer to the fact that God created him but that God made him what he is. In the previous verses we read about God's goodness as the basis for affliction; here we read about the testimony of a life that is the result of this affliction. The Psalmist looked at his own life with amazement and he came to the conclusion that the result of God's work in him began to become visible. One *Commentary* writes about this section "They glorified God in me."

There is a danger in such a discovery. The problem is that our testimony ought to be, at least partly, unconscious. As with humility, the more we are aware of it, the less we become it. Oswald Chambers writes in *My Utmost for His Highest*: "We want to be conscious saints and unconscious sinners, but God makes us conscious sinners and unconscious saints."

If God makes us what we are, the restriction will remain that we will not see ourselves as others see us and as we really are. The weakness of our flesh would make it difficult for us to realize the full work of grace in us. We have the tendency to credit ourselves too easily for things we did not bring about ourselves and which often surpass our own abilities and power. We should be constantly aware of this danger.

The Psalmist's prayer in verse 73 is very realistic. He realizes that he is what he is because of the work of God in him and not as the result of his own doing and perseverance. He is also aware of the fact that his own intelligence is insufficient to understand this fact. Actually, he admits that he is too dumb to handle the things God has entrusted to him. His prayer for understanding proves that he understands more than he thinks.

God is the Creator of my body, my soul and my spirit. I am not autonomous. I have to give account to Him for my life, my acts, and my thoughts. If I don't understand my origin, I miss the goal and purpose of my life; and I will be doomed to go astray. How we live is always connected to the understanding of our origin and goal. The decisive factor in the conversion of the prodigal son was the remembrance of his father's house.

The intent of God's commands is to show us who we are and where we are going. The only way the world can understand anything about God is if God's commands are demonstrated in our lives. We must be living advertisements of God's grace. Mahatma Gandhi once said: "I would have become a Christian if I could find one." Am I one, are we?

Psalm 119:81-88

"Though I am like a wineskin in the smoke, I do not forget your decrees."

In these verses the Psalmist undoubtedly reached the lowest point in the Psalm. The cries he uttered are not so much a sign of despair as of exhaustion. He was burnt out because his physical strength fails him. The condition of our body often influences the health of our spirit. But if the relationship between these two brings us to despair, something is wrong. Tensions may become too much for us to bear. But frequently, when we think that the pressures become too heavy, we come to the realization that it is not our duty to stand up in our own strength. The Psalmist had not come to this liberating insight yet.

In His struggle in Gethsemane, our Lord Jesus Christ took upon Himself a burden that went far above His physical abilities to bear. Obviously, He was at the point of collapse when an angel came to give Him strength. We read how "an angel from heaven appeared to him and strengthened him" (Luke 22:43).

Sooner or later every child of God will have to learn that the real Christian life can only be lived in a supernatural way. Often physical energy and spiritual vitality are antipodes. Paul made this discovery in his own life. He wrote: "To keep me from becoming conceited because of these surpassingly great revelations, there was given me a thorn in my flesh, a messenger of Satan, to torment me. Three times I pleaded with the Lord to take it away from me. But he said to me, 'My grace is sufficient for you, for my power is made perfect in weakness.' Therefore I will boast all the more gladly about my weaknesses, so that Christ's power may rest on me. That is why, for Christ's sake, I delight in weaknesses, in insults, in hardships, in persecutions, in difficulties. For when I am weak, then I am strong" (II Corinthians 12:7-10). At the most difficult point in our life salvation is often closer to us than ever.

Bible scholars disagree about the meaning of the image of "a wineskin in the smoke." Some think that wineskins were hung up in smoke to harden them, others believe that the skins become unusable. We get the impression that the Psalmist felt dried out and dirty, a burnt out case. Without God's decrees his situation would be hopeless. Like the angel that touched our Lord in Gethsemane, God is there to touch us at our deepest point. Jesus knows what it means to be burnt out. When we cry out, we will find a sympathetic ear.

Psalm 119:89-96

"If your law had not been my delight, I would have perished in my affliction."

With this twelfth stanza we have arrived at the mid-way point of the Psalm. The subject that is celebrated here is the eternal character of the law. Up to this point, the Psalmist had been struggling with his emotions and despairs. He realized that the essence of man's misery, that which causes him the deepest suffering is the temporal, transitory, and corruptible character of life. Life is fenced in by death, which makes life senseless. In the present stanza the Psalmist breaks through this impasse.

"Your word, O LORD, is eternal; it stands firm in the heavens." He understood that truth is absolute and that there is an eternal point of reference by which all our actions will be measured. There is no such concept as situational ethics, the principle that states, "If it feels good, do it!" What is good or evil on earth is good or evil in the whole universe.

Our moral condition is a decisive factor in the place we occupy in this creation. Jesus stilled the wind and the waves, walked on water, and conquered death by the power of His holiness. And the Bible says about us: "the man who does the will of God lives forever" (I John 2:17).

The Psalmist makes no distinction between God's relationship with material creation and His covenant with man. Laying the foundation of the earth and God's faithfulness toward generations of men are treated as poetical parallels. "Your faithfulness continues through all generations; you established the earth, and it endures." We may look at the stability of visible things and take them as a guarantee of the quality of God's dealing with us. We have to understand that if God's faithfulness toward us would cease, the atoms would split apart. The fact that the sun rises proves that God is who He is. That insight ought to widen our horizon.

The Psalmist states that he delights in God's law. That is not an indulgence in a hobby for regulations or a finding of security in knowing the do's and don'ts, but an understanding of the greatness of the One who created the universe and showed us how to live in it.

That is why sinners actually don't belong in this world, and that is why the land spews out those who steal and lie and murder.

On the other hand, we can be pure inwardly only if we are able to delight in God's creation. That is why our ability to reign over God's creation is closely connected to our redemption in Jesus Christ. "Blessed are the meek, for they will inherit the earth" (Matthew 5:5). It is God's law in which we may delight that puts us here and gives us the authority.

Psalm 119:89-96

"Save me, for I am yours."

The great theme of these verses is the contrast between God's eternal Word and the transience of human life. This section ends with the words "To all perfection I see a limit; but your commands are boundless." As one commentator observes, "the verse gives the message of the book of Ecclesiastes in a nutshell." The Psalmist didn't live long enough on earth to say this from experience. The Holy Spirit put these words in his mouth, and the Holy Spirit knew what He was talking about.

It is good to know that we live in the shadow of death. The person who lives as if he will never die is a fool. As Christians we belong to the resurrection, and we are looking forward to eternal life.

The statement "I am yours" presupposes an act of personal surrender. It would be impossible to draw the conclusions the Psalmist drew in this stanza, if there were no act of surrender. We cannot see ourselves as a fitting part of creation without personal abandon to the will of God. Harmony is only possible through submission of our will to the will of God. How would it be possible to be God's own and God not save us and keep us? In the parable of the lost sheep, the shepherd looks for the sheep because it is his. Our surrender and obedience are not the reasons God saves us; the reason is in God, not in us. Solomon sings: "I belong to my lover, and his desire is for me" (Song of Songs 7:10).

In the light of the theme of this stanza, the eternal character of God, the plot of the wicked to destroy the Psalmist comes to stand in a different light. The Word of God puts the efforts of the devil in the right perspective. This is important, because otherwise we would easily be overwhelmed by the propaganda of the enemy. We should not underestimate the threats of the Evil One. We read in Acts that the apostles prayed: "Now, Lord, consider their threats and enable your servants to speak your word with great boldness" (Acts 4:29). If the threats of the enemy influence our testimony, if we do not do what we should and if we are not what we should be, we are defeated. But if we belong to Jesus Christ because we have willingly signed over the rights of our life to Him, our protection will be God's business. Satan will not be able to get to us over Jesus' dead body. And since the death of Christ meant the end of the devil's power, He will stay away from us.

Psalm 119:97-104

"I have more insight than all my teachers, for I meditate on your statutes. I have more understanding than the elders, for I obey your precepts."

Some young people tend to have an overblown concept of their own knowledge. Reading the words of our text, one wonders whether the Psalmist simply made a youthful overstatement and that he may have changed his mind as he grew older.

But true wisdom does not always come with age. Many people gather experience that they are unable to digest. Some people gather experiences as others collect junk. The beginning of all wisdom is the fear of the Lord. If at one point, we do not align our lives with the will of God through an act of personal surrender, we will remain fools all our life.

Some teachers are highly educated and yet lack the basic wisdom needed in life. I once spoke with a family member who was an intelligent person, a math teacher in high school, about the need to invite Jesus in his life. He answered that the Gospel was not for him because he was an intellectual.

An accumulation of knowledge is not the same as wisdom. Wisdom consists of the skillful use of knowledge and that skill can only be learned from God.

As a twelve-year old boy, Jesus stayed in the temple after His parents had started on their journey home. The cream of theologians was there and the young boy wanted to learn more about His heavenly Father. It turned out that He understood more about God than they did. We read that His parents found Him, "sitting among the teachers, listening to them and asking them questions. Everyone who heard him was amazed at his understanding and his answers" (Luke 2:46-48).

Wisdom belongs to God alone and not to man. A teacher cannot pass on God's wisdom to others. He may demonstrate the wisdom God has given him; he may explain the principles, and he may show the way, but he cannot give to others what is not his.

We must respect our teachers, but we are not obliged to swallow everything they teach us. If what we are taught puts a wedge between God and our soul, we must turn to the statutes and precepts God has given us and abide with them. We must go after wisdom more than knowledge.

Psalm 119:97-104

"How sweet are your words to my taste, sweeter than honey to my mouth!"

These words suggest that there is a similarity between natural and spiritual nourishment. We find this comparison in other place in the Bible also. Moses said to the Israelites: - "He humbled you, causing you to hunger and then feeding you with manna, which neither you nor your fathers had known, to teach you that man does not live on bread alone but on every word that comes from the mouth of the LORD" (Deuteronomy 8:3). And Jeremiah told God: "When your words came, I ate them; they were my joy and my heart's delight, for I bear your name, O LORD God Almighty" (Jeremiah 15:16).

We not only *need* food, we also *enjoy* eating it. Everybody likes delicious food. God created food for the stomach and the stomach for food. All functions of the human body, when used for the purpose for which God created them, are enjoyable.

When we compare food for the physical needs with food for the soul, the Word of God is far superior and gives the greatest enjoyment. Our spirit is more than our body, and its capacity for enjoyment is greater. God created our heart, as Augustine said, more than for anything else, for the purpose that we would find rest in Him. There is no greater satisfaction than to rest in God.

In our calorie conscious society the Psalmist's words may have lost some of its vibrant meaning. People with a sweet tooth and chocoholics are considered oddballs in our world of trim health and fitness.

The topic becomes even more peculiar when we consider that the Psalmist actually speaks about obedience to the law of God. He enjoys the Word of God so much because he obeys it. Our minds may have become so warped that we treat any kind of obedience as an infringement on our personal liberty We do not realize that true liberty is in obedience to God. And if the basis for our obedience is love for God, the Word of God will be the greatest satisfaction of our life. Jesus said to His disciples: "I have food to eat that you know nothing about. My food is to do the will of him who sent me and to finish his work" (John 4:32-35).

A healthy daily diet of God's Word read in a spirit of loving obedience will assure us of excellent spiritual health and fitness --the most enjoyable experience we can have!

Psalm 119:105-112

"Your word is a lamp to my feet and a light for my path."

This Verse is probably the most quoted verse of this Psalm. The Psalmist concluded the last stanza with the statement "I hate every wrong path." The wrong path is the path that lies in the dark, but on the path that lies before the Psalmist in these verses shines the light of God's Word. Just as on the wrong path we encounter the power of darkness and sin, of hypocrisy and sham, so the path upon which the light of God shines is the way of truth and sincerity.

Actually, the path itself lies in the dark; a lamp would have no effect at midday. Light and darkness are moral realities. Darkness not only represents that which is unknown, but also the confusion and degeneration which are the result of the break with God. Similarly, the light of the Word is an image of fellowship with God and of obedience to His will, through which we obtain moral insight and guidance. The light not only shows the way, it also conquers darkness.

The picture of the path speaks of a journey, of progress, and of a purpose. The light goes before us only if we ourselves go forward. Victory keeps in step with us. The dynamo of a bicycle lamp may be the best example of what is meant, although of course, the Psalmist was not familiar with the gadget. The light shines only as we go on.

Jesus identifies Himself with this light: "I am the light of the world. Whoever follows me will never walk in darkness, but will have the light of life" (John 8:12). "As long as it is day, we must do the work of him who sent me. Night is coming, when no one can work. While I am in the world, I am the light of the world" (John 9:4,5). "Are there not twelve hours of daylight? A man who walks by day will not stumble, for he sees by this world's light. It is when he walks by night that he stumbles, for he has no light" (John 11:9,10).

We will only know where we are going in this life if we walk in the path our Lord Jesus Christ has traced for us. As we walk with the Lord, one step at the time, the light of His Word will always shine exactly on the place where we must take the next step. If we cannot see ahead of us it is time to wait for Him. God does not want us to walk in the dark.

Psalm 119:105-112

"Your statutes are my heritage forever; they are the joy of my heart."

The Bible tells us that a two-fold heritage is involved in God's plan of salvation. Moses prayed God to: "forgive our wickedness and our sin, and take us as your inheritance" (Exodus 34:9). God said to Aaron: "I am your share and your inheritance among the Israelites" (Numbers 18:20). Moses also confirmed: "For the LORD's portion is his people, Jacob his allotted inheritance" (Deuteronomy 32:9). So God is our inheritance and we are His.

There is no doubt about it but that we get the better deal in this. Even if we would inherit all the riches of the richest person in the world, it would not compare to inheriting the riches of God. God's statutes, as we saw earlier, are the expression of God's character. In inheriting His statutes we come into possession of the eternal attributes of God who is perfect. The statutes, more than anything else, express that this is fixed and immovable; it is engraved in stone and poured in concrete. If ever we are looking for a reason to rejoice, here it is!

But what does God win in all of this? Why would the Almighty rejoice in inheriting us? We imagine that if God were like any of us He would feel burdened by having us, so to speak, unloaded on Him. Having the people of Israel as an inheritance was not any unadulterated joy for the Lord. Having us can hardly be considered a treasured possession either. Yet, like the father in the Parable of the Prodigal Son, God is filled with compassion for us and He throws His arms around us and kisses us" (See Luke 15:20).

God considers us a treasure and a perfect pearl of great value. Like the two men in the parable, He sold everything in order to possess us (See Matthew 13:44-46). Looking at ourselves with the stains of sin on us and in us, we can hardly understand why God does this.

The strange problem with us— human beings— is that we are worth much less than we think and much more than we can imagine. We are created in God's image and it is this smirched and defaced image that God is looking for.

The real dilemma we may have to face is that statutes are made to be obeyed. Without obedience there will be no inheritance, neither for God nor for us. Israel's history testifies to this.

Psalm 119:113-120

"I hate double-minded men, but I love your law."

In talking about "double-minded men," the Psalmist speaks not necessarily about other people. In verse 112 he said: "My heart is set on keeping your decrees to the very end." But here he realizes that it is easier to set goals than it is to reach them.

Two powers were struggling in the Psalmist's life. He tried to identify with only one, but that was impossible. This problem has not subsided for us. In Romans, the Apostle Paul describes this condition: "I do not understand what I do. For what I want to do I do not do, but what I hate I do. And if I do what I do not want to do, I agree that the law is good. I know that nothing good lives in me, that is, in my sinful nature. For I have the desire to do what is good, but I cannot carry it out. For what I do is not the good I want to do; no, the evil I do not want to do-- this I keep on doing" (Romans 7:13-26).

If we try to deny this condition we are not realists. All our promises or intentions cannot change this condition. We are responsible for the whole of our being. We don't mind accepting responsibility for the righteousness of Christ that is imputed to us, but not for the lusts of the flesh in us. The only solution is a complete surrender to the authority of Christ.

The dividing line between good and evil is not drawn between one person and another; it goes through everyone's heart.

That makes the pressure of the "evildoers" so painful, because there is so much within us that responds to it. If God is our refuge and our shield, He protects us—first of all—against ourselves.

The problem is linked to our human nature as a whole, not necessarily to our sinful nature alone. As human beings, like Adam when God created him, we are susceptible to temptation. Since we are descendants of the one who introduced sin in this world, we are carriers of the disease also, which makes us even more prone to fall. But we see the same struggle and susceptibility in Jesus Christ. Even after having been filled with the Holy Spirit at His baptism, He was exposed to temptation; the uncorrupted was exposed to corruption. And He was, obviously, not immune to the attacks. The devil knew this. Victory over temptation was not automatic for Jesus. We see this in His temptation in the desert (Matthew 4:1-11). Jesus only found immunity in the Word of God. The same principle was as relevant for the Psalmist as it is for us. We must realize what our condition is and what could happen to us if we don't take God as our refuge and shield and do not hope in His Word.

Psalm 119:113-120

"My flesh trembles in fear of you; I stand in awe of your laws."

The Psalmist confesses that he is afraid of God. This seems inconsistent with the message of the Bible that God is love. Our problem may be that our concept of what love is suffers from distortion. We think of love in terms of soft, fuzzy things, as if God is an old grandfather who is too weak to become angry with us. When Moses asked to see God's glory, God told him: "You cannot see my face, for no one may see me and live" (Exodus 33:20). And when the apostle John saw Jesus in His glory, he said: "When I saw him, I fell at his feet as though dead" (Revelation 1:17). If we would be taken to heaven in our present condition, it would be a most horrifying experience.

The Psalmist saw himself as he really was, with the image of God in which he was created, besmirched and soiled, standing before the glory of God, and he cried: "My flesh trembles in fear of you."

We must understand who God is, in whose image we are created and what the caricature we made of it looks like. Paul says: "Do not be deceived: God cannot be mocked" (Galatians 6:7). And in Hebrews we read: "It is a dreadful thing to fall into the hands of the living God" (Hebrew 10:31).

We shouldn't think that this is only a danger to which unbelievers are exposed. Peter says: "For it is time for judgment to begin with the family of God; and if it begins with us, what will the outcome be for those who do not obey the gospel of God? And, if it is hard for the righteous to be saved, what will become of the ungodly and the sinner? So then, those who suffer according to God's will should commit themselves to their faithful Creator and continue to do good" (I Peter 4:17-19). We must, therefore, as Paul expresses it: "Continue to work out [our] salvation with fear and trembling" (Philippians 2:12).

Our fellowship with God should always be a mixture of intimacy and deep respect. The key to this is confession of sin and receiving of forgiveness. It is only in as much as we are saturated with the love of Christ that fear will disappear from our lives. The apostle John states: "God is love. Whoever lives in love lives in God, and God in him. In this way, love is made complete among us so that we will have confidence on the day of judgment, because in this world we are like him. There is no fear in love. But perfect love drives out fear, because fear has to do with punishment. The one who fears is not made perfect in love" (I John 4:17,18). God's love is awesome!

Psalm 119:121-128

"Ensure your servant's well-being; let not the arrogant oppress me."

We may get the wrong impression when we read these words, as if the Psalmist wanted God to bless him with good health and an easy life. The New King James Version translates the original better: "Be surety for Your servant for good; do not let the proud oppress me." A surety is a person who takes responsibility for other people's debts.

Jesus Christ is our surety. Isaiah says of Him in Chapter Fifty-three of his prophecy: "Surely he took up our infirmities and carried our sorrows" (Isaiah 53:4), "But he was pierced for our transgressions, he was crushed for our iniquities; the punishment that brought us peace was upon him, and by his wounds we are healed" (v.5) "We all, like sheep, have gone astray, each of us has turned to his own way; and the LORD has laid on him the iniquity of us all" (v.6), "For the transgression of my people he was stricken" (v.8), "And he will bear their iniquities," (v.11), "He poured out his life unto death, and was numbered with the transgressors. For he bore the sin of many, and made intercession for the transgressors" (v.12).

Evidently, the Psalmist knew who was the source of his righteousness. Even in the Old Testament with its incomplete knowledge of justification and redemption, people knew that righteousness consisted in the covering of their sin and in being clothed with a righteousness that did not originate in themselves. How much more then may we boast in the righteousness of Jesus Christ. In the words of the apostle Paul: "God made him who had no sin to be sin for us, so that in him we might become the righteousness of God" (II Corinthians 5:21).

Because of what Christ did for us, we can withstand the pressure of godless people upon our lives. As Paul states: "What, then, shall we say in response to this? If God is for us, who can be against us? Who will bring any charge against those whom God has chosen? It is God who justifies" (Romans 8:31,33).

Since God is our surety, we can be the most secure people in the world. God guarantees to pay our debts; He already did. Therefore, we owe Him everything we possess; we owe Him ourselves.

Psalm 119:121-128

"It is time for you to act, O LORD; your law is being broken."

Who does this Psalmist think he is? He tells God when to act and he probably would tell Him also what to do!

People have broken God's law ever since the fall. There has never been a time when people did not break the Ten Commandments.

But there have been periods in world history when godlessness was more openly demonstrated than at other times, so that God had to pass judgment upon peoples and places. There was such a time when the flood of Noah occurred, which wiped out all of mankind, but for eight souls. The cities Sodom and Gomorrah were destroyed because of the heinous crimes that were committed in them.

There are times when God considers that the measure of iniquity is full and so He acts. God told Abraham about the inhabitants of Canaan: "In the fourth generation your descendants will come back here, for the sin of the Amorites has not yet reached its full measure" (Genesis 15:16). Four centuries later, God ordered the Israelites to take possession of Canaan and execute the sentence He had pronounced earlier.

Centuries later there was the captivity when Israel spent seventy years in Babylon, because they themselves had consistently disregarded God's command. There are times for God to intervene in world history and punish individuals as well as nations.

But God not only acts by punishing. Actually, ever since sin entered the world God has acted. God called Adam after he sinned. We read: "Then the man and his wife heard the sound of the LORD God as he was walking in the garden in the cool of the day, and they hid from the LORD God among the trees of the garden. But the LORD God called to the man, 'Where are you?' " (Genesis 3:8,9). Jesus states: "My Father is always at his work to this very day, and I, too, am working" (John 5:17). God's work is in the first place a work of redemption. John says: "For God did not send his Son into the world to condemn the world, but to save the world through him" (John 3:17). This doesn't mean that there is no judgment, but judgment is not what God wants.

For us, who are in Jesus Christ, judgment is already passed. Jesus said: "I tell you the truth, whoever hears my word and believes him who sent me has eternal life and will not be condemned; he has crossed over from death to life" (John 5:24). God has acted already!

Psalm 119:129-136

"The unfolding of your words gives light; it gives understanding to the simple."

The word "unfolding" suggests the reading of a scroll, or the opening of a book. The reports of the facts of salvation, as recorded in the Bible, are put on the same level with the facts themselves. The written Word is just as much a monument of God's grace as is the Word Incarnate.

When the apostle Peter wrote his second epistle, he told what he had experienced when he was with Jesus and he states: "So I will always remind you of these things, even though you know them and are firmly established in the truth you now have. I think it is right to refresh your memory as long as I live in the tent of this body... And I will make every effort to see that after my departure you will always be able to remember these things. We did not follow cleverly invented stories when we told you about the power and coming of our Lord Jesus Christ, but we were eyewitnesses of his majesty. For he received honor and glory from God the Father when the voice came to him from the Majestic Glory, saying, 'This is my Son, whom I love; with him I am well pleased.' We ourselves heard this voice that came from heaven when we were with him on the sacred mountain. And we have the word of the prophets made more certain, and you will do well to pay attention to it, as to a light shining in a dark place, until the day dawns and the morning star rises in your hearts" (II Peter 1:12-19). He reports about the facts of which he had been an eyewitness for the purpose "to refresh your memory." Peter put his prediction and the following report of events on the same line. Like the Psalmist, he speaks about light, comparing prophecy with a light shining in a dark place. The light itself is a prophecy about the dawn in our heart. God's light starts to shine if we open His Word, if we read it and apply it.

The thrill one experiences in nature at the rising of the sun can be compared to the emotions of a person who opens the Bible and sees darkness disappear at the dawn of the new morning. "The path of the righteous is like the first gleam of dawn, shining ever brighter till the full light of day" (Proverbs 4:18).

Psalm 119:129-136

"Make your face shine upon your servant and teach me your decrees."

This prayer is borrowed from the priestly blessing: "The LORD bless you and keep you; The LORD make his face shine upon you and be gracious to you; the LORD turn his face toward you and give you peace" (Numbers 6:24-26). God shared His glory with Moses and from the words of this blessing we understand that it was His intention that every Israelite would share in this blessing also.

When God's face shone upon Moses, his face reflected some of that glory. We read: "When Moses came down from Mount Sinai with the two tablets of the Testimony in his hands, he was not aware that his face was radiant because he had spoken with the LORD. When Aaron and all the Israelites saw Moses, his face was radiant, and they were afraid to come near him" (Exodus 34:29,30).

When we ask Jesus to come into our heart, our faces will not light up in the same way Moses' face did. In the Old Testament this was an outward demonstration; in the New Testament it is the presence of Jesus Christ within us by the Holy Spirit. Paul calls this: "Christ in you, the hope of glory" (Colossians 1:27). Some of the glory of Jesus ought to be visible in our lives, if we have surrendered to Him. We may be as Moses, who was not aware that his face was radiant, but it will be noticeable to others. Paul writes: "And we, who with unveiled faces all reflect the Lord's glory, are being transformed into his likeness with ever-increasing glory, which comes from the Lord, who is the Spirit" (II Corinthians 3:18). It is for this glory the Psalmist prays here.

In our present condition, we cannot see God's face and stay alive. God's ultimate purpose is that we shall see Him and partake of His character. We read in Revelations: "They will see his face, and his name will be on their foreheads" (Revelation 22:4). Great changes will have to take place within us before we will be able to see Him. This metamorphosis is slowly taking place in our present situation if we live a life of obedience and of fellowship with God. The Psalmist establishes a clear link between glory and obedience.

We have little idea what it will mean for us to share God's glory, yet this is God's plan for our life. If we could catch one glimpse of what heaven will be like, we would never for one moment entertain the idea of disobeying the Lord of glory.

Psalm 119:137-144

"My zeal wears me out, for my enemies ignore your words."

There is a danger that we burn out in doing the work of the Lord. We only possess a limited supply of energy and if we spend it all on God's cause, we may become like the virgins in the parable, in Matthew 25:1-12, whose lamps had gone out because they were out of oil. They missed out on what it was all about, the arrival of the bridegroom and the wedding feast.

The Psalmist looked at the world around him and found it filled with people who didn't care about God or His Word. He spent himself evangelizing and trying to convert people, but no one seemed to be interested. At the end he was exhausted.

When Jesus chose His co-workers, we read: "He appointed twelve-designating them apostles-that they might be with him and that he might send them out to preach" (Mark 3:14). When God calls us, He calls us primarily to Himself, to be with Him and to enter into a relationship of love and friendship with Him.

In our daily life it is much easier to do something for God than to "be with Him." Unless we love Him with all our heart, soul, mind, and will, we will turn into spiritual workaholics and it will wear us out. If we feel burned out, we must check and see if we have allowed our zeal for the Lord to substitute for our love for the Lord. If we are with Him, His Spirit will work through and it will not wear us out. He will provide the oil for our lamps. When the apostles Peter and John performed the miracle of the healing of the paraplegic, the members of the Sanhedrin who wanted to punish them "took note that these men had been with Jesus" (Acts 4:13).

If we enter into an intimate relationship with Jesus Christ, He will transfer His passion for souls to us. Jesus loves the lost more than we ever can. We read: "When he saw the crowds, he had compassion on them, because they were harassed and helpless, like sheep without a shepherd" (Matthew 9:36). We ought not to try to work ourselves up to Jesus' level of compassion; it will wear us out. He will communicate to us His love for a lost world. Then and only then we can do something.

Psalm 119:137-144

"Your promises have been thoroughly tested, and your servant loves them."

An alternate reading of this verse is: "Your word is very pure." The Hebrew word refers to the process of smelting and purifying metal.

Purity means absence of particles that do not belong to the element. Human words and motives are never completely pure. We have ulterior motives in everything we think, do, or say. The Holy Spirit may say various things with one word, but that does not diminish its purity in any way. In Jesus' conversations we see this purity demonstrated. The Lord must have made the impression upon everyone with whom He entered into conversation that what He said was one hundred percent true and pure. That is why His words always penetrate immediately to the core of the matter. God's Word proves that there are no hidden things or incomprehensible matters for Him.

The Psalmist tells us that God's promises have been in the crucible and withstood the most severe testing; they came out vindicated. Everything God promised turned out to be true.

The smelting pots in which God's truths are tested are the hardships of our life on earth. There are no circumstances in human life that can prove God's promises wrong and unreliable. There may be seeming inconsistencies in which it appears as if God is letting us down, but when we look back upon our darkest hours, we see that God was closer to us then than at any other moment in life. God said to Isaiah: "When you walk through the fire, you will not be burned; the flames will not set you ablaze. For I am the LORD, your God, the Holy one of Israel, your Savior" (Isaiah 43:2,3). For Shadrach, Meshach and Abednego this became literally true when King Nebuchadnezzar tried to cremate them alive. When they came out of the king's oven, we read: "the fire had not harmed their bodies, nor was a hair of their heads singed; their robes were not scorched, and there was no smell of fire on them" (Daniel 3:26,27).

And the apostle Paul assures us that he is "convinced that neither death nor life, neither angels nor demons, neither the present nor the future, nor any powers, neither height nor depth, nor anything else in all creation, will be able to separate us from the love of God that is in Christ Jesus our Lord" (Romans 8:38,39).

My wife and I spent approximately thirty-eight years in the jungle of Indonesia. We can testify that the Lord never let us down.

Psalm 119:145-152

"I rise before dawn and cry for help; I have put my hope in your word. My eyes stay open through the watches of the night, that I may meditate on your promises."

These verses indicate that the Psalmist followed a strict daily routine in his devotional life: "I rise before dawn and cry for help; I have put my hope in your word. My eyes stay open through the watches of the night, that I may meditate on your promises." Early in the morning and late at night he set aside fixed periods of meditation and prayer. A profound spiritual life is in no way in conflict with the keeping of a strict daily routine. Without a program of regularity our enthusiasm will soon ebb away.

We may all be created equal but not everyone fits in the same pattern. We are not all night owls or morning persons. It is good to create habits, devotional and otherwise, that fit our personality and stamina. Yours truly usually goes "brain dead" rather early in the evening and having my quiet time of Bible reading and prayer late at night, just before going to bed, would be detrimental for my spiritual health. But one colleague of mine who was in the habit of having devotions in the evening argued that her pattern was more biblical. According to my friend, the day begins in the evening: "And there was evening, and there was morning--the first day!" (Genesis 1:5).

The important thing is that we seek the Lord on a daily basis and spread out the details of our life before Him. Having fixed times keeps us from forgetting. Regular eating habits are said to promote health. The principle applies to our spiritual appetite also.

Forming spiritual disciplines does not have to kill spontaneity. Routine and rut are not identical. If we want twenty-four hour coverage of God's presence, seven days a week, we do well to check that the line is clear, at least once a day.

When Daniel's colleagues plotted to have him removed from office and killed, we read: "Now when Daniel learned that the decree had been published, he went home to his upstairs room where the windows opened toward Jerusalem. Three times a day he got down on his knees and prayed, giving thanks to his God, just as he had done before" (Daniel 6:10). It was this faithful fellowship with God that accounts for his miraculous salvation in the lions' den. Who knows what kind of protection we will need one day. Faithfulness pays off.

Psalm 119:145-152

"Hear my voice in accordance with your love; preserve my life, O LORD, according to your laws."

The Psalmist equates God's love with God's law. In our thinking we often see the two as opposites. God's law is the rulebook that states the dos and don'ts, and that metes out severe and indiscriminate punishment to offenders. God's love, we think, is the warm sentiment that makes Him overlook our faults and shortcomings. Our mistake is not only due to the fact that God's thoughts are higher than ours, but also we misunderstand the quality and essence of God's love and justice. Isaiah states, in connection with God's thoughts: " 'Let the wicked forsake his way and the evil man his thoughts. Let him turn to the LORD, and he will have mercy on him, and to our God, for he will freely pardon. For my thoughts are not your thoughts, neither are your ways my ways,' declares the LORD. As the heavens are higher than the earth, so are my ways higher than your ways and my thoughts than your thoughts.' " (Isaiah 55:7-9).

The Hebrew word, translated here "love" is God's "covenant love," sometimes rendered "lovingkindness." It is God's motivation to enter into a legal relationship with us. It is reflected in the love that impels human beings to exchange vows when they marry.

God's love and justice were fully expressed in the fact that Jesus Christ took upon Himself our sins and paid the penalty in full when He died on the cross. On the basis of that act of love, we have the right to be forgiven, we have the right to be protected and guided on our way to glory.

God's love for us is unlike human love in that He falls in love with us and can fall out of it again. His relationship with us is based on legal grounds. In Paul's words: "If we are faithless, he will remain faithful, for he cannot disown himself" (II Timothy 2:13). Since Jesus died and rose for us, we have a right to participate in His life. As Paul also says to Timothy: "Here is a trustworthy saying: If we died with him, we will also live with him" (II Timothy 2:11). We have a right to the new life in Christ, not on the basis of our crying but because of the work Jesus Christ accomplished for us.

Psalm 119:153-160

"Defend my cause and redeem me; preserve my life according to your promise."

As the Psalmist approaches the conclusion of the Psalm, his tone becomes more intense. The theme of this stanza is "preserve my life," or as some other versions read: "give me life," "revive me," or "quicken me." We find these words three times in this stanza, in verses 154, 156, and 159. The Hebrew word means, "make to live" or "let live."

The fact that the Psalmist stresses the point so much shows that the issue in this Psalm is not the knowing of God's law as an academic pursuit, but that it is a matter of life or death. When Moses spoke his last words to the Israelites, he said: "See, I set before you today life and prosperity, death and destruction. This day I call heaven and earth as witnesses against you that I have set before you life and death, blessings and curses. Now choose life, so that you and your children may live" (Deuteronomy 30:15,19). The issue is not a series of rules and regulations. God's Word means life.

Real life consists of knowing God and of obeying Him on the basis of a personal relationship of love. That is why Jesus said: "Now this is eternal life: that they may know you, the only true God, and Jesus Christ, whom you have sent" (John 17:3).

The life mentioned here is not mere physical life, which is only part of it. It is possible to be alive physically and be spiritually dead. The point made is the spiritual life that is brought about by the presence of the Holy Spirit within us. Speaking about the coming of the Holy Spirit Jesus said to His disciples: "You will see me. Because I live, you also will live" (John 14:9). His physical resurrection from the dead played an important role in their seeing Him, but that was not all. Physical life without spiritual life amounts to nothing; it is worse than death. Actually, it *is* death. The life the Psalmist speaks of is the very life of God, the life that cannot die.

God told Adam he would die the day he sinned. Although Adam kept on living for almost a millennium, his spirit died that day. His lifeline with God was cut. A cut flower is a dead flower, even if it looks alive in a vase. When God's Spirit moves into our life, we are quickened. When we pray for "life," we ask for a lot --we ask for God Himself!

Psalm 119:161-168

"Rulers persecute me without cause, but my heart trembles at your word."

We don't know when this Psalm was written and who was the king that ruled over Israel during the Psalmist's lifetime. It appears that the government was not one that sought to prioritize the law of God. The Bible states about several of the kings of Judah and Israel: "He did evil in the eyes of the LORD" (I Kings 15:26). One commentary renders this verse: "The authorities persecute me without reason."

It could be that the Psalmist was more the victim of slander than of open persecution and physical abuse. But spiritual and emotional pressure is often harder to endure than corporal mistreatment. The author of this Psalm, however, takes the attitude on which Jesus would later expound: "Do not be afraid of those who kill the body but cannot kill the soul. Rather, be afraid of the One who can destroy both soul and body in hell" (Matthew 10:28).

If our eyes remain open to the spiritual reality, we keep things in their right perspective. Fear of man and fear of God are mutually exclusive. Our fear of man is related to our fear of death, which the devil manipulates cleverly. Human beings can do horrible things to one another. We cannot always prevent them from harming us physically, but we have the power to keep them from killing our soul. No one can take away from us our integrity and our faith in God unless we allow them to do so.

Elie Wiesel survived the Nazi concentration camp of Auschwitz in which his whole family perished, but his faith in God did not survive. When he witnessed the executing by hanging of a young angel-faced boy, he confessed that God died within him. Corrie ten Boom went through similar experiences in another camp where her sister died. Not only did her relationship with God not suffer, but she confessed that she came out "more than conqueror."

Jesus frees us from the fear of death. "Since the children have flesh and blood, he too shared in their humanity so that by his death he might destroy him who holds the power of death-that is, the devil- and free those who all their lives were held in slavery by their fear of death" (Hebrews 2:14,15). If we are afraid of other people, we are still their slaves and they can make us do what they want. If our heart trembles at the Word of God, we are more than conquerors.

October 22

Psalm 119:161-168

"Great peace have they who love your law, and nothing can make them stumble. I wait for your salvation, O LORD, and I follow your commands."

When the Psalmist states that he loves God's law, he doesn't speak about words written on a scroll or in a book. He was not like a lawyer who has made it his hobby to study law in order to find escape holes in it for a client. He saw the law as a reflection of God's character. The Ten Commandments are the constitution of God's righteousness and the ceremonial law expresses God's love for the sinner who needs atonement for his sins.

The love of God stills the storm in the human heart and creates peace. The application of God's righteousness to our lives means an end to our inner conflicts. If we have peace with God, we are at peace with ourselves and with our neighbors. Jesus invites us: "Come to me, all you who are weary and burdened, and I will give you rest. Take my yoke upon you and learn from me, for I am gentle and humble in heart, and you will find rest for your souls. For my yoke is easy and my burden is light" (Matthew 11:28-30). Obeying the law of God will lift the heavy burden of our life.

Those who carry the yoke of Jesus will not stumble on the narrow path to heaven. Jude states: "To him who is able to keep you from falling and to present you before his glorious presence without fault and with great joy; to the only God our Savior be glory, majesty, power and authority, through Jesus Christ our Lord, before all ages, now and forevermore! Amen" (Jude 1:24).

When the Psalmist says: "I wait for your salvation, O LORD" he doesn't mean that he is still lying under the burden of sin and that God has not yet set him free. There is a salvation that is waiting for us, the seed of which has been planted in our heart when we turned to God and asked Him to forgive us and to come into our heart. At the end of his life, when Jacob gave his blessing to his children, he interrupted himself and said to God: "I have waited for your salvation, O LORD!" (Genesis 49:18 NKJV). The apostle Paul indicates that our salvation will only be complete when God has resurrected our bodies. He writes: "We wait eagerly for our adoption as sons, the redemption of our bodies. For in this hope we were saved" (Romans 8:23,24). Between now and that glorious day to come, we can walk on the way to heaven without stumbling if we love God and obey His Word.

Psalm 119:169-176

"May my cry come before you, O LORD; give me understanding according to your word. May my supplication come before you; deliver me according to your promise."

We have entered into the last stanza of this magnificent Psalm. We have arrived at the last letter of the Hebrew alphabet, the letter *Taw*. The Psalmist recapitulates his theme for the last time. Everything that had come to him before comes back with the exception of the adversaries. What the author is probably saying is that the greatest hindrance for fellowship with God doesn't come from the outside, but from the inside. He considered himself to be his own greatest enemy.

His prayer is for access into the presence of God and for certainty that God hears him. This prayer is an expression of faith; it shows insight into God's character.

What reason do we have to presume that the Creator of heaven and earth would listen to us? There is even no guarantee that God would allow the request to be heard, let alone that He would do something about it. Yet, the Psalmist's prayer is far removed from the agnostic cry: "God! If there is a God..."

The Bible not only guarantees us that God hears our prayers, but also that He hears immediately. Jesus says: "And will not God bring about justice for his chosen ones, who cry out to him day and night? Will he keep putting them off? I tell you, he will see that they get justice, and quickly" (Luke 18:7,8).

The most glorious perspective of what happens when our prayers reach the throne of God is given in Revelation: "Another angel, who had a golden censer, came and stood at the altar. He was given much incense to offer, with the prayers of all the saints, on the golden altar before the throne. The smoke of the incense, together with the prayers of the saints, went up before God from the angel's hand" (Revelation 8:3,4). Our prayers reach God as a sweet fragrance that delights Him and makes Him ecstatic.

We ourselves may enter the place that was off limits to any of the Old Testament saints, with the exception of the high priest, whose symbolic access to God's throne room was limited to one day a year. The writer of Hebrews encourages us: "Therefore, brothers, since we have confidence to enter the Most Holy Place by the blood of Jesus, by a new and living way opened for us through the curtain, that is, his body, and since we have a great priest over the house of God, let us draw near to God with a sincere heart in full assurance of faith, having our hearts sprinkled to cleanse us from a guilty conscience and having our bodies washed with pure water. Let us hold unswervingly to the hope we profess, for he who promised is faithful" (Hebrews 10:19-23).

Psalm 119:169-176

"I have strayed like a lost sheep. Seek your servant, for I have not forgotten your commands."

The Psalm ends with the parable of the Good Shepherd, as Jesus tells it (See Matthew 18:12-14; Luke 15:4-7). It ends where the New Testament begins. The whole Psalm is actually one great confession of lostness, but the Psalmist could not yet see the light that shines through in Isaiah's prophecy – "We all, like sheep, have gone astray, each of us has turned to his own way; and the LORD has laid on him the iniquity of us all," (Isaiah 53:6). Our Lord Jesus Christ is the Good Shepherd, who gives His life for the sheep, as is stated in John's Gospel: "I am the good shepherd. The good shepherd lays down his life for the sheep" (John 10:11). Paul said to the elders of Ephesus: "Keep watch over yourselves and all the flock of which the Holy Spirit has made you overseers. Be shepherds of the church of God, which he bought with his own blood" (Acts 20:28).

If we never come to the point in our life where this Psalmist came, that is -- the realization of our lostness --we will never experience either what the death of Jesus means for us. We need to make ours the Psalmist's confession in order to realize that God laid on Him the iniquity of us all. God does seek us and if He has not found us, it is because we don't want to be found.

As lost sheep we were all like hostages of a foreign hostile power, a power that intends to destroy us. Our ransom has been paid and we have a right to be free.

In conclusion: This Psalm covers the whole Hebrew alphabet of twenty-two letters. Most Western languages have more letters in their alphabet, but that is not important. With the letters of our alphabet, we can make any word in our language we want. Jesus Christ calls Himself "the Alpha and the Omega" (Revelation 1:8). Those are the first and the last letters of the Greek alphabet. If He is the first and the last letter, He is also all the letters in between. In Him God says all He has to say to us. If God speaks to us through this Psalm, it is because He speaks through us in His Son.

Psalm 120

"I am a man of peace; but when I speak, they are for war."

This Psalm is the first in a series of fifteen Psalms, which are known as "Psalms of Degrees," or "Songs of Ascent." Bible scholars are divided about the meaning of those titles. Some think that they may have been sung by pilgrims traveling to the temple in Jerusalem.

The theme of this Psalm suggests a pilgrimage that leads from the lie to the truth. Sin entered our world because our first parents were led to doubt the veracity of the Word of God and they believed a lie. The devil's lie has pursued and hunted us ever since. We no longer mean what we say and our words have become devoid of meaning.

Before sin overran the world, the Word of God had been the instrument of His self-revelation. Heaven and earth were created by the Word of God. The Word has become flesh. In using the word to tell a lie, Satan has caused immeasurable damage to the human mind. The word has become a mere sound that has no immediate relation to reality. The devaluation of the word is the basis of most human anguish.

As far as we know, the Psalmist was not exposed to physical danger. We may, therefore, see this Psalm partly as a prophecy about Jesus, who was driven to the cross because of "lying lips" and "deceitful tongues."

The spiritual and emotional damage that the lie can do to us is much greater than physical death. Spiritual death is the first death that man died. All other forms of death are derived from it. In using the word, the devil did not rob the Word of God from its power but, because man believed the lie, he became separated from the Word. This is the cause of all angst. The lie causes distress and despair.

The fact that human beings hurt and kill each other is the result of the lie, the mistrust of God's Word that marked the beginning of the history of our fallen race.

When we return to the Word of God and to the one who personifies it, Jesus Christ, peace is restored in our life. We will have peace with God and peace with ourselves. And, eventually, when the Father of Lies, the one who invented the lie, is put in chains, there will be peace on earth.

Psalm 121

"I lift up my eyes to the hills--where does my help come from? My help comes from the LORD, the Maker of heaven and earth."

Sometimes we read more in a Scripture verse than we are supposed to. It seems as if the Psalmist's looking up to the hills is part of his search for God. But the hills in his day were often the places where people had built altars for the worship of pagan gods. Those who had given up on God lifted up their eyes to the hills to ask for the help of their idol.

The Psalmist's hope is in the One who made the hills and the valleys, the heavens and the earth.

Mountains may remind us of God's majesty, but they are not identical to it. God is far more glorious than any snow-covered mountain peak.

Both the worshipper of idols and the believer in God, the Creator of heaven and earth, know that they need help. In looking for help the Psalmist makes a choice to put his trust in God, instead of in anything else.

When the Psalmist states from where he expects help to come, he uses the Name LORD, Yahweh, or Jehovah in Hebrew. It is the Name God used to reveal Himself to Moses at the beginning of the history of salvation. God's acts of creation demonstrate the power that guarantees the help. He is the God who redeemed His children from slavery in order to bring them to liberty and human dignity and who redeems us from the power of darkness in order to bring us into the freedom of Jesus Christ. It is, in Paul's words, the "God, who said, 'Let light shine out of darkness,' [who] made his light shine in our hearts to give us the light of the knowledge of the glory of God in the face of Christ" (II Corinthians 4:6). That is, in the first place, the help that is spoken of here.

The Psalmist gives a personal testimony when he states: "*My* help comes from the LORD, the Maker of heaven and earth."

People, who worship idols and seek help from them, are looking at lifeless objects they have made with their own hands. Idols are manmade. That means they can be manipulated. Idols only help those who help themselves.

If we are in real need of help (and who isn't?) we do well to go to the One who is the Maker of heaven and earth, who made us and who is our salvation.

Psalm 121

"He will not let your foot slip--he who watches over you will not slumber; indeed, he who watches over Israel will neither slumber nor sleep."

One thought that keeps some people from becoming a Christian is that they would never be able to live the Christian life. How true this is! No one can walk on the narrow path of the Gospel on his own steam. The Christian life is a supernatural life that can only be lived by the power of God. We can only live as a Christian if we trust God to live in and through us.

The Psalmist assures us that God is more than willing to keep us on the road and to see us through: "He will not let your foot slip." Jude writes in his epistle that God "is able to keep [us] from falling and to present [us] before his glorious presence without fault and with great joy" (Jude v.24). He will do it if we trust Him instead of trusting ourselves.

The Psalmist calls God "He who watches over you," and "He who watches over Israel." In Hebrew this is expressed in one single word, which has the meaning of putting a protecting fence around a property.

While my wife and I were teaching in a Bible school in Indonesia, many of our students became sick with malaria and several of them died. In one year we had eight deaths. We began to pray and asked others to pray that God would put a fiery fence of protection around the campus of the school and He did. The next year, we had no death. We realized though that fences have to be kept up and we couldn't allow our prayer vigil to slacken.

God keeps His vigil if we keep ours. God doesn't doze off or lose His concentration, as we often do. He may lead us on paths that are rocky and slippery, but if we put our trust in Him, He will keep our foot from slipping.

God is Israel's watchman. But Israel's history, which is a chronicle of being lost, indicates that God's protection is not automatic. The majority of Israel was lost because the people didn't want to be kept by God. Without our trusting surrender, God's protection will have no effect for us. God forces His protection on no one.

The light that God shines upon us casts a shadow on our side. The position of the shadow is of no importance here, but the fact of God's nearness and our walking in the light certainly is. If God is our shadow, we are blessed. Our shadow is not part of our body but it cannot be separated from our person and our actions. It is an image of the influence we have upon our surrounding. If God is our shadow, we spread the odor of Christ around us.

Psalm 121

"The LORD will keep you from all harm--he will watch over your life; the LORD will watch over your coming and going both now and forevermore."

This short Psalm is rich enough to go back to it three times. The Psalmist promises God's protection "from all harm." Our personal experience tells us that God's protection against "all harm" does not mean that we will always be protected against pain and suffering. God protects our souls in those circumstances. In everything we undergo, God will keep us from being lost or from suffering spiritual damage. It is absolutely necessary to realize this in order to be kept from despair. When Jesus tells us: "Do not be afraid of those who kill the body but cannot kill the soul" (Matthew 10:28), He implies that we may be killed. Such considerations are only meaningful in the light of eternity. If we keep staring at the present, the importance of our physical well-being will take on enormous proportions. We will only be able to see things in their right perspective in the light of eternity. God's protection reaches into eternity; "both now and forevermore." It sounds contradictory to say that God protects the whole man and, at the same time, that our bodies turn out to be so vulnerable. This paradox demonstrates the two sides of our life as a child of God in a torn world. I don't know how the two pieces fit together, but I have known both periods of sickness and instances of divine healing.

The "coming and going" in Verse Eight (mark the sequence!) probably refers primarily to the coming and going through the temple gate. But "both now and forevermore" places it against the background of eternity. Interestingly, it also covers the time that is spent outside the temple. God also protects us in those periods in which we are not in His immediate presence. We are not called to spend all of our life on earth in the temple. God sends us out with the promise: "And surely I am with you always, to the very end of the age" (Matthew 28:20). Life with God does not only consist of prayer and meditation. We have a daily life to live in which we go out into the world, rub shoulders with other people, make money, make mistakes, make up for them. God wants us to experience His presence in all these details. It takes effort to enter into God's presence in prayer; it takes determination and perseverance to experience God in the marketplace and everywhere else.

Psalm 122

"I rejoiced with those who said to me, 'Let us go to the house of the LORD'."

These Songs of Ascent show a clear progression of thought, yet each of them forms an independent poem. The theme of the first Psalm was a flight from fear. In the second one, the pilgrim was on the way, and in this one he arrives at his destination.

Sometimes there is as much joy in preparation as in reaching the goal. Hope can be as stimulating as receiving that which is hoped for. A strange characteristic of this Psalm is that the actual goal of the pilgrimage is not mentioned; only the setting is alluded to. God's presence is implied but not stated explicitly. It is, however, clear that the glory of Jerusalem is derived from the glory of God.

The Psalm intones a melody of joy, praise, and peace. The joy is related to fellowship. Others, of the same persuasion, invite the Psalmist to the pilgrimage. The joy is not merely personal or individual. There are signs of brotherly love and a passion for souls; otherwise, the others would not have bothered to ask the poet to join them. When I was a young man and a non-Christian, my peers invited me to a youth retreat that would change my life. I reacted differently from this Psalmist. Inwardly, I resisted strongly. The Psalmist accepted the invitation with joy because He knew God, which I didn't.

Every Israelite was required to appear before the Lord three times a year, according to Deuteronomy 16:16. In practice, this commandment was not always observed. We read of Jesus' parents: "Every year his parents went to Jerusalem for the Feast of the Passover" (Luke 2:41). This Psalm suggests that the average Israelite did not routinely go up to Jerusalem.

The impressions upon the Psalmist are too vivid and overwhelming to account for a routine visit. His description sounds more like a once-in-a-lifetime experience. The poet wants to tell us how our reaction ought to be. For that reason he paints a picture of Jerusalem seen through the eyes of someone who had never seen it before. The twelve-year-old Jesus must have seen it that way. In our fellowship with God there is no place for a "déjà vu."

If our fellowship with God has lost its luster, the Lord may allow us to go through a time of crisis and loss. After Jeremiah had witnessed the destruction of Jerusalem, he wrote: "Because of the LORD's great love we are not consumed, for his compassions never fail. They are new every morning; great is your faithfulness" (Lamentations 3:22,23). God has His ways to get our attention!

Psalm 122

"There the thrones for judgment stand, the thrones of the house of David."

It has been objected that, if David had written this Psalm, he would not have mentioned "the thrones of the house of David." We know, however, that David had received a prophecy about the house that God would build him. The prophet Nathan had told David: "The LORD declares to you that the LORD himself will establish a house for you" (II Samuel 7:11). For David, Jerusalem was not only the place of God's revelation of Himself; it was also the place of the fulfillment of God's promises. David had wanted to build a house for God. God responded by saying: "I will build you a house."

When we come to God, He makes us what He wants us to be. When we surrender our lives to Him and tell Him we want to become His servants, He serves us. Jesus said: "The Son of Man did not come to be served, but to serve, and to give his life as a ransom for many" (Matthew 20:28). When we surrender to Jesus, He washes our feet!

The thrones of the house of David are called "the thrones for judgment." This Psalm speaks about judgment, which is the application of righteousness, before it speaks of the peace of Jerusalem.

I will never forget a sermon I once heard on a verse in Hebrews. The writer, speaking about Melchizedek says: "First, his name means 'king of righteousness'; then also, 'king of Salem' means 'king of peace' " (Hebrews 7:2). The topic of the message was "First righteousness, then also peace." The preacher pointed out that this sequence is consistently mentioned in the Bible. There cannot be peace without righteousness, no peace with God and no peace among men. It is because of the righteousness of Jesus Christ that we can have peace with God.

The pilgrims went up to Jerusalem to have fellowship with God, but the throne for judgment of the house of David was a human throne. The actual throne for judgment is the cross of Jesus Christ. That is the place where judgment was executed onto the Son of David. "The punishment that brought us peace was upon him" (Isaiah 53:5). The Apostle Paul writes about both aspects when he says: "Therefore, since we have been justified through faith, we have peace with God through our Lord Jesus Christ," (Romans 5:1) and "For he himself is our peace, who has made the two one and has destroyed the barrier, the dividing wall of hostility, by abolishing in his flesh the law with its commandments and regulations. His purpose was to create in himself one new man out of the two, thus making peace" (Ephesians 2:14,15). Part of this righteousness is the confession of sin, which gives us inner peace.

Psalm 122

"Pray for the peace of Jerusalem."

It is not wrong to love certain places on earth if we have precious memories about them. What is wrong is to love a place instead of loving God. The Psalmist loved Jerusalem because God said that He would dwell there.

The greatest judgment in the entire universe took place in Jerusalem, but that did not, automatically, provide peace for Jerusalem. Ever since the crucifixion, the city has been the center of war and destruction. We must pray for peace for Jerusalem. God's plans are only accomplished through the prayers of His children. There will be no peace for Jerusalem unless we ask for it.

There will be no peace for Jerusalem without the righteousness of our Lord Jesus Christ. Today, the city is still far from the peace this Psalm speaks about.

The peace of Jerusalem is, first of all, the peace of those who have found peace with God. Jesus prayed for the peace of Jerusalem when He said: "Holy Father, protect them by the power of your name-the name you gave me-so that they may be one as we are one... My prayer is not for them alone. I pray also for those who will believe in me through their message, that all of them may be one, Father, just as you are in me and I am in you. May they also be in us so that the world may believe that you have sent me" (John 17:11,20,21).

When the glory of the Lord departed from Jerusalem, as we read in Ezekiel's prophecy and in Matthew's Gospel (Ezekiel, chapters 9-11; Matthew 24:1-3), nothing was left but an empty hull, a dead decomposing body. This doesn't mean that Israel no longer has a place in God's plan. Zechariah prophesied: "And I will pour out on the house of David and the inhabitants of Jerusalem a spirit of grace and supplication. They will look on me, the one they have pierced, and they will mourn for him as one mourns for an only child, and grieve bitterly for him as one grieves for a firstborn son" (Zechariah 12:10). Israel will partake in the redemption of Jesus. The Apostle Paul writes: "I do not want you to be ignorant of this mystery, brothers, so that you may not be conceited: Israel has experienced a hardening in part until the full number of the Gentiles has come in. And so all Israel will be saved, as it is written: 'The deliverer will come from Zion; he will turn godlessness away from Jacob' " (Romans 11:25,26). This change, however, will not occur without repentance and conversion and without our prayers. We as Christians have little in common with modern day Jerusalem. The Jerusalem whose peace we covet is the place of God's revelation.

Psalm 123

"As the eyes of slaves look to the hand of their master, as the eyes of a maid look to the hand of her mistress, so our eyes look to the LORD our God, till he shows us his mercy."

In the previous Psalm, the pilgrim let his eyes roam over the city in which God had promised to reveal Himself. His gaze wandered over his surrounding. As we have seen, Jerusalem owed her glory to the presence of God, but this presence was never mentioned directly in these Psalms. In this Psalm, the poet penetrates to the core. Not only did he recognize that God's presence in Jerusalem is an image of the heavenly reality but he directly addressed God in heaven. This is no roving glance but a deep concentration.

God is seated on the throne of the universe. Isaiah saw this vision: "I saw the Lord seated on a throne, high and exalted, and the train of his robe filled the temple" (Isaiah 6:1). And the apostle John reports: "There before me was a throne in heaven with someone sitting on it. And the one who sat there had the appearance of jasper and carnelian. A rainbow, resembling an emerald, encircled the throne" (Revelation 4:2,3). When we lift up our eyes, we do not look at a projection of our own fantasy but we look up to Him whose throne is in heaven, we see reality. Everything else that is visible to our eyes is a shadow of this reality.

It is impossible to see God, to see His reality and not obey Him. The Psalmist pledged total obedience to God as a slave to his master. He considered himself to be owned by God and indebted to Him. As a Hebrew slave he may have had the option to be free after a period of seven years. But he said to God: "I love my master and my wife and children and do not want to go free" (Exodus 21:5).

We owe our life and redemption to the fact that Jesus died for us and paid for our lives with His own blood. It would only be natural for us to say to Him: "'I love you, my Master, I do not want to go free." The apostle Paul reminds us: "Do you not know that your body is a temple of the Holy Spirit, who is in you, whom you have received from God? You are not your own; you were bought at a price" (I Corinthians 6:19,20). If we do consider ourselves to be God's slave, Jesus responds: "I no longer call you servants... Instead, I have called you friends" (John 15:15).

Psalm 124:1-5

"If the LORD had not been on our side when men attacked us, when their anger flared against us, they would have swallowed us alive."

The Psalmist uses three images to depict Israel's situation: ferocious wild animals, a river in flood stage, and a bird caught in a snare. The three pictures show what human beings can do to each other under the dominion of sin.

A child of God always lives in enemy territory. We are like spies sent to a foreign country. Jesus characterizes the situation with the words: "I am sending you out like sheep among wolves" (Matthew 10:16). What happens to us is never an accident. We are attacked because we have been sent. Without this commission and without Jesus' assurance that He is with us, we would have no chance of survival.

Our problem is that we realize so seldom what our condition is. Jesus' admonition to "be as shrewd as snakes and as innocent as doves" (Matthew 10:16[b]) is not superfluous. The fact that God is with us does not give us license to be careless.

The opening verse: "If the LORD had not been on our side..." is an admission that what happens to us can only be explained supernaturally. This is the core of the matter. It is the only explanation for the continued existence of Israel. It is also the only key to the understanding of the life of every Christian. The Psalmist wanted Israel to live by this understanding. Insight in God's intervention in history is the best guarantee of hope for the future. Israel did not understand that their history was the world's history of salvation. Israel still does not understand this fact at present. The meaning of Israel's history can only be understood in Jesus Christ.

The Psalmist also demonstrated that the actual struggle is "not against flesh and blood, but against the rulers, against the authorities, against the powers of this dark world and against the spiritual forces of evil in the heavenly realms" (Ephesians 6:12,13). The fact that the struggle takes on the form of human opposition is only a smoke screen. People who oppose us are being manipulated by higher powers.

God's presence with us provides the ultimate protection for our souls. As Paul states: "If God is for us, who can be against us? He who did not spare his own Son, but gave him up for us all-how will he not also, along with him, graciously give us all things? (Romans 8:31,32). This does not mean, however, that there will be no physical or emotional suffering. Paul also writes: "For your sake we face death all day long; we are considered as sheep to be slaughtered." It is in the midst of such circumstances, not because of their absence, that "we are more than conquerors through him who loved us" (Romans 8:36,37).

Psalm 124:6-8

"Our help is in the name of the LORD, the Maker of heaven and earth."

The three illustrations in this Psalm bring the problem closer to home. We do not only experience hardship and opposition because we represent the Kingdom of Heaven in a broken and rebellious world. There is the matter of sin within that has to be dealt with before we can do any work or representation.

As far as our experience is concerned, the images are given in a reversed order. We begin by being trapped in a snare, then we are swept away by the current, and finally the monster will devour us. But our salvation in Jesus Christ begins at the other end. Because Jesus overcame the monster, our snare is broken. Victory is not incidental; it occurred at the basis. We experience personal deliverance because death has been conquered and the teeth of the animal are broken.

We do well to realize where we would have been if God's grace had not intervened in our lives. It not only helps us to steer away from a judgmental attitude toward others, it helps us to treasure the wonder of our deliverance. We are never above temptation and to believe that we could never commit the sins that others commit leads us into dangerous illusions. It was after Peter had declared: "Even if I have to die with you, I will never disown you," that he denied knowing his Master (Matthew 26:35). Keeping a clear picture of what we were makes us confess: "Amazing grace, how sweet the sound that saved a wretch like me!"

It is tragic that this Psalm that is so applicable to Israel's condition no longer has any meaning for the average Jew of our time. It has, however, lost none of its meaning for us as Christians.

As a child of God we encounter opposition of cosmic proportions. It is not only a question of what one person does to another but of what the prince of the kingdom of darkness in heavenly places does against the representatives of the Kingdom of Heaven on earth. But "our help is in the name of the LORD, the Maker of heaven and earth." There is help in that Name. This does not mean that we are protected by a mantra but by the very character of God; the very being of Jehovah is our guarantee. We are protected by the righteousness of Jesus Christ. He is in us as the hope of glory. Satan will not try to break his teeth on this. He tried it once and it was enough.

A clear concept of what God has done for us will qualify us to represent Him on earth. We will know that the Lord who created heaven and earth will use His same creative power to keep us and lead us.

Psalm 125:1-2

"Those who trust in the LORD are like Mount Zion, which cannot be shaken but endures forever."

The theme of this Psalm is faith; that is, trust in God as a practical way of life. Faith in the Lord means acting on the basis of God's promises and being certain that He will do what He promised. The classic manifesto of faith is found in the eleventh chapter of the Epistle to the Hebrews.

We must note that this kind of faith is seldom found in its pure form. Those people, who are presented as heroes of faith in Hebrews, and elsewhere in Scripture, often turn out to have groped for the truth and stumbled. The only person who ever demonstrated a completely pure and consistent faith is our Lord Jesus Christ. I know of no one else who ever walked on water or who moved mountains. This fact does not make this Psalm worthless. To the contrary, it stimulates us to reach for what God has for us.

Faith is a fundamental need in our pilgrimage. Even when our hopes are fulfilled and we have reached the reality of things unseen, faith will remain a lasting element in eternity.

The Psalmist tells us that faith makes us like Mount Zion. Mount Zion, probably, stands for the temple, the place of God's revelation of Himself. The pilgrim who traveled to Jerusalem, himself became Jerusalem. In the same manner, the heavenly Jerusalem turns out to be the bride of the Lamb. In Revelation, one of the angels says to the apostle John: "Come, I will show you the bride, the wife of the Lamb." John reports: "And he carried me away in the Spirit to a mountain great and high, and showed me the Holy City, Jerusalem, coming down out of heaven from God" (Revelation 21:9,10). Thus the individual members of the body of Christ become the place of God's revelation.

It is obvious that the Psalmist said more than he himself could know or understand. The Word of God which we handle and proclaim far surpasses our own comprehension.

That which begins as simply trusting that God will do for us what He has promised, will bring about a complete change in our lives. We will be transformed from the inside out and eventually the glory of God will become flesh and blood in us as it was in Jesus Christ Himself. All that is needed is faith, as large as a mustard seed.

Psalm 125:3-5

"Do good, O LORD, to those who are good, to those who are upright in heart."

Is God only good to those who are good? And who is good? Does the Psalmist make the same mistake the rich young ruler made, to whom Jesus replied: "Why do you call me good? No one is good-except God alone" (Luke 18:19)? We must not take that verse out of its context. Jesus spoke to a young man who thought that he was good enough for God. The Psalmist speaks about people who put their trust in the Lord and who, on the basis of their faith, do not buckle under the pressure of the enemy to "use their hands to do evil." The goodness of those people is not their inborn tendency but the application, by faith, of the goodness of Jesus Christ to their lives. They "do good works, which God prepared in advance for [them] to do" (Ephesians 2:10). This goodness is the fruit of the confession of their sin and the forgiveness they received.

God's goodness is not a preferential treatment for friends. God gave His Son for the salvation of a world that hates Him. "While we were still sinners, Christ died for us" (Romans 5:8). God is always good to all men. What the Psalmist meant to say is that the man who is saved and forgiven receives a taste of God's goodness which remains hidden to those who cling to their sins. Only those who have received a new heart "are upright in heart."

We rarely realize how ingrained in us is the tendency to believe that we can do something for God for which He owes us something. As if, on the Day of Judgment, our good deeds will be put on one of the scales and our sins on the other and, if the balance tips to the good, we'll go to heaven, if not, we enter hell. We may pay lip service to Isaiah's statement that "All of us have become like one who is unclean, and all our righteous acts are like filthy rags" (Isaiah 64:6). Deep down in our hearts we believe that God will find something of value, something that is worth saving in us.

If we have a picnic and sit under a tree with a plate of food and a bird in that tree drops something right in the middle of our plate, which part of the food do we throw away? To God our sin means total pollution. He has thrown away our old plate and has given us a new one. It is to that new creation God responds with His good deeds to us.

November 6

Psalm 126:1-3

"The LORD has done great things for us, and we are filled with joy."

The Hebrew text rendered "When the LORD brought back the captives to Zion" can also be translated "when the LORD restored the fortunes of Zion." Since this Psalm is part of the "Songs of Ascent," hymns that were sung by pilgrims as they approached the temple in Jerusalem, the second reading makes more sense. When Israel returned from captivity in Babylon there was no temple pilgrims could visit.

We read in the story of Job: "And the LORD restored the fortunes of Job, when he had prayed for his friends" (Job 42:10 – RSV).

We find in this Psalm the double theme of a supernatural intervention which brought about a sudden and complete deliverance, and of the process of the growing of fruit which is the result of man's toil. In the life of a child of God, both elements are present, the heavenly and the earthly. There is a marvelous relationship between the two: laughter and weeping!

Whether this Psalm speaks of a return from captivity, or the exodus from Egypt, or whatever miracle of redemption is meant, the historical facts are all an image of a greater spiritual reality. The apostle Paul states: "For he has rescued us from the dominion of darkness and brought us into the kingdom of the Son he loves, in whom we have redemption, the forgiveness of sins" (Colossians 1:13,14). And Peter writes: "But you are a chosen people, a royal priesthood, a holy nation, a people belonging to God, that you may declare the praises of him who called you out of darkness into his wonderful light"

(I Peter 2:9).

What God has done for us in saving us from perdition and restoring to us honor and dignity seems too good to be true. When this reality penetrates to us, we will burst out in laughter and praise. We should never forget and come to the point where the miracle of our redemption has become a "déjà vu."

However strange this may seem, the reality of our redemption is often more easily recognized by outsiders than by us. We may, initially, react with laughter and songs of joy, but other people will recognize that God was behind these supernatural phenomena. It seems as if there is a lapse of time before we come to the same conclusion. Deep inside, we often say to ourselves that God could reach His goal with us because He had such good material to work with. But outsiders often know better than that! We must never lose sight of the miracle that happened to us! We must never forget that we are God's miracle!

Psalm 126:4-6

"Those who sow in tears will reap with songs of joy."

As we saw yesterday, the words "restore our fortunes" in Hebrew are the same as "bring back the captives." Verse One recounts the surprising miracle God performed in the past, the deliverance from a captivity of sin and slavery. In Verse Four, the Psalmist asks that God would repeat that miracle.

After Israel was freed from Egypt, they found themselves in the desert. It is not uncommon that we find ourselves in a desert after the initial overwhelming joy of our salvation. Speaking about his conversion, the apostle Paul wrote to the Galatians: "When God, who set me apart from birth and called me by his grace, was pleased to reveal his Son … I went immediately into Arabia" (Galatians 1:15-17). After Jesus was baptized and His Father called from heaven, saying: "This is my Son, whom I love; with him I am well pleased," we read "Then Jesus was led by the Spirit into the desert to be tempted by the devil" (Matthew 3:17-4:1).

After the overwhelming experience of salvation and of God's love for us, there must be a time of dryness in which we are put to the test. We need quietude to develop the character the Holy Spirit wants to produce in us. The feeling of being arid inside doesn't mean that our conversion wasn't real. It means that God has work to do in us. The sowing of the Word of God in our hearts will cause us pain and tears. When we sow the same Word in the hearts of others, it will make us weep also.

When members of the Salvation Army went out as missionaries overseas and hit upon hardhearted people who didn't respond to their preaching, General Booth sent them a telegram that read: "Try tears!"

"Those who sow in tears will reap with songs of joy. He who goes out weeping, carrying seed to sow, will return with songs of joy, carrying sheaves with him." God can make our deserts bloom, both inside us and around us. Isaiah prophesied that these things will happen. "The desert and the parched land will be glad; the wilderness will rejoice and blossom. Like the crocus, it will burst into bloom; it will rejoice greatly and shout for joy… Water will gush forth in the wilderness and streams in the desert. The burning sand will become a pool, the thirsty ground bubbling springs" (Isaiah 35:1,2,6,7).

Psalm 127:1-2

"Unless the LORD builds the house, its builders labor in vain."

This Psalm is, first of all, a song of ascents. It is part of a pilgrimage, a search of fellowship with God. It establishes the relationship between fellowship with God and everyday life, especially family life.

We see that the Psalmist uses three pictures to illustrate this truth: the building of a house, the protection of a city, and the raising of a family, all illustrations of the same truth. The unity of the three images means that the founding of a family is like the building of a house, like the guarding of a city. The purpose of building a house is more than providing living space. A house must be a home. A family is a protected unity. A city symbolizes safety. In the olden days, city walls and gates kept the enemy out. The sense of uncertainty with which most people go through life can always be traced back to a lack of security in the family in which they grew up.

Everyone builds something in this world. We all leave something behind when we die. The question is how much of it consists of matter that has lasting value. The apostle Paul writes: "By the grace God has given me, I laid a foundation as an expert builder, and someone else is building on it. But each one should be careful how he builds. For no one can lay any foundation other than the one already laid, which is Jesus Christ. If any man builds on this foundation using gold, silver, costly stones, wood, hay or straw, his work will be shown for what it is, because the Day will bring it to light. It will be revealed with fire, and the fire will test the quality of each man's work. If what he has built survives, he will receive his reward. If it is burned up, he will suffer loss; he himself will be saved, but only as one escaping through the flames" (I Corinthians 3:10-15).

The foundation is the most important part of every construction, whether of a house, a city, or a family. That is why Jesus ended His Sermon on the Mount with the words: "Therefore everyone who hears these words of mine and puts them into practice is like a wise man who built his house on the rock. The rain came down, the streams rose, and the winds blew and beat against that house; yet it did not fall, because it had its foundation on the rock. But everyone who hears these words of mine and does not put them into practice is like a foolish man who built his house on sand. The rain came down, the streams rose, and the winds blew and beat against that house, and it fell with a great crash" (Matthew 7:24-27).

Psalm 127:3-5

"Like arrows in the hands of a warrior are sons born in one's youth."

We must not wrongly draw the conclusion from the Psalmist's words that what matters in life is to have a family that mainly consists of boys. There are civilizations in this world that value boys to the point that girls are neglected, sometimes to the point of abandon. That is not the philosophy propagated here.

In Old Testament culture, as in modern society, the boy carries on the family name. This was considered important because every father eventually dies and loss of the name of a family in Israel meant a loss of the heritage in the Promised Land. The birth of a male child was seen as if one carrier of the family name jumped over the wall of separation death had erected and carried on the heritage beyond.

The enemy in this Psalm is death, the same enemy we face in our time. It is the one the apostle Paul calls "the last enemy" (I Corinthians 15:26). It is about death that the Psalmist says to the fathers of a son: "They will not be put to shame when they contend with their enemies in the gate."

We know that having sons, or children of any sex, is no guarantee against death. We do not lose the heritage God gives us when we only have daughters or when we have no children at all, or remain single all of our life. Our defense against death is in our relationship with Jesus Christ, who said: "I am the resurrection and the life. He who believes in me will live, even though he dies; and whoever lives and believes in me will never die" (John 11:25,26). This Word of God is the sharpest arrow in our struggle against death. The apostle John adds to this: "the man who does the will of God lives forever" (I John 2:17). If we use the Word of God as our weapon against the last enemy, the Psalmist calls us blessed. "Blessed is the man whose quiver is full of them."

It is ultimately the presence of God in our life that counts. We must constantly repeat to ourselves, as we are on our pilgrimage, that if the Lord doesn't build our house, if the Lord doesn't protect our life, if the Lord doesn't bless our family, we live in vain. God wants to bless; we must be willing to be blessed.

Psalm 128:1-4

"Blessed are all who fear the LORD, who walk in his ways."

This Psalm contains the first direct beatitude in the series of Songs of Ascent. As in the previous Psalm, the family is the core of this poem as an image of a heavenly reality. The relationships in this Psalm, however, are not depicted in terms of defense and security but as a growing, flourishing joy, expressed in the word "blessed." The fear of the Lord is synonymous with the recognition that God is the deciding factor and the only value-denominator in the life of man.

The word "fear" is another term to describe the reality of our fellowship with God. It has nothing to do with angst but with the realization that God is the one for whose presence earth and sky will fly (Revelation 20:11). This elevates our relationship with Him to the highest level, far above what we can think or imagine. Fellowship with God is the deepest satisfaction of our being, and a harmonious family is an earthly expression of this fellowship.

We have to be careful not to see in this Psalm a fiat for a "God-wants-you-to-be-rich" theology. The fact that spiritual blessing is expressed in terms of material prosperity does not mean that material blessing is essential. Absence of prosperity is not necessarily an indication that something is wrong in our fellowship with God. It is true that poverty, sickness, death, strife, and discord are not parts of God's original plan with man. On this point also, sin has caused a lot of havoc. The Lord of Glory Himself said: "Foxes have holes and birds of the air have nests, but the Son of Man has no place to lay his head" (Luke 9:58). Why then do we have to assume that we have a right to affluence and to a happy family life? God guarantees us the essentials, which does not mean, necessarily, the material expression of blessing. He "has blessed us in the heavenly realms with every spiritual blessing in Christ" (Ephesians 1:3). Sometimes material blessings are added to this.

God desires to bless us but sin has come in between. We live no longer in the same paradise in which Adam and Eve were placed. We eat our bread by the sweat of our brow. It takes hard work, not only to bring in the food but also to have a family sitting around the table, the mother as a fruitful vine and the children as olive shoots, a truly happy and harmonious fellowship of people who love each other. That takes more than just the sweat of our brow; it takes the blessing of the Lord.

The Beatles used to sing a song about a girl who left her parents' home after "having lived alone" there for sixteen years. Evidently, God did not live in that home.

Psalm 128:5-6

"Peace be upon Israel."

Poetry consists of the use of images to illustrate the truth and reality of something else. It is obvious that children are not olive shoots and wives are not grapevines (or at least not all wives!) Zion is not heaven. But the points of comparison are clear.

The pilgrim had arrived at destination and yet he hasn't. Even if we set out to present-day Jerusalem, we have not experienced what Jerusalem and Zion represent of a heavenly reality. The best our earthly pilgrimage can give us is a foretaste of glory, enough to make us long for more.

Zion, Jerusalem, Israel, and even our families are representations of a heritage that will be ours when we get to heaven.

The Psalmist began this Psalm by pronouncing a blessing upon those who fear God. In the last part of this Psalm, he prays that God would bless us so that we, in turn, would bless Israel.

"Peace be upon Israel." Without peace there will be no true happiness. And without righteousness there can be no peace.

God established righteousness in Jerusalem when Jesus died on the cross, just outside the city walls. That foundation is sufficient to create peace worldwide. That there is no world peace at present, neither in Jerusalem, nor anywhere else, is not because God didn't lay the foundation for it, but because people reject it. If we allow God to place our life upon the foundation of the cross, we will experience God's peace and joy and we will be able to pray that Israel will become what God always wanted it to be: "a kingdom of priests and a holy nation" (Exodus 19:6).

Prayer for the peace of Israel does not focus primarily on the small strip of land on the east coast of the Mediterranean. It pertains to everything Israel stands for, which is to be a vehicle of God's revelation on earth. Prayer for the peace of Israel means that we ask God to make us all a light in this dark world, a city on a hill. Jesus says: "You are the light of the world. A city on a hill cannot be hidden" (Matthew 5:14). Let us all pray for one another that God make us what He wants us to be. He blesses us from Zion to be a blessing to the rest of the world.

Psalm 129:1-4

"Plowmen have plowed my back and made their furrows long. But the LORD is righteous; he has cut me free from the cords of the wicked."

This Psalm gives us a very graphic picture of suffering. "Plowmen have plowed my back and made their furrows long." The Psalmist compares himself and his people to a plowed field. But it is one thing to turn the earth; it is something else to be beaten to the point where your back is ripped open.

We don't know to what particular period of oppression and torture the poet refers here. We know that the Jews have a long history of pogroms and holocausts, but most of those occurred after the time this Psalm was written.

Oppression experienced in our youth marks us for the rest of our life, as does every youth-experience, whether good or bad. There are things from our youth we will never forget. Sexual or emotional abuse, suffered in childhood can maim people for the rest of their life.

The Psalmist doesn't blame God for what happened to him and his people. He states: "But the LORD is righteous." He recognized that what happened to him was the work of other human beings, inhumane people. As a matter of fact, God came into human history and suffered the same punishment Himself. Prophesying about what Jesus suffered at the hands of Roman soldiers, Isaiah wrote: "I offered my back to those who beat me, my cheeks to those who pulled out my beard; I did not hide my face from mocking and spitting" (Isaiah 50:6). And: "Just as there were many who were appalled at him--his appearance was so disfigured beyond that of any man and his form marred beyond human likeness..." (Isaiah 52:14).

The important lesson in this Psalm is not the suffering but the Psalmist's reaction to it. He testified: "God cut me free from the cords of the wicked." The whip cut his back, but not his integrity. He did not respond with wickedness to those who hurt him.

The apostle Peter comments: "To this you were called, because Christ suffered for you, leaving you an example, that you should follow in his steps. 'He committed no sin, and no deceit was found in his mouth.' When they hurled their insults at him, he did not retaliate; when he suffered, he made no threats. Instead, he entrusted himself to him who judges justly. He himself bore our sins in his body on the tree, so that we might die to sins and live for righteousness; by his wounds you have been healed" (I Peter 2:21-25).

The example of Jesus' suffering for us may not always provide physical healing, but it will help us to heal emotionally.

Psalm 129:5-8

"May those who pass by not say, "The blessing of the LORD be upon you; we bless you in the name of the LORD."

The curse pronounced in this Psalm is one of the strangest in the whole Bible. It cuts so deeply because it implies what could have been. In the background we see the abundantly rich harvest that is gathered in under God's blessing. But God is not directly mentioned in this context. The Psalmist draws a comparison without specifying the second factor. That is what makes these lines such powerful poetry.

In a previous Psalm, Israel gathered in its harvest with rejoicing while being oppressed at the same time. We read: "He who goes out weeping, carrying seed to sow, will return with songs of joy, carrying sheaves with him" (Psalm 126:6). Here the wicked are not even compared with a meager harvest but with grass on the roof that withers before it is thrown away. The image makes the wicked a parody of reality. On the Day of Judgment, the angels will not even pay any attention to such people. In the Book of Ruth, Boaz greeted the harvesters with: "The LORD be with you!" and they called back: "The LORD bless you!" (Ruth 2:4). There will be no question of the usual greeting which one reaper will call to another at harvest time.

During the suffering of Jesus, the Roman soldiers mocked Him by treating Him for a moment as if He were a king. They did this on the assumption that He could make no claim to such an honor. The wicked, backed up by Satan and his hordes, lay claim to an honor they do not possess. The Psalmist exposes them here in their shameful nakedness. There can be no question of honor because there is no question of God's blessing. This is the doom of those who hate Zion.

We are not called to curse our fellowmen. When God blesses us, He makes us a blessing. What the Psalmist portrays in this "blessing in reverse" is what happens when we do not recognize the image of God in our fellowmen. In the Parable of the Sheep and the Goats, Jesus says: " 'I tell you the truth, whatever you did not do for one of the least of these, you did not do for me.' Then they will go away to eternal punishment, but the righteous to eternal life." (Matthew 25:41-46).

The only worse thing that could happen to us would be that God doesn't even take the trouble to take a closer look at us. "Though the LORD is on high, he looks upon the lowly, but the proud he knows from afar!" (Psalm 138:6).

Psalm 130:1-2

"Out of the depths I cry to you, O LORD; O Lord, hear my voice. Let your ears be attentive to my cry for mercy."

We are still looking at a Psalm of Ascent, a hymn sung by pilgrims as they approached the temple, the place of God's revelation. Why does someone who draws close to God consider himself to be so low as to cry "out of the depths?" What depths are meant here?

The following verse shows that the Psalmist was conscious of his sin. It is out of this depth, this slimy pit of iniquity that he cried to God.

It is a common phenomenon that the closer we draw to God, the dirtier we get. Not that the amount of sin increases, but our awareness of it does. When we are in a dark room, we cannot see the dirt. When we turn on the light, some will become visible. But when the sun shines through the window, we can see the dust particles dance in the air. It is when we get close enough to God and His light shines upon our lives, that we become conscious of the pollution in our life. When Isaiah saw God in a vision, we read that he cried: "Woe to me! I am ruined! For I am a man of unclean lips, and I live among a people of unclean lips, and my eyes have seen the King, the LORD Almighty" (Isaiah 6:5).

We would have expected to find this Psalm earlier in the series of Songs of Ascent, when the pilgrim set out to encounter God. Our problem is that we don't know ourselves, and we are usually unaware of the extent of our sinfulness. As long as we are far enough away from God, as long as we are in the shade, our sinfulness will not bother us. We know we are not perfect, but then who is? It is as we get close that the Holy Spirit will send us His warning signals, and we become uncomfortable with ourselves to the point where it gets to be unbearable.

If we become enough realistic to see our true condition in the light of God, we are getting close to salvation. God cannot give us forgiveness for sins we don't own up to. But if we cry: "God, have mercy on me, a sinner" (Luke 18:13), salvation is ours instantaneously. We obtain knowledge of salvation through the forgiveness of our sins (Luke 1:77). All it takes is to cry out of the depths of our misery.

Psalm 130:3-4

"But with you there is forgiveness; therefore you are feared."

Forgiveness of our sin creates in us a biblical fear of God. This goes against the grain of our human reasoning. We tend to believe that fear belongs to the realm of evil. So we start from the assumption that we are good. If we project this kind of reasoning upon God, we become good and God is evil and wants to harm us. When it turns out that in reality the opposite is true, it becomes clear that our interpretation of "the fear of the Lord" was wrong. We read in Revelation: "Then the kings of the earth, the princes, the generals, the rich, the mighty, and every slave and every free man hid in caves and among the rocks of the mountains. They called to the mountains and the rocks, 'Fall on us and hide us from the face of him who sits on the throne and from the wrath of the Lamb! For the great day of their wrath has come, and who can stand?' " (Revelation 6:15-17).

Forgiveness draws us out of the realm of evil into the realm of good, out of darkness into light. God's awesomeness does not diminish in this process. To the contrary! When John says: "There is no fear in love. But perfect love drives out fear, because fear has to do with punishment. The one who fears is not made perfect in love" (I John 4:18), he does not contradict the above because he uses the word "fear" in its popular meaning, not in the biblical sense.

The realization of forgiveness increases our sense of awe of God because we begin to understand some of the depth of God's love. When, for example, we are asleep in a house that is on fire and someone runs in to rescue us, and while doing so succumbs to smoke and heat, that person becomes awesome to us. Even if he would only risk his life to save ours, we would owe him an immense debt, but if he perishes for our salvation we consider him our greatest hero. Jesus perished for our salvation; we stand in awe before Him.

If the kings of the earth, the princes, the generals, the rich, the mighty, and every slave and every free man flees for fear in the presence God because of their sin, how much greater must our awe be for Him who lost His life in order to gives us ours!

Psalm 130:5-8

"I wait for the LORD, my soul waits, and in his word I put my hope."

The Psalmist expresses his hope in God by using the image of a night watchman who waits for daybreak. Few things are more certain on earth than the rising of the sun. The weatherman can tell us exactly at what time the sun rises today or tomorrow. We have it all down to a science. God's mercy, His pardon of our sin is even more predictable and reliable than the astronomical phenomena that determine the hours of daylight and the seasons on our planet.

But the day will come when our whole solar system will disintegrate and the sun will no longer rise. In the words of Peter: "But the day of the Lord will come like a thief. The heavens will disappear with a roar; the elements will be destroyed by fire, and the earth and everything in it will be laid bare. That day will bring about the destruction of the heavens by fire, and the elements will melt in the heat" (II Peter 3:10,12). But God, who created us and the planet on which we live, will still be there and extend His mercy to us.

We must remind ourselves that this Psalm is a song of ascents, a pilgrims' song. The Psalmist was on the road to Jerusalem. He either had with him the sacrificial animals or he carried enough money to buy them in Jerusalem. Soon, he would bow down before the altar of Jehovah and bring his sacrifice. He was absolutely certain that God would receive him on the basis of this sacrifice. The writer of Hebrews states: "How much more, then, will the blood of Christ, who through the eternal Spirit offered himself unblemished to God, cleanse our consciences from acts that lead to death, so that we may serve the living God!" (Hebrews 9:14). God promises: " 'Though the mountains be shaken and the hills be removed, yet my unfailing love for you will not be shaken nor my covenant of peace be removed,' says the LORD, who has compassion on you" (Isaiah 54:10).

We have so much more to hope and wait for than this Psalmist ever had. Not only is God's mercy more secure that the rising of the sun, so is our destiny in Jesus Christ. In the words of the apostle John: "The world and its desires pass away, but the man who does the will of God lives forever" (I John 2:17).

Psalm 131

"But I have stilled and quieted my soul; like a weaned child with its mother, like a weaned child is my soul within me."

We can hardly imagine a greater difference in tone than between the previous Psalm and this one. In Psalm One hundred thirty, the pilgrim called to God "out of the depths," here he is quiet and satisfied like a child cradled upon his mother's breast. We could call this Psalm "God's lullaby." The difference with other lullabies is that it is the child who sings it. It is a picture of quietude and satisfaction, of peace and intimacy.

The mother here is God upon whose shoulder we lay our souls after He has fed us to our full satisfaction.

To the woman at the well in Samaria, Jesus said: "Whoever drinks the water I give him will never thirst. Indeed, the water I give him will become in him a spring of water welling up to eternal life" (John 4:14). And to a larger audience, He said "I am the bread of life. He who comes to me will never go hungry, and he who believes in me will never be thirsty" (John 6:35).

Let's forget for a moment the picture we have about a child who is weaned. A weaned infant often goes through a struggle to switch from mother's milk to other food and cries in resistance. This Psalm is a picture of peace and satisfaction. The Hebrew word translated "to wean" means more than being refused the mother's breast; it also has a connotation of ripening.

The Psalmist confesses that he had trouble with pride and haughtiness. Taking his nourishment from God, his restless soul was quieted to the point where he could completely relax against God's shoulder. This takes us beyond what Peter states: "Like newborn babies, crave pure spiritual milk, so that by it you may grow up in your salvation, now that you have tasted that the Lord is good" (I Peter 2:2,3).

Once we get a taste of God's goodness, our pride and haughtiness will disappear and we will experience an intimacy with God, our Father and our Mother, that goes beyond a comparison of being breastfed by our mother when we were first born. We may not remember that far back, but none of us ever lost the memory completely. There is more than one meaning to the word "pacifier." When God feeds and satisfies us, we will realize that we were made for that purpose.

Psalm 132:1-5

"O LORD, remember David and all the hardships he endured."

As the pilgrim approached the temple in Jerusalem, his thoughts went back in history to David, who had been ultimately responsible for the building of that magnificent edifice. In the process he gives God a condensed history lesson, or at least it seems that way.

The word "remember" strikes us as strange; God cannot forget. The Hebrew word translated "remember" means more than "don't forget," it also means: "to recognize." In the story of Noah's flood, for instance, we read: "But God remembered Noah... and he sent a wind over the earth, and the waters receded" (Genesis 8:1). When God remembers, He acts.

Most of David's life had been consumed by a passion to find a place where the Ark of the Covenant could be put, a place were God could reveal Himself on earth. As soon as his kingdom was established, David set to work on detailed plans and at the end of his life, when he entrusted the actual construction to Solomon, he had gathered billions of dollars in gold, silver, and other material for the realization of his vision. He died without ever seeing the fulfillment of his dreams.

These thoughts occupied the mind of the pilgrim as he neared the end of his journey. He may have thought, "If the zeal for God's house consumed David, how does that compare to my life?" We realize how important the question is for us. If the passion of our life is to seek the Kingdom of God and its righteousness, we live our life to the full. Those who have a passion for God's glory are the richest people on earth. We may not see the edifice of God's glory go up during our lifetime, but we will leave behind a monument that will become a compass and a point of reference for others.

That is what faith is all about. The writer of Hebrews states about the Old Testament heroes: "These were all commended for their faith, yet none of them received what had been promised. God had planned something better for us so that only together with us would they be made perfect" (Hebrews 11:39,40). People with a passion for God's glory become trailblazers. Even if we don't see the fulfillment of our vision in our lifetime, devoting our life for the only cause that matters in this world will make us complete persons. We will not die a premature death, even if it may seem that way to others.

Psalm 132:6-9

"We heard it in Ephrathah, we came upon it in the fields of Jaar."

In these verses the Holy Spirit lets us make a giant leap from a pilgrimage, to the temple in Jerusalem to the place where the Christmas story unfolded. We are brought to the field, just outside of Bethlehem, where the shepherds were on the night Jesus was born.

Centuries earlier, young David may have tended his father's sheep in this same field. After Samuel had anointed him as the future king of Israel, "the Spirit of the LORD came upon David in power" (I Samuel 16:13). As David went back to the sheep after this experience, he must have dreamed about his future as the new king. The first thoughts about what to build for the glory of God, once he had become king, must have occurred to him at this very place.

When the glory of the Lord shone around the shepherd and the angel announced to them the birth of the Son of God, and after they had heard the chorus "Glory to God in the highest, and on earth peace to men on whom his favor rests," they got up and said: "Let's go to Bethlehem and see this thing that has happened, which the Lord has told us about" (Luke 2:15). They made the ultimate pilgrimage to the stable and the manger where the Lord of glory had come to reveal Himself in this world.

The bringing of the Ark of the Covenant to Jerusalem and the building of the temple to house it are all pictures that illustrate the greatest event in the history of the universe. "The Word became flesh and made his dwelling among us" (John 1:14). Jesus Christ is the real temple of God, the only place of God's revelation on earth.

Bethlehem and Ephrata are still there, but they are no more, at present, than tourist attractions. Our true pilgrimage can take place anywhere. We can worship God even in our own bedroom. Nowadays Christ wants to be born in human hearts. God wants to reveal Himself in and through us. As a German poet once expressed: "If Christ were born one thousand times in Bethlehem and never in our heart, we would still be lost."

In Verse 9 of this Psalm, the author uses the words "priests" and "saints" as parallels. When God saves us, we become saints and priests at the same time. As saints we worship God, as priests we serve Him and bless people. God gives us a status and a ministry as we make the pilgrimage.

Psalm 132:10-18

"The LORD swore an oath to David, a sure oath that he will not revoke: 'one of your own descendants I will place on your throne'."

The Psalmist places David's oath to God next to God's oath to David. When David told God that he wanted to build a house for Him, God answered that He would build a house for David. We know that the word "house" has more than one meaning. When we speak of the house of Jones, we mean the place where the Jones live. When we mention "the house of Windsor" we mean the dynasty that rules Great Britain. After David had told the prophet Nathan about his plans to build the temple, God sent Nathan to the king with the word: "The LORD declares to you that the LORD himself will establish a house for you" (II Samuel 7:11).

The temple that was built on David's vision and initiative was one of the marvels of the ancient world. As we saw earlier, David had saved billions of dollars for the project. He couldn't know what it would cost God to build "the house of David." What is gold and silver in comparison with heavenly glory? David invested a lot of money, most of his riches to realize his vision for the glory of God. But David never went to bed hungry because of it. God laid aside all of His glory to become a human being. He left nothing to fall back on while living on earth. The Lord of glory testified: "Foxes have holes and birds of the air have nests, but the Son of Man has no place to lay his head" (Matthew 8:20). That was not all; He surrendered His body as a ransom to pay for our salvation. He died on a Roman cross as an outcast, as a common criminal. "He was pierced for our transgressions, he was crushed for our iniquities; the punishment that brought us peace was upon him" (Isaiah 53:5).

God's house cost David a lot, David's house cost God all! When we say to God: "Take my life and let it be consecrated, Lord, to Thee," God bows down before us and washes our feet; He consecrates Himself to us! Amazing love! "No eye has seen, no ear has heard, no mind has conceived what God has prepared for those who love him" (I Corinthians 2:9).

We are God's temple; we are the house God built for David.

Psalm 133

"How good and pleasant it is when brothers live together in unity! For there the LORD bestows his blessing, even life forevermore."

As the pilgrim approached the temple and drew closer to God, he also drew closer to his fellowmen. Fellowship with God binds people together. This is why there was such spontaneous love and unity in the early church after the coming of the Holy Spirit. We read in the Book of Acts: "All the believers were together and had everything in common. Selling their possessions and goods, they gave to anyone as he had need. Every day they continued to meet together in the temple courts. They broke bread in their homes and ate together with glad and sincere hearts" (Acts 2:44-46).

The ideal situation depicted in this Psalm is seldom or never seen on earth. As the ditty goes:

"To live above, with saints we love, that will be bliss and glory.
To live below, with saints we know, is quite a different story!"

The picture of the anointing of Aaron, the high priest, speaks of the work of the Holy

Spirit. Unity of love and fellowship with fellow believers is only possible in the Holy Spirit. It is not a case of some people who live together because they happen to like each other but of a supernatural influence that binds people together. This is the reason fellowship with our fellowmen depends on each person's personal relationship with God.

It is through the new birth that we are born into a new family, the family of God. When God saves us, we acquire new brothers and sisters. We will soon discover that our new family members have idiosyncrasies and rough edges that make us feel uncomfortable. It is only when we realize that God loves and accepts us in spite of our idiosyncrasies and rough edges, that we can begin to love our brothers and sisters in Christ. It is only in loving God that we can begin to love others.

The apostle John shows us how important this is. "This is love: not that we loved God, but that he loved us and sent his Son as an atoning sacrifice for our sins. Dear friends, since God so loved us, we also ought to love one another. No one has ever seen God; but if we love one another, God lives in us and his love is made complete in us" (I John 4:10-12). Love is a choice. Since God chose to love us and we accepted His love, we must be consistent and let His love flow through us.

Love is also very expensive. "This is how we know what love is: Jesus Christ laid down his life for us. And we ought to lay down our lives for our brothers" (I John 3:16).

Psalm 134

"Praise the LORD, all you servants of the LORD who minister by night in the house of the LORD."

This Psalm is the last in the series of Songs of Ascent. The pilgrim has arrived at the temple and he sees the priests and the Levites who served the Lord day and night. We read in the Book of Chronicles: "Those who were musicians, heads of Levite families, stayed in the rooms of the temple and were exempt from other duties because they were responsible for the work day and night" (I Chronicles 9:33). Serving God is a full-time job.

The pilgrim particularly addresses those who were doing the night shift. The night brings out some specific aspects of this service. In more than one sense it takes a special effort to serve God in the dark. During the day, we can see what we are doing and where we are going; at night our vision is limited and we have to trust what we cannot see. Darkness is the domain of the enemy; Satan operates in the dark.

Praising God in the dark is the most effective weapon we can use against the attacks of the enemy. We read about Paul and Silas as they had been put in prison in Philippi and were sitting shackled in their dungeon with bleeding backs: "About midnight Paul and Silas were praying and singing hymns to God, and the other prisoners were listening to them" (Acts 16:25). They fought the powers of darkness with praise and won. God answered their hymn singing with an earthquake that shook the foundation of the prison and of the jailer's life, so that the door of his heart opened and the Lord could move in.

God's light will shine in our darkness if we praise Him. Light is always stronger than darkness. If we cannot see what is ahead of us and we feel God is beyond our reach, we do well to lift up our hands in the sanctuary and praise the LORD. It will lighten up our night.

All children are scared in the dark; it is natural. But no child is afraid to walk in dark places when someone takes his hand and walks with him. That is what God does for us. As Asaph sang: "Yet I am always with you; you hold me by my right hand. You guide me with your counsel, and afterward you will take me into glory" (Psalm 73:23,24). Praise God who takes our hand in the dark!

Psalm 135:1-7

"Praise the LORD, for the LORD is good; sing praise to his name, for that is pleasant."

Almost every verse in this Psalm is a quote from a different Psalm. The author must have gone through the whole hymnal, gathering a bunch of flowers which he presents here as a whole bouquet. But this Psalm is not merely a collection of Bible verses; it teaches its own lesson. Its theme is "praise."

Praise and worship are not only meant for professionals. The fact that the task had been delegated to the priests and the Levites in order to assure that it would be done without interruption doesn't mean that laymen are under no obligation to praise God. The day-and-night praise in the temple gave an eternal character to it within the framework of time. This is, undoubtedly, why the four living creatures in Revelation never cease their praise. We read: "Each of the four living creatures had six wings and was covered with eyes all around, even under his wings. Day and night they never stop saying: 'Holy, holy, holy is the Lord God Almighty, who was, and is, and is to come' " (Revelation 4:8).

The most urgent reason for praising God is the goodness of His character. God is the only Person in the whole universe who is perfectly good. There are in God no ulterior motives as in human demonstrations of goodness. It is precisely the fact that human goodness is not unadulterated and pure that makes it difficult for us to conceive of God's perfect goodness. If we can envision God's perfect goodness, we will have a life-changing experience. Asaph stated: "Surely God is good to Israel, to those who are pure in heart" (Psalm 73:1). Concentration on God's goodness will purify our heart. That is why praising God for His goodness becomes so pleasant to us.

We may not always experience God's goodness as pleasant because we live in a broken world and our own goodness is polluted. The hardships of life tend to limit our vision and prevent us from seeing the whole picture. We blame God for the consequences of sin in our own life and in the world around us. Praising God's goodness will help us break through the impasse and bring us into the wide space of spiritual liberty that we experience as pleasant. Singing about God's Name will do us good. If we make praise a practice, regardless of our circumstances, we will fare well ourselves.

Psalm 135:8-12

"He struck down the firstborn of Egypt, the firstborn of men and animals."

It may be difficult for us to see what God did to the people of Egypt and the kings of Canaan as demonstrations of His goodness and greatness. God's judgment over Egypt was not against the Egyptians as human beings but against the spiritual powers to whom the Egyptians had surrendered themselves. We read in the account of Exodus that God said: "On that same night I will pass through Egypt and strike down every firstborn--both men and animals--and I will bring judgment on all the gods of Egypt. I am the LORD" (Exodus 12:12). The Psalmist elevated history above a struggle between man and man to a confrontation between spiritual powers. Both Egypt and Canaan with their surrounding kingdoms were manifestations of the power of the Evil One. Demonic activity was primarily directed against Israel as the guardian of God's revelation. Satan knew much better why God had chosen Jacob than Israel knew. He could see the coming Messiah from afar, and he knew that the seed of the woman would, eventually, crush the head of the serpent. God's acting in this period did not mean that He did not love the Egyptians and the inhabitants of Canaan, but the way in which they were completely possessed by the powers of darkness made them unacceptable to God's holiness.

The tenth plague of Egypt was a terrible event, a national catastrophe of enormous proportions. It did not come about, though, without previous warning. God only wiped out a whole generation after having issued nine severe warnings which were all ignored. In this way, Egypt learned the lesson that the God of Israel is great upon the whole earth and that His goodness does not tolerate evil. Those in Egypt, who wanted to disassociate themselves from the evil practices of their government, could have applied the blood of the lamb on their doorposts also.

God warns us: "Do not follow the crowd in doing wrong" (Exodus 23:2). We must disassociate ourselves from the evil practices of others, even if they are government endorsed. Those who are guilty by association, whether in Egypt, Canaan, or North America fall under the judgment that is reserved for Satan and his minions. We still have the option of having the blood of the Lamb applied to the door of our heart and placing ourselves under the protection of God's love and goodness.

Psalm 135:13-21

"The LORD will vindicate his people and have compassion on his servants."

The Psalmist knew his history and the facts of salvation. He knew that God intervenes in history to vindicate His people. Vindication suggests payment of debt and rehabilitation, and it supposes the presence of an enemy who oppresses. Israel had experienced a great deal of oppression. Some of it had been their own fault. We read in the Book of Judges that God allowed the Promised Land to be invaded and His people tyrannized by hostile neighbors. This happened because they had abandoned God and turned to idols. "Then the Israelites did evil in the eyes of the LORD and served the Baals. They forsook the LORD, the God of their fathers, who had brought them out of Egypt. They followed and worshiped various gods of the peoples around them. They provoked the LORD to anger because they forsook him and served Baal and the Ashtoreths. In his anger against Israel the LORD handed them over to raiders who plundered them. He sold them to their enemies all around, whom they were no longer able to resist. Whenever Israel went out to fight, the hand of the LORD was against them to defeat them, just as he had sworn to them. They were in great distress" (Judges 2:11-15).

But it had also happened that oppression occurred when the people did follow the Lord and obeyed His commands.

The apostle Paul assures us that "everyone who wants to live a godly life in Christ Jesus will be persecuted" (II Timothy 3:12,13). People who suffer through their own fault may yet experience God's compassion, but those who endure hardship because of their godly testimony have the assurance that God will vindicate them. Jesus pronounces His blessing upon us if we find ourselves in that condition. We read: "Blessed are those who are persecuted because of righteousness, for theirs is the kingdom of heaven. Blessed are you when people insult you, persecute you and falsely say all kinds of evil against you because of me. Rejoice and be glad, because great is your reward in heaven, for in the same way they persecuted the prophets who were before you" (Matthew 5:10-12). Peter states: "But if you suffer for doing good and you endure it, this is *commendable* (the actual Greek word is 'grace') before God." And "But even if you should suffer for what is right, you are blessed" (I Peter 2:20,21; 3:14). Some of us might wish to be less blessed in this regard!

We ought to consider it a compliment when God's enemy pays attention to us; it means that our life and testimony are a threat to his dominion. If Satan notices us, how much more will God! We are caught in the war between God and Satan; as long as we are on God's side, He will save and vindicate us.

Psalm 136:1-9

"Give thanks to the LORD, for he is good. His love endures forever."

It is difficult to read this Psalm without getting caught up in the rhythm of it. The recurring words *His love endures forever* give it a beat that makes us want to clap our hands, or stamp our feet, or swing our hips. The Hebrew text is actually more compelling than our English translation because it is shorter: *"Forever His love!"* The word, rendered "love" is elsewhere translated "lovingkindness." It is the word that is used in connection with the covenant God made with Abraham and later with Israel. In other meditations, we called it the love of the marriage vows. God has pledged His love to us as in a relationship of husband and wife. This love is everlasting. As far as God is concerned, divorce is not an option; God loves us eternally.

This realization brought the writer of the Psalm to ecstasy. There is no trace of monotony in the repetition of the refrain; it gets louder, wilder, and faster as the Psalm moves on.

The first thought that brings about this outburst of praise is God's goodness, His character. God is good and only that which is related to God is good. Everything that does not belong to God is evil. He is the source of all goodness. James writes in his epistle: "Every good and perfect gift is from above, coming down from the Father of the heavenly lights, who does not change like shifting shadows" (James 1:17). God's goodness rains down upon us the form of blessings that give light and glory to life on earth.

The Psalmist invites us to look up into the heavens, and then toward the horizon to see the way the ocean displays its vastness and the earth its grandeur. Look at the sun, that mighty life-sustaining ball of fire, that faithfully moves through the sky! Look up at the sky at night, at the moon, the planets, and the twinkling stars and think of Him who created all this and gave us the gift to enjoy it all! We must come to the conclusion that the Creator of all this beauty is worth knowing and praising. He is not a cold intellectual genius who created but doesn't care. He is the one who loves us to the point where He gave His life in order for us to live eternally at His side. "Give thanks to the LORD, for he is good. His love endures forever!"

Psalm 136:10-22

"To him who struck down the firstborn of Egypt, His love endures forever, and brought Israel out from among them His love endures forever, with a mighty hand and outstretched arm; His love endures forever."

As we saw elsewhere, the striking down of Egypt's firstborn sons went beyond punishment of human beings; it struck at the spiritual powers that had incited the Egyptians to cruelly oppress the people of Israel. Those, who had forced the Israelites to throw their babies in the river to drown or be eaten by crocodiles or hippopotamuses, lost their children to God's angel of death. God's act of retribution was an act of righteousness.

No one has the right to treat a fellow human as slave. Those who do, demonstrate that they have lost in their lives the image of God, according to which they were created. We will only treat others as God's child if we are a child of God ourselves.

When God delivered Israel out of Egypt and brought them into the Promised Land, He restored them to freedom and dignity. In doing so, God demonstrated His eternal love.

Yet, when Israel left Egypt, they didn't leave Egypt behind in their hearts. When they were in the desert, they kept on looking back instead of ahead. When God fed them supernaturally, they complained. "The rabble with them began to crave other food, and again the Israelites started wailing and said, 'If only we had meat to eat! We remember the fish we ate in Egypt at no cost--also the cucumbers, melons, leeks, onions and garlic. But now we have lost our appetite; we never see anything but this manna!' " (Numbers 11:4-6). They had been freed from slavery in Egypt but they were still slaves of sin. Jesus says: "I tell you the truth, everyone who sins is a slave to sin. Now a slave has no permanent place in the family, but a son belongs to it forever. So if the Son sets you free, you will be free indeed" (John 8:34-36).

God shows His eternal love to us in that He not only frees us from the evil powers that oppress us on the outside but also from the sin that enslaves us on the inside. He wants to bring us into a life of dignity and "into the glorious freedom of the children of God" (Romans 8:21).

This is one of the greatest proofs that "His love endures forever."

November 28

Psalm 136:23-26

"To the one who remembered us in our low estate. His love endures forever."

Sin demeans us as human beings, but God's righteousness, which is bestowed upon us in Jesus Christ, elevates us. When God became a human being in Jesus Christ, the angel Gabriel appeared to the virgin Mary and the priest Zechariah. Both Mary and Zechariah refer to humiliations to which they were subjected. Mary stated: "He has been mindful of the humble state of his servant" (Luke 1:48). And Zechariah sang: "Praise be to the Lord, the God of Israel, because he has come and has redeemed his people" (Luke 1:68).

When God created Adam and Eve He intended them to be the crown of His creation. Adam was lord of this earth and king of the animals. He and Eve were the highest form of life God had made. As human beings our first parents ranked above the angels. The writer of Hebrews states: "Are not all angels ministering spirits sent to serve those who will inherit salvation?" (Hebrews 1:14). And David sings: "What is man that you are mindful of him, the son of man that you care for him? You ... crowned him with glory and honor. You made him ruler over the works of your hands; you put everything under his feet" (Psalm 8:4-6).

Somehow mankind never completely lost this notion of its importance. We may have taken it out of the context of our relationship with God, and we may be bragging about it in an inappropriate manner, but the concept has never completely left us. Some of the most primitive people, still living in the Stone Age in Indonesia, called themselves "Lords of the Earth."

But the revelation of God's grace makes us realize how far we have strayed from the position God originally intended for us. When Gabriel visited Mary to tell her that she would become the mother of the Savior of the world, she realized how much of a nobody she really was. Before God spoke to her Mary of Nazareth was a teenage girl nobody knew. It takes the grace of God to understand how deeply we have fallen; it takes the grace of God also to make us see how high He lifts us up. "Because of his great love for us, God, who is rich in mercy, made us alive with Christ even when we were dead in transgressions-it is by grace you have been saved. And God raised us up with Christ and seated us with him in the heavenly realms in Christ Jesus, in order that in the coming ages he might show the incomparable riches of his grace, expressed in his kindness to us in Christ Jesus" (Ephesians 2:4-7). "Give thanks to the God of heaven. His love endures forever!"

Psalm 137:1-6

"How can we sing the songs of the LORD while in a foreign land? If I forget you, O Jerusalem, may my right hand forget [its skill]. May my tongue cling to the roof of my mouth if I do not remember you, if I do not consider Jerusalem my highest joy."

We can hardly imagine the despair that must have marked the Babylonian captivity. The destruction of Jerusalem and the disappearance of the ark must have seemed to be the death of God's revelation in this world. The darkness of this period in world history is only surpassed by the death of our Lord Jesus Christ on the cross of Golgotha and His lying in the grave.

This is a poem that might have been written in a Nazi extermination camp. We will be better able to understand it if we see it against the background of a place like Auschwitz. This is a descent into hell. God is dead and the only grip on reality this Psalm offers is that this is impossible. Only survivors of the Holocaust can appreciate what the writer of this Psalm must have experienced.

The cruelty of the condition of the captives was accentuated by the way their captors wanted them to sing the Hallelujah chorus while they were being tortured. The people who had robbed the temple and had destroyed it, who had murdered the infants of the captives, asked the stunned survivors to sing them a song! This defied all human compassion. These poor Jews were in the hands of sadists, people who found pleasure in the pain they caused others.

According to some archeologists, "the rivers of Babylon" were canals in the desert that connected the Euphrates with the Tigris. It was the place where, centuries earlier, Paradise must have been located and where the Tree of Life grew. But the Psalmist does not reach beyond the destruction of the temple and of the city of Jerusalem. The only thing remaining was the empty spot where God had dwelt and where the covenant had been made. The Jews in Babylon had lost more than their temple and their holy city; they had lost Paradise.

As members of a fallen human race we all find ourselves "East of Eden."

When Jesus, the Lord of glory, hung on the cross, one of the criminals who was crucified with Him turned to Him and said: "Jesus, remember me when you come into your kingdom." Jesus answered him, "I tell you the truth, today you will be with me in paradise" (Luke 23:42,43).

There was in fact a moment in world history when God was dead. But He conquered death and thus opened for us the door of Paradise. This leads us beyond Jerusalem and the temple to the place where it all went wrong to start with. That is where healing of our deepest wounds takes place.

Psalm 137:7-9

"O Daughter of Babylon, doomed to destruction, happy is he who repays you for what you have done to us--he who seizes your infants and dashes them against the rocks."

I wish we could skip verses like these. Is this part of the inspired Word of God? Not everything that is written in the Bible expresses the feelings of the Holy Spirit. God's grief about the murder of Jewish children was as great as the smashing of the infants of Babylon. The Holy Spirit grieved over the massacre of the infants in Bethlehem five centuries before it took place! When Matthew recorded King Herod's dastardly act, he quoted Jeremiah's prophecy. We read: "When Herod realized that he had been outwitted by the Magi, he was furious, and he gave orders to kill all the boys in Bethlehem and its vicinity who were two years old and under, in accordance with the time he had learned from the Magi. Then what was said through the prophet Jeremiah was fulfilled: 'A voice is heard in Ramah, weeping and great mourning, Rachel weeping for her children and refusing to be comforted, because they are no more" (Matthew 2:16-18 and Jeremiah 31:15). God was not responsible for Herod's crime, or for the cruelty of the Babylonians toward Israel. One Bible commentator states about these words of the Psalmist that they have the shocking immediacy of a scream, to startle us into feeling something of the desperation that produced them.

We note that the Psalmist reversed curse and blessing; he cursed himself in order to keep his love for Jerusalem alive, and he pronounced a blessing upon those who pay Babylon back in the same coin. The Holy Spirit wants to show us that the key to understanding the mystery is hidden in this paradox. Vengeance is left to a third person.

A robber once attacked me; a night watchman shot and killed the thief. I couldn't have done this myself. I actually cried for the young man who was killed, but I couldn't reproach the watchman for shooting him and saving my life.

The message of the New Testament is based on a similar reversal. Paul writes that Christ was cursed so we could receive the blessing: "Christ redeemed us from the curse of the law by becoming a curse for us, for it is written: 'Cursed is everyone who is hung on a tree.' He redeemed us in order that the blessing given to Abraham might come to the Gentiles through Christ Jesus, so that by faith we might receive the promise of the Spirit" (Galatians 3:13,14). The subject is different from what this Psalm says but the principle is the same. The Psalmist puts himself under a curse so that God's righteousness could be administered to the enemies. In the same way, Christ became a curse for us in order that God's righteousness could be applied to our lives.

Psalm 138:1-3

"I will praise you, O LORD, with all my heart; before the 'gods' I will sing your praise."

The Hebrew word for "praise" implies the use of hands. It must be seen in connection with the bringing of a thank-offering as the sacrifice described in Leviticus. Thanksgiving never consists in the mere use of words. What we see is the gesture that accompanies the bringing of a sacrificial animal upon which the person who brought the sacrifice laid his hands and which was then killed and burned on the altar. For us, praise and thanksgiving consists in our identification with the death on the cross of our Lord Jesus Christ.

David said that he praises God with all his heart; that includes his mind and his will. The great command in Deuteronomy reads: "Love the LORD your God with all your heart and with all your soul and with all your strength" (Deuteronomy 6:5). The whole man must be involved in praise. We understand that praise of God doesn't only express itself in what we say, but even more in what we are. Paul states that God has chosen us so that we "might be for the praise of his glory" (Ephesians 1:12). If we identify ourselves with Jesus Christ who died for us on the cross and rose for us from the grave, we are God's praise.

It is difficult to determine what is meant with the words "before the 'gods.'" The Hebrew word has multiple meaning. It can denote God, angels, or even magistrates. I like to think that David saw himself before the throne of God in the presence of the four living creatures, who never stop singing: "Holy, holy, holy is the Lord God Almighty, who was, and is, and is to come" (Revelation 4:8). If that is not what David intended to say, that is what he ultimately ended up doing. Our being God's praise will translate itself in our singing God's praise and joining everything God has ever created in an eternal hymn or chorus of worship.

We must understand, however, that we cannot sing God's praise if we aren't the praise of His glory. Our lips cannot say what our life doesn't say.

One of the reasons David sings God's praises is because God has exalted above all things His Name and His Word. This may sound awkward and different translations don't give much clarity. The New King James Version reads: "You have magnified Your word above all Your name." The best interpretation I have heard is that God signed His Name under His promises. We have God's signature as a guarantee that He will do for us what He promises. He will make us what He intends us to be: people created for His glory.

Psalm 138:4-5

"May they sing of the ways of the LORD."

Very few kings of this world have ever praised God and sung of the ways of the LORD. A more typical description of the powers of this world is found in another Psalm: "The kings of the earth take their stand and the rulers gather together against the LORD and against his Anointed One. 'Let us break their chains,' they say, 'and throw off their fetters.'" (Psalm 2:2,3). David prophesies that at least some of the world leaders will have a change of heart and will praise God not only for what He has done but also for the way He does it.

Most people have difficulty at this point. It seems to us that God's way is not always the shortest line between two points. A good illustration is the story of the exodus of Israel from Egypt. God told the people to "encamp near Pi Hahiroth, between Migdol and the sea" (Exodus 14:2). Taking the route from Egypt to Canaan via the Red Sea seemed to be a fatal mistake. Yet, once the people were on the other side of the sea, they burst out in song. They sang the song of Moses. Thus we will all, one day, sing "the song of Moses the servant of God and the song of the Lamb" (Revelation 15:3). If we can really rejoice, not only in what God does, but also in the way He does it, we demonstrate we understand the secret of victory. Jacob did this at the end of his life. "Israel worshiped as he leaned on the top of his staff" (Genesis 47:31[b]). The book of Revelation is one whole illustration of this point. When the Lamb opens the seals of the scroll and the reign of the antichrist begins, it seems that enormous catastrophes occur. Yet the greatness of God's glory becomes evident and the way it is revealed is the only possible way.

We cannot see beyond the horizon of our life; we don't even know how what happens to us today will look tomorrow. It takes a step of faith to believe that "the bad things" we experience now will look good in the light of eternity. If God would make mistakes He would no longer be God. Even if we cannot find beauty and joy in a bankruptcy, the loss of a job, a broken relationship, or the loss of a loved one, we may take comfort in the assurance that what God allows to happen to us on our way to glory will indeed increase that glory. To sing of the ways of the Lord is the greatest praise we can bring to God.

Psalm 138:6-8

'The LORD will fulfill [his purpose] for me; your love, O LORD, endures forever--do not abandon the works of your hands."

Another translation of the above verse reads: "The LORD will perfect that which concerns me" (The New King James Version). The Living Bible paraphrases this: "The Lord will work out his plans for my life."

It is obvious that we are on earth for a purpose. No one is born by accident or without the will of God. Even unwanted pregnancies and babies who are born out of wedlock are included in God's plan. This doesn't excuse sin, but it redeems the fruit. Unfortunately, few people ask the question what God has in mind with their life. Most of us are too busy to fulfill our own purposes to wonder about what God's purpose with us could be. That is one of the reasons so many of us miss out on God's love.

There is a general purpose for mankind as a whole. The first question in *The Westminster Catechism* is "What is the chief and highest end of man?" Answer: "Man's chief and highest end is to glorify God, and fully to enjoy him forever." But God also has an individual plan for each of us, a specific way for us to enjoy and serve Him and a particular place to do it. Missing out on that plan means missing what life is all about. God will not force His blueprint on us. He loves us with an eternal love, and real love never forces itself upon anyone. God only reveals His purpose for our life if we commit ourselves to Him in an act of surrender. It is always a matter of "not my will but yours" and "not my plan but yours." To renounce our own plans and hand God a clean sheet of paper, asking Him to write on us what He wants us to do brings us to a point of crisis. If we ask God to reveal His will to us so that we can see if we like it or not, we will probably never receive an answer. God will only speak to us clearly if we make the commitment to obey before the order is given.

Our decision will set our course for eternity. If we abandon our way, we surrender to the One whose love endures forever. Even if we retract our promise, He will remain faithful because He cannot deny Himself. There is no fear that He will ever abandon the work of His hands.

Psalm 139:1-6

"O LORD, you have searched me and you know me."

This Psalm tells us just as much about ourselves as about God. We cannot get to know God unless we allow Him to know us. There is a sense in which God knows all about us, infinitely more than we know ourselves, but that is not what this Psalm is all about, or at least not quite. Jesus says: "And even the very hairs of your head are all numbered" (Matthew 10:30). That is just a fraction of our own data we don't know and God does. Ever since sin came into the world it made our relationship with God more complicated. God has become a stranger to us and we have become a stranger to ourselves.

God knows us through and through, but we don't really want to be known. We are afraid that God will discover inside us the things we want to keep hidden from ourselves and from everyone else. We know enough about ourselves to know that there is filth and corruption in us, which we'd rather keep covered and lie about. We lie to ourselves, because we hate what is inside us. And we are afraid that if God discovers our secrets, He will hate us too.

When David realized that God knew all about Him, regardless of David's willingness to be known, his fear changed into wonder. God knew him through and through and yet God loved him. When he felt God's hand upon his shoulder, he felt a loving touch that no one had ever given him in that manner. David had never been touched like that before.

As a young man I had decided that God was not coming into my life. I was afraid that, if I would open the door for Jesus, He would come in, take inventory of all the dirty laundry and then make a public announcement of all the filth He found inside me. That would have been too embarrassing for me to endure. Once, however, during a chapel meeting, I thought I could experiment and open the door a crack. I could always close it if I didn't like what I saw. God immediately put His foot in the door and flooded me with a joy I had never known. He seemed unwilling to talk about the dirty laundry, saying that it had been taken care of when Jesus died on the cross.

It is good to be known, because we get to know God. The more we allow ourselves to be known the more will we experience His love.

Psalm 139:7-12

"Where can I go from your Spirit? Where can I flee from your presence?"

Vv. 7-12 suggest that David didn't feel quite comfortable in this intimacy with God. Fleeing from God's presence may not have been a real option but the thought crossed his mind. The word "flee" is an indication of the presence of sin. In C. S. Lewis' book Perelandra, one of the main characters has an encounter with an angel whom he recognizes as good. He reacts by asking himself if "good" is what he really wants. Such duplicity is characteristic of our relationship with God. On the one hand, we yearn for God's love but there is also a little inner voice that urges us to escape.

God is in heaven and He is in hell. He is where the sun rises and where it sets. He is in the darkness and in the light.

These words give greater depth to what was said in v.5, "You hem me in--behind and before." David wanted to express the nearness of God rather than His presence. He tried to imagine all the possible places where he could go himself, but at none of those would he be out of the presence of God. Francis Thompson in the beautiful poem The Hound of Heaven expresses well what David went through:

> *"I fled Him, down the nights and down the days;*
> *I fled Him, down the arches of the years;*
> *I fled Him, down the labyrinthine ways*
> *of my own mind; and in the mist of tears*
> *I hid from Him, and under running laughter,*
> *Up vistaed hopes, I sped;*
> *And shot, precipitated,*
> *Adown Titanic glooms of chasmed fears,*
> *From those strong Feet that followed, followed after,*
> *But with unhurrying chase,*
> *And unperturbed pace,*
> *Deliberate speed, majestic instancy,*
> *They beat-and a Voice beat*
> *More instant than the Feet-*
> *'All things betray thee, who betrayest Me.' "*

We may never completely lose this tendency to flee and evade God's guidance. But the certainty that flight is impossible gives us at the same time a comforting assurance. We need this kind of protection against ourselves. We will only find salvation and fulfillment when we allow ourselves to be found. It is up to us how long the chase lasts. Happiness is only found if we "Trust in the LORD with all [our] heart and lean not on [our] own understanding; in all [our] ways acknowledge him, and he will make [our] paths straight" (Proverbs 3:5,6).

Psalm 139:13-18

"For you created my inmost being; you knit me together in my mother's womb. I praise you because I am fearfully and wonderfully made; your works are wonderful, I know that full well."

These verses describe the miracle of the creation of a human being from the conception through the resurrection. David mentions the soul before he even speaks of the embryo. The idea that the human soul would only start to develop in a later stage of pregnancy is unbiblical nonsense. The conception of every living being is a great miracle and the forming of man as the crown of creation is the crown of all miracles. Few human beings realize that they are part of an ongoing miracle.

David proves his depth in the way he describes his own conception and the existential miracle of his person. Nothing is as beneficial to our self-image as to praise God for the way in which He created us. That person is truly spiritually dead who is blind to the miracle of his own body and soul. Ironically, we often begin to realize the importance of the normal functions of our organs when something goes wrong with them.

The words "woven together in the depths of the earth" sound strange to us. They are obviously a poetical metaphor. The mother's womb hides as many mysteries as mother earth. Understanding of our origin is the key to the understanding of the purpose of life. Those who believe that life occurred through a series of coincidences and that we are the product of random events will never be able to make sense out of life. If we understand that God created us and that our bodies are wonders of complexity in which we will always find something new to amaze us, and that the miracle of our souls is even greater than that, we cannot escape the conclusion that all this must be geared to a definite goal. And if we accept God as the origin, it is a small step to seeing Him as the goal also.

The fact that sickness and death do not fit in the picture, as the Bible clearly explains, cannot be called an insurmountable obstacle. Death, not the absence of death, is the problem! A temporary one! "When I awake, I am still with you?" speaks in a cryptic fashion about our ultimate resurrection from the dead. Elsewhere we read: "And I--in righteousness I will see your face; when I awake, I will be satisfied with seeing your likeness" (Psalm 17:15). That will be a real awaking.

During our waking hours on earth our consciousness is still rather limited. Seeing God will place everything in God's light. Not only shall we be like Him, for we shall see Him as He is (I John 3:2), but we will also see everything else as it is and that will change us.

Psalm 139:19-24

"Search me, O God, and know my heart; test me and know my anxious thoughts. See if there is any offensive way in me, and lead me in the way everlasting."

Some Bible scholars believe that Verses 19-22, about hating those who hate God, don't belong in this Psalm. David's outburst may be unexpected but it is not inexplicable. The contrast is between God who creates life and brings human beings into this world, and man who sheds blood and murders his fellowmen. David does not paint a completely black-and-white picture. He had committed murder himself and some of the hatred of these "blood-thirsty men" may have been self-hatred.

The human soul is one of God's most glorious creations; it is also one of the most vile and despicable ones. In Jesus' words: "Out of the heart come evil thoughts, murder, adultery, sexual immorality, theft, false testimony, slander" (Matthew 15:19). And Jeremiah testifies: "The heart is deceitful above all things and beyond cure. Who can understand it?" (Jeremiah 17:9). There is a sense in which we are our own worst enemies. Trusting our own heart is the most foolish thing we can do.

David was aware of the fact that sin was not only something that threatened him from the outside, but that the enemy was also inside. The idyll of the creation of man is besmirched by the realization that man is not what he ought to be.

The depth of these last verses is emphasized by the almost literal repetition of the opening words: "O LORD, you have searched me and you know me," and "Search me, O God, and know my heart." God's omniscience will not benefit us unless we surrender ourselves to it wholeheartedly. God doesn't come to us with a search warrant; we must ask for it. If we deny the Holy Spirit access to our innermost being that doesn't mean that He doesn't know us completely. But if we do not ask Him to search us, we will not experience the healing effect of His presence. No self-knowledge is possible without opening oneself to the scrutiny of the Spirit of God. Self-analysis can even be dangerous without the presence of the Lord in our lives. In asking for this, David confessed that he did not know himself. He also admitted that he could not trust himself. Only when God leads us out of this labyrinth of our own mind can we walk the straight and narrow way that leads to life. Without God we will never be able to make the right moral choices.

Psalm 140

"Keep me, O LORD, from the hands of the wicked; protect me from men of violence who plan to trip my feet."

This world is full of evil men, "men of violence." David does not mention any names here and there is no indication what the cause of the writing of this Psalm may have been. It can be applied to several episodes in David's life. We have to look to the principle more than to one particular incident; it calls for a broader application.

The word "sin" is written with large letters over this poem, sin as it influences human relations. God's intention has always been that human beings would love each other and live together in harmony, thus complementing and fulfilling one another. Through the atonement in Christ believers in their fellowship together give expression to the love and unity of the divine Trinity. In praying for His disciples Jesus said: "Holy Father, protect them by the power of your name-the name you gave me-so that they may be one as we are one ... that all of them may be one, Father, just as you are in me and I am in you. ... I have made you known to them, and will continue to make you known in order that the love you have for me may be in them and that I myself may be in them" (John 17:11,21,26).

In this Psalm, we see the other extreme "Dog-eat-dog!" The ultimate result of sin is that one human being devours another spiritually and emotionally and, sometimes literally, as in cannibalism. The book *That Fateful Shore* describes in gruesome detail how escaped prisoners in Australia ate one another. We can imagine the panic and hatred the last two survivors of such a party must have felt for one another. The apostle John writes: "This is how we know what love is: Jesus Christ laid down his life for us. And we ought to lay down our lives for our brothers" (I John 3:16). Paul warns against the alternative when he says: "If you keep on biting and devouring each other, watch out or you will be destroyed by each other" (Galatians 5:15). There is no reason to believe that, if we do not demonstrate the love of Christ to one another, we will not come to the point of devouring each other.

Most hatred is inspired by fear. Fear of God will cancel our fear of man. As Jesus said: "Do not be afraid of those who kill the body but cannot kill the soul. Rather, be afraid of the one who can destroy both soul and body in hell" (Matthew 10:28).

Psalm 141:1-4

"Set a guard over my mouth, O LORD; keep watch over the door of my lips."

It can be a very disturbing discovery when we realize that we are not the kind of stable persons we thought ourselves to be. We cannot trust ourselves as far as temptation to sin is concerned. Even our prayers are not one hundred percent pure. More than anywhere else, in the Book of Psalms the Psalmist bares his heart here. As in the beginning of the history of man, nakedness and sin caused shame, so it is here a feeling of deep shame. This is what makes this prayer so urgent.

The tongue is sin's greatest tool. When Isaiah had a vision of God he blurted out: "Woe to me! ... I am ruined! For I am a man of unclean lips, and I live among a people of unclean lips, and my eyes have seen the King, the LORD Almighty" (Isaiah 6:5).

Jesus says: "Out of the overflow of the heart the mouth speaks" (Matthew 12:34). And the heart harbors a wealth of evil. James adds to this: "If anyone is never at fault in what he says, he is a perfect man, able to keep his whole body in check" (James 3:2). And Solomon observes: "The tongue has the power of life and death, and those who love it will eat its fruit" (Proverbs 18:21).

The tongue is the most destructive weapon we can use against our fellowmen. The great difference between the Word of God and our words is that God's Word creates but we cannot call anything into being with our words, and we seldom use them to build up. We can, however, be very effective in the use of words to destroy. Nothing can do so much damage to a human life as a lie.

The greatest problem is that our tongue becomes an instrument of duplicity. James warns us: "With the tongue we praise our Lord and Father, and with it we curse men, who have been made in God's likeness. Out of the same mouth come praise and cursing. My brothers, this should not be. Can both fresh water and salt water flow from the same spring? My brothers, can a fig tree bear olives, or a grapevine bear figs? Neither can a salt spring produce fresh water" (James 3:9-12). As Christians we have the double task of on the one hand placing ourselves under God's protection as David did in this Psalm, and of offering our tongue to God as an instrument of righteousness (Romans 6:13). When God gives us a new heart He also wants us to have a new tongue.

Psalm 141:5-10

"Let a righteous man strike me--it is a kindness; let him rebuke me--it is oil on my head. My head will not refuse it."

Criticism is not always easy to accept, but the Book of Proverbs states: "Wounds from a friend can be trusted, but an enemy multiplies kisses" (Proverbs 27:6). The apostle Paul may say that "Love is patient, love is kind. It does not envy, it does not boast, it is not proud. It is not rude, it is not self-seeking, it is not easily angered, it keeps no record of wrongs. Love does not delight in evil but rejoices with the truth. It always protects, always trusts, always hopes, always perseveres" (I Corinthians 13:4-7), but he doesn't say that love is blind. It may be true that love "keeps no record of wrongs" and that "it always protects," but true love knows what it protects. This passage doesn't deal with criticism in general but with criticism for unrighteousness. David asks for a righteous man to strike him, someone who knows fellowship with God and who sees that his friend needs help.

Ultimately it is the Holy Spirit who convicts us of sin. Sometimes the Spirit of God must delay His convicting work in our hearts because we are not willing to be convicted. Often when other people point out to us our mistakes, we tend to bristle and become defensive. But God also uses others to keep the checks and balances we need in our life. Sometimes those checks come in the form of having to work or live with a person who is abrasive and rude. "As iron sharpens iron, so one man sharpens another" (Proverbs 27:17). We may have difficulty accepting the other person's idiosyncrasies as being God-sent for our polishing and perfection.

Not all sharpening is abrasive. As the old English divine John Donne said: "No man is an island entire of itself; every man is a piece of the Continent." We are members of the body of Christ. The apostle Paul stated: "The eye cannot say to the hand, 'I don't need you!' And the head cannot say to the feet, 'I don't need you!' " (I Corinthians 12:21). We can turn this around. The eye does need the hand, and the head the feet.

It is good advice to find a friend to whom we can be accountable and who is willing to tell us honestly and clearly where we went wrong. A loving friend will do this and when our fellowship with God is restored, we will experience it as an anointing by the Holy Spirit Himself.

Psalm 142

"I cry to you, O LORD; I say, 'You are my refuge, my portion in the land of the living'."

David composed this Psalm when he fled from King Saul and hid in the cave of Adullam. The story is recorded in the I Samuel 22:1,2. The Psalm was probably written while David was still by himself, before his family came to him and a group of four hundred gathered around him. In the confinement of the cave, David was subject to strong mood changes. God had just saved him from a precarious situation when he escaped death at the court of King Achish (I Samuel 21:10-15) to which we owe the beautiful Thirty-fourth Psalm. Now, he found himself safely between four walls, and he cried out to God in his distress!

It is often difficult to keep emotionally abreast of what God is doing for us. It is much easier to look back at experiences and then to praise God, than to praise Him while we are in the midst of trouble and are trying to digest what goes on.

David was safe in the cave, but the closed-in space oppressed him. When outward pressure recedes, the inner turmoil begins to reveal itself. Only when we are inwardly free, it no longer makes any difference in what circumstances we find ourselves. Comparing David with the apostle Paul, we see that David had more liberty in the cave of Adullam than Paul had in prison in Rome. Yet in that confinement Paul wrote his greatest epistles. David did not get beyond the point of "Set me free from my prison, that I may praise your name." Paul and Silas were praying and singing hymns to God in prison at midnight (Acts 16:25).

What counts is our inner freedom, not our circumstances. When God confines us to a wheelchair or to any other kind of imprisonment, we have the choice to rebel or to glorify Him in our circumstance. Joni Eareckson Tada who is unable to move any muscle below her neck testifies that she is free in her wheelchair. In the period between World War One and Two, a wonderful spiritual revival took place in Möttlingen, a little village in the Black Forest in Germany. God used a simple farmhand, Friederich Stanger, to bless a great many people. I owe my own salvation indirectly to that movement. When Stanger laid his hands on people to pray for them, many were healed. Stanger himself suffered a stroke and someone else had to lift up his hand and put it on the head of people to be prayed for. They were healed, but he was not. This raised many questions. Stanger's answer was: "I no longer need my hands to glorify God." There is no reason why we wouldn't praise God in prison.

Psalm 143:1-5

"Do not bring your servant into judgment, for no one living is righteous before you."

This Psalm is the spiritual companion of the previous one. In the preceding Psalm, David felt oppressed in the cave of Adullam because his physical liberty was curtailed. Here he feels shackled by sin. David appealed to God's faithfulness and righteousness, as qualities that are not found in himself. His solitude in the cave brought him to have a new look at his inner self, and he realized that there was a worse enemy inside him than those who threatened him from the outside. When Jesus said: "You will know the truth, and the truth will set you free" (John 8:32), He spoke these words in the context of conviction of sin. Immediately following these words we read: "I tell you the truth, everyone who sins is a slave to sin. Now a slave has no permanent place in the family, but a son belongs to it forever. So if the Son sets you free, you will be free indeed" (John 8:34-36). Knowing the truth means the truth about ourselves, the discovery that we are sinners in need of being liberated from the evil power within us.

Calling upon God's righteousness would be dangerous for us apart from the atonement in Jesus Christ. In Christ we are, in the eyes of God, identified with His righteousness. If God is just, He punishes us for our sins instead of forgiving us. But Jesus has already paid the fine for our sin when He died on the cross. If God charges us again, it would mean that our sins would be paid for twice and that would not be just. That is why the apostle John writes: "If we confess our sins, he is *faithful* and *just* and will forgive us our sins and purify us from all unrighteousness" (I John 1:9). Therefore, God's pardon of our sin is proof of God's righteousness. David didn't know about the ultimate payment for his unrighteousness. He sacrificed an animal while confessing his sin, and on that basis he asked God to forgive him.

Yesterday we said that God sometimes puts physical limitations on us, and that we could choose to blame Him or praise Him. God also allows handicaps in order to make us understand who we are and what we ought to do about it. The inner freedom we talked about is the freedom of the Lord Jesus Christ. If we submit to the searching ministry of the Holy Spirit in our heart, our conviction of sin will change into a conviction of being forgiven. Inner freedom consists in the understanding that "God made him who had no sin to be sin for us, so that in him we might become the righteousness of God" (II Corinthians 5:21).

Psalm 143:6-12

"I spread out my hands to you; my soul thirsts for you like a parched land."

David packs a series of poetical images in this section in order to describe his emotional and spiritual condition. He sees himself as a traveler in the desert, dying of thirst. He feels himself being lowered in a pit, representing death and perdition. Darkness envelops him and he longs for the light of dawn. He has also lost his way in life and doesn't know in what direction to go. Enemies surround him who will shoot on sight. The cave in which he finds himself is in the mountains and the steep climb is difficult. We can understand David's confusion when we realize that God had anointed him to be the next king of Israel. In David's mind, that revelation ought to have given him the right to be protected and safe from threats upon his life. The problem was that Saul was still on the throne, and he didn't accept the fact that God would replace him with his own army general. Saul had tried twice to pierce David with his spear. And when David fled for his life Saul pursued him in order to kill him.

It is often difficult to reconcile the high calling God has given us in Jesus Christ with the hardships and pressures of daily life. If "God raised us up with Christ and seated us with him in the heavenly realms in Christ Jesus" (Ephesians 2:6), why then do we have financial problems, why do our intimate relationships break down, and why do we become terminally ill? We feel like the prodigal son who looked at the pods the pigs were eating while his stomach was empty and said to himself: "How many of my father's hired men have food to spare, and here I am starving to death!" (Luke 15:17). Like David, we need a new vision of glory in order to pull us through painful and desperate circumstances.

At the end of his life, David realized that Saul never succeeded in killing him and that in all those tight situations God had seen him through. The walls of the cave of Adullam that confined and oppressed him were ultimately the walls of God's protection.

The enemy of our soul will not be able to reach us when we cry out to God in our confinement. He may roar and shout outside, but inside we are safe. "For in the day of trouble he will keep me safe in his dwelling; he will hide me in the shelter of his tabernacle and set me high upon a rock" (Psalm 27:5).

Psalm 144:1-8

"Praise be to the LORD my Rock, who trains my hands for war, my fingers for battle."

The opening words sound shocking to us. People tend to demonstrate against wars, not praise the Lord for them. To understand the issue, we have to take a closer look at the names David used to address God. He called God "My Rock," "My loving God," or "My Love." The Hebrew word is derived from the word that is usually translated "lovingkindness." The other names are related to an experience of protection. It is important to see David's remarks about war against the background of God's lovingkindness. It means that David's war was a war against hatred and malice. David saw in the physical wars he fought a model of the spiritual battle in which he was involved, just as he saw the cave as a symbol for God's protection. We are in a state of war in this world. We must not go through life as if all is well or that a ceasefire has halted all hostilities. Our lives are in danger.

Four things are important in the war we are involved in: On whose side are we fighting? How do we live? What strategy do we follow? Who is the enemy?

When the Israelites made the golden calf in the desert, we read: "Moses saw that the people were running wild and that Aaron had let them get out of control and so become a laughingstock to their enemies. So he stood at the entrance to the camp and said, 'Whoever is for the LORD, come to me.' And all the Levites rallied to him" (Exodus 32:25,26). If we are for the LORD we must make it known clearly.

Fighting the Lord's war will change our lifestyle. Paul wrote to Timothy: "Endure hardship with us like a good soldier of Christ Jesus. No one serving as a soldier gets involved in civilian affairs-he wants to please his commanding officer" (II Timothy 2:3,4).

As far as the strategy is concerned Paul states: "The weapons we fight with are not the weapons of the world. On the contrary, they have divine power to demolish strongholds. We demolish arguments and every pretension that sets itself up against the knowledge of God, and we take captive every thought to make it obedient to Christ" (II Corinthians 10:4,5). That involves also our own arguments and thoughts.

We must know who the enemy is. "Our struggle is not against flesh and blood, but against ... the spiritual forces of evil in the heavenly realms." We must "put on the full armor of God so that [we] can take your stand against the devil's schemes." "And pray in the Spirit on all occasions with all kinds of prayers and requests. With this in mind, be alert and always keep on praying for all the saints" (see Ephesians 6:10-18).

Psalm 144:9-15

"Blessed are the people of whom this is true; blessed are the people whose God is the LORD."

David had not yet experienced the deliverance from "the deadly sword." But he had learned to know God as "the One who gives victory to kings." This was enough for him to join his voice in this new song, the song of resurrection. For him the singing of this song was an act of faith, not of seeing. When David challenged Goliath he said to the Philistine: "You come against me with sword and spear and javelin, but I come against you in the name of the LORD Almighty, the God of the armies of Israel, whom you have defied. All those gathered here will know that it is not by sword or spear that the LORD saves; for the battle is the LORD's, and he will give all of you into our hands" (I Samuel 17:45,47). And when King Jehoshaphat faced the enemy God told him: "You will not have to fight this battle. Take up your positions; stand firm and see the deliverance the LORD will give you, O Judah and Jerusalem. Do not be afraid; do not be discouraged. Go out to face them tomorrow, and the LORD will be with you" (II Chronicles 20:17).

Our lives are based upon a victory that is not our own. Jesus defeated our enemy when He died on the cross. Paul states: "And having disarmed the powers and authorities, he made a public spectacle of them, triumphing over them by the cross" (Colossians 2:15).

David's conclusion is that if God's victory over our enemies is the foundation of our life, it must also be the basis upon which our family is built. In spite of this logical conclusion, David didn't give us a model of a happy and healthy family. Polygamy and adultery caused an almost complete ruin for him and his children.

Even if our personal lives are built upon the resurrection of the Lord Jesus Christ, it doesn't mean that our family relations will reflect this. God has laid for us the foundation, but it is up to us to build on it with the material that God wants us to use. As Paul says again: "If any man builds on this foundation using gold, silver, costly stones, wood, hay or straw, his work will be shown for what it is, because the Day will bring it to light. It will be revealed with fire, and the fire will test the quality of each man's work. If what he has built survives, he will receive his reward" (I Corinthians 3:12-14).

"Blessed are the people of whom this is true; blessed are the people whose God is the LORD." O, for a nation of families like this; O, for a world like that!

December 16

Psalm 145:1-13

"Great is the LORD and most worthy of praise; his greatness no one can fathom."

This Psalm is the last one in the book that bears the name of David. It is also the last acrostic Psalm, using one of the 22 letters of the Hebrew alphabet at the beginning of each verse. The Psalm is a great song of praise. Most of the words David uses to describe the acts of God refer to redemption.

One of the outstanding features of the Psalm is the illusion of space David creates in calling upon the next generation to join in an antiphonal chorus. This makes this Psalm into a three-dimensional poem. The form gives expression to content and we get the impression of standing between the centuries, as if we find ourselves already in eternity. David calls and the answer echoes back from a generation not yet born. The effect is very impressive.

Words are insufficient to praise God as He ought to be praised. God's greatness is such that not even one human being or one generation can give God the glory that is due to Him.

We might even question if God needs our praise. God's glory certainly doesn't depend upon our recognition of it. Although it is true that we cannot add anything to God's perfection and that even an endless chain of generations doesn't add up to eternal praise, praising God is valid and good. However strange and impossible this may sound, man's praise does add something to the being of God. When God created man and placed him on this planet, He planted a seed. Our praise and worship are the fruit of the growing and flourishing of that seed. We will probably never fully understand how the eternal God reveals Himself in time and space. When we exalt God, we do nothing more than acknowledge reality. This in itself means deliverance from the bondage of the lie, because sin distorts reality. Seeing God "high and exalted" proves that our eyes have been opened. It is an indication of forgiveness of sin. This also opens the gates of praise for us.

Even when all who were ever born and all who will yet be born, when all ages join together in praise of God's greatness, it will take eternity-- and nobody knows how long that is! If we don't begin now, we may miss out in the end.

357

Psalm 145:14-16

"You open your hand and satisfy the desires of every living thing."

Every time a farmer feeds his livestock or we feed our pets, we act out by way of a weak shadow what God does universally on a much higher plane. Our pets recognize us as their masters because we feed them every day at the same time. Our dogs may show more appreciation than our cats do; they usually behave as if they own us and do us a favor by allowing us to feed them. David's picture shows us what reality ought to be like. Often animals come closer to this reality than humans. Jesus had this image in mind when He spoke those moving words about the birds of the air and the lilies of the field in His Sermon on the Mount (See Matthew 6:25-34). We only approach this reality if we first seek God's kingdom and His righteousness.

In a movie entitled Shenandoah Valley, the actor Jimmy Stewart says a prayer before each meal in which he reminds God that the food on the table is more the result of his hard labor than of God's blessing. In saying this, he translates the general feeling of modern man quite correctly. Elsewhere in the Book of Psalms, however, this matter is put in its right perspective with the addition: "When you hide your face, they are terrified; when you take away their breath, they die and return to the dust" (See Psalm 104:29).

Verse sixteen goes one step beyond the physical feeding that provides satisfaction. When God opens His hand, He satisfies with more than just food. The Hebrew word rendered "desire" means "delight." The act of eating is, of course, a natural function that provides satisfaction and joy, like the fulfillment of all the functions for which God created our bodies. But "delight" seems to suggest more than mere satisfaction. Man's deepest hunger is not physical but spiritual. "Man does not live on bread alone, but on every word that comes from the mouth of God" (Deuteronomy 8:3; Matthew 4:4). Our Lord Jesus Christ confirmed Moses' words during His temptation in the desert. When God opens His hand, He satisfies our deepest longings. We have the advantage over the animals in that we can hear and understand the Word of God.

It isn't just our hard labor that brings food to the table. "Unless the LORD builds the house, its builders labor in vain. Unless the LORD watches over the city, the watchmen stand guard in vain" (Psalm 127:1). We must realize that "when God gives any man wealth and possessions, and enables him to enjoy them, to accept his lot and be happy in his work-this is a gift of God" (Ecclesiastes 5:19).

Psalm 145:17-21

"The LORD is near to all who call on him, to all who call on him in truth."

The fact that one of God's attributes is His omnipresence means that He is everywhere. There is no place on earth or in the whole universe where God is not. As David expressed in another Psalm: "If I go up to the heavens, you are there; if I make my bed in the depths, you are there" (Psalm 139:8). Therefore, when we read here: "The LORD is near to all who call on him, to all who call on him in truth" David doesn't state an objective fact but a subjective experience. If the subjective experience were not based on an objective reality, it would, of course, be a mere illusion.

What David is saying here is that if we want to experience God, we have to call upon Him in truth. First of all, it is usually quite a discovery for us modern people that calling on God is an option that is open to us. We have to get used to the fact that we can in reality speak to God and receive an answer. A dialogue is possible.

Secondly, the condition is truth. By accepting the lie, as Adam and Eve did, God's presence becomes a frightening experience and after that it tends to become more and more vague. The realization of God's presence comes back again only when the lie is broken in our lives by means of a confession of sin. Truth always begins with confession. Life in fellowship with God in Jesus Christ is the only way we can live spiritually, both on earth and in heaven.

Thirdly, calling upon God in truth means that we really want it. That may be the biggest obstacle to experiencing God's presence. An ardent and all consuming desire is ninety percent of the realization. "As the deer pants for streams of water, so my soul pants for you, O God. My soul thirsts for God, for the living God" (Psalm 42:1,2). The experience of God's presence doesn't depend on God; it depends on our thirst for Him. Calling on God in truth goes together and grows together with loving God. Jesus calls this "the first and greatest commandment." Not only the Law and the Prophets hang on these two commandments, but our whole existence also.

Psalm 146:1-6

"Do not put your trust in princes, in mortal men, who cannot save."

This Psalm is the first in a series of "Hallelujah Psalms" that concludes the Book of Psalms. In every one of these Psalms the accent on praise differs. The praise of this Psalm confines itself to life on earth. In Psalm 147, Jehovah is praised for His help; in Psalm 148 the rejoicing takes on a cosmic character; in Psalm 149 the church does the singing and the doxology of Psalm 150 is for "everything that has breath."

It has been said that in life it is more important *who* you know than *what* you know. Those who are known by people in high places are those who get the better-paid jobs and acquire influence in society. What more can mere man wish for than to be noted in Buckingham Palace or in the White House? The tendency to make friends with people of influence and to manipulate connections is widespread.

The Psalmist understands that there is a higher authority than the one we look up to and that it is more important to be known in heaven than on earth. What have we gained if we have occupied on earth a position that influenced foreign policy or world opinion and on the Day of Judgment we hear Jesus say: "I never knew you. Away from me, you evildoer!" (Matthew 7:23).

Praise is an expression of trust. The context of this Psalm confirms this. The lack of trust in princes supposes trust in God. It is important to keep in mind the limits the Psalmist has set himself in this Psalm. The topic is life on earth, or rather, staying alive on earth. The poet may have been concerned about making ends meet. There is also a note of disappointment in the advice not to trust people who are in authority. Evidently, the author tried it and experienced disappointments.

The Hebrew has an interesting play on word between the words "man" and "earth." The word for "man" is *'adam* and for "earth" *'adamah*. The reference here is to Genesis, Chapter Three, where God said to Adam: "By the sweat of your brow you will eat your food until you return to the ground, since from it you were taken; for dust you are and to dust you will return" (Genesis 3:19).

Not all human authority is corrupt; there are some favorable exceptions. There are some world leaders whose example we may follow, but we should never put our trust in man instead of in God. The Netherlands owes its existence, and several centuries of freedom and prosperity to the fact that William of Orange (the "father of the country") had made a covenant with "the Potentate of all potentates." The Bible commands us to pray for those in authority, both for the good and the bad ones.

Psalm 146:1-6

"Blessed is he whose help is the God of Jacob, whose hope is in the LORD his God."

In this Psalm, the Psalmist draws specifically the boundaries of life on earth and he makes his song of praise rise from those limitations. This does not mean that he doesn't believe in the resurrection from the dead. But in putting the accent on life on earth, he demonstrates that God is the God of the "here and now."

As we saw earlier, praise never comes to us spontaneously. Sin has blurred the realization of the reason for our existence. We have to arouse ourselves from our lethargy in order to become what we ought to be. Praise always begins with an act of the will. The Jerusalem Bible renders verse two: "I mean to praise Jehovah."

"Blessed is he whose help is the God of Jacob" is the last beatitude in the Book of Psalms. The setting is life on earth in which man is faced with the struggle of survival. There is some irony in the title "the God of Jacob." Jacob was not the hero of faith Abraham was. Jacob tried to keep his head above the water by deceit. He tried to make deals with God, and he wanted to give God a hand in receiving the blessing of the firstborn. I suppose God smiles when we call Him "the God of Jacob." When we call for help to "the God of Jacob," we put ourselves on Jacob's level and we confess our moral weakness and our lack of confidence in God. God is the God of those who worry! But if we go to Him for help, He immediately becomes "the God of Israel" because as soon as we confess our weaknesses to Him, He declares us to be victors. Our deliverance consists in the fact that we confess our deception and that God helps us to become victorious over ourselves. This is the first kind of help and the most fundamental kind that God gives us. Our reaction to the discovery of who God is and who we are ourselves may be the same as that of Peter. We read in Luke's Gospel: "When Simon Peter saw this, he fell at Jesus' knees and said, 'Go away from me, Lord; I am a sinful man!' " (Luke 5:8). Praise God, He doesn't go away from us.

Psalm 146:7-10

"The LORD sets prisoners free."

Prisons were not Israelite institutions. Nobody paid for a crime by serving a prison sentence. According to some Bible scholars, people were only incarcerated briefly in preparation for capital punishment. All other criminals had to pay fines or make restitution. The mention of prisoners supposes an invasion by foreign powers or a foreign influence in the life of Israel. The taking of Israel into Babylonian captivity is an example in case. Another form of imprisonment was demonic possession. In our modern world we have come to accept the existence of prisons as part of everyday life. In our slow-working judicial systems people are often locked up for months even before a judge and a jury look at the matter of guilt or innocence.

Human beings, like the birds of the air, are meant to be free. Limitation of freedom is an insult to our human dignity. Our revulsion to taking a human life is understandable, but the Bible is quite adamant that there are some crimes that require the ultimate retribution. God considers every murder to be a personal insult. "Whoever sheds the blood of man, by man shall his blood be shed; for in the image of God has God made man" (Genesis 9:6). In God's eye even the violation of the sanctity of marriage, the most precious image in human relations of our fellowship with God in Jesus Christ, is a capital offense. "If a man commits adultery with another man's wife--with the wife of his neighbor--both the adulterer and the adulteress must be put to death" (Leviticus 20:10). It would be hard for us to imagine a modern-day society in which that rule would be enforced.

Adultery is not punishable by modern law, but neither is mankind free anymore. The ultimate captivity is the imprisonment of sin. The freedom God offers is the inner freedom from sin and the restoration of our human dignity in Jesus Christ. Physically we may be in captivity or prison, we may be confined to a bed or a wheelchair. In Jesus Christ we can enjoy the freedom for which God created us. Some people in prison enjoy more freedom than their jailers. We must never be confined in prisons of our own making. There is no bondage God cannot break if we allow Him to do it for us.

Psalm 147:1-9

"He heals the brokenhearted and binds up their wounds. He determines the number of the stars and calls them each by name."

In this amazing Psalm the poet first allows his gaze to wander to the limits of the universe, and then he swings back to zoom in on a particular incident on earth. The effect of this sweeping motion is overwhelming because it gives us some understanding as to who the one is who heals our broken hearts and binds up our wounds. The distance between the outer limits of space and the smallness of human existence seems to us an unbridgeable gap. We remember David's words of amazement: "When I consider your heavens, the work of your fingers, the moon and the stars, which you have set in place, what is man that you are mindful of him, the son of man that you care for him?" (Psalm 8:3,4). We cannot conceive of a God who created heavenly bodies that are thousands of light years away from us and who also created the atoms with their tiniest particles. Our God is often too small and too great at the same time.

Yet it is this God, the Creator of infinity, who stoops to where we are to heal our broken hearts and bind up our wounds.

By mouth of Isaiah God says to us: " 'To whom will you compare me? Or who is my equal?' says the Holy One. 'Lift your eyes and look to the heavens: Who created all these? He who brings out the starry host one by one, and calls them each by name. Because of his great power and mighty strength, not one of them is missing. Why do you say, O Jacob, and complain, O Israel, 'My way is hidden from the LORD; my cause is disregarded by my God' '? He gives strength to the weary and increases the power of the weak. Even youths grow tired and weary, and young men stumble and fall; but those who hope in the LORD will renew their strength. They will soar on wings like eagles; they will run and not grow weary, they will walk and not be faint" (Isaiah 40:25-27,29-31). If this doesn't give us hope, what will?

Our God is never too busy with the bigger things to pay attention to our small needs. He is the God who has counted the hairs on our head (Matthew 10:30), and who knew us from the time we were an embryo and before. In David's words: "You created my inmost being; you knit me together in my mother's womb" (Psalm 139:13). We can trust Him.

Psalm 147:10-20

"His pleasure is not in the strength of the horse, nor his delight in the legs of a man; the LORD delights in those who fear him, who put their hope in his unfailing love."

The strength of the horse and the legs of a man represent the cavalry and the infantry, the military power that wages wars. God is not impressed by human armament and power. This pertains to both those wars that we call primitive as well as to our modern warfare. The prophet Zechariah said to the miserable little group of returned exiles from Babylonian Captivity: "This is the word of the LORD to Zerubbabel: 'Not by might nor by power, but by my Spirit,' says the LORD Almighty" (Zechariah 4:6). This is the topic of this Psalm. God says to Mao Zedong that power does not come from the barrel of a gun. Those who fear God and who put their hope in His unfailing love are stronger than any military power on earth. The Berlin Wall came down because of a prayer meeting in the city of Leipzig. And "By faith the walls of Jericho fell, after the people had marched around them for seven days" (Hebrews 11:30).

These verses speak about more than horsepower and manpower; they refer to human energy as opposed to the power of God. As a young boy, I used to ride a bicycle that had a small dynamo on it to provide light when I went somewhere in the dark. As I peddled my bike, the light would shine. At home I never tried to produce my own electricity. We had outlets in the wall where we could plug in our appliances and use the energy provided by the bigger dynamos of the city. Trying to produce our own energy where outside power is available would make no sense in daily life. Yet in the spiritual domain, that is what most people try to do. We can't even produce the low voltage that is used to keep our heart pumping. Jesus says to us what He said to the Sadducees: "You are in error because you do not know the Scriptures or the power of God" (Matthew 22:29). If God doesn't trust our power supply, why should we? We do better to plug in to His eternal energy, if we want to participate in the resurrection. "We eagerly await a Savior from there, the Lord Jesus Christ, who, by the power that enables him to bring everything under his control, will transform our lowly bodies so that they will be like his glorious body" (Philippians 3:20,21).

Psalm 148:1-6

"Praise him, sun and moon, praise him, all you shining stars. Praise him, you highest heavens and you waters above the skies. Let them praise the name of the LORD, for he commanded and they were created. He set them in place for ever and ever; he gave a decree that will never pass away."

This Psalm speaks as much about God as about His creation, about the stars and about us. Sin does not cast its shadow over this Psalm. This Psalm follows the same design as the Incarnation of the Son of God, beginning in the highest heaven, coming down to earth, and lifting man up.

Yet the call for praise comes from the earth and is directed to the highest heavens. This is an indication of the unique position of man. On the basis of what God has done for man, nothing is so fitted to call for praise as man is. We could be baffled by the presumptuous and holy arrogance of man who addresses heaven with a call to praise God. If a tiny ant addressed a similar call to mankind, it would have the same effect. Added to this, God has already been praised for eons in heaven more than anywhere else. Yet the very fact that this Psalm is included in the written Word of God proves that the call is not futile and that it has been heard. When our voice speaks through the microphone of God's glory, it is heard throughout the universe. I once saw a TV show of a Dr. Seuss story in which a creature on earth heard a very soft voice that was calling. When he began to pay attention to the voice, he discovered a whole microcosm that was just as complete as the universe in which he lived. The story ends with a creature of this miniature microcosm who in turn hears a similar voice from yet another creation contained in his. This story depicts our position in God's creation quite well. To the inhabitants of the heavens we must be like creatures living in a microcosm. We are like Gulliver in Jonathan Swift's book *Gulliver's Travels*. But this does not change the truth of our calling. It makes no difference to us whether the heavenly beings praise God uninterruptedly or not. We have discovered how vitally important this praise is, and we want all of creation to join in. This makes the cosmic hymn of praise our example to follow.

So far, we have not been able to see what the effect of all this is. The fact that the voice of man is heard throughout the universe elevates man above himself. But our elevation is caused by God's glory and not by something in us. The Psalm correctly begins in heaven and comes down to earth; the movement is symbolic.

Psalm 148:7-14

"He has raised up for his people a horn, the praise of all his saints, of Israel, the people close to his heart."

The Psalmist seems to say that the earth has more reason to praise God than any other place in the whole universe. Astronauts tell us that our planet is the only one that possesses color in our solar system. All the other celestial bodies are black-and-white. Color is the expression of God's glory. John saw a rainbow that encircled the throne of God (Revelation 4:3). God's Name stands for God's character and the essence of His character is glory. The seraphs in Isaiah called to one another: "Holy, holy, holy is the LORD Almighty; the whole earth is full of his glory" (Isaiah 6:3). God's majesty, His greatness, and His might are proof of the link between the earth and the universe of which we are part.

What is most unique, however, is that God "has raised up for his people a horn." As far as we know, such a thing has never happened on any other planet in the universe. We interpret the word "horn" in the light of Zechariah's hymn of praise: "He has raised up a horn of salvation for us in the house of his servant David" (Luke 1:49). Zechariah, undoubtedly, quoted this Psalm as he spoke about the coming of the Messiah. The exclusive position of Israel in this world is solely based on the fact that the Savior of the world was born from them. The unique feature of our planet is that God became man on this earth, that He dwelt among us, and that the blood of an eternal covenant was shed on our soil. It is on our planet that the war between God and Satan was decided. God became a member of the human race in order to crush the head of the serpent. He has involved us in this cosmic struggle and in His victory over evil.

The battle between God and Satan is being fought out in human lives. What God did here has elevated man to a level that surpasses everything else. We have to remember that God's unique meddling in human affairs began with man's fall into sin. That should keep us from becoming proud about that which is our deepest shame. The fact that we have been redeemed from this condition enables us to call upon heaven and earth to shout with us a thundering HALLELUJAH!

Psalm 149:1-5

"For the LORD takes delight in his people; he crowns the humble with salvation."

This *Hallelujah* Psalm is a new song, sung by the church of Jesus Christ. It is a prophecy about the new song that will be sung in heaven (Revelation 5:9; 14:3). It is the song of a new creation, related to the resurrection from the dead, the Lord Jesus Christ's resurrection and ours.

The song of praise has to be intoned by the saints. The Hebrew word translated with "saints" is derived from a word that means: "to bow the neck." The word refers to those who take their relationship with God seriously. The Psalmist does not speak about individuals but about the Church. He envisions more than Israel as a nation.

When Israel rejoices in its Maker, it does much more than recognize that God is the Creator of man. God is Israel's Maker in the sense that He called Abraham, and delivered Israel out of the slavery of Egypt, and gave it identity as a nation in the conquest of Canaan, and entrusted it with the law of His self-revelation. The topic is Israel as a theocracy. God is their King.

In a sense, Israel never was a genuine theocracy. They were never a nation composed of members who completely accepted God's reign over their individual lives. The Israel mentioned in this Psalm is the group of people that has surrendered to God's reign. It is, what the apostle Paul calls: "the Israel of God" (Galatians 6:16). It is the new creation in Jesus Christ. The new song is sung by those who have the Word of God and who "hear the word of God and obey it" (Luke 11:28). These are the ones who are invited to dance, sing, and play the orchestra. It is an exuberant ecstasy of dance and song. There is nothing sedate in this joy.

The Lord takes delight in His people. We mean something to Him. We make Him happy. We would never be able to love God if He had not loved us first. This miracle amazes us every time we think of it. God loves me! He takes delight in me!

And "He crowns the humble with salvation." This corresponds to what Jesus calls "the poor in spirit" in the Sermon on the Mount (Matthew 5:3). God elevates those who confess their sins to the highest level possible. This miracle of being elevated by God's grace never ceases to amaze us. Jesus Himself set the tone by being born in a stable and by dying on a cross. Heaven chooses that which is lowly. That is the content of humility. The real power belongs to the victims of evil. God elevates what the world rejects.

Psalm 149:6-9

"May the praise of God be in their mouths and a double-edged sword in their hands ... This is the glory of all his saints."

Our praise of God is a double-edged sword. It has a different effect upon different people. The Apostle Paul explains: "We are to God the aroma of Christ among those who are being saved and those who are perishing. To the one we are the smell of death; to the other, the fragrance of life" (II Corinthians 2:15,16). The way the sword cuts depends on how people react to our praise of God. We do no harm to those who in their hearts have longed for forgiveness of sin and rehabilitation. Those who reject the Word of God throw themselves upon their sword as King Saul of old did (See I Samuel 31:4).

God's wrath expresses itself on man in a confrontation of the sinful person with His Word. This places a person who is created in the image of God next to the original. Man then realizes that God's image in him has become a caricature. He reacts to this by crying out to the mountains and the rocks, "Fall on us and hide us from the face of him who sits on the throne and from the wrath of the Lamb!" (Revelation 6:16).

What it amounts to is that when we are saved by the Gospel, God appoints us as judges and juries over our fellowmen and over the heavenly powers. The First Psalm states: "The wicked will not stand in the judgment, nor sinners in the assembly of the righteous" (Psalm 1:5). And Paul extends this by saying: "Do you not know that the saints will judge the world? And if you are to judge the world, are you not competent to judge trivial cases? Do you not know that we will judge angels?" (I Corinthians 6:2,3). And Jesus explains: "The men of Nineveh will stand up at the judgment with this generation and condemn it" (Matthew 12:41).

Heaven will have many surprises for us. Instead of sitting throughout eternity playing our harps, we will find that God will place us in a position and give us an authority which will make our work on earth seem like child's play. Jesus says: "Whoever can be trusted with very little can also be trusted with much, and whoever is dishonest with very little will also be dishonest with much. So if you have not been trustworthy in handling worldly wealth, who will trust you with true riches?" (Luke 16:10,11). Evidently the true riches, the real things are what await us still. Whether we will take our place and exercise our ultimate responsibility depends on how much we praise God with what we do here and now.

Psalm 150

"Praise God in his sanctuary; praise him in his mighty heavens."

The whole Book of Psalm is divided into five books, each of which ends with a doxology. At the end of the first book we read: "Praise be to the LORD, the God of Israel, from everlasting to everlasting. Amen and Amen" (Psalm 41:13). The second book closes with "Praise be to the LORD God, the God of Israel, who alone does marvelous deeds. Praise be to his glorious name forever; may the whole earth be filled with his glory. Amen and Amen (Psalm 73:18,19). The third book concludes with: "Praise be to the LORD forever! Amen and Amen (Psalm 89:52) and the fourth with: "Praise be to the LORD, the God of Israel, from everlasting to everlasting. Let all the people say, 'Amen!' Praise the LORD" (Psalm 106:48). The whole Psalter ends, not with one or two verses of praise but with a whole Psalm. This is a "Hallelujah for Choir and Orchestra." It is the greatest and loudest hymn of praise in the whole Bible. It is a mighty fortissimo that brings the Book of Psalms to a triumphant end.

Yet, this Psalm is not a hymn of praise in the strictest sense of the word; it is a call to praise God. God is never addressed personally in this Psalm but the addressed are "Everything that has breath." This constitutes a fundamental difference between this doxology and the ones that concluded the previous four books. The call to praise suggests that the *Hallelujah* ought to be like this, not that it actually is so.

"*Hallelujah*, Praise God in his sanctuary." We see here again the same kind of holy arrogance as in Psalm 148. A human being on earth calls upon heaven to praise God. There was also a sanctuary on earth. In the Old Testament it was the Ark of the Covenant in the tabernacle or the temple. It was the place God had chosen to reveal Himself. The implication is that God ought to be praised at the place of *His* choosing and in the way *He* prescribes. It is not up to us to praise God where and how we like. For us New Testament Christians, it means that we ought to praise God in Jesus Christ. He is God revealed in the flesh. Even more, God's sanctuary is the body of Christ, which is the Church. That means that this Psalm also constitutes a New Testament call to praise. The Psalmist's primary intention, however, is that God should be praised in heaven.

We don't know what the Psalmist thought when he mentioned heaven. With our present knowledge of the universe, our God may even be greater than the One David knew. The God we praise is the God of the mighty heavens. Millions of light-years are as one day to Him.

Psalm 150

"Praise him for his acts of power; praise him for his surpassing greatness."

We are not asked to praise God without a reason. The British Bible scholar, John Stott, once said that the Bible never uses the word *Hallelujah* without giving a reason for it. I had a friend who, whenever his phone rang, he would never pick it up and say "hello," but "Praise the Lord" without giving a reason. God prefers us to know what we are doing when we praise Him. He doesn't want us just to use a polite phrase. The reason we have for our *Hallelujah* is God's acts of power and His incomparable greatness.

The Psalmist speaks about God's acts of power in the most general terms. He clearly includes all of God's deeds. He is the creator of heaven and earth but also the Savior of fallen mankind. He is the Word that became flesh and that dwelt among us. The Psalmist didn't know yet the mightiest of God's act when he said: "Praise him for his acts of power." We know that we owe our salvation to God's greatest act of power in the resurrection from the dead of Jesus Christ. We have more reason to shout *Hallelujah* than the Psalmist ever had.

As human beings we will never come to the end of our amazement about God's greatness. His perfect character, His glory, and the infinity of all His attributes will throughout eternity be for us an inexhaustible source of adoration. We will penetrate deeper and deeper into the meaning of "holy, holy, holy is the LORD Almighty." When we share in His glory, we will only begin to sound the depths of His holiness.

In this life, we don't even have a definition of holiness. The only thing we can determine on earth is that we have nothing we can use as a standard to measure holiness. Even this very hiatus makes us realize that we are dealing with a God who is infinitely great. The image of God in us keeps us from disregarding God because we cannot define Him. It is particularly the fact that we are related to Him that makes us fall on our knees, realizing that God defies all concepts and definitions. If we deny this, we deny our own humanity. We must praise the Lord, if not for His sake then for our own.

Psalm 150

"Praise him with the sounding of the trumpet, praise him with the harp and lyre, praise him with tambourine and dancing, praise him with the strings and flute, praise him with the clash of cymbals, praise him with resounding cymbals."

Here comes the orchestra! Eight instruments are mentioned, plus dancing. The first instrument is the trumpet, or rather, the shophar which is a ram's horn. There is a lyre or a lute, a harp or a zither, and a tambourine. There is a stringed instrument, maybe comparable to our violin, and a reed-instrument like the flute. Whether the fact that the first instrument mentioned is the ram's horn has any theological significance is open for discussion. The instrument is the part of an animal that was killed, which suggests a sacrifice that was laid on the altar. Even if this is not the underlying thought behind the use of the horn, it remains true that all our praise is based on the fact that the Lamb is slain. The words "sin" and "atonement" are not used in this Psalm but the "acts of power" or "mighty acts," and the mention of the ram's horn point in that direction.

The lute and zither are soft-sounding instruments. David's playing of the harp had a soothing influence on the demon-possessed King Saul (I Samuel 16:23). There is in the presence of God a place for quietness and peace in praise. Quietness ought not to be absent from our worship.

In contrast to this, we find the exuberance of "tambourine and dancing," which is more a matter of rhythm than of melody. The first time tambourine and dancing are mentioned in the Bible is in the Song of Moses. We read: "Then Miriam the prophetess, Aaron's sister, took a tambourine in her hand, and all the women followed her, with tambourines and dancing" (Exodus 15:20). We may, therefore, assume that although harps are only mentioned in that context, the same demonstration of exuberance will be seen at the singing of "the song of Moses the servant of God and the song of the Lamb" (Revelation 15:3). In our praise, we are often as far removed from the tambourines and dancing as we are from the miracle at the Red Sea.

Thinking of all these instruments, we must remember that one needs skill to play an instrument. No one picks up a musical instrument for the first time and plays it perfectly. We have to exercise our gifts in order to praise God as virtuosos. Praise is not only spontaneous; it is also an art that has to be practiced. We have to put time and effort into our gifts. God has given us a gift of praise.

Psalm 150

"Let everything that has breath praise the LORD. Praise the LORD."

We concluded our last meditation with the words: "Praise is an art that has to be practiced. We have to put time and effort into our gifts. God has given us a gift of praise." But there is also a song of praise that comes effortlessly. "Let everything that has breath praise the LORD." There is not one living human being that does not have breath. Breath and life are identical. Breathing is one of the most fundamental functions of the human body. "The LORD God formed the man from the dust of the ground and breathed into his nostrils the breath of life, and the man became a living being" (Genesis 2:7).

God's breath also made man into a spiritual being. The Hebrew word, rendered "breath" also means "spirit." Breathing, therefore, means more than merely inhaling oxygen and exhaling carbon dioxide. It also means worshipping God in spirit and in truth. "Let everything that has breath praise the LORD" is at the same time the most unsophisticated form of worship as well as "Life on the Highest Plane."

The human spirit died when Adam fell in sin and it is resurrected from the dead in the regeneration through the Holy Spirit. This is the reason we can praise God with our breath. Let everything that has breath realize what is involved in the call of this Psalm and answer: "Hallelujah!"

This brings us to the end of our Walking through the Psalms this Year. If you joined me on this walk by reading one page of this book every day, you have come to the end of the year. It is good to look back in more than one way and see where we have been. Like the authors of this hymnal, we may have enjoyed the beauty of God's creation and experienced some of the glory of the Creator. We may also have gone through valleys of the shadow of death, or felt that God had forsaken us like they did. Drawing the balance of the whole gamut of experiences, we end up with this doxology. If we are still breathing, it means that we are still alive. When we stop breathing we will find ourselves more alive than ever and in the presence of Him to whom all praise is due. The password to make our transition is Hallelujah! Let's practice it here!